DIGESTIV
WELLNESS

Other books by Elizabeth Lipski:

Leaky Gut Syndrome (A Keats Good Health Guide)

DIGESTIVE WELLNESS

Second Edition

Elizabeth Lipski

M.S., C.C.N.

Foreword by Jeffrey S. Bland, Ph.D.

KEATS PUBLISHING

LOS ANGELES

NTC/Contemporary Publishing Group

Digestive Wellness is intended solely for education and information and not as medical advice. Please consult a medical or health professional if you have any questions about your health.

Library of Congress Cataloging-in-Publication Data

Lipski, Elizabeth.
   Digestive wellness / by Elizabeth Lipski.
      p. cm.
   Includes bibliographical references.
   ISBN 0-87983-679-2
   ISBN 0-87983-984-8 (second edition)
   1. Digestion—Popular works. 2. Indigestion—Popular works.
OP145.L57   1996
616.3—dc20   95-49689
                                      CIP

Published by Keats Publishing
A division of NTC/Contemporary Publishing Group, Inc., 4255 West Touhy Avenue, Lincolnwood, Illinois 60646-1975 U.S.A.

Printed and bound in the United States of America
International Standard Book Number: 0-87983-984-8
99 00 01 02 03 04 RRD 18 17 16 15 14 13 12 11 10 9 8 7 6 5 4 3 2 1

*This book is dedicated to my mother and father
who taught me that I could fly
and to Stephen
who soared beside me for so long.*

DISCLAIMER

THE THERAPIES IN this book have been helpful for many people and have been scientifically researched and documented. Because I do not know you or your particular needs, they may or may not be appropriate for you. This book is not intended to displace proper medical care. Do not stop taking medications without discussion with your physician. If you want to try the approaches discussed, take this book to your physician and ask her to help you by ordering the appropriate laboratory tests and monitoring your progress. Teamwork can often bring the best results.

Contents

PART 3
A NEW WAY OF IDENTIFYING
THE PROBLEM

PART 4

THE DIGESTIVE WELLNESS PROGRAM:
You Can Change The Way You Feel!

PART 5

A FUNCTIONAL APPROACH TO
THERAPEUTICS/SELF-CARE

PART 6

RESOURCES

FOREWORD

I'VE HAD THE pleasure of having a professional exchange with Liz Lipski for nearly fifteen years and have been impressed with the way that she has kept abreast of the latest knowledge and information in nutritional sciences—and how it applies to nutritionally related chronic health problems. Her book, *Digestive Wellness*, opens the door to a new chapter in nutritional science. The result will be the alleviation of a number of health problems that many people have experienced for years, not knowing what to do about them. We now recognize that the intestinal tract plays an important role in determining our health other than just digesting our food and getting rid of waste products. We are not "what we eat" but rather "what we absorb from what we eat." It is this aspect of our digestive system that may, in fact, determine our immune function, glandular activity, and neurological function. I believe that Ms. Lipski's book identifies these relationships well and gets the reader to understand the complex interrelationships of our digestive process—and the bacteria living in our digestive tract that are in constant communication with us.

It may come as a great surprise to many readers of this book to learn that the bacteria that live in our digestive tract are the largest organ of the body, even though they're not directly tied to the body through the blood supply. Bacteria in our intestinal tract weigh nearly 3½ pounds and are metabolically active, releasing many substances into our blood which are absorbed across the intestinal barrier. A number of these substances, such as vitamins and amino acids, may be beneficial to our health, and others, which come from harmful bacteria, may, in fact, alter our immune, nervous, or glandular system in such a way as to increase our susceptibility to chronic illness. Liz Lipski, in this book, defines these relationships and indicates how an individual might utilize nutritional intervention to reduce some of these problems.

This book will make a positive contribution to people's understanding of the important relationship between gastrointestinal physiology, diet, and health. For many readers who are not familiar with this exciting and important topic, this book will provide an introduction and a guide as to how they can gain better control over their digestive function and its relationship to their health. It seems hard to believe that our health is, to a great extent, controlled by that thin, three millimeter lining of our intestinal tract that we call the gastrointestinal mucosa. The maintenance of its integrity so that it does not become "leaky" is of tremendous importance. Ms. Lipski's book helps the reader to understand how to approach this objective with precision.

Jeffrey Bland, Ph.D.

PREFACE TO
THE SECOND EDITION

I ORIGINALLY WROTE *Digestive Wellness* because I felt this
information was important and should be in the hands of
people who need it. I still feel that way. It is a gratifying
feeling to be stopped in the grocery store and told "My
fibromyalgia is gone since I read your book and followed the
advice," or to be told "I sell *Digestive Wellness* in my office so
that my patients can really understand what we are doing."

This book was conceived at the first International Symposium on Functional Medicine. I received my first copy at the
third symposium; I am revising it on the sixth. In the past
six years, the concepts presented in *Digestive Wellness* have
stood the test of time, gaining more recognition and solidity
each year. Research on the gut/immune system connections
grows. For example, we now know that at least 60 percent
of the immune system is located in our Gut Activated Lymphatic System (GALT). A disordered gut can translate into
a disordered immune response; and so in nearly every autoimmune condition, we are finding a digestive connection.

Research has also shown that there are more nerve cells
in the digestive system than in the spine. This helps explain
why anxiety and nervousness play such a large part in digestive conditions. The digestive system even has its own auton-
omous nervous system, called the *enteric nervous system*, which
can function on its own without help from the brain. In fact,
the digestive system has been called "the second brain."

In this edition I have included additional healing options
and functional lab tests. I've also added new sections on

illnesses that are now known to have definite digestive components: attention deficit disorder (ADD), asthma, autism, and schizophrenia. Time has also reinforced the concept of biochemical individuality. What works for one person doesn't necessarily work for the next. Health practitioners must look to the underlying causes and triggers of illness, and then tailor treatment to the person and his lifestyle. This is the underlying basis of a functional approach.

Sartre said "Life is the sum of all of our choices." Health, to a great extent, is also the sum of choices. Each of us is predisposed to certain genetic typing, but individual destiny is determined by how we live our lives. If we choose to eat healthful foods and think pleasing thoughts, our genetics respond to that. And if we choose to spray our homes and yards with pesticides and eat processed foods, our genetics also respond. Some of us were born with strong genetic constitutions and can withstand much of late twentieth-century culture, but others are like canaries in a coal mine and are unusually susceptible to the many contaminants in our culture, from microwaves to stain retardant in carpeting. As we embrace modern technology and urban living, more and more of us become "canaries."

Ultimately, the way we treat our own bodies mirrors in our world view. We are really a web of one being, and the more we use this weblike approach, the greater chance we have to live healthful, meaningful lives. In the original edition of *Laurel's Kitchen*, a vegetarian cookbook, the authors tell this story: Once there was a woman who was given a beautiful bouquet of flowers. She put them in a vase, but noticed that the vase was dirty. She washed and dried the vase and placed it on a table in the living room. She then noticed that the table needed polishing, so she polished the table. Once the table was polished she noticed that the other furniture looked shabby, so she polished and dusted it. But then the floor needed a good vacuuming, and the rugs shampooing. Once the living room was clean, she noticed that other rooms in the house had also been neglected. Room by room she cleaned until her whole house was spotless.

Paying attention to food and health is like receiving that bouquet of flowers. Health conditions are the body's way of shouting to us to pay attention! When you slow down enough to focus on your own health, you begin to notice that other parts of your "world" are also in need of attending. This can ripple out to love of community, of place, and of earth itself. This is much needed today in our quickly expanding global community where so few have so much, and so many also want to enjoy the benefits we in wealthy countries take for granted.

I do hope that you will enjoy the journey through *Digestive Wellness*. Remember, your job is to live each day fully, open to the glory of the surprises within it, to feel deeply, to appreciate the love and kindness in your life, and to let people you care about know it. Be real. And inhale the divine.

E. Lipski
P.O. Box 1459
Hanalei, Hawaii 96714
(808) 826-2562
Lipski@aloha.net
www.innovativehealing.com

ACKNOWLEDGMENTS

MY GRATITUDE AND THANKS TO:

My husband, Stephen Long, who opened the space in my life so I could write this book and for his many devoted hours of editing my work.

My children, Kyle and Arthur, who missed me.

Gabrielle Resnick who kept my life in order.

Stephen Barrie, N.D., and Marty Lee, Ph.D., who generously gave me access to information and illustrations for my book.

Russell Jaffe, M.D., who helped me shape my ideas in the earliest phase and whose ideas have greatly influenced my work.

Jeff Bland, Ph.D., who was my first nutrition teacher and continues to amaze me with the depth of his knowledge decades later.

Lori Feiss for drawing the illustrations.

Nathan Keats and Don Bensen at Keats Publishing for putting their trust in an unknown author.

Susan E. Davis for shaping my manuscript into a real live book.

Peter Hoffman, Hudson Perigo, and Claudia McCowan for their work on the second edition.

And to the many people who shared their knowledge, time, and work with me: Leo Galland, M.D., Corey Resnick, N.D., Bill Shaddle, Bob Smith, Natasha Trenev, and Billy Crook, M.D.

Part I

Digestive Health

Chapter 1

WHO CAN BENEFIT FROM THIS BOOK?

"If the patient has been to more than four physicians, nutrition is probably the medical answer."

ABRAHAM HOFFER, M.D., PH.D.

THERE IS CURRENTLY an epidemic of digestive illness in our country, an epidemic that is directly related to the foods we eat and the way we live. One-third to one-half of all adults have digestive illness—over 62 million people. According to a May 1994 study, 69 percent of the people studied reported having at least one gastrointestinal problem within the previous three months. Except for the common cold, digestive problems are the most common reason people seek medical advice. They are the third largest category of illness in the United States, at a cost of $41 billion, and result in 229 million days of lost productivity, at a cost of $14.5 billion per year. Constipation plagues our nation. Americans each average over $500 a year on laxatives alone. Year after year, medications for digestive illness top the pharmaceutical best-seller list. Zantac, an ulcer medication, is the best-selling drug of all time, with sales of well over $1 billion annually.

When I first began studying nutrition, I remember going to meetings where the old-time nutritionists would lecture in evangelistic style, foretelling "death begins in the colon" while pointing to posters of enormous colons. At the time I thought they were being overly dramatic, but I have slowly come to learn that they were right. For many of us, disease and death do begin in the digestive system.

Most of us don't think much about digestion unless it isn't working well. We don't have to because it works automatically. The function of digestion is to break down foods into basic components for the cells to use for energy, as building materials and as catalysts. The uninterrupted flow of these nutrients into our system is critical to our long-term health. When we eat poorly or our digestion becomes blocked and sluggish, we compromise the ability of *all* our cells to work efficiently and healthfully. While it may seem obvious to some that what we eat affects the health of our digestive systems and our bodies, it is a revolutionary idea to many. There is a consensus of agreement among health organizations and professionals that we can reduce the risk of heart disease, diabetes, and cancer by eating more healthful foods. But many people with chronic digestive problems continue to eat poorly, never realizing that their food choices are causing their ill health.

This book is a resource for people with faulty digestion and the people who care about them. Some of you may have serious digestive illness, like Crohn's disease, irritable bowel syndrome, or ulcerative colitis, while others may have simpler problems of heartburn, indigestion, or constipation. In addition to obvious digestive problems, many other medical problems are caused by faulty digestion. Arthritis, many autoimmune diseases, eczema, food sensitivities, and psoriasis are digestive in origin. People with migraine headaches nearly always have food sensitivities that trigger the problem. Chronic fatigue syndrome, while initially triggered by a virus, has a major digestive component as well. When digestive competence is restored, many of these problems are resolved.

ANNUAL BURDEN OF SELECTED DIGESTIVE DISEASES
IN THE UNITED STATES

Disease	Number of people with this condition, in millions	Days of restricted activity, in millions	Deaths caused by this condition
GI infections	8.3	22.8	456
GI cancers	0.258	14	79,854
Hemorrhoids	10.36	8.2	22
Esophageal disease	0.546	2.4	1,600
Ulcer	4.491	28.8	6,715
Gastritis and duodenitis	2.793	7.2	641
Hernia	4.741	32.5	1,391
Inflammatory bowel disease	2.308	20.3	628
Diverticular disease	1.9	9.2	2,933
Constipation	4.458	1.9	31
Irritable bowel	1.379	2.2	63
Chronic liver disease	0.552	10.6	32,107
Gallstones	0.956	8.8	2,975
Other GI conditions	18.958	60.1	61,584
Total GI conditions	**62**	**229**	**191,000**

Digestive Diseases in the United States: Epidemiology and Impact, U.S. Department of Health and Human Services, Public Health Service, National Institutes of Health, Publication No. 94-1447, May 1994, p. 19.

DIGESTIVE HEALTH PROBLEMS

Mouth ulcers	Tongue problems	Periodontal disease
Heartburn	Belching	Hiatal hernia
Ulcers	Gastritis	Bloating and gas
Irritable bowel syndrome	Crohn's disease	Ulcerative colitis
Celiac disease/ Sprue	Gallbladder problems	Indigestion
Constipation	Diarrhea	Diarrhea and constipation
Chronic fatigue	Food sensitivities	Arthritis, all types
Yeast infections	Migraine headaches	Ankylosing spondilitis
Eczema	Psoriasis	

New medical research and clinical studies indicate that digestive illness is often caused by things we can control:

Poor food choices
Lack of dietary fiber
High levels of daily stress
Pharmaceuticals, both over-the-counter and recreational drugs
Alcoholic beverages
Cigarette smoking
Environmental irritants and toxins

In fact, the only factor we can't control is our genetic makeup.

Dennis Burkitt, father of the fiber revolution, found almost no appendicitis, colon disease, diabetes, or hiatal hernia in people eating traditional diets. When these people move to cities or change to a Westernized diet—of high sugar, highly processed, low-fiber, and low-nutrient-density foods—they develop these illnesses in the same amounts as do Westerners. Other studies show that ulcerative colitis and Crohn's disease are increasing in cultures that switch to a Western diet.

In the past decade, research has yielded surprising results, turning the arena of digestive health on its head. The food that we eat is our most intimate contact with the environment. We take food inside of our bodies and turn it into us! Each day several pounds of this "foreign" matter must be processed. Recent research shows that over 60 percent of the immune system is located in or around the digestive system. The digestive system is often called the "second brain" because if has more nerves than the spine. What we once thought of as a simple system becomes more complex with each advance of knowledge.

Ulcers, long believed to be a disease of high stress and high stomach acidity, are now known to be caused by bacteria. Of people with ulcers, 79 to 90 percent have a bacteria called *Helicobacter pylori*. When it takes hold, the mucus layer of the stomach is digested, and the acid comes into direct contact with the unprotected stomach lining, causing it to burn and develop sores called ulcers. Though Zantac and Tagamet, the most commonly used medications for ulcers, are the best-selling drugs of all time, the latest recommendations from the National Institutes of Health put these medications in the background and focus instead on killing the *Helicobacter* bacteria.

Ulcers haven't been the only surprises in the field of digestive health. Unfortunately, we often lose some of our ability to function long before a disease is present. Now medical laboratories are developing new tests that focus on function rather than disease. They are able to give us information that can serve as an early warning device, letting us know when our organs are losing their abilities. These labs are asking new questions and getting new answers that are changing internal medicine.

Innovative stool testing has shown that about a quarter of the people tested harbor parasites. Some may be harmless, while others cause illness that resolves when the parasitic infestation is treated. Parasites cause a wide range of symptoms, including gastrointestinal complaints of constipation, diarrhea, gas, and bloating, as well as allergies, anemia, fatigue, immune system problems, joint and muscle aches and pains, nervousness, skin conditions, and sleep disturbances.

Research on microbes provides a new view of the symbiosis of our own bodies and the organisms dwelling there. Now we can look inside without invasive techniques to see which microbes are present and how well we are digesting food. There are ten times more bacteria in our intestinal tract than cells in our body. They do important work like producing vitamins, digesting the sugar in milk, and keeping our intestines acidic, which protects us from disease-producing viruses and bacteria. Antibiotics, stressful living conditions, and poor dietary habits destroy this balance, and opportunistic microorganisms can take over. We call this imbalance *intestinal dysbiosis*.

These microorganisms can also travel out of the digestive tract and create havoc throughout the body. One theory especially intrigues me: displaced bacteria, fungi, or parasites can set up a local immune reaction that mimics specific gene markers. The immune system sees the gene markers as something to attack and autoimmune diseases develop. It is believed that this mechanism underlies some serious diseases like rheumatoid arthritis and ankylosing spondylitis.

We are becoming more sensitive all the time to the foods we eat. Leaky gut syndrome (also called *increased intestinal permeability*), another new concept in digestive health, plays a large role in these sensitivities. Our intestines have a dual function: to let nutrients into our bloodstream while blocking the absorption of other materials. When foods aren't digested properly, they ferment and rot in our intestines, producing toxic by-products that irritate and inflame the intestinal lining, causing tiny tears. The intestinal lining loses its ability to act properly as a filter and leaks, hence the name leaky gut syndrome. It is a contributing factor in Crohn's disease, celiac disease, irritable bowel, and ulcerative colitis. It is often responsible for illness in distant tissues and organs, including problems like chronic fatigue syndrome, food sensitivities, eczema, migraine headaches, psoriasis, and osteoarthritis.

Digestive Wellness provides you with a step-by-step plan for making healthful changes in your lifestyle. The approach is from a biological rather than a medical viewpoint. The standard medical approach is to diagnose and provide "appropriate" treatment, either drugs or surgery. The biological approach involves cleansing, feeding, and nurturing your entire being—simple but effective tools to improve the way you feel. By understanding the function of the various parts of the gastrointestinal (GI) tract and looking for underlying causes of disease rather than mere treatment of symptoms, we can begin to understand how to correct our problems.

In the first part of the book we explore the causes of digestive illness due to the American lifestyle. Then we take a trip through the digestive tract where we find a beautifully orchestrated system of integrated harmony. Then we look at the microbes that populate our digestive universe. When they are out of balance, we feel the effects. We move on to discuss dysbiosis and leaky gut syndrome, which often underlie digestive illness and many seemingly unrelated health problems. These chapters provide the groundwork so you can really understand the causes and effects of poor lifestyle choices and medical therapies on your condition.

In the next part we move on to self-improvement, with information and practical tips on how to develop a wellness lifestyle. Information about exercise, stress reduction programs, food choices, and shopping lists are provided. We'll focus on a personal exploration of what makes you feel better or worse and recommend approaches that support your body's ability to evoke its natural healing response. You will discover which habits make you feel vibrant and energetic and which drain you. The biological approach, which treats you as a whole person with unique needs, is based on the concept of "biochemical individuality." Just as each of us has a unique face, body, and personality, so too do we each have a unique biochemistry. One person's need for a specific nutrient, for example, can be thirty-fold higher or lower than another person's. When it comes to food, one person's pleasure is another's poison. Although you may believe that it's important to eat certain foods—like bread, eggs, meat, milk, oranges, and tomatoes—they may or may not be healthy for you. It depends on how well *your* body can use them. Detoxification programs are discussed: why you need to incorporate them into your life, recommended programs, and what to expect during detoxification.

Functional medicine, which is concerned with early intervention in health problems, is presented next. Early intervention improves your chances of returning to full health. Information on functional lab tests is detailed. This information is new, and most physicians will be unfamiliar with many of these laboratory tests. Take this book to your doctor's office, and ask your doctor to work with you in this new way.

The next part of the book discusses self-care strategies for digestive and digestively-related health problems, including information about the latest research on nutritional and herbal therapies. This part is divided into two chapters. The first discusses common digestive illnesses and conditions, and the second explores problems that are the consequence of faulty digestion, like arthritic conditions, migraine headaches, and skin problems. Research has been gathered from clinicians and researchers who are striving to learn how your body works and why it fails. The goal is to help your body reach its own natural balance, which will allow it to heal. Day in and day out, cell by cell, your body continually replaces itself. With the correct balance of work, rest, and nutrients, your body can become healthier each year. If you build your "house" with excellent materials, it will wear better!

Finally, a resource guide is included. It lists professional organizations that can refer you to nutritionally oriented physicians, health professionals, and laboratories. For those who want to read more on a specific topic, a suggested reading list is also provided.

Throughout the book are exercises and questionnaires designed to increase your self-awareness of mind and body, help you shop more wisely, breathe more deeply, relax more fully, and live more freely. Even though we may not be aware of it, we all practice medical self-care. When we get a headache, we take an aspirin or go for a walk. If we have indigestion, we take an Alka-seltzer or drink ginger tea. We know when we're too sick to go to work. Most of the time, we make our own assessment and treatment plan, expecting that the problem will pass with time. When these plans fail, we seek professional help. This book will expose you to more plans, new ideas, and the tools to be your own health expert. Just as one tool won't work for every job, not all of these tools will work for you. But some will, and even the failures may give you useful information.

The good news is that you can change the way you feel. The bad news is that it takes work and personal commitment. The good news about the bad news is that the journey can be an amazing voyage of self-discovery and self-mastery. This book provides you with some of the tools you need. In fact, the voyage is as interesting as the destination. So work, relax, laugh, and remember to look out the window and enjoy the scenery. This book is about taking control of your lifestyle to increase your chances of getting healthier and more vibrant each year.

Exercise 1

DIGESTIVE HEALTH APPRAISAL QUESTIONNAIRE

DATE: _____

This questionnaire will help you assess your digestive status. It is not meant as a replacement for a physician's care. The answers will help you focus your attention on specific areas of need.

MEDICATIONS USED CURRENTLY

Circle any of the following medications you are taking. Write down the dosage and frequency:

Antacids	Laxatives	Cortisone
Antibiotics	Oral contraceptives	Prednisone
Antifungals	Ulcer medications	Tylenol
Anti- inflammatories	Aspirin	Stool softeners

OTHER _____

FOOD, NUTRITION AND LIFESTYLE

Circle if you eat, drink, or use:

Alcohol	Luncheon meats
Candy	Margarine
Cigarettes	Soft drinks
Coffee	Sweets/pastries
Fast foods	Chew tobacco
Fried foods	

Circle if you:

Diet often
Do not exercise regularly
Are under excessive stress
Are exposed to chemicals at work
Are exposed to cigarette smoke

This part of the questionnaire will help you discover where your digestive system is having problems. It is a screening tool and does not constitute an exact diagnosis of your problem. However, it can point you in the right direction in determining where the highest priorities lie in your healing process.

Instructions: Circle the number which best describes the intensity of your symptoms. If you do not know the answer to a question, leave it blank. Add the totals for each section to assess which areas need your attention.

0 = **Symptom is not present/**   **2** = **Moderate/often**
     rarely present   **3** = **Severe/almost always**
1 = **Mild/sometimes**

SECTION A:
HYPOACIDITY OF THE STOMACH

1	Burping	0	1	2	3
2	Fullness for extended time after meals	0	1	2	3
3	Bloating	0	1	2	3
4	Poor appetite	0	1	2	3
5	Stomach upsets easily	0	1	2	3
6	History of constipation	0	1	2	3
7	Known food allergies	0	1	2	3
	Total:				

Score 0–4: Low priority   **Score 5–8: Moderate priority**
Score 9+: High priority

SECTION B:
HYPOFUNCTION OF SMALL INTESTINES AND/OR PANCREAS

1	Abdominal cramps	0	1	2	3
2	Indigestion one to three hours after eating	0	1	2	3
3	Fatigue after eating	0	1	2	3

Hypofunction of Small Intestines and/or Pancreas (con't)

4	Lower bowel gas	0	1	2	3
5	Alternating constipation & diarrhea	0	1	2	3
6	Diarrhea	0	1	2	3
7	Roughage & fiber causes constipation	0	1	2	3
8	Mucus in stools	0	1	2	3
9	Stool poorly formed	0	1	2	3
10	Shiny stool	0	1	2	3
11	Three or more large bowel movements daily	0	1	2	3
12	Dry, flaky skin &/or dry brittle hair	0	1	2	3
13	Pain in left side under rib cage	0	1	2	3
14	Acne	0	1	2	3
15	Food allergies	0	1	2	3
16	Difficulty gaining weight	0	1	2	3
17	Foul-smelling stool	0	1	2	3
	Total:				

Score 0–4: Low priority   **Score 5–8: Moderate priority**
Score 9+: High priority

Section C:
Ulcers/Hyperacidity of the Stomach

1	Stomach pains	0	1	2	3
2	Stomach pains just before or after meals	0	1	2	3
3	Dependency on antacids	0	1	2	3
4	Chronic abdominal pain	0	1	2	3
5	Butterfly sensations in stomach	0	1	2	3
6	Difficulty belching	0	1	2	3

ULCERS/HYPERACIDITY OF THE STOMACH (con't)

7	Stomach pain when emotionally upset	0	1	2	3
8	Sudden, acute indigestion	0	1	2	3
9	Relief of symptoms by carbonated drinks	0	1	2	3
10	Relief of stomach pain by drinking cream/milk	0	1	2	3
11	History of ulcer or gastritis	0	1	2	3
12	Current ulcer	0	1	2	3
13	Black stool when not taking iron supplements	0	1	2	3
	Total:				

Score 0–4: Low priority   **Score 5–8: Moderate Priority**
Score 9+: High priority

SECTION D:
COLON/LARGE INTESTINE

1	Seasonal diarrhea	0	1	2	3
2	Frequent and recurrent infections (colds)	0	1	2	3
3	Bladder and kidney infections	0	1	2	3
4	Vaginal yeast infection	0	1	2	3
5	Abdominal cramps	0	1	2	3
6	Toe and fingernail fungus	0	1	2	3
7	Alternating diarrhea/constipation	0	1	2	3
8	Constipation	0	1	2	3
9	History of antibiotic use	0	1	2	3
10	Meat eater	0	1	2	3
11	Rapidly failing vision	0	1	2	3
	Total:				

Score 0–4: Low priority   **Score 5–8: Moderate priority**
Score 9+: High priority

SECTION E:
LIVER/GALLBLADDER

1	Intolerance to greasy foods	0	1	2	3
2	Headaches after eating	0	1	2	3
3	Light-colored stool	0	1	2	3
4	Foul-smelling stool	0	1	2	3
5	Less than one bowel movement daily	0	1	2	3
6	Constipation	0	1	2	3
7	Hard stool	0	1	2	3
8	Sour taste in mouth	0	1	2	3
9	Gray-colored skin	0	1	2	3
10	Yellow in whites of eyes	0	1	2	3
11	Bad breath	0	1	2	3
12	Body odor	0	1	2	3
13	Fatigue and sleepiness after eating	0	1	2	3
14	Pain in right side under rib cage	0	1	2	3
15	Painful to pass stool	0	1	2	3
16	Retain water	0	1	2	3
17	Big toe painful	0	1	2	3
18	Pain radiates along outside of leg	0	1	2	3
19	Dry skin/hair	0	1	2	3
20	Red blood in stool	No			Yes
21	Have had jaundice or hepatitis	No			Yes
22	High blood cholesterol and low HDL cholesterol	No	Unknown		Yes
23	Is your cholesterol level above 200?	No	Unknown		Yes
24	Is your triglyceride level above 115?	No	Unknown		Yes
	Total:				

Score 0–2: Low priority   **Score 3–5: Moderate priority**
Score 6+: High priority

Section F:
Intestinal Permeability/Leaky Gut Syndrome, Dysbiosis

1	Constipation and/or diarrhea	0	1	2	3
2	Abdominal pain or bloating	0	1	2	3
3	Mucus or blood in stool	0	1	2	3
4	Joint pain or swelling, or arthritis	0	1	2	3
5	Chronic or frequent fatigue or tiredness	0	1	2	3
6	Food allergy or food sensitivities or intolerance	0	1	2	3
7	Sinus or nasal congestion	0	1	2	3
8	Chronic or frequent inflammations	0	1	2	3
9	Eczema, skin rashes, or hives (urticaria)	0	1	2	3
10	Asthma, hayfever, or airborne allergies	0	1	2	3
11	Confusion, poor memory, or mood swings	0	1	2	3
12	Use of nonsteroidal anti-inflammatory drugs (aspirin, Tylenol, Motrin)	0	1	2	3
13	History of antibiotic use	0	1	2	3
14	Alcohol consumption, or alcohol makes you feel sick	0	1	2	3
15	Ulcerative colitis, Crohn's disease, or celiac disease	0	1	2	3
	Total:				

Score 1–5: Low priority   **Score 6–10: Mild case**
Score 7–19: Moderate priority   **Score 20+: High priority**

SECTION G:
GASTRIC REFLUX

1	Sour taste in mouth	0	1	2	3
2	Regurgitate undigested food into mouth	0	1	2	3
3	Frequent nocturnal coughing	0	1	2	3
4	Burning sensation from citrus on way to stomach	0	1	2	3
5	Heartburn	0	1	2	3
6	Burping	0	1	2	3
7	Difficulty swallowing solids or liquids	0	1	2	3
	Total:				

Score 0–3: Low priority   Score 4–6: Moderate priority
Score 7+: High priority

INTERPRETATION OF QUESTIONNAIRE

MEDICATIONS

- Medications are good indicators that your body is in some sort of imbalance.
- Medications have drug/nutrient interactions. Some nutrient needs may be increased, some decreased; some nutrients may block absorption or usefulness of the drug.

FOODS, DRINKS, TOBACCO

- Candy, alcohol, sweets, and soft drinks: These "empty calorie foods" contain few nutrients, but nutrients are needed to metabolize them, and they replace healthy foods in our diets. These foods have a detrimental effect on most digestive problems; for instance, simple sugars feed *Candida*, bacteria, and parasites.

- Cigarettes and chewing tobacco: Make sure to take a good antioxidant supplement and lots of vitamin C to compensate for the stress the tobacco causes. Tobacco has a negative effect on the digestive system.
- Luncheon meats, pastries, fast-foods, and margarine: If you eat these foods you are probably getting too much fat, especially saturated fat. Margarine and most pastries also contain "hydrogenated oils," which are absorbed into our cells but are detrimental to our health. They make the cell membranes stiff and stifle the intake of nutrients and outgo of wastes, promote free radical activity, and contribute to atherosclerosis and inflammatory diseases.

LIFESTYLE

- Diet often: Weight problems can be caused by a hypoactive thyroid, food sensitivities, poor food choices, sedentary lifestyle, and emotional and social overeating. Chronic dieting leads to further metabolic slowdown. A wellness-centered approach works best for the overweight person.
- Lack of routine exercise: Exercise is the great stress reducer and enhances the health of our whole body, including our digestive system. Regular exercise at least three times a week for twenty to thirty minutes can significantly reduce the risk of cardiovascular disease and increase our total sense of well-being.
- High stress level: This indicates the need for a good exercise program, ways of nurturing oneself, and training to increase emotional heartiness. Food choices usually

suffer during stressful periods, while nutrient needs are increased. Supplementation may be indicated.

- Exposure to chemicals: Prolonged exposure to chemicals can cause environmental illness, which can manifest as obvious illness or as nondiagnosable complaints of confusion, chronic fatigue, headaches, or just not feeling right. Many women with breast cancer have had prolonged exposure to chemicals. Metabolic clearing and low-temperature saunas are important.

- Exposure to cigarette smoke: Research indicates that second-hand smoke is detrimental to a healthy respiratory system. If you cannot get away from smokers, buy them "smokeless" ashtrays, open windows whenever possible, and take antioxidant supplements.

- Focus your attention on the sections where you scored in either the moderate or high priority range. They are the greatest arenas for health enhancement of your digestive system.

Chapter 2

THE AMERICAN WAY OF LIFE IS HAZARDOUS TO YOUR HEALTH

"Of the ten leading causes of death in the United States, four, including the top three, are associated with dietary excess: coronary heart disease, some types of cancer, stroke, non-insulin-dependent diabetes mellitus. Together these conditions account for nearly two-thirds of the deaths occurring each year in the United States."

BETTY FRZAZO, "THE HIGH COST OF POOR DIETS,"
USDA FOOD REVIEW, JANUARY–APRIL 1994, 17(1): 2

WE EAT VERY differently than did our great-grandparents. Food production began to change during the Industrial Revolution, making refined sugar and white flour, previously a luxury of the rich, affordable and available to everyone. However, in processing, fiber and nutrients are lost. This was just the beginning of the changes introduced into our food supply—frozen foods, packaged foods, microwave ovens, foods shipped globally! Today we are part of a massive, uncontrolled science experiment. What happens when people are fed highly processed foods, lacking in nutrients and fiber and loaded with chemicals, over three generations? What happens when you put these same people under high levels of stress, in sedentary jobs, with poor air and water quality? Is it a coincidence that infertility rates are up, that Americans are fatter than ever before, that we are more violent than ever before, and that more people are committing suicide? Is it a coincidence that more children have attention deficit syndrome, a condition that never existed previously, and that children and adults have more allergies and chronic ear infections? Is it a coincidence that our immune systems are breaking down or that diabetes and heart disease rates have changed dramatically over the past eighty years? I don't think so.

If you add up the calories we consume each day of high-calorie, nutrient-poor foods, *nearly half of our caloric intake comes from nutritionally depleted foods.* In addition, we also drink 2.65 gallons of pure alcohol per person each year, which equals 50 gallons of beer, 20 gallons of wine, or more than 4 gallons of distilled liquor. No wonder, the *S*tandard *A*merican *D*iet is SAD!

According to the United States Department of Agriculture (USDA) in 1988–1989, Americans each ate on average:

365 servings of soda pop or 638 cans per year for people aged 12–29
134 pounds of refined sugar excluding honey
 90 pounds of fats and oils
 63 dozen donuts
 60 pounds of cakes and cookies
 23 gallons of ice cream
 22 pounds of candy
  8 pounds of corn chips, popcorn, and pretzels
  7 pounds of potato chips

In 1978, for the first time, a U.S. Senate subcommittee chaired by George McGovern made recommendations about healthy eating. They proposed cutting fat intake by a third, doubling fiber intake, eating at least 2½ cups of produce daily, focusing on whole grains and legumes, viewing meat as a sidedish rather than the main course, integrating more vegetarian meals, and cutting sodium. Lobbyists from the food industry were up in arms and defended the status quo.

In 1993, the USDA released a new food pyramid, which is an updated but watered down "improvement" of the 1978 recommendations. The numbers have been removed, so they won't offend anyone, but that made the guidelines ambiguous. Bland as they were, even this provoked controversy. The meat and dairy lobbies exerted their clout so that meat and dairy play a more prominent part in a daily menu than is optimal. The resulting pyramid provides a new shape, but offers little change to the old four basic food groups.

Even disguised, the U.S. dietary guidelines were heard loud and clear by the media and food manufacturers. You'd have to live in a cave to be unaware of why low-fat, fat-free foods are on the market. Clever packaging claims—"no cholesterol" or "low fat"—sway purchasing decisions. But despite increased awareness of what we ought to eat, Americans still don't eat right. According to the latest USDA food consumption study, although many of us seem to understand the concepts, we are still not making healthy choices. For example, we eat 10 percent fewer vegetables than we did just ten years ago, and in the same decade use of soft drinks has grown by 60 percent. We're consuming more sugar—a whopping 135 pounds per person per year, up from 126 pounds in 1976 and only 15 pounds in 1850. Only 9 percent of the population eats five servings of fruits and vegetables a day.

Though Americans have significantly decreased the amount of fat in their diets, only a quarter of us meet the recommendations to reduce fat to 30 percent of total calories. High-fat diets are a primary factor in gallbladder and heart diseases, and they contribute to obesity, which raises the risk of all degenerative illnesses. Of women aged thirty to seventy-four, 30 to 35 percent are overweight and getting fatter. Almost as many men are overweight. We weigh more now than we did just ten years ago.

Even though most Americans still eat too much fat, we also eat the wrong kind. In 1910, a process called hydrogenation was invented which turned liquid oils into solid fat that was inexpensive, suitable for frying and baking, and didn't go rancid. Since then, manufacturers replaced healthy oils with hydrogenated fats in thousands of products, until they now comprise about 8 percent of daily calories. These restructured fats are detrimental to our health and have been implicated in cancer, heart disease, and inflammatory conditions. And although we eat too much fat, many of us are deficient in essential fatty acids, especially the omega-3 fatty acids that are in seafoods, grains, nuts, seeds, and flaxseeds. These essential fatty acids are critical for growth, healing, reduction of pain and inflammation, healthy skin, reproduction, nervous system functioning, and overall well-being.

There have been significant reductions in the incidence of heart disease since 1970. Most researchers attribute this to changes in diet, plus an overall increase in exercise. Cholesterol is one of many risk factors for heart disease; the higher your levels, the more likely you are to have cardiovascular problems. But reducing dietary cholesterol may not solve the problem. In fact, only 30 percent of all people who overeat cholesterol have a significant rise in serum cholesterol levels. Kilmer McKully, M.D., who discovered that elevated homocysteine levels are another risk factor for heart disease, believes that high serum cholesterol may be a symptom of oxidative stress in our arteries, not the real culprit. Increasing dietary and supplemental levels of vitamin B_6, B_{12}, and folic acid can normalize homocysteine levels. These nutrients are stripped from the contemporary American diet. Some progressive physicians look at high serum cholesterol levels as a sign of liver distress. The liver is on a feedback loop: if we eat more cholesterol, it makes less; if we eat less, it makes more. So high cholesterol levels may indicate a need for liver-supportive nutrients and herbs. Many researchers believe that an increase in vitamin C consumption may be the reason for the large decline in cardiovascular disease. In countries where vitamin C intake has risen, heart disease has fallen. Oxidization of cholesterol in the vessels is caused by free radical damage. Vitamin C keeps LDL cholesterol from oxidizing, helps normalize serum cholesterol levels and reduces atherosclerosis. Dr. Matthias Rath, Director of Cardiology Research at the Linus Pauling Institute, discovered in 1989 that lipoprotein A exists in abnormal amounts in people with heart disease: "There is a direct relationship between vitamin C and lipoprotein A which leads to the conclusion that vitamin C deficiency is the primary cause of heart disease." Another recent study concluded that men who took 300 milligrams or more of vitamin C daily had a 30 percent reduction in mortality from all causes.

The average person consumes 12 grams of fiber daily, according to studies done by the USDA and the National Institutes of Health. This falls far short of the recommendation of 20 to 30 grams and is half of what people ate 150 years ago. Dietary fiber, found in fruits, vegetables, legumes, and whole grains, is beneficial to our digestive tract and reduces risk of GI illness. In fact, short-chained fatty acids (like butyrate, the main fuel of the colon) are manufactured directly from fiber-rich foods and protect us against diseases of the colon.

Not only what we eat, but the way we eat has changed—for the worse. Often, we eat the same way we put gas in our cars: stop, fuel, go. We eat 45 percent of meals away from home, up from 39 percent in 1980 and 34 percent in 1970. Many of us skip breakfast, and others skip breakfast and lunch. Studies show that school-aged children perform better when they've eaten breakfast. Adults are no different. In fact, small, frequent meals keep our energy levels even and our minds alert. We need to treat our bodies like a wood stove. You light the stove in the morning so it will warm the house while you work. Throughout the day you put small amounts of wood into the stove, and at nighttime, you fuel the stove and then let it die down before going to sleep. Our bodies work the same way. If we eat small meals and nutritious snacks throughout the day, they are burned efficiently.

Americans often overeat socially and emotionally. How commonly we hear that someone went to a party or out to dinner and just "stuffed themselves sick" or "ate like a pig." At home we eat when we aren't hungry because we are bored, lonely, angry, depressed, sad, frustrated, procrastinating, and a million other reasons that have nothing to do with hunger or nourishing our bodies. We stuff feeling inside with food rather than feel the hurt inside. This too contributes to digestive illness.

We eat to give nourishment to our bodies, but meals are also a time for relaxation, rest, refreshment, and renewal. If we are relaxed while eating, we digest food better. Numerous studies show that our mental state while eating has bearing on how well we digest food. People seem to know this intuitively. Saying grace or taking a couple of moments to center ourselves before eating is a global custom.

FOOD AND THE ENVIRONMENT

Thousands of years ago, people foraged and hunted for food. When populations increased, people learned how to farm and propagate plants and animals, so that more people could be fed with regularity. Farmers used to grow many foods, rotate crops, and use "natural" fertilizers. Foods grown nearby were eaten fresh and primarily in season.

Today, we depend on the global economy to produce and supply our food. It seems perfectly normal to buy Granny Smith apples from New Zealand, dried Turkish apricots, salmon from Norway, and drink mineral water and wine imported from France or California. We have grown accustomed to nectarines in winter and oranges in summer.

Are foods shipped from far away just as nutritious as foods that are grown locally? A ripe, juicy tomato from your backyard has about the same measurable nutritional value as those whitish-orange hothouse tomatoes on sale in winter. But even though they have the same "scientific" measurements, our intuitive measurement tells us they are different.

The life force in foods gives us vitality and life. If you photograph foods with Kirlian photography, living foods have large energy fields, while processed foods have little or none. I recently had an opportunity to watch Valerie Hunt's videotape on using Kirlian photography to show the effects of various activities on the human aura: First a man was videotaped sitting and eating denatured junk food. Both the food's aura and his aura were nil—about 2 inches. Then the same man was videotaped eating fresh fruits, fresh vegetables, and natural foods. His aura and the food's aura were bright, extended out about 2 feet in every direction, and were intertwined. Although I have always believed that natural foods have more vital energy, to see it documented was a thrill.

Once a plant is picked or an animal killed, a grain split or milk homogenized, it begins to lose its essential life force. Transporting foods over long distances diminishes their life-giving capacity. Statistically, canned, frozen, and packaged foods often contain great nutrients, but we know instinctively that they're different from fresh or homemade foods. In fact, processed foods are enzyme-deficient. They don't have the essential enzymes that are critical aids in digestion and metabolism. Fresh fruits, vegetables, local fish and game, grains, beans, nuts, and seeds give us these necessary enzymes. If your body doesn't have to work overtime making enzymes, it has more energy for other processes. Whole foods are in balance with themselves and with nature. When we eat them, we benefit from their balance.

Today our soils are being depleted. Most food in America is grown on corporate agrifarms that grow monocrops.

Chemical fertilizers add only the nutrients necessary for healthy plants, not nutrient-rich foods. In fact, use of pesticides and herbicides to limit crop loss has skyrocketed over the past thirty years. The average person consumes 1 pound of these chemicals each year. These pesticides have neurotoxic effects and can cause damage to our nervous systems. They are especially harmful to children whose small bodies are exposed to more pesticides per unit of weight than adults. The good news is that organic farming and integrated pest management are gaining momentum.

Most of our produce is hybridized. Its nutrient value is often sacrificed for pesticide resistance, ease of transportation, or appearance. Many of these hybridized foods look or taste better than their old counterparts, but corn, for instance, has 14 percent less protein now than it did forty years ago.

In Hawaii, tiny wild bananas are much more flavorful than commercial bananas. Throughout the world groups of people now collect seeds from these nonhybrid food plants and grow them. Someday we may be very grateful for these pioneers who are helping to protect biodiversity.

FOOD PREPARATION AND TECHNOLOGY

Linked to changes in food production and distribution are changes in food preparation. Valuable nutrients are taken out of foods, while chemicals and processes that change the very genetic makeup of foods are used to preserve and "enhance" them.

Food processing destroys nutrients. For example, whole wheat contains twenty-two vitamins and minerals that are removed to make white flour. After the bran and germ are removed from the whole wheat kernel, so too are 98 percent of pyridoxine (vitamin B_6), 91 percent of manganese, 84 percent of magnesium, and 87 percent of fiber. One of the many lost nutrients is chromium, which is critical for maintenance of blood sugar levels, normalizing high serum cholesterol levels, and fat burning. The average American diet is seriously depleted in many nutrients due to food processing.

From the earliest times, people salted meats and other foods to cure them. Later they canned foods with sugar, salt, and vinegar to keep them from perishing. Today, because food is produced and shipped from afar, manufactured chemical additives are put into foods to stabilize and preserve them. More than three thousand food additives are used in the United States alone—dyes, artificial flavors, dough conditioners, texturing agents, anticaking agents, and so on—to extend shelf life and enhance flavor, appearance, consistency and texture. The average person eats an alarming 14 pounds of additives each year.

Current research indicates that only a tiny percentage of the population is sensitive to food additives, but I have seen many people in my practice with sensitivities. One fifteen-year-old client went into anaphylactic shock within ten minutes if she ate a single drop of food coloring. Another client could no longer eat in restaurants because of severe reactions to monosodium glutamate. It is well documented that sulfites cause asthma and respiratory problems in sensitive individuals.

The long-term effects of food additives on children are of special concern. They consume more harmful substances per body weight than do adults. Ben Feingold, among others, found that many additives caused significant behavior and learning problems in sensitive children. The potential for long-term damage is clearly greater for children than for adults.

Additives have been tested singly, but never in combination. What are the long-term effects? No one really knows. The chemistry experiment going on inside of us reminds me of my favorite experiment with a childhood chemistry set. I used to mix two chemicals together and watch the test tube explode. Although food additives have been tested singly, they have never been tested in combinations. We have no idea what their synergistic effect really is. Healthy people can handle most food additives, but why burden your body with having to detoxify them? Minimize them by reading labels carefully.

Americans love the convenience of frozen foods. But if you read the labels, you'll find that most frozen foods contain additives that make the foods less perishable or less expensive. With careful shopping, you can find good quality frozen foods.

Microwave cooking has spread like brush fire over the last two decades. Yet there is no scientific consensus about the safety of microwaved food. Many researchers find that although there are some particles in microwaved food that aren't ordinarily found in nature, the food remains nutritious and healthful. Others feel that microwaved food is denatured and therefore detrimental to our health. Studies show that when breast milk has been microwaved to 98.6 degrees Fahrenheit, almost all the antibodies and lysozymes that protect us from infection are destroyed. Still other studies are conflicting. One thing is for sure: microwaving foods is too recent an innovation to know what the long-term effects are. It really doesn't take that much longer to cook food in the oven or on the stove.

For the first time, we now have genetically engineered foods. Technologists are splicing genes into dozens of foods to make them last longer, be juicer, taste sweeter, grow bigger, and be more pest-resistant. Some experts are opposed to bioengineering. They are concerned that people with allergies to specific foods will react to gene-spliced foods. What will these foods do to the long-term ecological balance of the world?

Food irradiation is now being used in food production. It's a "clever" way to use nuclear wastes—to keep food fresh longer, and to decrease the incidence of food poisoning. Irradiation kills all bacteria, like *Salmonella*, and leaves no radiation in the food itself. But many researchers are opposed to irradiation. For instance, milk loses 70 percent of vitamin A, thiamin, and riboflavin. Moreover, irradiated foods have molecules that are found nowhere in nature. The Food and Drug Administration (FDA) dubs them "radiolytic by-products" and separates them into two categories: "known radiolytic products," such as formaldehyde and benzene, which are known carcinogens, and "unique radiolytic products," which are new molecules that haven't been characterized. What's frightening is no one knows what the long-term effects of these molecules will be on health. Many people are opposed to such massive experimentation done at our risk. They are also worried about the risk of having small irradiating facilities throughout the country, which will have all the problems associated with handling nuclear materials.

THE CHANGING AMERICAN LIFESTYLE

Though many people have a high standard of living today, the price is a hurried life that takes its toll on our bodies. Studies show we actually have less leisure time than people had just twenty years ago—despite an array of time-saving appliances. Because our bodies and our minds work together, the stresses we feel in either one affects the other. The synergy can help calm us down or stress us out. The mind/body connection plays an important role in digestive wellness. Stress makes our stomach feel like it has rocks in it. Stress plays a large role in ulcerative colitis, skin conditions, and autoimmune problems. In fact, nearly all health problems are due to stress: physical, emotional, or environmental.

Commonly used drugs also play a role in the development of many digestive illnesses. Seventy million prescriptions for nonsteroidal anti-inflammatory drugs (NSAIDs) are written each year. The cost this contributes to the development of gastric ulcers is estimated to be over $100 million a year. Aspirin is especially hard on the stomach lining and overuse can contribute to the development of ulcers. NSAIDs, like Tylenol, Motrin, Advil, and dozens of others, are gentler on the stomach lining but much more irritating to the intestinal

lining. They cause damage to the lining by blocking prostaglandins that stimulate repair. They are a direct cause of
leaky gut syndrome, food sensitivities, and inflammatory
problems like arthritis and eczema.

Antibiotics kill not only disease-causing bacteria, but
healthy ones as well. Healthful bacteria, like *Lactobacillus acidophilus*, attach tightly to the intestinal lining so that no parasites or disease-producing organisms can get a foothold.
Antibiotics kill these friendly bacteria, allowing pathogenic
microbes, viruses, and fungi to take hold. Antibiotics also
disrupt the natural symbiosis of the gut and can cause gross
imbalance of the natural flora, leading to chronic and systemic illness. According to S. M. Wolfe, "After Congres-
sional hearings and numerous academic studies on this issue,
it has become the general consensus that 40 to 60 percent
of all antibiotics in this country are misprescribed."

We live in a toxic environment. Air quality is questionable,
and water, our most precious resource, is becoming polluted.
Although various localities are cleaning up their natural resources, the global balance is on average deteriorating. Our
soils are becoming contaminated. Vast numbers of grazing
livestock are destroying many habitats and causing erosion.
World population has exploded, demanding material needs
that are stripping the planet.

Many physicians believe that the underlying cause of digestive illness is a combination of poor nutrition and exposure to
toxic substances. We are exposed daily to hundreds of chemicals: side-stream smoke, chlorine and fluoride from water, air
pollution, cosmetics, toiletries, household cleaning supplies,
medications, and workplace toxins. Healthy people can handle
them fairly well, but when the liver gets overloaded, it fails to
adequately protect us. Many holistic therapies integrate detoxification programs, which enhance the liver's ability to carry us
through this chemical minefield. If our livers are functioning
suboptimally, our digestion doesn't work optimally, which leads
to increased work for the already overtaxed liver, which leads
to more digestive problems, and on and on.

We have yet to find the balance between the miracles that technology offers and the health of our environment. Our greatest challenge is to increase the standard of living in a way that everyone on earth can reap the many benefits of modern technology without destroying our ecosystems and biodiversity.

THE WILL TO CHANGE

Most people are unaware of how closely their health problems are related to their lifestyle. We are overfed and undernourished. Poor food choices, use of alcohol and cigarettes, a sedentary lifestyle, and chronic stress shorten our lives and contribute to degenerative illness as well as how we feel daily. People are born with reserves of nutrients in their organs, but a lifetime of low-nutrient foods will deplete those reserves, weakening the body's ability to heal. We like to think of ourselves living robustly, rooting and tooting until we die, but the truth is most of us limp along, accepting poor health and declining quality of life for the last twenty years of our lives as though it were normal and customary. Many of us have come to accept digestive illness as an integral part of our lives. But we can change the way we feel by making changes in our way of life.

It's time to focus on health rather than convenience and develop better habits. Instead of asking, Does it look and taste good?, we should ask: Is this food healthful, will it contribute to my biochemical balance and help me feel better, and will it taste good? We need to exercise regularly and think positive thoughts. We need to relax by ourselves and with friends. We need to create balance in our lives.

Your digestive problems offer you an opportunity to change. You can see this as a curse or a blessing. When you get sick and tired of being sick and tired, you're willing to make some real changes! This involves commitment on your part. Remember: no pain, no gain!

Exercise 2

FOOD DIARY

Write down everything you eat and drink in a diary and keep track of how your body feels. If you have diarrhea or pain after you eat or feel like a million bucks, write it down. See if you can correlate specific foods to the way your digestive system works. Keep track of where you were, who you were with, and your moods. Digestive problems are often related to how comfortable or uncomfortable we feel in a situation. Does a specific person make you nervous? Keeping a chart will help you find out. A sample chart looks like this:

DAY

Time of day	What did I eat?	Where was I? Who was I with? What was my mood?	How does my GI tract feel?

EXAMINING YOUR FOOD DIARY_____

1. Do you eat breakfast every day? Breakfast provides the fuel we need to get our bodies going for the day. It literally means "break the fast."
2. Is your indigestion better or worse at specific times of the day? This can be a clue to indigestion. Maybe it's something you ate, how fast or how much you ate, or where you ate.
3. Do you eat when you aren't really hungry? If so, examine the reasons, and try to find other outlets for your energies.
4. How often do you eat? Most people feel best when they eat three meals daily plus nutritious snacks. This meal plan keeps blood sugar levels even and facilitates digestion.
5. Do certain foods/beverages provoke symptoms? Eliminate suspicious foods for a week and note any differences in how you feel.
6. Are you relaxing at mealtimes or rushing? Eating more slowly aids digestion.
7. Do you get at least five servings of fruits and vegetables each day? A serving is a piece of fruit, a half cup of most vegetables, or a cup of lettuce. Five servings is a minimal requirement.
8. What percentage of your foods and beverages were high-sugar, high-fat, low-fiber, or highly processed? Replace these with fresh, wholesome foods.
9. Do you consume enough high-fiber foods? We find fiber in whole grains, fruits, vegetables, and legumes.
10. Do you drink enough—6 to 8 cups—water, herb teas, and juices? Soft drinks and coffee don't count!

Part 2

HEALTHY DIGESTION/
FAULTY DIGESTION

Chapter 3

A Voyage Through the Digestive System

"The surface area of the digestive mucosae, measuring up and down and around all the folds, rugae, villi, and microvilli, is about the size of a tennis court."

SYDNEY BAKER, M.D.

THE DIGESTIVE SYSTEM is self-running and self-healing. Because this beautiful, intricate system works automatically, the average person knows very little about it. Let's take a trip through the digestive system to see what miraculous events occur inside us every moment of our lives.

Think of the digestive tract as a 25- to 35-foot hose that runs from the mouth to the anus. Its function is to turn the foods we eat into microscopic particles that the cells can use for energy, maintenance, growth, and repair. The old saying "You are what you eat" is primarily true. From birth to death, we continually create and recreate ourselves from the nourishment we put inside the body.

Whatever we eat is squeezed through the digestive system by a rhythmic muscular contraction called peristalsis. Sets of smooth muscles contract, alternately pushing food through the esophagus to the stomach and through the intestines. There it is acidified, liquefied, neutralized, and homogenized until it's broken down into usable particles. From the time you swallow, this process is involuntary and can occur even if you stand on your head. My seven-year-old son demonstrated this by eating upside-down. Yes, the food went down—or rather up—as usual!

The digestive system is like an irrigation system. A large source of water gets narrower and narrower, finally getting water to each tiny portion of a field. If the water becomes blocked upstream, the plants wither and die. In the body, the unblocked flow of nutrients is critical for optimal health and function. Along the way, the body breaks down food—protein into amino acids, starches into glucose, and fats into fatty acids and glycerol. Enzymes, vitamins, and minerals are also absorbed. The cells use these raw materials for energy, growth, and repair. If digestive wellness is compromised, our cells lose their capacity to function fully. Unlike a field, the body is innovative and will try to find ways to make things work. Eventually, however, its ability to seek new pathways fails, and we feel unwell. This is especially apparent in the lining of the digestive tract, which repairs and replaces itself every three to five days.

YOU AREN'T ONLY WHAT YOU EAT

Nutritious foods are the right place to start on the path to digestive wellness. But many people eat all the "right" foods and still have digestive problems. The best diet in the world won't help if you aren't digesting properly. You must be able to digest foods; break them down into tiny particles; absorb the food mash; take that through the intestinal lining and into the bloodstream; assimilate nutri-

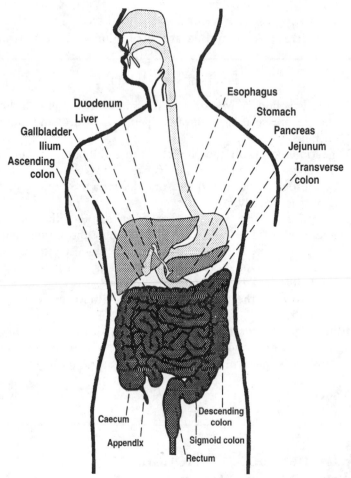

Duodenum
Liver
Gallbladder
Ilium
Ascending
colon

Esophagus
Stomach
Pancreas
Jejunum
Transverse
colon

Caecum
Appendix

Descending
colon
Sigmoid colon
Rectum

The human digestive system.

ents and calories into the cells where they can be used; and eliminate waste products through the kidneys, bowels, lymph system, and skin. Health can and does break down at any of these phases. For example, people with lots of intestinal gas are fermenting their food. Difficulty with absorption can cause people to have food sensitivities, fatigue, skin rashes, and migraine headaches. Diabetics have a problem with assimilation of glucose into the cells. Constipation and diarrhea are problems of elimination.

THE DIGESTIVE PROCESS

Eating is voluntary when materials are put in the mouth. Food choices are related to lifestyle, personal values, and cultural customs.

Digestion occurs in the stomach and small intestine and requires cooperation from the liver and pancreas. Proper levels of hydrochloric acid and intestinal bacteria are critical for full digestive capacity.

Absorption occurs when food is taken through the intestinal lining into the bloodstream, and through the portal vein to the liver where it is filtered. From the bloodstream it passes to the cells. Until food is absorbed, it is essentially outside the body—in a tube going through it.

Assimilation is the process by which fuel and nutrients enter the cells.

Elimination of waste products happens through the kidneys, bowels, lymph system, and skin. We absorb and excrete many substances through the skin, which is the second largest organ in the body.

Water is essential to the digestive process. It softens foods and dissolves many components.

A GUIDED TOUR THROUGH THE DIGESTIVE SYSTEM

To gain a thorough understanding of how the digestive system works, let's take a guided tour starting at the brain and ending at the colon.

Brain

Digestion begins before we even put food into our mouths! Any sound, sight, odor, taste, or texture associated with food

Digestive Process	Where in the Body	Function
Eating/food choices	Mouth/mind	Portal for all nutrients/materials to enter the body
Digestion	Stomach/small intestine; to a lesser degree, saliva in the mouth	Breaks down food into basic components for use by the cells
Absorption	Small intestine/ large intestine, bloodstream, liver	Food comes through the intestinal wall into the bloodstream
Assimilation	Cellular	Nutrients enter cells and are used for energy, storage, and structure
Elimination	Colon, kidneys, skin, lymph system, cells, and bloodstream	Wastes are excreted

can trigger the body to prepare for the food that will arrive. Digestive juices, saliva, enzymes, and digestive hormones begin to flow in anticipation of the food to come. In addition, the body "revs up" to prepare for the work of digestion, and the heart rate and blood flow can change.

Although this phase of digestion only lasts a short time, it emphasizes the importance of eating in a relaxed manner and of appreciating the food you are about to ingest. Some people find that taking time to say grace and to look at and smell the food, as well as making a special time and place for eating, can dramatically enhance their total digestive function more completely than can enzymes, bitters, or other digestive supplements.

DIGESTIVE SYSTEM
ABSORBTION

LOCATION	ENTER	EXIT TO BLOOD
Mouth and Esophagus	Salivary amylase	
Stomach	Gastric juice pepsin and HCL	Ethyl alcohol
Small Intestine		
Duodenum	Pancreatic juice, bicarbonate enzymes	1. Chlorine and Sulfuric Acid, Calcium, Magnesium, Iron, Zinc, Copper, Manganese
		2. Monosaccharides, Glucose, Galactose, Fructose
		3. B_1, B_2, B_6, Folate, C
		4. Fat (i.e., short-chain fatty acids, long-chain fatty acids, and partially split glycerides)
	Bile	5. Fat soluble vitamins A, D, E
Jejunum	Intestinal brush border enzymes	6. Disaccharides sucrose, maltose, lactose
		7. Water-soluble vitamins: thiamine, pyridoxine, riboflavin, folic acid
		8. Proteins and amino acids
Ileum		9. Cholesterol
		10. Vitamin B_{12}
		11. Bile salts
Large Intestine Colon		12. Potassium
		13. Water
		14. Sodium Chloride
		15. Vitamin K formed by colonic bacteria
		16. Short-chain fatty acids and volatile fatty acids from fiber digestion

Mouth

The main function of the mouth is chewing and liquefying food. The salivary glands, which are located under the tongue, produce saliva which softens food, begins dissolving soluble components, and helps keep the mouth and teeth clean. Saliva contains amylase, an enzyme for splitting carbohydrates. Only a small percentage of starches are digested by amylase, but if you keep a piece of bread in your mouth for a long time, you can begin to taste the increased sweetness that comes from splitting the starch into simple sugars. Chewing also stimulates the parotid glands, behind the ears in the jaw, to release hormones that stimulate the thymus to produce T-cells, which are the core of the protective immune system.

Healthy teeth and gums are critical for proper digestion. Many people eat so fast, they barely chew their food at all and then wash it down with liquids. So the stomach receives chunks of food instead of mush. This undermines the function of the teeth, which is to increase the surface area of the food. These people often complain of indigestion or gas. In *May All Be Fed*, John Robbins describes three men who survived in a concentration camp during World War II by chewing their food very well, while their compatriots perished. Simply by chewing food thoroughly we can enhance digestion and eliminate some problems of indigestion.

The most common problems that occur in the mouth are sores on the lips or tongue—usually canker or cold sores (herpes)—and tooth and gum problems.

Esophagus

The esophagus is the tube which passes from the mouth to the stomach. Here peristalsis begins to push the food along the digestive tract. Well-chewed food passes through the esophagus in about six seconds, but dry food can get stuck and take minutes to pass. At the bottom of the esophagus is a little door called the cardiac or esophageal sphincter. It separates the esophagus from the stomach, keeping stomach acid and food from coming back up. It remains closed most of the time, opening when a peristaltic wave, triggered by swallowing, relaxes the sphincter. The most common esophageal problems are heartburn (also called gastric reflux) and hiatal hernia.

Stomach: The Body's Blender

The stomach is the body's blender. It chops, dices, and liquefies as it changes food into a soupy liquid called chyme, which is the beginning of the process of protein digestion. The stomach is located under the rib cage, just under the heart.

Protein molecules are composed of chains of amino acids—up to 200 amino acids strung together. Hydrochloric acid (HCl), produced by millions of parietal cells in the stomach lining, begins to break apart these protein chains. HCl also kills microbes that come in with food, effectively sterilizing it. HCl is so strong that it would burn our skin and clothing if spilled on us. Yet, the stomach is protected by a thick coating of mucus (mucopolysaccharides), which keeps the acid from burning through the stomach lining. Prostaglandins, small chemical messengers, help keep the mucous layer active by sending messages to replace and repair the stomach lining and provide a protective coating. When this mucous layer breaks down, HCl burns a hole in the stomach lining, causing a gastric ulcer.

The stomach also makes pepsin, a protein-splitting enzyme, which cuts the bonds between specific amino acids, breaking them down into short chains of just four to twelve. The stomach also produces small amounts of lipase, enzymes that digest fat. Most foods are digested and absorbed farther down the gastrointestinal tract, but alcohol, water, and certain salts are absorbed directly from the stomach into the bloodstream. That's why we feel the effects of alcohol so quickly.

Food stays in the stomach two to four hours—less with a low-fat meal, more with a high-fat or high-fiber meal. When the stomach has finished its job, chyme has the consistency of split pea soup. Over several hours it passes in small amounts through the pyloric valve into the duodenum, the first 12 inches of the small intestine. Chronic stress lengthens the amount of time that food stays in the stomach, while short-term stress usually shortens the emptying time. Most of us have experienced a nervous stomach, or a feeling in the pit of the stomach, or a stomach that feels like it's filled with rocks.

VITAMIN B_{12} AND INTRINSIC FACTOR

Before vitamin B_{12} even had a name, scientists knew that there was something in food that joined with something in the stomach that helped its absorption. They named these two substances intrinsic factor and extrinsic factor. Later, extrinsic factor was discovered to be vitamin B_{12}, which is essential for blood formation, energy, growth, and cell division and function. Intrinsic factor is made in the stomach in the parietal cells, and binds vitamin B_{12} so that it can be readily absorbed in the intestines. Hydrochloric acid is also produced by the parietal cells. As the parietal cells become less efficient, the production of both hydrocholoric acid and intrinsic factor falls.

As we age, the ability to manufacture hydrochloric acid decreases. Intrinsic factor is likewise decreased and vitamin B_{12} deficiencies occur. Many elderly people have vitamin B_{12} deficiencies which affect the body's ability to get oxygen into each cell. The main symptoms are muscle weakness and fatigue. Many people benefit from vitamin B_{12} injections, under a physician's care, even though many do not have low serum B_{12} levels or pernicious anemia (anemia caused by B_{12} deficiency). I remember one elderly woman who had normal serum B_{12} levels, but she felt enormously different when B_{12} shots were added to her regimen. This simple, inexpensive therapy can dramatically affect quality of life for those who need it. More sensitive tests of vitamin B_{12} status are also available—homocysteine and methylmalonic acid.

The most common problems associated with the stomach are gastric ulcers and underproduction of hydrochloric acid.

THE MAN WITH A WINDOW IN HIS STOMACH

We owe early information about how digestion works to a man who had a "window" in his stomach. In 1822, Alexis St. Martin, a young Canadian trapper, was shot at close range in his left side. A U.S. Army doctor, William Beaumont, successfully treated St. Martin but was unable to close the wound completely. Over the next eight years Dr. Beaumont observed the activity of St. Martin's stomach through the hole, watching what happened when various foods were eaten and how his emotions affected his digestive activity. Until this time, people had no idea what happened to food after it was swallowed. Science owes much to these two men.

Small Intestine

The small intestine is hardly small. If this coiled-up garden hose were stretched out, it would average 15 to 20 feet long. If spread flat, it would cover a surface the size of a tennis court. Here food is completely digested and absorbed. Nutrients are absorbed through hundreds of small fingerlike folds called villi in the intestinal wall, which are covered, in turn, by millions of microvilli. (Think of them as small loops on a velvety towel which then have smaller threads projecting from them.) The villi and microvilli are only one cell layer thick, but perform multiple functions of producing digestive enzymes, absorbing nutrients, and blocking absorption of substances that aren't useful to the body.

The intestinal lining repairs and replaces itself every three to five days. The sloughed material contains enzymes and fluids which are recycled to help digestion. The intestinal wall has a paradoxical function: it allows nutrients to pass into the bloodstream while blocking the absorption of foreign substances found in chemicals, bacterial products, and other large molecules found in food. Some foods we eat and medications we use cause the intestinal wall to lose the ability to discern between nutrients and foreign substances. When this occurs, there is a problem of intestinal permeability, or leaky gut syndrome. This newly recognized syndrome contributes to skin problems, food sensitivities, osteoarthritis, migraine headaches, and chronic fatigue syndrome.

The small intestine has three parts: the duodenum, the jejunum, and the ileum. The duodenum is the first 12 inches of the small intestine, the jejunum is the next 40 percent, and the ileum is the last segment. Each nutrient is absorbed at specific parts of the small intestine. For instance, the duodenum has an acidic environment which facilitates absorption of some nutrients, including calcium, copper, iron, folic acid, thiamin, manganese, vitamins A and B_2, and zinc. People with low hydrochloric acid levels may become deficient in one or more of these nutrients.

Pancreas

The pancreas has two main roles: production of digestive enzymes and insulin. When food passes from the stomach to the duodenum, the pancreas secretes bicarbonates, essentially baking soda, which neutralizes the acidity of the chyme so it won't burn the tissues of the intestines. Then it manufactures and secretes specific enzymes that digest fats, carbohydrates, and protein. These enzymes are lumped into three categories: lipase, amylase, and protease. Lipase breaks fats into fatty acids and glycerol; amylase splits carbohydrates into simple sugars; and protease digests the links between amino acids from protein. Once digested, these nutrients can be absorbed into the bloodstream and used by the cells. Low secretion of pancreatic enzymes can also lead to nutritional deficiencies. For example, vitamin B_{12} requires protein-splitting enzymes to separate

RELATIVE IMPORTANCE OF SITE ABSORBTION
WITHIN THE SMALL INTESTINE

LOCATION	LENGTH	EXITS TO BLOOD
Duodenum	12-18 inches	Chlorine , Sulfuric acid, Calcium, Magnesium, Iron, Zinc, Copper, Manganese
		Monosaccharides, Glucose, Galactose, Fructose
		B_1, B_2, B_6, Folate, C
		Fat (i.e., short-chain fatty acids, long-chain fatty acids, and partially split glycerides)
		Fat soluble vitamins A, D, E, H
Jejunum	10 feet	Disaccharides sucrose, maltose, lactose
		Water-soluble vitamins: thiamine, pyridoxine, riboflavin, folic acid
		Proteins and amino acids
Ileum	12 feet	Cholesterol
		Vitamin B_{12}
		Bile salts

it from its carrier molecule, so poor pancreatic function can lead directly to vitamin B_{12} deficiencies.

The second role of the pancreas is hormonal regulation of blood sugar levels. When the blood sugar is too high, the pancreas secretes insulin which signals the cells to store glucose. When this mechanism fails, people develop diabetes.

Gut-Associated Lymphatic Tissue (GALT)

Current research indicates that 70 percent of the immune system is located in or around the digestive system. Called *gut-associated lymphatic tissue*, it's located in the lining of the digestive tract and in the intestinal mucus. If the digestive system is presented with a foreign substance, an *antigen*, specialized cells called *M-cells* carry the antigen to the lining of the digestive tract. There they are "checked out," or sampled, by specialized cells called *Peyer's patches* in the intestinal lining. These cells in turn alert B- and T-cells to begin processing the antigens. The B- and T-cells carry the antigens back to the intestinal mucosa, where they are gobbled up by macrophages. Secretory IgA, which are like sentinels on constant alert for foreign substances, are also present in the gut mucosa. Their arousal signals cytokines to begin the inflammatory process designed to rid our bodies of antigenic materials.

The Liver: The Body's Fuel Filter

The liver is the most overworked organ in the body because it plays many roles. It manufactures bile to emulsify fats for digestion; it makes and breaks down many hormones, including cholesterol, testosterone, and estrogens; it regulates blood sugar levels; it processes all food, nutrients, alcohol, drugs, and other materials that enter the bloodstream and lets them pass, breaks them down, or stores them. In our culture, the job of neutralizing environmental pollution inside the body is no small task—one which the liver never evolved to handle. Yet, the liver can lose as much as 70 percent of its capability and not show diagnosable liver disease. The quality of virtually every body function depends on the liver.

The 4½ pound liver manufactures 13,000 chemicals and has 2,000 enzyme systems, plus thousands of synergists that help with body functions. With these chemicals and enzymes, it "humanizes" nutrients so that the cells can use them. Practically all vitamins and minerals we take in need to be enzymatically processed by the liver before we can use them. If the liver is too congested to enzymatically process these nutrients, we do not get the benefit from them.

Bile, manufactured by the liver and stored by the gallbladder, buffers the intestinal contents due to its high concentration of bicarbonates. It also emulsifies fats. Bile is a soaplike substance made of bile salts, cholesterol, and lecithin. It makes fats more water-soluble, increasing their surface area so that the enzymes can split them for the cells to use.

The liver has three lobes: main, left, and lower. The main lobe organizes and humanizes nutrients. It is the main chemical factory, producing enzymes and chemicals necessary for body functions. The left lobe regulates and maintains body functions. People with toxic left lobes are often environmentally sensitive or pan-allergic—allergic to nearly everything. Many times allergic people crave what they are sensitive to. The body gets used to having nicotine, alcohol, wheat, dairy, or whatever, and when we remove it, the body's balance is disturbed. The left lobe works to maintain body homeostasis (staying the same) without the "missing" substance. The craving is, in some part, the liver's way of trying to get us what we "need." As Jack Tips writes in *The Liver Triad*, "As long as toxic residues from these substances are present in this lobe, the body will get a subtle signal to continue the addiction, to want to respond to allergens."

The lower lobe is where the essential fatty acids and fat-soluble vitamins A, D, E, and K are stored so the liver and other glands can produce cholesterol and hormones. This is also where the liver stores environmental toxins like radioactive substances, pesticides, herbicides, food preservatives, and dyes. The liver will detoxify what it can, but if it can't break down a particular substance, it stores it there and in tissues throughout the body. It is important to detox the liver on a regular basis, perhaps twice a year, to help maintain its function. Many systems have been developed to help detoxify the liver, which we discuss at length in chapter 9.

Gallbladder: A Holding Tank for Bile

The gallbladder is a pear-shaped organ that lies just below the liver. The gallbladder's function is to store and concentrate bile, which is produced by the liver. Bile emulsifies fats, cholesterol, and fat-soluble vitamins by breaking them into tiny globules. These create a greater surface area for the fat-splitting enzymes (lipase) to act on during digestion. When we eat, the gallbladder and liver release bile into the common duct which connects the liver, gallbladder, and pancreas to the duodenum. Between meals the gallbladder concentrates bile. The most common problem of the gallbladder is gallstones. When bile becomes too concentrated, stones may form, which can cause pain and discomfort. Gallbladder disease is directly related to diet.

The Large Intestine or Colon

When all nutrients have been absorbed, water, bacteria, and fiber pass through the ileocecal valve to the large intestine or colon. The ileocecal valve is located by your right hipbone and separates the contents of the small and large intestine. The appendix is a small, fingerlike sac which extends off the beginning of the colon. Until recently, the function of the appendix was a mystery. Now we know it contains a great deal of lymphatic tissue and is thought to be part of the immune system.

The colon is short, only 3 to 5 feet long. Its job is to

absorb water and remaining nutrients from the chyme and form stool. Two and a half gallons of water pass through the colon each day, two-thirds of which come from body fluids. The efficient colon pulls 80 percent of the water out of the chyme, which is absorbed into the bloodstream.

The large intestine has three main parts: the ascending colon (up the right side of the body), the transverse colon (straight across the belly under the ribs), and the descending colon (down the left side of the body) to the rectum, where feces exit the body. Stool begins to form in the transverse colon. If the chyme passes through the colon too quickly, water is not absorbed, causing diarrhea. Stool that sits too long in the colon becomes dry and hard to pass, leading to constipation. About two-thirds of stool is composed of water and undigested fiber and food products. The other third is composed of living and dead bacteria.

The large intestine contains trillions of bacteria. Helpful bacteria, called probiotics, lower the pH of the colon, killing disease-causing microbes. Probiotics also produce vitamins A, B, and K, protect us from illness, enhance peristalsis, and make lactase for milk digestion. Probiotic bacteria ferment the dietary fiber, producing short-chained fatty acids—butyric, propionic, acetic, and valerate. Butyric acid is the main fuel of the colonic cells. Low butyric acid levels or an inability of the colon bacteria to properly metabolize butyric acid has been associated with ulcerative colitis, colon cancer, active colitis, and inflammatory bowel disease.

When the stool is finally well formed, it gets pushed down into the descending colon and then into the rectum. It is held there until there is sufficient volume to have a bowel movement. Two sphincters—rings of muscle—control bowel movements. When enough feces have collected, the internal spincter relaxes and your mind gets the signal that it's time to relieve yourself. The external sphincter opens when you command it. Because this is voluntary, you can have the urge to defecate, but wait until it's convenient. If you ignore the urge, water keeps being absorbed back into the body and the stool gets dry and hard. Some people are chronically constipated because they don't want to take the time to have a bowel movement or don't like to have bowel movements at work. This book is about listening to your body signals. Take the time when your body calls you, not when it's convenient or ideal.

Many health problems arise in the colon: appendicitis, constipation, diarrhea, diverticular disease, Crohn's disease, ulcerative colitis, rectal polyps, colon cancer, irritable bowel syndrome, parasites, and hemorrhoids.

What Goes In, Must Come Out!

We can learn a lot about ourselves from stool. Dennis Burkitt, M.D., father of the fiber theory, found that on average people on Western diets only excreted 5 ounces of stool daily, whereas Africans eating traditional diets passed 16 ounces. Well-formed stool tells us when it wants to come out; we don't need to coax it. It looks like a brown banana with a point at one end, is well-hydrated, and just slips out easily. Stool that looks like little balls all wadded together has been in the colon too long. The longer waste materials sit in the colon, the more concentrated the bile acids become; concentrated bile acids irritate the lining of the colon. Hormones that have been broken down by the body are also excreted via our feces. If the stools sit in the colon for too long, these hormones are reabsorbed into the bloodstream, increasing the risk for estrogen-dependent cancers. Beta-glucuronidase, an enzyme that may activate formation of cancer-causing substances in the colon, can be measured as a marker of hormone reabsorption.

Frequency of bowel movements is a good health indicator. How often do you have a bowel movement? People on good diets generally have one to two each day. If you are not having a daily bowel movement, there can be many causes.

First, take a close look at your diet. You probably aren't eating enough fiber. If not, increase your intake of fruits, vegetables, whole grains, and legumes. These foods are generally high in magnesium, which helps normalize peristalsis. Make sure that you are drinking enough fluids. Coffee and soft drinks don't count! And get regular exercise!

Another good indicator of your colon's health is your bowel transit time—how long it takes food to move from the first swallow until it exits the body. When your system is working well, the average amount of time is twelve to

---

TESTING BOWEL TRANSIT TIME

Transit time is how long it takes from the time you eat a food until it comes out the other end. Buy charcoal tablets at a drug or health food store, and take twenty grains (or 1 gram)—anywhere from five to twelve depending on how big they are. Note exactly when you took the charcoal. When you see darkened stool (charcoal will turn the stool black), calculate how many hours since you took the charcoal tablets. That is your transit time. You can also do the test with beets. Eating three or four whole beets will turn stool a deep garnet red.

The Results
Less than twelve hours: This usually indicates that you are not absorbing all the nutrients you should from your food. You may have malabsorption problems.

Twelve to twenty-four hours is optimal.

More than twenty-four hours: This indicates that wastes are sitting inside your colon too long. Poor transit time greatly increases the risk of colon disease. Substances that were supposed to be eliminated get absorbed back into the bloodstream, and they can interfere with and irritate your system. Take action now! Increase your fiber intake by eating more fruit, vegetables, whole grains, and legumes. Drink lots of water every day. Get thirty minutes of exercise at least three times a week.

twenty-four hours. On average, Americans have a transit time that is way too long—forty-eight to ninety-six hours—because we don't eat enough high-fiber foods or drink enough water. You can do a simple home test to determine your transit time, which gives you important information about the way your body works.

Exercise 3

CLEAN UP YOUR DIET!

Let's take a look at what foods you are eating and begin the process of cleaning up your diet. Take last week's diary. Get out some crayons or markers. You're going to color!

Circle the following foods:

Sugar, caffeine, alcohol, junk foods, fried foods, high-fat foods, pastries, donuts, chips, microwave popcorn, highly processed foods, soft drinks, diet soft drinks, diet foods   Circle them red

Dairy products: milk, cheese, yogurt, ice cream, frozen yogurt, ice milk   Circle them blue

Fruits and vegetables   Circle them green

Protein foods: fish, poultry, beef, pork, lamb, veal, legumes, soy products   Circle them yellow

Nuts and seeds, oils, butter, margarine   Circle them purple

Grains: wheat, bread, corn, rice, millet, buckwheat, bulghur, quinoa, amaranth, barley, oats, rye   Circle them black

Look at those circles. Is there one food group that dominates your diary? If you eliminated one of these categories from your diet, which would be the easiest to give up and which would be the most difficult? Sometimes the ones which are the hardest to give up are the ones that are causing us the most trouble. They temporarily make us feel better, even though they are really making us sicker. Why? Our bodies react negatively to cigarettes, dairy products, caffeine, sugar, wheat, pork, beef, citrus fruits, or any other foods, yet we crave them.

Tackle the Sweet Tooth

This week, focus on the foods you circled in red and eliminate all of them. Sugars ferment and can contribute to your digestive problems. Get rid of soft drinks, cookies, pastries, donuts, and sugar added to coffee or tea. We're not talking about perfection here. Let's just make some progress. Why? Because these foods make it harder for your body to be healthy. High-sugar foods deplete our nutrient stores. We need most of the B-complex vitamins, chromium, manganese, and potassium to metabolize these foods properly, but sweets don't have any of these nutrients. So we take nutrients out of storage, and eventually our tissues become depleted.

After a couple of weeks, fruit begins to taste really sweet, which is just how it ought to taste. Once, I realized that it had been months since I had had any chocolate. I began to feel deprived, so I bought a big chocolate bar for my family and friends. I ate a few squares and was totally satisfied. I hope that eventually you can be satisfied with just a little bit, too. But if you can't, you're really better off without any. Once I was sick and was craving sweets like crazy. My doctor told me it was the bacteria—both good and bad—that wanted the energy. So starve those bad guys out. The helpful bacteria can adapt with real food.

Chapter 4

The Bugs in Your Body!
Intestinal Flora

"There are more bacteria in our intestinal tract than cells in our body."

JEFFERY BLAND

WE HAVE 400 TO 500 types of bacteria in our digestive systems, each of which has many types of strains. This variety may seem overwhelming, but 20 types make up three-quarters of the total. The most common are bacteroides, bifidobacteria, eubacterium, fusobacteria, lactobacillus, peptococcaceae, rheumanococcus, and streptococcus. Most of these bacteria are anaerobic, meaning they do not need oxygen to thrive; some are aerobic, which do need oxygen for survival; and a third group produces lactic acid and can be either aerobic or anaerobic. Lactic acid-producing bacteria help acidify the intestinal tract and protect us from overgrowth of harmful bacteria. A total of one hundred trillion bacteria live together in our digestive system, in either symbiotic or antagonistic relationships. Their total weight is about 4 pounds—the size of the liver.

There are billions of bacteria in our mouths. While the stomach has few due to its high acid content, which prohibits their growth, the small intestine has many billions of bacteria. The overwhelming majority of intestinal flora reside in the colon—trillions and trillions. Each day we produce several ounces of these microbes and eliminate several ounces in stool. These bacteria manufacture substances that raise or lower our risk of disease and cancer, effect of drugs, immune competence, nutritional status, and rate of aging. Some of these bacteria cause acute or chronic illness. Other bacteria cause illness in people who are genetically susceptible, but no problems in other people.

Another group of bacteria offer us protective and nutritive properties. These friendly bacteria are called *intestinal flora, probiotics*, or *eubiotics*—the last two terms mean "healthful to life." The term "probiotics" is commonly used to refer to supplemental use of these bacteria in powder or capsule form. The two most important groups of flora are the *lactobacilli*, found mainly in the small intestine, and bifidobacterium, found primarily in the colon. These bacteria live symbiotically within us in a mutually beneficial relationship that has evolved to enhance our health and theirs. *Saccharomyces boulardi*, a yeast, is also used as probiotic health enhancing. They live at about 98.6 degrees Fahrenheit and thrive on the constant nourishment we provide in a warm, dark, moist environment. We allow them to inhabit us because they give us valuable preventive and therapeutic benefits.

MAIN BACTERIA TYPES IN OUR BODIES

Type	Aerobic/ Anaerobic	Percent
Bacteroides, twenty species	Anaerobic	Almost 50
Bifidobacterium	Anaerobic	11
Pepto streptococcus	Anaerobic	8.9
Fusobacteria, five species		7
Rheumanococcus, eleven species		4.5
Lactobacillus	Both	2–2.5
Clostridia		0.6
Enterobacteria, E. coli, Klebsiella, Aerobacteraerobacter, etc.		Less than 0.5

Where did these trillions of bacteria come from? Up until birth, we receive predigested food from our mothers and are born with a sterile digestive tract. The trip down the birth canal initiates us into the world of microbes that thrive everywhere. Babies are exposed to bacteria in breast milk and formula and when sucking on nipples, fingers, and toes. With every breath and touch, bacteria enter the body to colonize on the skin and mucous membranes. In no time, every conceivable space in the colon is occupied by microbes. The microbes set up homogeneous neighborhoods which push out competing microbes that try to break into their territories. This normally happens in a predictable way, and once established, the colonies flourish. When babies are unable to properly colonize friendly flora, they become irritable, colicky, have gas pains, and eczema in their diaper area. As we age, the specific types and strains of dominant flora change from *Bifidobacteria infantus* in infants to other strains of *Bifidobacteria* in children and adults.

THE MANY BENEFITS OF INTESTINAL FLORA

Flora play an important role in our ability to fight infectious disease, providing a front line in our immune defense. As noted in the 1988 report of the U.S. Surgeon General, "Normal microbial flora provide a passive mechanism to prevent infection." Friendly flora also manufacture many vitamins including the B-complex vitamins biotin, thiamin (B_1), riboflavin (B_2), niacin (B_3), pantothenic acid (B_5), pyridoxine (B_6), cobalamine (B_{12}), and folic acid, plus vitamin A and vitamin K.

Lactic acid-secreting acidophilus and bifidus increase the bioavailability of minerals which require acid for absorption—calcium, copper, iron, magnesium, and manganese.

Farm animals are routinely given supplemental flora which enhance absorption of both vitamins and minerals.

Friendly flora help increase our resistance to food poisoning. In 1993 the United States reported 20 to 40 million cases of food poisoning, although the FDA estimates the true total to be 80 million. Many cases go unreported because the symptoms closely resemble the flu. Some food-borne infections lead to chronic illness, causing heart and valve problems, immune system disorders, joint disease, and possibly even cancer. Use of supplemental acidophilus and bifidus can help prevent food poisoning by making the intestinal tract inhospitable to the invading microbes. It is a common misconception that friendly flora kill invading microbes. What they actually do is change the environment by "competitive exclusion"—they secrete large amounts of acids (acetic, formic, and lactic acids) which make the area unsuitable for pathogens.

Benefits of *Bifidobacteria*

1. Prevent colonization of the intestine by pathogenic bacteria and yeasts by protecting the integrity of the intestinal lining.
2. Produce acids which keep the pH balance in the intestine. This acid environment prevents disease-producing microbes from getting a foothold.
3. Lessen side effects of antibiotic therapy.
4. Are the primary bacteria in infants, which helps them grow.
5. Inhibit growth of bacteria which produce nitrates in the bowel. Nitrates are bowel-toxic and can cause cancer.
6. Help prevent production and absorption of toxins produced by disease-causing bacteria, which reduces the toxic load of the liver.
7. Manufacture B-complex vitamins.
8. Help regulate peristalsis and bowel movements.
9. Prevent and treat antibiotic-induced diarrhea.

PROBIOTIC BACTERIA HELP US IN MANY WAYS

Nutritional	Manufacture vitamins in our foods and bodies: B_1, B_2, B_3, B_5, B_6, B_{12}, A, and K.
Digestive	Digest lactose. Allow some people with lactose intolerance to eat yogurt and cultured dairy products. Help regulate peristalsis and regular bowel movements. Digest protein to free amino acids. Establish good digestion in infants, preventing colic, diaper rash, and gas.
Immune	Produce antibiotics and antifungals which prevent colonization of harmful bacteria and fungus. Manufacture essential fatty acids, 5–10 percent of all short-chained fatty acids. Increase the number of immune system cells. Create lactic acid which balances intestinal pH. Break down bacterial toxins and prevent production of bacterial toxins and colitis. Have antitumor and anticancer effects. Protect from xenobiotics like mercury, pesticides, radiation, and harmful pollutants. Break down bile acids. Manufacture hydrogen peroxide which has antiseptic effects.
Heart	Play a role in normalization of serum cholesterol and triglycerides.
Metabolism	Break down and rebuild hormones. Promote healthy metabolism. Convert flavonoids (useful as antitumor factors and to reduce inflammation) to useable forms.

Benefits of *Lactobacillus acidophillus*

1. Prevent overgrowth of disease-causing microbes: *Candida* species, *E. coli, H. pylori* and *Salmonella.*
2. Prevent and treat antibiotic-associated diarrhea.
3. Aid digestion of lactose and dairy products.
4. Improve nutrient absorption.
5. Maintain integrity of intestinal tract and protect against macromolecules entering bloodstream and causing antigenic response.
6. Lessen intestinal stress from food poisoning.
7. Acidify intestinal tract; low pH provides a hostile environment for pathogens and yeasts.
8. Help prevent vaginal and urinary tract infections.

In addition to these nutritional and digestive benefits, probiotics enhance immune function. They manufacture antibiotics, like acidophilin produced by acidophillus, which are effective against many types of bacteria, including Streptococcus and staph. *Lactobacillus acidophillus* and *Lactobacillus bulgaricus* have been shown to be effective in laboratory testing against the following pathogens: *Bacillus subtilis, Clostridium botulinum, Clostridium perfringens, Escherichia coli, Proteus mirabilis, Salmonella enteridis, Salmonella typhimurium, Shigella dysenteriae, Shigella paradysenteriae, Staphylococcus aureus,* and *Staphylococcus faecalis.*

Candida albicans, a fungus which causes infections in nails and eyes, thrush, and "yeast infections," is controlled by acidophilus. This works in at least two ways. First, acidophilus bacteria ferment glycogen into lactic acid which changes the pH of the intestinal tract. Since *Candida* and many other disease-causing microbes thrive in alkaline environments, this action discourages many disease-producing microbes. Second, specific strains of *Lactobacillus* produce hydrogen peroxide which kills *Candida* directly. Studies show that supplementation with a hydrogen peroxide-producing strain of acidophilus, DDS-1, reduced the incidence of antibiotic-induced vaginal yeast infections threefold. Other probiotics have antitumor and anticancer effects. Probiotics also help us metabolize foreign substances, like mercury and pesticides, and protect us from damaging radiation and harmful pollutants.

Friendly bacteria also help us in other ways. Studies have repeatedly shown that *Lactobacillus* bacteria can help normalize cholesterol levels. Probiotics also rebuild and break down hormones like estrogen. Probiotics aid digestive function, improve peristalsis, and help normalize bowel transit time. Finally, bacterial balance is essential for healthy metabolism. Many super-thin people have been able to gain weight when their bacteria were rebalanced, although the mechanism is not yet understood.

L. bulgaricus and *Streptococcus thermophilus* are two other friendly inhabitants of our digestive tracts. Transient residents of the digestive tract, these flora are not native to it. They "vacation" in us for up to twelve days, which gives them time to have a beneficial effect on the intestinal ecology. Their most obvious function is enhancing the production of *Bifidobacteria*. They have also been shown to have antitumor effects, and *L. bulgaricus* has antibiotic and antiherpes effects as well. They are found in cultured dairy products or can be taken supplementally.

Saccharomyces boulardii is a friendly fungus which enhances levels of secretory IgA. In France it's called "yeast against yeast." Clinically, it has been found to be useful for clearing the skin and controlling diarrhea caused by antibiotics, *Clostridium difficile*, and traveling. *Saccharomyces* has also been used effectively in people with Crohn's disease, significantly reducing the number of bowel movements. Animal studies indicate that it may be used against toxins formed by cholera bacteria.

NOT ALL INTESTINAL BACTERIA ARE FRIENDLY!

Friendly bacteria comprise only a small percentage of our total bacteria. You could call the rest the okay, the bad, and the ugly! Most intestinal residents are "commensal" bacteria; they have neither good nor bad effects on how we feel. Other intestinal bacteria are pathogens causing acute illness (*Salmonella* causes food poisoning) or chronic illness (*Helicobacter pylori* causes ulcers). Disease-causing microbes produce bothersome gas and toxic secretions which irritate the intestinal lining and get absorbed into the bloodstream, making us sick. Some bacteria are extremely virulent and cause sudden and violent illness. Our body's reaction to a strong bacteria like *Salmonella* is diarrhea, fever, loss of appetite, and vomiting. The body is screaming, "Get this stuff out of me!" So it attempts to rapidly flush it out of the body and starve it out. Most disease-causing microbes thrive at human body temperature, while fever kills them by overheating them.

Bacteria that cause chronic illness are generally weak organisms of low virulence. They are often found in small quantities in all of us and have been assumed to be harmless. But when large colonies are given the opportunity to thrive, they can and do cause illness. This type of illness is called intestinal dysbiosis, which is discussed in the next chapter.

PREBIOTICS

A prebiotic is a substance which enhances beneficial intestinal flora in the gut. The two most well-documented prebiotics are fructooligosachharide, commonly known as FOS, and inulin. These fibers have been shown to increase levels of bifidobacteria in the colon. In addition, FOS has been shown to increase acidophilus. Foods containing FOS and inulin include Jerusalem artichokes, onions, chicory, garlic, leeks, bananas, fruit, soybeans, burdock root, asparagus, sugar maple, Chinese chive, and (in small amounts) whole rye and whole wheat.

Because of their health-building qualities, inulin and FOS are being researched as possible functional food additives by companies throughout the world. Be prepared to see them as additives in foods. Dosages as low as 2.75 grams will dramatically increase bifidobacteria. They have also been shown to be antagonistic to at least eight disease producing microbes including salmonella, listeria, campylobacter, shigella, and vibrio.

A new term that is now showing up in the literature is *synbiotics*, the simultaneous use of both probiotics and prebiotics.

BACTERIA AND YEASTS USED AS PROBIOTIC SUPPLEMENTS

Bifidobacterium	Lactobacillus	Streptococcus	Other
B. bifidum	L. acidophilus	S. thermophilus	Enterococcus faecium
B. breve	L. bulgaricus	S. facium	Saccharomyces
B. infantis	L. rhamnosus	S. faecali	boulardii
B. bifidum	L. casei	S. lactis	Lactococcus cremoris
B. adolescentis	L. gasseri		
B. pseudocate-	L. brevis		
nulatum	L. debreuckii		
B. catenulatum	L. lactis		
B. angulatum	L. kefir		
B. longum	L. yoghurti		
	L. plantarum		
	L. salavarius		

Note: Some supplements contain soil-based probiotic organisms such as *Bacillus laterosporus*, *Bacillus subtilis*, and *L. sporonges* (also known as *Bacillus coagulous*). Although there are many anecdotal stories of great success with these soil-based organisms for many digestive problems, there is no research yet to substantiate the claims.

FOODS AND HERBS THAT ENHANCE
INTESTINAL FLORA

Cultured foods, like yogurt, have significantly increased nutritional content over milk. The bacteria commonly used to produce yogurt—*Lactobacillus bulgaricus* and *L. thermophilus*—produce biotin, a B-complex vitamin. The bacteria make this nutrient for their own benefit, but we benefit as well. By using cultured foods such as sauerkraut rather than cabbage, cottage cheese and yogurt rather than milk, tofu, miso, natto, tamari or shoyu sauce and tempeh rather than soybeans, wine rather than grapes, we get higher levels of vitamins A, B-complex, and K. In addition, fermented foods have increased probiotic content, aid digestion, and provide health-building enzymes and higher nutritional value.

ENHANCED NUTRIENT CONTENT OF SELECTED DAIRY FOODS		
Original Food	**Fermented/Cultured Food**	**Increased Nutrition**
Milk	Cheddar cheese	Vitamin B_1, 3x
Milk	Cottage cheese	Vitamin B_{12}, 5x
Milk	Yogurt	Vitamin B_{12}, 5–30x
Milk	Yogurt	Vitamin B_3, 50x
Skim milk	Low-fat yogurt	Vitamin A, 7–14x

People have long recognized the benefits of fermented foods. Although indigenous people didn't know the science behind their use, they easily noticed the healthful benefits. Sauerkraut, a traditional European food, has a long history of use by people with ulcers and digestive problems. Asian cultures traditionally use pickles and fermented foods as condiments—kimchee, pickled daikon radish, or a sweet rice drink called *amasake*. Due to the high incidence of people who are lactose-intolerant around the world, people have relied on cultured dairy products—cottage cheese, kefir, yogurt—for centuries. In India, a fermented dairy drink called *lassi* is a household staple, and in Israel *leban*, which is similar to yogurt, is served daily.

Chinese green tea and ginseng also increase friendly flora. Polyphenols are believed to be the enhancing substance in green tea, which has beneficial effects on serum cholesterol, tumors, and ulcers. When polyphenols were tested to see their effect on intestinal flora, they increased the number of beneficial bacteria, such as lactobacilli and bifidus, while decreasing the number of disease-causing *Clostridium*. A significant increase in beneficial flora was also found when ginseng extract was tested in vitro on 107 types of human bacteria.

The traditional Japanese diet takes advantage of several fermented foods—miso, tempeh, and tamari or soy sauce—that have antibiotic properties. Miso, a fermented soybean paste, was found to contain 161 strains of aerobic bacteria. Almost all of these were found to compete successfully with *E. coli* and *Staphylococcus aureus*, two main food-poisoning agents. Many lactic acid-producing bacteria were also found. Another positive property of miso is that it helps reduce the negative effects of radioactivity and electromagnetic resonance. Several microbes, including yeast and *L. acidophillus*, are used in the fermentation process of soy sauce, also called shoyu or tamari, which produces a health-giving food. However, in the United States most soy sauce is manufactured from inorganic acids such as hydrochloric acid that break down the soybeans, rather than from living microbes. This type of soy sauce doesn't have the same benefits as traditionally brewed soy sauce.

PROBIOTIC SUPPLEMENTS

Since flora do not permanently stay in the gut, we have need to get them either in our foods, such as yogurt or kefir, or to take supplementally. The composition of intestinal flora usually remains fairly constant in healthy people, but it can become unbalanced by aging, diet, disease, drugs, poor health, or stress. In fact, problems due to imbalanced flora have become widespread. Eating yogurt and cultured dairy products can maintain healthful friendly flora colonies in people who are already healthy, but once disease-producing microbes have colonized, probiotic supplements are necessary.

Taking daily probiotics increases our body's ability to protect itself from illness. Due to their acid-loving nature, they easily survive the high-acid environment of the stomach. Once in the intestinal tract, they colonize and replace less desirable residents. However, not all probiotic supplements provide the same benefits. According to expert Natasha Trenev, various strains of acidophillus can differ genetically by as much as 20 percent. This is a huge difference, when you consider that the genetic difference between mice and man is about 2 percent.

What to Look for in a Probiotic Supplement

1. Look for *Lacobacillus acidophilus* and *bifidum*.
2. Choose an age-appropriate product. For a baby or toddler, *Bifidobacteria infantis* is appropriate; for children and adults, the most-studied strain of *L. acidophillus* is DDS-1.
3. Because these bacteria are delicate, they must be refrigerated—when shipped, at a store, and in your home—to ensure the lifespan of the product and to maintain the greatest potency.
4. Bacteria multiply very quickly, but they need enough food and protection to survive the trip through the stomach and into the intestinal tract. Many manufacturers include FOS or inulin to feed the flora; check to make sure they are included. Some people bloat from FOS.
5. There is controversy about whether to buy bacteria mixed in one jar or to buy them separately. Most manufacturers produce combination supplements with several types of flora. However, if these flora compete with each other for

food, they can limit each other's growth. The only truly cooperative bacteria are the two used in making yogurt: *L. bulgaricus* and *L. thermophilus*. Either purchase acidophilus and bifidobacteria separately or purchase freeze-dried supplements. Freeze-drying puts the flora into suspended animation, keeping them dormant until placed in water.

Dosage

For preventive measures, take about a billion microbes of each protective species once a day. This is usually about a ¼ to ½ teaspoon or one to three capsules. For therapeutic purposes, take this amount three times a day. If you take probiotic supplements and have sudden bloating, diarrhea, gas, or worsening of symptoms, this is not necessarily a bad sign. As the disease-producing bacteria and fungus are killed, they release chemicals that aggravate symptoms. If this happens, begin again with tiny amounts and build up your dosage slowly to avoid the die-off reaction.

Probiotic supplements are also important for the prevention of traveler's diarrhea. If you plan to travel outside the United States, take a probiotic supplement daily. Studies show that it significantly increases your ability to withstand the new microbes you will be exposed to.

Chapter 5

Dysbiosis: A Good Neighborhood Gone Bad

"Within these regions battles rage; populations rise and fall, affected just as we are by local environmental conditions, industry thrives and constant defense is exercised against interlopers and dangerous aliens who may enter unannounced; colonists roam and settle some permanently, some only briefly, in general we have in miniature many of terrestrial life's vicissitudes, problems and solutions."

NATASHA TRENEV AND LEO CHAITOW, *PROBIOTICS*,
THORSONS PUBLICATION, 1990

EARLY IN THIS century, Dr. Eli Metchnikoff popularized the theory that disease begins in the digestive tract due to an imbalance of intestinal bacteria. He called this state "dysbiosis," which comes from "symbiosis," meaning living together in mutual harmony, and "dys," which means *not*! Dr. Metchnikoff was the first scientist to discover the useful properties of probiotics. He won the Nobel Prize in 1908

73

for his work on lactobacilli and their role in immunity and was a colleague of Louis Pasteur, succeeding him as the director of the Pasteur Institute in Paris.

Dr. Metchnikoff found that the bacteria in yogurt prevented and reversed bacterial infection. (He named it *Lactobacillus bulgaricus* after the long-lived, yogurt-loving peasants of Bulgaria.) His research proved that lactobacilli could displace many disease-producing organisms and reduce the toxins they generated. He believed these endotoxins—toxins produced from substances inside the body—shortened lifespan. He advocated use of lactobacillus in the 1940s for ptomaine poisoning, a widely used therapy in Europe.

In recent decades, Metchnikoff's work has taken a back seat to modern therapies like antibiotics and immunization programs, which scientists hoped would conquer infectious diseases. For instance, due to an aggressive worldwide immunization program, the World Health Assembly formally declared on May 8, 1980, that smallpox had been eradicated worldwide, which was an enormous triumph for science and humankind. But subsequent efforts at eradicating other diseases have been unsuccessful. While parents in America routinely immunize their children against measles, mumps, and polio, parents in poor nations are coping with the loss of half their children by age ten. Worldwide we are finding an increase in new and deadly viruses for which there are no vaccines.

Viruses and bacteria are extremely adaptable. In our efforts to eradicate them we have pushed them to evolve. Long before chemists created antibiotics, yeasts, fungi, and rival bacteria were producing antibiotics to ward each other off and establish neighborhoods. They became adept at evading each other's strategies and adapting for survival. Because people have used antibiotics prophylactically and indiscriminately in humans and animals, the bacteria have had a chance to learn from it, undergoing rapid mutations. As they shuffle their components, learning new evolutionary dance steps, superstrains of bacteria have been created which no longer respond to any antibiotic treatment. For instance, our immune systems normally detect bacteria by information coded on the cell walls. Now in response to antibiotics some bacteria have survived by removing their cell walls, so they're able to enter the bloodstream and tissues unopposed, causing damage in organs and tissues. Bacteria can also turn on specific genes when exposed to specific antibiotics.

Resistant strains of bacteria are communicating with each other, and passing resistance information on to other types of bacteria. For example, we now have antibiotic-resistant gonorrhea, leprosy, staph, and strep. Similarly, many bacteria that cause disease primarily in the digestive tract—cholera, dysentery, *E. coli, Enterobacteriaceae, Enterococcus faecium, Klebsiella, Proteus, Pseudomonas, Salmonella, Serratia marcenscens,* and *Shigella*—have mutated to become resistant to specific antibiotics. (For a lengthy but fascinating look at the world through the eyes of virologists, read Lori Garret's *The Coming Plague*.) In 1992, 13,300 hospital patients died of infections that resisted every drug doctors tried.

The sexual revolution also helped the evolution of microbes. Multiple sex partners allowed bacteria, fungi, and virus more opportunity to replicate, increasing the possibility of mutation. Some of these mutant microbes became better at causing infection or deepening illness. Given people's rapid movement between countries, these new microbes are spread quickly throughout the world, increasing the risk of even more mutation and enhancement of the microbial defense system.

In *The Coming Plague*, Laurie Garrett spends nearly 700 pages discussing microbes, their increasing virulence, and the devastation of their epidemics. There is little optimism in her solutions. But she has neglected half the equation: If microbes are becoming more resistant and virulent, we must increase our own resistance and strength to outsmart them. We must boost immune function so that people will be less receptive to infection. We need to take a new look at Metchnikoff's work—at probiotic bacteria and the many immune-strengthening benefits they confer.

Optimum nutrition is a logical starting point. Nutrients, by definition, are essential for growth, immune function, repair, and maintenance of our bodies. But the SAD diet of Americans will not protect our immune function. New research has shown that diets deficient in just one nutrient, in this case either selenium or vitamin E, could cause a benign virus to mutate to a disease-producing organism. Today, less than 80 percent of women and children meet the RDA for vitamin E and zinc. Less than 80 percent of American women meet the RDA for magnesium. A study of high school runners found that 45 percent of girls and 17 percent of boys were deficient in iron, while 31 percent of female college athletes were also found to be iron-deficient. A recent survey of nutritional status in elderly Americans showed that 25 percent of all elderly patients were malnourished, and 50 percent of all hospitalized elderly suffer from malnutrition.

Dysbiosis weakens our ability to protect ourselves from disease-causing microbes, which are generally composed of low-virulence organisms. Unlike Salmonella, which causes immediate food-poisoning reactions, low-virulence microbes are insidious. They cause chronic problems which go undiagnosed in the great majority of cases. If left unrecognized and untreated, they become deep-seated. For instance, if joint pain is the most obvious symptom, we stop movement. If we have diarrhea, then we try to eat differently. In other cases, the effects are much more severe, resulting in chronic fatigue syndrome or colon disease. The dysbiosis causes us to adapt our lifestyle to new limitations.

Because most doctors in our culture do not yet recognize dysbiosis, symptoms are treated with medication, but the underlying cause is never dealt with, and ultimately people do not get well. Published research has listed dysbiosis as the cause of arthritis, autoimmune illness, B_{12} deficiency, chronic fatigue, cystic acne, the early stages of colon and breast cancer, eczema, food allergy/sensitivity, inflammatory bowel disease, irritable bowel syndrome, psoriasis, and steatorrhea. These problems were previously unrecognized as being microbial in origin. Common dysbiotic bacteria are *Aeromonas, Citrobacter, Helicobacter, Klebsiella, Salmonella, Shigella, Staphylococcus aureus, Vibrio,* and *Yersinia. Helicobacter,* for example, is commonly found in people with ulcers. Citrobacter is implicated in diarrheal diseases. A common dysbiosis culprit, the *Candida* fungus, causes a wide variety of symptoms that range from gas and bloating to depression, mood swings and PMS (premenstrual syndrome).

SOME BACTERIA AND THEIR RELATIONSHIP TO DIGESTIVE & AUTOIMMUNE PROBLEMS

Bacteria	Gastrointestinal Effect
Citrobacter freundii and diversus	Implicated in diarrheal diseases. Possess an antigen similar to some strains of salmonella which may cause cross-reactive immune reactions. May invade the intestinal mucosa, causing irritation and inflammation.
E. coli	Indicate intestinal flora imbalance when low levels found in stool samples. Look for diet, drugs, environmental stress, excessive yeast, parasites, and pathogens as possible causes.
Enterobacter	Associated with diarrhea in children, when found in large numbers. Indicator of imbalanced flora.
Klebsiella	Can cause bacteremia, cystitis, pneumonia, prostatitis. Linked with such autoimmune diseases as ankylosing spondylitis and myasthenia gravis. Usually asymptomatic in the intestine, although it can cause diarrhea. Generally very resistant to antibiotics. Infections often acquired in hospitals, mainly in patients with low resistance.

Lactobacillus	Low levels indicate flora imbalance. Look for diet, drugs, environmental stress, excessive yeast, parasites, and pathogens as possible causes.
Nonlactose E. coli	90 percent of normal strains of *E. coli* produce lactase, which ferments lactose. Half of the pathogenic strains fail to do so. May be causing symptoms if found in a stool culture in a patient with diarrheal symptoms.
Proteus	Normally found in flora of feces, soil, and water. In large numbers, may promote diarrhea and GI distress. *Proteus vulgaris* may be involved in the initiation of myasthenia gravis. Also associated with ankylosing spondylitis and rheumatoid arthritis.
Pseudomonas	May be acquired from contaminated water and lead to diarrhea and GI distress.
Salmonella	Most often reported cause of food poisoning from eggs, milk products, and raw meat; infects 38 percent of commercial uncooked chickens. May occur without symptoms in a carrier state. May also invade the mucosa and present as enteric fever, a focal disease with or without septicemia or gastroenteritis. Increasing health concern.
Staphylococcus aureus	Major cause of food poisoning, with abrupt onset of nausea and vomiting; may include diarrhea and abdominal cramps. Also implicated in pseudomembranous colitis and toxic-shock syndrome.
Yersinia enterocolitica	Implicated as a significant cause of gastroenteritis. Variable symptoms may resemble ulcerative colitis. Antigenic determinants, cross-reactive to the thyroid plasma membrane, may result in Grave's disease. Also associated with such autoimmune diseases as arthritis, erythema nodosum, or Sjögren's syndrome.

WHAT CAUSES DYSBIOSIS?

There are many causes of dysbiosis, but we generally bring it on ourselves. Constant high levels of stress, exposure to manufactured chemicals, poor food choices, oral contraceptives, surgery, and use of antibiotics and pain killers all change the healthy balance of the digestive tract.

The most common cause of dysbiosis is the use of antibiotics, which change the balance of intestinal microbes. Not terribly specific, antibiotics simultaneously kill both harmful and helpful bacteria throughout our digestive system, mouth, vagina, and skin, leaving the territory to bacteria, parasites, viruses, and yeasts that are resistant to the antibiotic that was used. In a healthy gut, parasites may be present in small numbers and not cause symptoms, but if allowed to flourish they can cause diarrhea, illness, and weight loss. Most people can recover fairly easily from a single round of antibiotics, but even those with strong constitutions have trouble regaining balance from repeated use of antibiotic drugs.

These microbes produce toxins that cause symptoms. The bacteria form chemicals that are poisonous to the cells around them and to the person they live in. A wide variety of substances are produced, including amines, ammonia, hydrogen sulfide, indoles, phenols, and secondary bile acids. These substances may hurt the intestinal lining directly by damaging the brush border and become absorbed into the bloodstream, causing systemwide effects. Initially, our body rushes white blood cells to the injured tissue to eat up the bacteria and carry away the debris via the lymphatic system. Inflammation, pain, and swelling are nature's message to stop and let your body heal. But we often ignore this basic instinct and reach for pain medication so we can continue our lives. If the pain and inflammation were initially caused by microbes and you never dealt with the cause, more endotoxins will be produced, causing chronic pain and inflammation, and setting up a continuing cycle.

Often, the pain medications we take become a factor in

the continuation and severity of the problem. Stephen Barrie, N.D., calls it a Machiavellian theme: The drug causes damage to the intestinal lining, causing more inflammation, irritation, and pain, so we take more pain medication, which causes further damage. The most common pain medications fall into two groups: steroidal drugs, like cortisone and prednisone, and nonsteroidal anti-inflammatories (NSAIDs), like aspirin, ibuprofen, and indomethacin. Let's look at the long-term effects of these medications on the digestive system and their consequences on health.

Corticosteroids are naturally produced by the adrenal glands. Synthetic corticosteroids like cortisone and prednisone are two of the most effective emergency drugs, used for a multitude of problems, including allergies, arthritis, asthma, Crohn's disease, eczema, lupus, poison ivy, psoriasis, and ulcerative colitis. They are generally prescription medications, but weaker over-the-counter remedies can be purchased everywhere. Because cortisone and prednisone have such powerful anti-inflammatory effects, they are used long-term by people with chronic illness. But long-term use of cortisone and prednisone depresses the immune system, causing side effects like lowered resistance to infection and parasites, stomach and duodenal ulcers, thinning of bones, and dozens of other problems. Steroids are contraindicated for anyone who has a fungal infection because they provide excellent nourishment for fungi. Yet, many people with *Candida* infections go undiagnosed. In turn, *Candida* damages the intestinal lining, causing a wide variety of symptoms, including bloating, chronic fatigue, constipation, depression, diarrhea, fatigue, hypoglycemia, and premenstrual syndrome, to name but a few. Because corticosteroids are so strong, they suppress your body's ability to work through an illness on its own. They are best suited for an emergency, not daily use.

NSAIDs like aspirin, ibuprofen, and indomethacin work by blocking prostaglandins, which are small protein messengers that circulate throughout the body. Some prostaglandins cause pain and inflammation; others cause healing and repair.

NSAID drugs block all prostaglandins. The pain is gone, but the healing process is blocked. Since the intestinal lining repairs and replaces itself every three to five days, prolonged use of NSAIDs blocks its repair. The GI side effects are well known: the lining becomes weak, inflamed, and "leaky," causing leaky gut syndrome, or intestinal permeability. NSAID use also increases the risk of ulcers of the stomach and duodenum. These drugs also cause bleeding, damage to the mucous membranes of the intestines, and GI inflammation.

Because aspirin is hard on the stomach lining, doctors and advertisers have advised us to switch to anti-inflammatory drugs like ibuprofen. What we aren't told is NSAIDs cause irritation and inflammation of the intestinal tract, leading to colitis and relapse of ulcerative colitis. NSAIDs can cause bleeding and ulceration of the large intestine and may contribute to complications of diverticular disease. Even with moderate use, NSAIDs increase gut permeability. In fact, use of NSAIDs, steroids, antacids, and antibiotics are probably the greatest contributors to leaky gut syndrome.

Poor diet also contributes to dysbiosis. A diet high in fat, sugar, and processed foods may not have enough nutrients to optimally nourish the body or repair and maintain the digestive organs. The nutrients most likely to be lacking are the antioxidants—vitamins C and E, beta-carotene, coenzyme Q10, glutathione, selenium, the sulfur amino acids, and zinc—the B-complex vitamins, calcium, essential fatty acids, and magnesium.

Poor ileocecal valve function can contribute to dysbiosis. The valve's job is to keep waste matter in the colon from mixing with the useful material that is still being digested and absorbed in the small intestine. When this valve is stuck, either open or closed, dysbiotic problems can occur. Chiropractors can adjust the ileocecal valve to alleviate this problem.

Many other factors contribute to dysbiosis. Low levels of hydrochloric acid (HCl) in the stomach encourage bacterial overgrowth. Poor transit time in the intestinal tract also encourages proliferation of bacteria. For example, in twenty-four hours one *E. coli* bacterium produces nearly 5,000 identical bacteria! The longer they sit inside us, the greater their potential to colonize.

PATTERNS OF DYSBIOSIS

There are four commonly recognized patterns of dysbiosis: putrefaction, fermentation, deficiency, and sensitization.

Putrefaction Dysbiosis

This is the most common type and occurs when food is not well digested, essentially rotting inside us. We may feel this as bloating, discomfort, and indigestion. The typical American high fat, high animal-protein, low fiber diet predisposes people to putrefaction. It causes an increase of bacteroides bacteria, a decrease in beneficial bifidobacteria, and an increase in bile production. Bacteroides cause vitamin B_{12} deficiency by uncoupling the B_{12} from the intrinsic factor necessary for its use. Other bacteria normally make vitamin B_{12} directly for their own purposes, but it too becomes unavailable to us. The most common signs of B_{12} deficiencies are depression, diarrhea, fatigue, memory loss, numbing of hands and feet, sleep disturbances, and weakness. Vitamin B_{12} deficiency is commonly seen in older people due to poor hydrochloric acid levels in the stomach.

Poor bifidobacteria levels decrease our body's ability to resist infection, affect bowel health, and reflect a decreased production of B-complex vitamins. Research has implicated putrefaction dysbiosis with breast and colon cancer. Bacterial enzymes change bile acids into thirty-three substances formed in the colon that are tumor promoters. Bacterial enzymes such as beta glucuronidase, recreate estrogens that were already broken down. These estrogens are reabsorbed into the bloodstream, increasing estrogen levels and estrogen-dependent breast cancers. Putrefaction dysbiosis can be corrected by increasing high fiber foods, fruits, vegetables, and grains in our diet while decreasing meats and fats.

Fermentation Dysbiosis

This is characterized by bloating, constipation, diarrhea, fatigue, and gas. People with fermentation dysbiosis have faulty digestion of carbohydrates: sugars, fruit, beer, wine, grains and fiber. Fermentation of carbohydrates provides food for multiplying bacteria and produces hydrogen and carbon dioxide gases and short-chained fatty acids, which can be tested. Fermentation dysbiosis is often characterized by flora that have been taken over by *Candida* fungi or other disease-causing microbes. These microbes damage the intestinal brush borders (microvilli) and lead to increased intestinal permeability. People with fermentation dysbiosis need to strictly avoid carbohydrate-containing foods. It is recommended that they receive therapeutic support to help regain bowel health. Up to 2,000 milligrams of citrus seed extract can be used daily. Use of probiotic supplements and repair of the intestinal mucosa are essential.

Deficiency Dysbiosis

This is characterized by a lack of beneficial flora like bifido-bacteria and lactobacillus. Use of antibiotics and low-fiber diets are the primary cause of poor flora. Deficiency dysbiosis is often seen in people with irritable bowel syndrome and food sensitivities. Deficiency dysbiosis is often coupled with putrefaction dysbiosis, and the treatment is the same. To restore balance, supplementation with beneficial flora and fructooligosaccharides (FOS) is also recommended. Up to 2,000 milligrams of citrus seed extract may be used daily.

Sensitization Dysbiosis

This occurs when the immune system reacts with abnormal or aggravated responses to the digestive process. Microbes in the gut and foods produce exotoxins that irritate the gut lining. Our bodies recognize these toxins as foreign substances and produce antibodies which signal the immune system to get rid of them. Unfortunately, this local reaction may be the cause of some autoimmune diseases. Rheumatoid arthritis, ankylosing spondylitis, and perhaps skin diseases like eczema and psoriasis are often the result.

The process works like this: Our body initially reacts to a "bug" of some sort, but the antibodies formed to fight it are the perfect keys that fit into *gene markers*. These markers make us more susceptible to certain diseases. The mechanism by which these are turned on or off is unclear, but it appears that specific microbes cause disease *only* in people with specific gene markers who are exposed to specific microbes, which are harmless in everyone else. Our body senses that as a systemic problem rather than just some imbalanced microbes in our intestines. It reacts with an all-out antibody reaction, attacking the body itself—an autoimmune reaction. What originated as a local infection becomes an autoimmune illness. For instance, rheumatoid arthritis has been linked to a prevalence of a bacteria called *Proteus* which mimics gene marker HLADR4; 50 to 75 percent of people with rheumatoid arthritis have this gene marker.

People with sensitization dysbiosis often have food intolerances, leaky gut syndrome, and increasing sensitivity to foods and the environment. Symptoms may include acne, bowel or skin problems, connective tissue disease, and psoriasis. Sensitization dysbiosis may accompany fermentation dysbiosis, and similar treatments may be helpful. Replacing probiotic bacteria and repair of the intestinal mucosa are essential.

CANDIDA: THE MASQUERADER

The most prevalent and obvious form of dysbiosis is candidiasis, a fungal infection. *Candida* is found in nearly everyone, and in small amounts is compatible with good health. *Candida* is usually controlled by friendly flora, our immune defense system, and intestinal pH. When the bacteria that normally balance *Candida* are killed, it causes what's commonly known as a yeast infection because it produces a smell like yeasty bread. Also called a yeast infection in the vagina and a fungal infection in the nailbeds and the eyes, it's called thrush in the throat. *Candida albicans* is the usual offender, but other species of *Candida* fungus may cause health problems as well.

In the early 1980s, Orion Truss, M.D. noticed that many of his patients' other problems resolved when he treated them with nystatin for fungal problems. Indeed, one patient had a complete reversal of multiple sclerosis. After hearing Dr. Truss lecture on his findings, Abraham Hoffer, a doctor in the field of orthomolecular psychiatry, tried his first yeast protocol on a psychiatric patient who had suffered from depression for many years. One month after initiating Truss's program she was mentally and emotionally normal.

What is less well recognized in contemporary medical practice is that *Candida* can also colonize in the digestive tract, causing havoc everywhere in the body. *Candida* colonies produce powerful toxins that are absorbed into the bloodstream and affect our immune system, hormone balance, and thought processes. The most common symptoms are abdominal bloating, anxiety, constipation, diarrhea, or both, depression, environmental sensitivities, fatigue, feeling worse on damp or muggy days or in moldy places, food sensitivities, fuzzy thinking, insomnia, low blood sugar, mood swings, premenstrual syndrome, recurring vaginal or bladder infections, ringing in the ears, and sensitivities to perfume, cigarettes, or fabric odors. Although these symptoms are the most prevalent, *Candida* has many faces, and many types of symptoms can occur.

American physicians recognize *Candida* in many forms, but in general they have been unwilling to recognize it in a systemic form. For those who do, it is a common diagnosis. In my own experience, I have found *Candida* to be an underlying cause in many clients. Abraham Hoffer, M.D. states that one-third of the world's population is affected by candidiasis.

Candida infections are usually triggered by use of antibiotics, birth control pills, steroid medications, and consumption of sugar. These drugs change the balance of the intestinal tract, kill the bacteria that keep *Candida* in check, and the fungus quickly takes hold. *Candida* are like bullies that push their way into the intestinal lining, destroying cells and brush borders. Greater numbers of *Candida* produce greater amounts of toxins, which further irritate and break down the intestinal lining. This damage allows macromolecules of partially digested food to pass through. The macromolecules are the perfect size for antibodies to respond to. Your immune system then goes on alert for these specific foods so the next time you eat them, your antibodies will be waiting! The net result is increased sensitivity to foods and other food substances and the environment.

There are many, many therapeutic programs that people may follow to rid themselves of *Candida*. The standard therapeutic diet allows beef, chicken, fish, eggs, poultry, yogurt, vegetables, oils, nuts, and seeds. No alcoholic beverages, fruit or dried fruits, flours, grains, mushrooms, sugar, vinegar, or yeasted breads are allowed. When I had *Candida*, I found that the worst foods for me were beer, sugar, and dried fruit. A sip of beer triggered symptoms within twenty minutes. At that time I was a bananaholic, consuming three to five daily. I now know that bananas are loaded with fructooligosaccharides, which feed *Lactobacillus* and *Bifidobacteria* but not *Candida*! Due to biochemical individuality, other people find other foods and substances to be the worst triggers for them. People are advised to go on a strict diet for three weeks and then reintroduce foods one at a time to test for reactions. If you know you're sensitive to a specific food, avoid it.

Candida often causes bowel problems—either diarrhea or constipation or both alternately—so it is essential that bowel transit time be normalized. Adding psyllium seed husks (found in fiber supplements) and probiotic supplements greatly helps to normalize this condition. Russel Jaffe, M.D. uses vitamin C flushes, which are described in chapter 9, Detoxification.

Many substances are helpful in killing off *Candida*. Garlic is my personal favorite—eat lots of it raw; women can use it as a vaginal suppository (make sure not to nick the garlic or it can sting!) or take in capsule form. Capryllic acid from coconuts, oleic acid from olive oil, oil of oregano, pau d'arco, and grapefruit seed extract are all valuable agents for killing *Candida*. Mathake, a South American herb, has been found to be extremely effective. While it isn't necessary to use all these health enhancers, you can buy many of them in combination products in health food stores or from health professionals. Probiotics help keep *Candida* in check.

When the *Candida* are killed, the protein fragments and endotoxins released trigger an antibody response. This can initially produce a worsening of the person's symptoms and is commonly known as a die-off reaction, or a Herxheimer reaction. Therefore, it is important to begin therapeutics gently with small doses and gradually increase. If your symptoms are still initially aggravated, cut back and gradually increase supplements. Most people begin to feel dramatically better within two weeks. If you don't, you're probably not dealing with a *Candida* problem. Ask your health professional to make therapeutic recommendations.

I recently advised a client to take probiotic supplements for peeling skin and burning sensation on her feet. Although she scored rather low on the *Candida* questionnaire, her symptoms fit those of *Candida*. I advised her to take probiotics slowly, beginning with ¼ teaspoon daily and working up gradually to a full teaspoon once or twice a day. Six days later, she told me her feet were improving, but she had a horrible headache every time she took a teaspoon of probiotics. After she began more slowly, she was soon relieved of both problems.

The following *Candida* questionnaire can help you determine if *Candida* is a factor in your own health. The selected reading list includes several informative books on *Candida*.

Exercise 4

YEAST QUESTIONNAIRE—ADULT

Answering these questions and adding up the scores will help you decide if yeasts contribute to your health problems. Yet you will not obtain an automatic "yes" or "no" answer.

For each "yes" answer in Section A, circle the point score in that section. Total your score and record it at the end of the section. Then move on to sections B and C and score as indicated.

Add the total of your scores to get your *Grand Total Score*.

SECTION A: HISTORY _____

	Point score
1. Have you taken tetracyclines (Sumycin®, Panmycin®, Vibramycin®, Minocin®, etc.) or other antibiotics for acne for one month (or longer)?	35
2. Have you, at any time in your life, taken other "broad spectrum" antibiotics* for respiratory, urinary, or other infections (for two months or longer, or in shorter courses four or more times in a one-year period)?	35
3. Have you taken a broad spectrum antibiotic drug*, even a single course?	6
4. Have you, at any time in your life, been bothered by persistent prostatis, vaginitis, or other problems affecting your reproductive organs?	25

*Including Keflex, ampicillin, amoxicillin, Ceclor, Bactrim, and Septra. Such antibiotics kill off "good germs" while they're killing off those which cause infection.

5. Have you been pregnant ...
   Two or more times?   5
   One time?   3
6. Have you taken birth control pills ...
   For more than two years?   15
   For six months to two years?   8
7. Have you taken prednisone, Decadron® or
   other cortisone-type drugs ...
   For more than two weeks?   15
   For two weeks or less?   6
8. Does exposure to perfumes, insecticides,
   fabric shop odors, and other chemicals
   provoke ...
   Moderate to severe symptoms?   20
   Mild symptoms?   5
9. Are your symptoms worse on damp, muggy
   days or in moldy places?   20
10. Have you had athlete's foot, ringworm, "jock
    itch," or other chronic fungus infections of the
    skin or nails?
    Have such infections been ...
    Severe or persistent?   20
    Mild to moderate?   10
11. Do you crave sugar?   10
12. Do you crave breads?   10
13. Do you crave alcoholic beverages?   10
14. Does tobacco smoke *really* bother you?   10
    Total Score, Section A.......................................

SECTION B:
MAJOR SYMPTOMS: _____

For each of your symptoms, enter the appropriate figure in the
Point Score column:
   If a symptom is *occasional or mild*...........................score 3 points
   If a symptom is *frequent and/or moderately severe*...score 6 points
   If a symptom is *severe and/or disabling*...................score 9 points
Add total score and record it at the end of this section.

Point score

1. Fatigue or lethargy
2. Feeling of being "drained"
3. Poor memory
4. Feeling "spacey" or "unreal"
5. Depression
6. Inability to make decisions
7. Numbness, burning, or tingling
8. Muscle aches or weakness
9. Pain and/or swelling in joints
10. Abdominal pain
11. Constipation
12. Diarrhea
13. Bloating, belching, or intestinal gas
14 Troublesome vaginal burning, itching, or discharge
15. Persistent vaginal burning or itching
16. Prostatitis
17. Impotence
18. Loss of sexual desire or feeling
19. Endometriosis or infertility
20. Cramps and/or other menstrual irregularities
21. Premenstrual tension
22. Attacks of anxiety or crying
23. Cold hands or feet and/or chilliness
24. Shaking or irritable when hungry
   Total Score, Section B.................................

SECTION C:
OTHER SYMPTOMS:* ————————————

For each of your symptoms, enter the appropriate figure in the point score column:
   If a symptom is *occasional or mild*............................ score 1 point
   If a symptom is *frequent and/or moderately severe*...score 2 points
   If a symptom is *severe and/or disabling*.................... score 3 points
Add total score and record it at the end of this section.

*While the symptoms in this section commonly occur in people with yeast-connected illness, they are also found in other individuals.

Point score

1. Drowsiness
2. Irritability or jitteriness
3. Uncoordination
4. Inability to concentrate
5. Frequent mood swings
6. Headache
7. Dizziness/loss of balance
8. Pressure above ears, feeling of head swelling
9. Tendency to bruise easily
10. Chronic rashes or itching
11. Numbness, tingling
12. Indigestion or heartburn
13. Food sensitivity or intolerance
14. Mucus in stools
15. Rectal itching
16. Dry mouth or throat
17. Rash or blisters in mouth
18. Bad breath
19. Foot, body, or hair odor not relieved by washing
20. Nasal congestion or postnasal drip
21. Nasal itching
22. Sore throat
23. Laryngitis, loss of voice
24. Cough or recurrent bronchitis
25. Pain or tightness in chest
26. Wheezing or shortness of breath
27. Urgency or urinary frequency
28. Burning on urination
29. Spots in front of eyes or erratic vision
30. Burning or tearing of eyes
31. Recurrent infections or fluid in ears
32. Ear pain or deafness
    Total Score, Section C ....
    Total Score, Section A...............................
    Total Score, Section B...............................

GRAND TOTAL SCORE...................................

The Grand Total Score will help you and your physician decide if your health problems are yeast connected. Scores in women will run higher as seven items in the questionnaire apply exclusively to women, while only two apply exclusively to men.

Yeast-connected health problems are almost certainly present in women with scores *over 180* and in men with scores *over 140*.

Yeast-connected health problems are probably present in women with scores *over 120* and in men with scores *over 90*.

Yeast-connected health problems are possibly present in women with scores *over 60* and in men with scores *over 40*.

With scores of less than 60 in women and 40 in men, yeasts are less apt to cause health problems.

YEAST QUESTIONAIRE—CHILD

Circle appropriate point score for questions you answer "yes." Total your score and record it at the end of the questionnaire.

	Point score
1. During the two years before your child was born, were you bothered by recurrent vaginitis, menstrual irregularities, premenstrual tension, fatigue, headache, depression, digestive disorders or "feeling bad all over"?	30
2. Was your child bothered by thrush? (Score 10 if mild, score 20 if severe or persistent.)	10 20
3. Was your child bothered by frequent diaper rashes in infancy? (Score 10 if mild, 20 if severe or persistent.)	10 20
4. During infancy, was your child bothered by colic and irritability lasting over three months? (Score 10 if mild, 20 if moderate or severe.)	10 20
5. Are his symptoms worse on damp days or in damp or moldy places?	20
6. Has your child been bothered by recurrent or persistent "athlete's foot" or chronic fungus infections of his skin or nails?	30

7. Has your child been bothered by recurrent hives, eczema, or other skin problems?   10
8. Has your child received:
   a. Four or more courses of antibiotic drugs during the past year? Or has he received continuous "prophylactic" courses of antibiotic drugs?   80
   b. Eight or more courses of "broad-spectrum" antibiotics ... (such as amoxicillin, Keflex®, Septra®, Bactrim®, or Ceclor®) during the past three years?   50
9. Has your child experienced recurrent ear problems?   10
10. Has your child had tubes inserted in his ears?   10
11. Has your child been labeled "hyperactive"? (Score 10 if mild, 20 if moderate or severe.)   10 20
12. Is your child bothered by learning problems (even though his early developmental history was normal)?   10
13. Does your child have a short attention span?   10
14. Is your child persistently irritable, unhappy, and hard to please?   10
15. Has your child been bothered by persistent ot recurrent digestive problems, including constipation, diarrhca, bloating, or excessive gas? (Score 10 if mild; 20 if moderate; 30 if severe.)   10 20 30
16. Has he been bothered by persistent nasal congestion, cough, and/or wheezing?   10
17. Is your child unusually tired or unhappy or depressed? (Score 10 if mild, 20 if severe.)   10 20
18. Has your child been bothered by recurrent headaches, abdominal pain, or muscle aches? (Score 10 if mild, 20 if severe.)   10 20
19. Does your child crave sweets?   10
20. Does exposure to perfume, insecticides, gas, or other chemicals provoke moderate to severe symptoms?   30
21. Does tobacco smoke really bother him?   20
22. Do you feel that your child isn't well, yet diagnostic tests and studies haven't revealed the cause?   10

TOTAL SCORE

Yeasts possibly play a role in causing health problems in children with scores of 60 or more.

Yeasts probably play a role in causing health problems in children with scores of 100 or more.

Yeasts almost certainly play a role in causing health problems in children with scores of 140 or more.

Source: Used with permission from Crook, William, *The Yeast Connection and the Woman*. Jackson, Tenn.: Professional Books, 1995.

Chapter 6

LEAKY GUT SYNDROME: THE SYSTEMIC CONSEQUENCES OF FAULTY DIGESTION

"The gut is a major, potential portal of entry into the body for foreign antigens. Only its intact mucosal barrier protects the body from foreign antigen entry and systemic exposure."

RUSSELL JAFFE, M.D., *ELISA/ACT CININICAL UPDATE* 2,

NO. 1 (JANUARY 1992)

LEAKY GUT SYNDROME is really a nickname for the more formal term *increased intestinal permeability*, which underlies an enormous variety of illnesses and symptoms. It's not a disease or an illness itself. Rather, it manifests itself in an enormous variety of ways depending on your genes and your personal ecology. The list of health conditions associated with increased intestinal permeability grows each year as we increase our knowledge of the synergy between digestion and the immune system.

A healthy intestinal lining allows only properly digested

95

fats, proteins, and starches to pass through so they can be assimilated. At the same time it also provides a barrier to keep out bacterial products, foreign substances, and large undigested molecules. This is called the "barrier function" of the gastrointestinal mucosal lining. This surface is often called the "brush border," because under a microscope its villi and microvilli look like bristles on a brush.

The intestinal lining lets substances move across this barrier in several ways. The process of "diffusion" is a simple one: it equalizes the concentrations inside and outside the cells. Diffusion is the way ions of chloride, magnesium, potassium, sodium, and free fatty acids pass into the cells. Most nutrients are moved through the brush borders via a process called "active transport." Carrier molecules, all of low molecular weight, transport nutrients like molecular taxis. Amino acids, fatty acids, glucose, minerals, and vitamins cross cell membranes through active transport.

In-between cells are junctions called "desmosomes." Normally, desmosomes form tight junctions and do not permit large molecules to pass through. But when the area is irritated and inflamed, these junctions loosen up, allowing larger

Tight Junction (Desmosome)

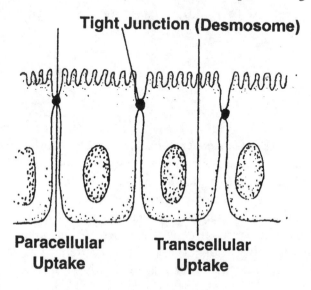

**Paracellular   Transcellular
Uptake   Uptake**

molecules to pass through. The substances that pass through the intracellular junctions are seen by our immune system as foreign, stimulating an antibody reaction. When the intestinal lining is damaged, larger substances of particle size are allowed to pass directly, again triggering an antibody reaction.

When the intestinal lining is damaged even more, substances larger than particle size—disease-causing bacteria, potentially toxic molecules, and undigested food particles—are allowed to pass directly through the weakened cell membranes. They go directly into the bloodstream, activating antibodies and alarm substances called cytokines. The cytokines alert our lymphocytes—white blood cells—to battle the particles. Oxidants are produced in the battle, causing irritation and inflammation far from the digestive system. That is the basis for a condition called increased intestinal permeability or leaky gut syndrome.

Intestinal mucus normally blocks bacteria from moving to other parts of the body. But when the cells are leaking, bacteria passes into the bloodstream and throughout the body. When intestinal bacteria colonize in other parts of the body, we call it bacterial translocation, and it is often found in people with leaky gut syndrome. For example, *Blastocystis hominis*, a bacteria that causes GI problems, has been found in the synovial fluid in the knee of an arthritis patient. Surgery or tube feeding in hospitals can also cause bacterial translocation.

Here's how leaky gut syndrome works. Imagine that your cells need a kernel of corn. They are screaming out, "Hey, send me a kernel of corn." The blood stream replies, "I have a can of corn, but I don't have a can opener." So the can goes around and around while the cells starve for corn. Finally, your immune system reacts by making antibodies against the can of corn, treating the corn as if it were a foreign invader. Your immune system has mobilized to finish the job of incomplete digestion, but this puts unneeded stress on it. The next time you eat corn, your body already has antibodies to react against it, which triggers the immune system, and so on. As time goes on, people with leaky gut syndrome tend to become more and more sensitive to a wider variety of foods and environmental contaminants.

Depending on our own susceptibilities, we may develop a wide variety of signs, symptoms, and health problems. Leaky gut syndrome is associated with the following medical problems: allergies, celiac disease, Crohn's disease, and malabsorption syndromes. It is also linked to autoimmune diseases like AIDS, ankylosing spondylitis, asthma, atopy, bronchitis, eczema, food and environmental sensitivities, other allergic disorders, psoriasis, Reiter's syndrome, rheumatoid arthritis, Sjögren's syndrome, and skin irritations.

COMMON CLINICAL CONDITIONS ASSOCIATED WITH INTESTINAL PERMEABILITY

Alcoholism	Aging
Autism	Childhood hyperactivity
Celiac disease	Malnutrition
Chemotherapy	Celiac disease
Crohn's disease	Giardia
Environmental illness	Multiple chemical sensitivities
HIV-positive	Ankylosing spondylitis
Hives	Chronic fatigue syndrome
Acne	Eczema
Cystic fibrosis	Psoriasis
Inflammatory joint disease/ arthritis	Food allergies and food sensitivities
Intestinal infections	Endotoxemia
Malnutrition	Liver dysfunction
Pancreatic insufficiency	Trauma
Schizophrenia	NSAIDs enteropathy
Thermal injury	Irritable bowel syndrome
Ulcerative colitis	

The conditions in the following chart can arise from a variety of causes, but leaky gut syndrome may underlie more classic diagnoses. If you have any of the common symptoms or disorders associated with leaky gut syndrome, ask your physician to order an intestinal permeability test to see if it is causing your problem. This test is best done in conjunction with a comprehensive digestive and stool analysis with parasitology, which checks for digestive function and dysbiosis.

In addition to clinical conditions, people with leaky gut syndrome display a wide variety of symptoms.

SYMPTOMS ASSOCIATED WITH LEAKY GUT SYNDROME

Abdominal pain	Diarrhea
Asthma	Bed wetting
Chronic joint pain	Recurrent bladder infections
Chronic muscle pain	Fevers of unknown origin
Confusion	Poor memory
Fuzzy thinking	Shortness of breath
Gas	Constipation
Indigestion	Bloating
Mood swings	Aggressive behavior
Nervousness	Anxiety
Poor exercise tolerance	Primary biliary cirrhosis
Poor immunity	Fatigue and malaise
Recurrent vaginal infections	Toxic feelings
Skin rashes	

Leaky gut syndrome puts an extra burden on the liver. All foods pass directly from the bloodstream through the liver for filtration. The liver "humanizes" the food and either lets it pass or changes it, breaking down or storing all toxic or foreign substances. Water-soluble toxins are easily excreted, but the breakdown of fat-soluble toxins is a two-stage process that requires more energy. When the liver is bombarded by inflammatory irritants from incomplete digestion, it has less energy to neutralize chemical substances. When overwhelmed, it stores these toxins in fat cells, much the same way that we put boxes in the garage or basement to deal with at a later date. If the liver has time later, it can deal with the stored toxins, but most commonly it is busy dealing with what is newly coming in and never catches up. These toxins provide a continued source of inflammation to the body.

WHAT CAUSES LEAKY GUT SYNDROME?

There is no single cause of leaky gut syndrome, but some of the most common are chronic stress, dysbiosis, environmental contaminants, gastrointestinal disease, immune overload, overuse of alcoholic beverages, poor food choices, presence of pathogenic bacteria, parasites and yeasts, and prolonged use of NSAIDs. Let's discuss some of these one at a time.

Chronic stress: Prolonged stress changes the immune system's ability to respond quickly and affects our ability to heal. It's like the story of "The Little Boy Who Cried Wolf." If we keep hollering that there's a wolf every time we're late for an appointment or we need to finish a project by a deadline, our bodies can't tell the difference between this type of stress and real stress—like meeting a vicious dog in the woods or a death in the family. Our body reacts to these stressors by producing less secretory IgA (one of the first lines of immune defense) and less DHEA (an antiaging, antistress adrenal hormone) and by slowing down digestion and peristalsis, reducing blood flow to digestive organs, and producting toxic metabolites. Meditation, guided imagery, relaxation, and a good sense of humor can help us deal with daily stresses. We can learn to let small problems and traumas wash over us, not taking them too seriously.

Dysbiosis: The presence of dysbiosis contributes to leaky gut syndrome. *Candida* push their way into the lining of the intestinal wall and break down the brush borders. They must be evaluated when leaky gut syndrome is suspected. *Blastocystisis hominis, Giardia, Helicobacter, Salmonella, Shigella, Yersinia enterocolitica,* amoebas, and other parasites also irritate the intestinal lining and cause gastrointestinal symptoms. People who have or have had digestive illness or liver problems have an increased tendency to leaky gut syndrome. Which came first: the chicken or the egg?

Environmental contaminants: Daily exposure to hundreds of household and environmental chemicals puts stress on our immune defenses and the body's ability to repair. This leads to chronic delay of necessary routine repairs. Our immune systems can only pay attention to so many places at one time. Parts of the body far away from the digestive system are affected. Connective tissue begins to break down, and we lose trace minerals like calcium, potassium, and magnesium. Environmental chemicals deplete our reserves of buffering minerals, causing acidosis in the cells and tissue and cell swelling. This is known as leaky cells—like having major internal plumbing problems!

Overconsumption of alcoholic beverages: Alcoholic drinks contain few nutrients but take many nutrients to metabolize. The most noteworthy of these are the B-complex vitamins. In fact, alcoholic beverages contain substances that are toxic to our cells. When alcohol is metabolized in the liver, the toxins are either broken down or stored by the body. Alcohol abuse puts a strain on the liver which affects digestive competency and also damages the intestinal tract.

Poor food choices: Poor food choices contribute to an imbalance of probiotics and pH. An intestinal tract that is too alkaline promotes dysbiosis. Low-fiber diets cause an increase in transit time, allowing toxic by-products of digestion to concentrate and irritate the gut mucosa. Diets of highly processed foods injure our intestinal lining. Processed foods invariably are low in nutrients and fiber, with high levels of food additives, restructured fats, and sugar. These foods promote inflammation of the GI tract. In fact, even foods we normally think of as healthful can be irritating to the gut lining. Milk, an American staple, can be highly irritating to people with lactose intolerance.

Use of medication: As was discussed more fully in chapter 5, NSAIDs damage brush borders, allowing microbes, partially digested food particles, and toxins to enter the bloodstream. Birth control pills and steroid drugs also create conditions that help feed fungi, which damage the lining. Chemotherapy drugs and radiation therapy can also significantly disrupt GI balance.

RESTORING GUT INTEGRITY

If you believe you suffer from leaky gut, it's best to work with a health professional who can help you determine the underlying factors. Fortunately, there are many ways to heal your gut. Some involve changing your habits, like chewing your food more completely; others involve taking specific supplements that will help your body repair itself. If you have food allergies or sensitivities, deal with them. Find out if you have dysbiosis or *Candida* and get appropriate treatment. Replenish your bacterial flora with probiotics and prebiotics such as FOS. You may need to support your digestive function with enzymes, bitters, or hydrochloric acid tablets.

Once the intestinal tract has been damaged, free radicals are often produced in quantities too large for the body to process. This causes inflammation and irritation, which exacerbate a leaky gut. Increasing use of antioxidant nutrients such as vitamin E, selenium, N-acetyl cysteine, superoxide dismutase, zinc, manganese, copper, Coenzyme Q10, lipoic acid, and vitamin C can help quench the free radical fire.

Supportive nutrients can help repair the mucosal lining

directly. Glutamine is the preferred food of the cells of the small intestine. Dosages can range from 1 gram to 30 grams daily, depending on your needs. Other nutrients and supplements that are helpful include: gamma-oryzanol, Seacure, vitamin A, vitamin C, panthothenic acid (vitamin B₅), deglycyrrhized licorice, folic acid, concentrated whey immunoglobulin concentrates, schizandra, and zinc.

(For more information on leaky gut see *Leaky Gut Syndrome*, E. Lipski, Keats Publishing, 1998.)

FOOD AND ENVIRONMENTAL SENSITIVITIES

Food and environmental sensitivities are usually the result of leaky gut syndrome. The prevalence of these sensitivities is more widely recognized today than in the past; 24 percent of American adults claim they have food and environmental sensitivities. These sensitivities, also called delayed hypersensitivity reactions, differ from true food allergies, also called Type 1 or immediate hypersensitivity reactions.

True food allergies are rare occurrences. They affect 0.3 to 7.5 percent of children and 1 to 2 percent of adults. The foods that most often trigger these reactions are eggs, cows' milk, nuts, shellfish, soy, wheat, and white fish. Food allergies trigger reaction of type IgE antibodies which bind to the offending food antigens. The IgE antibodies attach to mast cells which stimulates the release of cytokines and histamines. This results in closing of the throat, fatigue, tearing, hives, itching, respiratory distress, watery or runny nose, skin rashes, itchy eyes or ears, and sometimes severe reactions of asthma and anaphylactic shock. These symptoms occur within minutes after the food is eaten and people usually know what they are (hives or difficulty breathing). Physicians diagnose food allergies through the use of patch skin tests and RAST blood testing. These tests are great for testing for food allergies but do not accurately determine food sensitivities.

Sensitivity reactions, also called "delayed" or "hidden" hypersensitivities, occur when IgA, IgG, and IgM antibodies are triggered in response to foods, chemicals, and bacterial toxins. The most common antibody reactions are IgG to mold and foods; exposure to molds and foods is quite high compared to exposure to pollens. For example, in an entire hayfever season we may inhale a teaspoon of pollen, but we take pounds of food inside us each day. It is estimated that 95 percent of all food allergy is of this delayed type. In the past, these delayed allergies were called "serum sickness." The sensitivities cause symptoms which are delayed, taking several hours to several days to appear. This makes tracking them down very difficult. Food and environmental sensitivities cause a wide number of symptoms typical of a leaky gut reaction. Food particles enter the bloodstream through damaged mucosal membranes, the body recognizes them as foreign substances (antigens), and triggers an immune reaction. Prolonged antibody response can overwhelm the liver's ability to eliminate these food antigens. Subsequently, the antigens enter the bloodstream and trigger delayed hypersensitivity response, inflammation, cell damage, and disease. Almost any food can cause a reaction, although the most common are beef, citrus, dairy products, egg, pork, and wheat. These foods provoke 80 percent of food sensitivity reactions.

Antibodies and antigens form what is known as *immune complexes*. If you have lots of antibodies and few antigens, you have a small immune complex. Conversely, if you have lots of antigens and only a few antibodies, you also have a small immune complex. The worst symptoms and cravings appear when you have moderate amounts of both antibodies and antigens—when you have a large immune complex. When you try to eliminate foods while in this state, you are left with enormous cravings for these foods, and symptoms worsen before they improve. It can take seven to ten days to get through this stage. These large immune complexes can cause rashes in the skin and cheeks, as those seen in lupus.

Symptoms of Food & Environmental Sensitivity

The following symptoms occur because of many health conditions. Professional evaluation is necessary to uncover the source of these symptoms and to establish if food sensitivities are involved.

HEAD: Chronic headaches, migraines, difficulty sleeping, dizziness

MOUTH & THROAT: Coughing, sore throat, hoarseness, swelling/pain, gagging, frequently clearing throat, sores on gums, lips, and tongue

EYES, EARS, NOSE: Runny or stuffy nose, postnasal drip, ringing in the ears, blurred vision, sinus problems, watery and itchy eyes, ear infections, hearing loss, sneezing attacks, hay fever, excessive mucus formation, dark circles under eyes, swollen, red, or sticky eyelids

HEART & LUNGS: Irregular heartbeat (palpitations, arrhythmia), asthma, rapid heartbeat, chest pain and congestion, bronchitis, shortness of breath, difficulty breathing

GASTROINTESTINAL: Nausea and vomiting, constipation, diarrhea, irritable bowel syndrome, indigestion, bloating, passing gas, stomach pain, cramping, heartburn

SKIN: Hives, skin rashes, psoriasis, eczema, dry skin, excessive sweating, acne, hair loss, irritation around eyes

MUSCLES & JOINTS: General weakness, muscle/joint aches and pains, arthritis, swelling, stiffness

ENERGY & ACTIVITY: Fatigue, depression, mental dullness and memory lapses, difficulty getting your work done, apathy, hyperactivity, restlessness

EMOTIONS & MIND: Mood swings, anxiety and tension, fear, nervousness, anger, irritability, aggressive behavior, "binge" eating or drinking, food cravings, depression, confusion, poor comprehension, poor concentration, difficulty learning

OVERALL: Overweight, underweight, fluid retention, dizziness, insomnia, genital itch, frequent urination

---

ADDITIONAL SIGNS OF FOOD SENSITIVITIES IN CHILDREN

In addition to the symptoms listed above, children with food sensitivities may have:

Attention Deficit Disorder
Behavior problems
Learning problems
Reoccurring ear infections

These problems are often not recognized as being related to food sensitivities. Children with these problems will benefit from a food evaluation and environmental sensitivity testing.

Blood testing for IgG or IgG4 antibody reactions can help determine sensitivities to a variety of foods and environmental substances. You may want to screen for food allergies with IgE testing at the same time. Some labs do a test for another indicator of delayed hypersensitivity: white blood cell blastogenesis, where lymphocytes are stimulated and produce protein, DNA, and RNA at a rapid rate. Environmental screening panels measure antibody reaction to chemicals commonly found in our homes, yards, workplaces, and public places. People often test positive to household cleaning supplies and petroleum-based chemicals. Several laboratories perform antibody testing for foods, dusts, environmental chemicals, heavy metals, molds, and pollens. These labs are listed in the Resources section.

LECTINS

Lectins that are incompatible with our genetics can also cause negative reactions to foods. We each have a blood type—A, B, AB, or O—which is genetically determined. Our blood types contain specific antibodies which helped our ancestors live successfully in their environment. We no longer stick to our ancestor's specific environment and are continually exposed to new substances. When we eat a food that contains lectins which are incompatible to our blood type, the lectins target an organ or tissue and begin to collect blood cells in clumps, called agglutination.

Peter D'Adamo has developed a hypothesis that states that if we eat foods containing lectins incompatible with our blood type, we will experience negative health reactions. If, for example, I have type A blood and eat milk, my body will begin to agglutinate and reject that milk. When I drink milk, the next morning I wake up with a clump of mucus in my throat. I know this and usually avoid dairy products. The lectins don't get digested and then cause reactions. According to D'Adamo, the lectin proteins settle somewhere in our bodies and have a magnetic effect on the cells there. The cells clump together and are targeted for destruction as if they were foreign invaders. This can appear to us as irritable bowel syndrome, arthritis, or nearly any inflammatory condition. Lectin reactions mimic food allergies. The digestive system and nervous system are especially sensitive to lectin reactions. The people whose arthritis responds to elimination of the nightshade family of foods (potatoes, eggplant, tomatoes, peppers) probably have lectin sensitivities. If you want to know much more about blood type diets and lectins, read *Eat Right for Your Type*, by Peter D'Adamo.

ELIMINATION PROVOCATION DIET

If you wish to determine food and chemical sensitivities on your own, you can use the elimination provocation challenge. Only eat foods that you are unlikely to be sensitive to for a week and then add back the foods you normally eat to "challenge" your system. Removal of offending foods calms down symptoms, while careful addition of only one food each two days makes it easier to determine which foods caused the reaction. Although the elimination provocation challenge sounds simple, it can be tricky. People usually have no problem with the elimination part—a restricted food plan for a week is easy. Slowly adding foods back into your diet may be more difficult, because recipes and restaurant foods have many ingredients. Sometimes it's hard to determine which ingredient caused the distress. Reactions that are delayed for a day or two also complicate the situation. It then becomes necessary to remove all suspected foods for four days, and try them again one at a time. If you have the same reaction each time you add the food, you've found the culprit. Unfortunately, if you have sensitivities to one food, you are often sensitive to all foods in the same family. For example, some people who are sensitive to wheat are sensitive to all grains in the grass family. It is common to be sensitive to more than one food or food family.

To cure food and environmental sensitivities, you'll do best with a holistic approach. Begin by avoiding substances you are sensitive to for a period of six months, and your body will gradually stop reacting to most of them. That will help detoxify the body, especially the liver (detoxification programs are discussed in chapter 9). A comprehensive program of nutritional supplements will help in the healing process. *The Elisa/Act Handbook* reads: "Persons suffering from immune system dysfunction and overload due to delayed hypersensitivity reactions often have a need for even greater supplementation because of poor functioning of the body's normal biochemical pathways." Natural foods, organically grown and nutrient rich, also help repair the body. Exercise programs and use of stress management tools also play a part in recovery. With a holistic program you will find that over time you will become less and less sensitive to foods and the environment.

Part 3

A New Way of Identifying the Problem

Chapter 7

FUNCTIONAL MEDICINE/ FUNCTIONAL TESTING

"The best measure of quality is not how well or how frequently a medical service is given, but how closely the result approaches the fundamental objective of prolonging life, relieving distress, restoring function, and preventing disability."

LEMBEKE QUOTED IN JEFFERY BLAND, *FUNCTIONAL MEDICINE JOURNAL*, 1993

MEDICAL DISCIPLINES AND medical testing are like the ancient East Indian folktale of the six blind men touching the elephant. We test for what we "see." But each of us is "blind" because no matter how much we know, there is still so much that is unknown to us. Contemporary medicine offers a great deal, but there are other healing disciplines that lead to different explanations and interpretations. By pooling our information, we can have a fuller understanding that leads to better healing outcomes.

There is a new paradigm in nutritional healing called

functional medicine. Its primary concern is finding health problems before they become illnesses. Questionnaires and lab testing are used to determine how well organs and systems are functioning. Functional medicine recognizes that each of us has specific biochemical needs which are determined by our lifestyle, genetic structure, and environment. It focuses on restoration of health and health status, rather than progression of disease. It looks for improvement in the quality of life and an increase in a person's healthspan. The ultimate goal is for people to live a healthful existence throughout life.

Modern medicine equates the absence of disease with health. Often people walk into a doctor's office feeling tired and run down, have an exam, a battery of tests, and come back a week later to hear, "Nothing's wrong with you. You're perfectly healthy." While relieved, they still don't feel well. This is where functional, complementary, and alternative medicines play a critical role. People often seek "alternative" treatment as a last resort, but chiropractors, naturopathic physicians, nutritionally oriented MDs, nutritionists, and other holistic health practitioners offer a different view of health. Their work focuses on wellness and improved function.

As a nutritionist, I measure improved function by how people feel. When a client comes to me with symptoms or a diagnosed medical problem, I listen carefully to what the client tells me, record the information, and ask lots of questions. I was taught that if I listened carefully my clients would tell me 90 percent of what I need to know. While I can't do that with each of you, I have included several questionnaires which can help you discover more about yourself, your lifestyle, and your body. These questionnaires also provide valuable information for your health care provider.

When I still don't feel I have all the information I need, laboratory testing is my next resource. Tests give accurate measurements that can be compared with what is normal, average, and optimal. Each lab test looks for specific patterns and biochemical markers. Depending on their point of view and training, health care providers may order widely differing lab tests. Like blind men looking at an elephant, they don't always see the same thing.

Many years before most illnesses occur, people have a steady, cumulative, measurable decline in body function. To quantify this, holistic health practitioners require different tools than those most commonly used over the past fifty years. By the time you need a cardiogram, you already have heart symptoms. By the time you have a lower or upper GI test, you are experiencing some digestive problems. Even so-called "preventive medical testing" like mammograms and cholesterol screenings are really tests for early detection of disease rather than true prevention. Innovative people in medical laboratories worldwide have been designing tests to determine function rather than disease. The leading laboratories in functional testing are listed in the Resources.

There are numerous tests for functional medicine. The following are the ones I've found to be most useful for digestive problems. Most of these are laboratory tests, but a few are home tests you can perform on your own!

COMPREHENSIVE DIGESTIVE AND STOOL ANALYSIS

Comprehensive digestive and stool analysis (CDSA) is a test that checks for bacterial balance and health, digestive function, and dysbiosis. A CDSA is used to determine what types of bacteria are found and measures beneficial, possibly harmful, and disease-producing microbes. It also checks to see levels of *Candida*. If present, they are cultured to see if they grow and what agents will be most effective in eliminating them. In addition, the CDSA measures digestive function by determining how well a person can digest proteins, fats, and carbohydrates, the level of pancreatic enzymes produced, and the amount of short-chain fatty acids and butyric acid in the colon. Some labs also include a dysbiosis index, which uses the combined testing to give a measure of normalcy or abnormalcy. The CDSA provides a quick reference for your health care provider and can determine your therapeutic needs.

The CDSA test and associated research are very new. As recently as 1990, no one really knew what specific bacterial balance was normal, but since then, many thousands of stool analyses have been completed and the view of what is normal has become better defined. CDSA is useful for everyone who has digestive problems. If you only choose to do one test, do this one in conjunction with the comprehensive parasitology screening described below.

A recent client had ulcerative colitis characterized by bleeding with bowel movements, severe reactions to a large number of foods, rapid weight loss, and fatigue. In partnership with his gastroenterologist we ran a CDSA. The test showed that he had overgrowth of two dysbiotic bacteria (*Citrobacter* and *Klebsiella*) and *Candida parapsilosis* (a less common variety of *Candida*). Because lab technicians actually culture the client's microbes to see what works most effectively to kill them, the CDSA lists which medications the bacteria and fungi respond to most effectively, which the physician prescribed. In addition, we set up a dietary regime that eliminated foods which were irritating his digestive system. With proper diet, supplementation, and medication, his bleeding stopped, he had normal bowel movements, he gained weight consistently, and he is no longer taking prednisone. His physician had expected that he would need it for the rest of his life. The CDSA was validating to my client. He could finally "see" what was going on inside his body, which helped his self-esteem and his healing process tremendously. Because he has gotten so much better, he now has an optimistic view of his future health prospects and quality of life.

PARASITOLOGY TESTING

Though we think of parasites as something we get from traveling in other countries, it's not true. According to the June 27, 1978, *Miami Herald,* the Center for Disease Control (CDC) in Atlanta found that one out of six randomly selected people had one or more parasites. Great Smokies Diagnostics Laboratory in North Carolina has similar results. They find parasites in 20 percent of samples tested. Over 130 types of parasites have been found in Americans. Parasites have become more prevalent for many reasons, including contaminated water supplies, day care centers, ease of international travel, foods, increased immigration, pets, and the sexual revolution. Most people will meet a parasite at some point in their lives. Contrary to popular myths, having parasites isn't a reflection of your cleanliness. My family contracted *Giardia* in Chicago. We hadn't traveled and have absolutely no idea how we contracted it.

If you have prolonged digestive symptoms, you should really consider having a comprehensive parasitology screening. Some symptoms of parasites can appear to be like other digestive problems: abdominal pain, allergy, anemia, bloating, bloody stools, chronic fatigue, constipation, coughing, diarrhea, gas, granulomas, irritable bowel syndrome, itching, joint and muscle aches, nervousness, pain, poor immune response, rashes, sleep disturbances, teeth grinding, unexplained fever, and unexplained weight loss.

Many physicians request parasitology testing on random stool samples. This can be highly inaccurate, so repeated testing is often necessary to get definitive results. Since many parasites live further up the digestive tract, many labs now give an oral laxative to induce diarrhea to detect these parasites. Yet other parasites are found by using a rectal swab rather than a stool sample. The most accurate stool testing is usually done by labs that specialize in parasitology testing.

Parasite Questionnaire

Check If Yes

1. Have you ever been to Africa, Asia, Central or South America, China, Europe, Israel, Mexico, or Russia? _____

2. Have you traveled to the Bahamas, the Caribbean, Hawaii, or other tropical islands? _____

3. Do you frequently swim in freshwater lakes, ponds, or streams while abroad? _____

4. Did you serve overseas while in the military? _____

5. Were you a prisoner of war in World War II, Korea, or Vietnam? _____

6. Have you had an elevated white blood count, intestinal problems, night sweats, or unexplained fever during or since traveling abroad? _____

7. Is your water supply from a mountainous area? _____

8. Do you drink untested water? _____

9. Have you ever drunk water from lakes, rivers, or streams on hiking or camping trips without first boiling or filtering it? _____

10. Do you use plain tap water to clean your contact lenses? _____

11. Do you use regular tap water that is unfiltered for colonics or enemas? _____

12. Can you trace the onset of symptoms (intermittent constipation and diarrhea, muscle aches and pains, night sweats, unexplained eye ulcers) to any of the above? _____

13. Do you regularly eat unpeeled raw fruits and raw vegetables in salads? _____

14. Do you frequently eat in Armenian, Chinese, Ethiopian, Filipino, fish, Greek, Indian, Japanese, Korean, Mexican, Pakistani, Thai, or vegetarian restaurants; in delicatessens, fast-food restaurants, steak houses, or sushi or salad bars? _____

15. Do you use a microwave oven for cooking (as opposed to reheating) beef, fish, or pork? _____

16. Do you prefer fish or meat that is undercooked, i.e., rare or medium rare? _____
17. Do you frequently eat hot dogs made from pork? _____
18. Do you enjoy raw fish dishes like Dutch green herring, Latin American ceviche, or sushi and sashimi? _____
19. Do you enjoy raw meat dishes like Italian carpaccio, Middle Eastern kibbe, or steak tartare? _____
20. At home, do you use the same cutting board for chicken, fish, and meat as you do for vegetables? _____
21. Do you prepare gefilte fish at home? _____
22. Can you trace the onset of symptoms (anemia, bloating, distended belly, weight loss) to any of the above? _____
23. Have you gotten a puppy recently? _____
24. Have you lived with, or do you currently live with, or frequently handle pets? _____
25. Do you forget to wash your hands after petting or cleaning up after your animals and before eating? _____
26. Does your pet sleep with you in bed? _____
27. Does your pet eat off your plates? _____
28. Do you clean your cat's litter box? _____
29. Do you keep your pets in the yard where children play? _____
30. Can you trace the onset of your symptoms (abdominal pain, distended belly in children, high white blood count, unexplained fever) to any of the above? _____
31. Do you work in a hospital? _____
32. Do you work in an experimental laboratory, pet shop, veterinary clinic, or zoo? _____
33. Do you work with or around animals? _____
34. Do you work in a daycare center? _____
35. Do you garden or work in a yard to which cats and dogs have access? _____
36. Do you work in sanitation? _____

37. Can you trace the onset of symptoms (gastrointestinal disorders) to any of the above? ___
38. Do you engage in oral sex? ___
39. Do you practice anal intercourse without the use of a condom? ___
40. Have you had sexual relations with a foreign-born individual? ___
41. Can you trace the onset of symptoms (persistent reproductive organ problems) to any of the above? ___

Major Symptoms: Please note that although some or all of these major symptoms can occur in any adult, child, or infant with parasite-based illness, these symptoms might instead be the result of one of many other illnesses.

ADULTS

1. Do you have a bluish cast around your lips? ___
2. Is your abdomen distended no matter what you eat? ___
3. Are there dark circles around or under your eyes? ___
4. Do you have a history of allergy? ___
5. Do you suffer from intermittent diarrhea and constipation, intermittent loose and hard stools, or chronic constipation? ___
6. Do you have persistent acne, anal itching, anemia, anorexia, bad breath, bloody stools, chronic fatigue, difficulty in breathing, edema, food sensitivities, itching, open ileocecal valve, pale skin, palpitations, PMS, puffy eyes, ringing of the ears, sinus congestion, skin eruptions, vague abdominal discomfort, or vertigo? ___
7. Do you grind your teeth? ___
8. Are you experiencing craving for sugar, depression, disorientation, insomnia, lethargy, loss of appetite, moodiness, or weight loss or gain? ___

CHILDREN

1. Does your child have dark circles under his or her eyes? _____
2. Is your child hyperactive? _____
3. Does your child grind or clench his teeth at night? _____
4. Does your child constantly pick her nose or scratch her behind? _____
5. Does your child have a habit of eating dirt? _____
6. Does your child wet his bed? _____
7. Is your child often restless at night? _____
8. Does your child cry often or for no reason? _____
9. Does your child tear her hair out? _____
10. Does your child have a limp that orthopedic treatment has not helped? _____
11. Does your child have a brassy, staccato-type cough? _____
12. Does your child have convulsions or an abnormal electroencephalogram (EEG)? _____
13. Does your child have recurring headaches? _____
14. Is your child unusually sensitive to light and prone to blinking frequently, eyelid twitching, or squinting? _____
15. Does your child have unusual tendencies to bleed in the gums, the nose, or the rectum? _____

INFANTS

1. Does your baby have severe intermittent colic? _____
2. Does your baby persistently bang his or her head against the crib? _____
3. Is your baby a chronic crier? _____
4. Does your baby show a blotchy rash around the perianal area? _____

Interpretation of Questionnaire

1. If you answered "yes" to more than 40 items, you are at high risk for parasites.
2. If you answered "yes" to more than 30 items, you are at moderate risk for parasites.
3. If you answered "yes" to more than 20 items, you are at risk.
4. If you are not exhibiting any overt symptoms now, remember that many parasitic infections can be dormant and then spring to life when you least expect them. Be aware that symptoms that come and go may still point to an underlying parasitic infection because of reproductive cycles. The various developmental stages of parasites often produce a variety of metabolic toxins and mechanical irritations in several areas of the body—for example, pinworms can stimulate asthmatic attacks because of their movement into the upper respiratory tract.

Source: Used with permission from Ann Louise Gittleman, *Guess What Came To Dinner?* Garden City Park, N.Y.: Avery Publishing Group, 1993.

FOOD AND ENVIRONMENTAL SENSITIVITY TESTING

Elimination/provocation testing for food and environmental irritants is a two-stage process: an elimination diet and then a provocation challenge test. Elimination/provocation testing requires your determination and commitment because you must radically change your diet to find out which foods you are reacting to. Often the foods we are sensitive to are the ones we depend on most, so you may have to do without some of your favorite foods for awhile.

Over the past few years, I have been using an elimination diet that works well for nearly all of my clients (except those with *Candida*). This program allows all fruit (except citrus), all vegetables (except tomatoes, eggplant, potatoes, and peppers), and white rice. You can eat as much of these foods as you like, plus olive oil and canola oil for stir-frying and on salads. In addition, I use a rice-protein, nutrient-enriched drink that helps detoxify your system and ensures your protein needs are met. The foods allowed during the elimination are unlikely to cause food sensitivities. If food sensitivities are provoking symptoms, you'll find you feel terrific eating this way. In fact, some people feel better than they have in years! Elimination of the offending foods gives your digestive system a chance to heal over several months' time because you are no longer irritating it.

After seven to fourteen days on the elimination diet, you begin the provocation challenge. By slowly reintroducing foods into your diet, you can test yourself for your reactions. Do you become sleepy thirty minutes after eating wheat? Does cheese give you diarrhea? Do you itch all over after eating oranges? Do your joints ache after eating tomatoes? Through careful observation, you can detect many foods you have become sensitive to. Once you become familiar with your body's reaction, you can identify sensitivities, though it may be necessary to test a food several times to be certain of your reaction.

To enhance this process, it is best to also have a blood test for IgG4 and IgE antibody reactions to determine food and environmental sensitivities. Some labs also include testing for IgA and IgM antibodies. While many foods may be unmasked during the elimination/provocation challenge, others may remain hidden. If you suspect that chemicals, molds, or pollens are causing problems, you should also be screened for them. (Labs offer these tests either separately or as part of a complete screening package.) Sensitivities are rated from normal to severe reactions. In addition to a detailed readout documenting your personal reactions, most laboratories also include a list of foods which contain hidden sources of the offending foods, a rotation menu, and other educational material to help you in the healing process.

Leaky Gut Syndrome/Intestinal Permeability Testing

There are several ways to measure for leaky gut syndrome/ intestinal permeability. The method that has rapidly become the recognized standard is the mannitol and lactulose test. Mannitol and lactulose are water-soluble sugar molecules that our bodies cannot metabolize or use. They come in differing sizes and weights and are absorbed into the bloodstream at different rates. Mannitol is easily absorbed into cells by people with healthy digestion, while lactulose has such a large molecular size that it is only slightly absorbed. A healthy test shows high levels of mannitol and low levels of lactulose. If large amounts of mannitol and lactulose are present, it indicates a leaky gut condition. If low levels of both sugars are found, it indicates general malabsorption of all nutrients. Low mannitol levels with high lactulose levels have been found in people with celiac disease, Crohn's disease, and ulcerative colitis.

Your doctor can give you a test kit to collect urine samples. After collecting a random urine sample, you drink a mannitol/lactulose mixture and collect urine for six hours. The samples are then sent to the laboratory. This test is often done in conjunction with a CDSA or a parasitology test.

Secretory IgA Testing

Secretory IgA (sIgA), an immunoglobulin antibody, is found in saliva in the mouth, throughout the digestive tract, and in mucous secretions throughout the body. We normally don't think of the digestive system as being part of the immune system, but sIgA provides our first line of defense against bacteria, food residue, fungus, parasites, and viruses. By sitting on mucous membranes, it prevents invaders from attaching to them and neutralizes them. New technology has made it simple to measure sIgA levels throughout the body using saliva.

Deficiency of sIgA is the most common immunodeficiency. Low levels of sIgA make us more susceptible to infection and may be a fundamental cause of asthma, autoimmune diseases, candidiasis, celiac disease, chronic infections, food allergies, and more. In other words, if the sentry isn't standing at the gate, anyone can come in! A study examining people with Crohn's disease or ulcerative colitis found that all of them had low levels of sIgA. It concluded that raising sIgA levels might eliminate inflammatory bowel disease.

High levels of sIgA are found in people who have chronic infections and whose immune systems are overloaded. It often accompanies chronic viral infections like CMV, EBV, and HIV. It has also been found in people with rare medical problems like Berger's nephropathy, dermatitis herpetiformis, gingivitis, hepatic glomerulonephritis, IgA neoplasms, parotitis, and secretory antisperm Abs.

Lifestyle and nutritional factors can influence sIgA levels. A balanced lifestyle, which encompasses our ability to nurture ourselves, environmental considerations, exercise, good food choices, and moderate stress levels, can increase sIgA levels. Choline, essential fatty acids, glutathione, glycine, phosphatidylcholine, phosphatidylethanolamine, quercitin, vitamin C, and zinc are all required to maintain healthy sIgA levels. Detoxification programs and repair of intestinal mucosa help normalize sIgA. *Saccharomyces boulardii*, a nontoxic yeast often found in probiotic supplements, has been shown to raise sIgA levels. A recent study showed that visualization and relaxation techniques significantly increase sIgA levels.

Heidelberg Capsule Test

The Heidelberg capsule test is a radiotelemetry test for functional hydrochloric acid (HCl) levels. It is a simple, effective technique to determine how much HCl your stomach is producing. Normally produced by the parietal cells of the stomach, HC1 is necessary for the initial stage of protein digestion and the absorption of vitamin B_{12} and many minerals. Common symptoms of low-stomach acidity include belching or burning sensation immediately after meals, bloating, a feeling that the food just sits in the stomach without digesting, and an inability to eat more than small amounts at any one sitting. Poor HCl levels have been associated with childhood asthma, chronic hepatitis, chronic hives, diabetes, eczema, gallbladder disease, lupus erythematosus, osteoporosis, rheumatoid arthritis, rosacea, under- and overactive thyroid conditions, vitiligo, and weak adrenals. As we age, we produce less HCl. As many as half of all people over the age of sixty may be deficient in this important substance.

The Heidelberg test has proven to be accurate and sensitive in determining stomach pH levels. After you swallow a radio transmitter that's about the size of a B-complex vitamin, it measures the resting pH of your stomach, alternating with challenges of baking soda, which is very alkaline. By observing how well the stomach returns to an acid condition after administration of the baking soda, the physician can determine whether or not you produce adequate amounts of HCl.

Functional Liver Profile Testing

Liver profile testing is useful for determining how well you are able to handle toxic substances. The liver is responsible for transforming toxic substances into harmless by-products that the body can excrete. It does this in a variety of ways, including acetylation, conjugation, sulfation, sulfur transferase, and via the cytochrome P450 system. The functional liver profile looks at the total toxic load in your body and sees how well your body handles it by measuring the abilities of your liver detoxification systems.

When we are exposed to substances that the body sees as toxic, cytochrome P450 levels go up. Many substances can stimulate its production, including alcohol, barbiturates, carbon tetrachloride, charcoal broiled meats, dioxin, exhaust fumes, high-protein diets, niacin, oranges, organophosphorus pesticides, paint fumes, riboflavin, sassafras, saturated fats, steroid hormones, sulfonamides, and tangerines. The cytochrome P450 system transforms endotoxins (toxins produced within the body) and exotoxins (those taken into the body from outside) into water-soluble forms that can be excreted in urine. By measuring the cytochrome P450 levels and seeing how quickly the toxic materials are transformed, tests can provide useful information about how well the body is able to detoxify a wide variety of substances.

When cytochrome P450 is released, a second phase of detoxification is also activated, which causes an elevation of D-glucaric acid. D-glucaric acid is released by the liver and is a by-product of turning toxic substances into glucuronidase, which is excreted in urine. A sulfur/creatinine ratio is used to test this function. This ratio helps determine leaky gut syndrome, low glutathione levels, and the level of free radical activity.

For the test take small amounts of caffeine, aspirin, and acetaminophen at home and send urine samples off to the laboratory for analysis. By measuring your urine and saliva, it can be determined how well your liver is able to process toxins. Normal levels of cytochrome P450 are found in 50 percent of people tested. A low-caffeine clearance is found in about one-third of all people tested and indicates that your body is having difficulty detoxifying. High-caffeine clearance levels are found in people who have been exposed to high levels of toxins or smoke.

Another way to measure liver detoxification pathways is to measure D-glucaric acid and mercapturic acid in the urine. D-glucaric acid is a general marker for Phase 1/cytochrome P450 detoxification pathways. High levels of D-glucaric acid indicate the presence of environmental toxins such as pesticides, herbicides, fungicides, petrochemicals, and excessive alcohol intake. Mercapturic acid provides a measurement of glutathione conjugation. This test is easier on those who do not tolerate caffeine, aspirin, or acetaminophen.

INDICAN TEST

The Indican test measures the amount of putrefaction in your digestive system. This is a urinary test and gives a general indication of how well you are digesting foods. High indican levels are found in people with dysbiotic conditions and malabsorption. Indican testing offers a quick way to screen for faulty digestion, but does not give enough detailed information to know exactly why or where the problem originates. Some doctors find it a useful office screening test because it is inexpensive and noninvasive.

LACTOSE INTOLERANCE

Lactase is an enzyme that digests lactose, a sugar naturally found in milk products. The inability to digest lactose affects about 70 percent of the world's population and is highly prevalent in African Americans, Asian Americans, Caucasian Americans of Mediterranean and Jewish descent, Hispanics, and Native Americans. Lactose intolerance is caused by an enzymatic deficiency and is not a milk allergy, which is the inability to digest milk proteins. Lactose intolerance causes a wide variety of symptoms including abdominal cramping, acne, bloating, diarrhea, gas, headaches, and nausea. Most people with lactose intolerance fail to recognize that the food they eat has any relationship to how they feel.

There are two ways to test for lactose intolerance—a self-test and a laboratory test. To self-test, you must restrict intake of all dairy products for at least ten days. Obvious sources include milk, yogurt, cheese, ice cream, creamed soups, frozen yogurt, powdered milk, and whipped cream. Less obvious sources are bakery items, cookies, hot dogs, lunchmeats, milk chocolate, most nondairy creamers, pancakes, protein powder drinks, ranch dressings, and anything that contains casein, caseinate, lactose, sodium caseinate, and whey. If you're not sure what's in a food, avoid it during the testing period. It's probably best to eat all your meals at home or prepare all food yourself.

If lactose intolerance is causing your problems, you will probably notice your symptoms have disappeared significantly. Reintroduction of dairy products will trigger a return of symptoms. However, the results may be inconclusive because you may be sensitive to other foods in addition to dairy—in which case your symptoms won't change. A laboratory test would then be indicated.

Your doctor can order a simple, noninvasive hydrogen breath test to pinpoint if lactose intolerance is causing your problems. This challenge test is ideal for people who find it difficult to complete a self-test or are confused about their findings. After you breathe into a bag to collect a baseline sample, you drink a small amount of a lactose solution and breathe into a different bag. Lab technicians measure the levels of hydrogen and methane gas you exhaled in both samples. Normal methane levels are 0 to 7 parts per million (ppm). If levels increase at least 12 ppm between the two samples, it indicates lactose intolerance, even if your hydrogen production is normal. Normal hydrogen levels are 10 ppm.

Levels of 20 ppm or more are commonly found in people with lactose intolerance. When both methane and hydrogen are measured, false results are narrowed considerably. Use of antibiotics, enemas, and laxatives are common reasons for false negative results, which occur 5 percent of the time. This test has a few false positive results, which are generally caused by eating high-fiber foods before the test, exposure to cigarette smoke, or sleeping during testing.

HAIR ANALYSIS

Hair analysis is a useful tool to see how well you absorb essential minerals and what levels of toxic minerals have accumulated in your tissues. Hair is cut as close to your head as possible—only the 1 to 2 inches which grew closest to your head will be tested because it reflects your mineral status over the past few months. The lab burns your hair in an electrochromatography scan to measure the levels of minerals present. Low levels of six or more essential minerals indicate a problem with absorption of nutrients. This could be due to drug therapy, dysbiosis, low hydrochloric acid levels, or poor flora. Hair analysis is also an accurate test to determine whether you have high levels of toxic minerals like aluminum, arsenic, cadmium, lead, and mercury. It is also a recognized tool for detecting lead poisoning in children.

pH TESTING

Our body pH is maintained just above 7.0 for optimal health. Note that 7.0 is the pH of water, which is neither alkaline nor acidic. The pH is kept in balance by a variety of mechanisms which produce acid by-products. The alkaline mineral buffers, found in fruits and vegetables, help keep us healthy. Many disease conditions are helped by keeping pH at optimal levels.

The pH testing is a simple home urine test with a dipstick. You simply place a piece of pH-sensitive paper into your first morning urine and "read" it to see what your pH is. Optimally, the level will be between 6.5 and 7.5, or fairly neutral. By manipulating your foods, you can bring this into an optimal range, which will give support to your body's own innate healing and balancing capacities.

SMALL BOWEL BACTERIAL OVERGROWTH

The small bowel bacterial overgrowth test measures breath levels of hydrogen and methane to determine if there is a bacterial infection in the small intestine. This test differs from the comprehensive digestive and stool analysis in that it tests for dysbiosis of the small rather than the large intestine. Small bowel overgrowth occurs when bacteria in the large intestine travel to the small intestine. It is often the result of poor hydrochloric acid production in the stomach or an insufficient amount of pancreatic enzyme function. It is often found in conjunction with parasitic infections. Chronic pancreatitis, Crohn's disease, and lupus erythematosus can also cause small bowel overgrowth. People with small bowel bacterial overgrowth experience diarrhea, poor nutrient absorption, and weight loss. Other people who may be affected are those with poor ileocecal valve function, poor intestinal motility, scleroderma, or recent gastric surgery. People infected with small bowel overgrowth often have difficulty with digestion of fats, which come through undigested in the stool, called steatorrhea. They may also experience B_{12} deficiency, chronic diarrhea, and poor absorption of the fat-soluble vitamins A, D, E, and K.

Breath testing provides a simple, noninvasive alternative to the more widely used method of obtaining a small

Most Alkaline	More Alkaline	Low Alkaline	Lowest Alkaline
•Baking Soda	Spices/ Cinnamon	Herbs (most)	
Table salt (NaCl)	Sea salt		*Sulfite*
Mineral water	•Kambucha	•Green or mu tea	Ginger tea
	Molasses	Rice syrup	•Sucanat
	Soy sauce	Apple cider vinegar	•Umeboshi vinegar
•Umeboshi plums		•Sake	•Algae,blue-green
			•Ghee (clarified butter)
		•Quail eggs	•Duck eggs
			Oats 'Grain coffee' •Quinoa Wild rice
	Poppy seed	Primrose oil	Avocado oil
Pumpkin seed		Sesame seed	Seeds (most)
	Chestnuts	Cod Liver oil	Coconut oil
	Pepper	Almonds	Olive oil
Hydrogenated oil		•Sprouts	Linseed oil
Lentils	Kohlrabi	Potato/bell pepper	Brussel sprout
Yam	Parsnip/Taro	Mushroom/fungi	Beet
	Garlic	Cauliflower	Chive/cilantro
Onion	Kale/Parsley	Rutabaga	Okra
Daikon/•Taro root	Endive	•Salsify/•ginseng	Turnip greens
Sea vegetables (other)	Mustard green	Eggplant	Squashes
Burdock/Lotus Root	Ginger root	Pumpkin	Lettuces
Sweet potato/yam	Broccoli	Collard greens	Jicama
Lime	Grapefruit	Lemon	Orange
Nectarine	Canteloupe	Pear	Apricot
Persimmon	Honeydew	Avocado	Banana
Raspberry	Citrus	Apple	Blueberry
Watermelon	Olive	Blackberry	Pineapple
Tangerine	•Dewberry	Cherry	Raisin, currant
Pineapple	Loganberry	Peach	Grape
	Mango	Papaya	Strawberry

•Therapeutic, gourmet, or exotic items.   *Italicized items are NOT recommended.*
Used with permission of Russell Jaffe, M.D., *Health Collegieum.*

ACID/ALKALINE BODY CHEMICAL BALANCE

Food Category	Lowest Acid	Low Acid	More Acid	Most Acid
Spices/Herbs	Curry	Vanilla	Nutmeg	Pudding/Jam/Jelly
Preservatives	*MSG*	*Benzoate*	*Aspartame*	
Beverages	*Kona coffee*	*Alcohol*	Coffee	Beer
		Black tea		Yeast/hops/malt
Sweeteners	Honey/maple syrup		*Saccharin*	Sugar/cocoa
Vinegar	Rice vinegar	Balsamic vinegar		White/acetic vinegar
Therapeutics		*Antihistamines*	*Psychotropics*	*Antibiotics*
Processed dairy	Cream	Cow milk	•Casein, milk protein	*Processed cheese*
Cow/human	Yogurt	Aged cheese	New cheeses	Ice cream
soy		Soy cheese	Soy milk	
Goat/sheep	Goat/sheep/cheese	Goat milk		
Eggs	Chicken eggs	•Game meat		
Meat	Gelatin/organs	Lamb/mutton	Pork/veal	Beef
Game	venison	Boar/elk	Bear	
Fish/shell fish	Fish	Shell fish	•Mussles/squid	Lobster
Fowl	Wild duck	Goose/turkey	Chicken	•Pheasant
	Triticale	Buckwheat	Maize	Barley
Grains	Millet	Wheat	Barley groats	
Cereal	Kasha	•Spelt/teff	Corn	
Grass	Amaranth	Farina/semolina	Rye	
	Brown rice	White rice	Oat bran	
Nuts	Pumpkin seed oil	Almond oil	Pistachio seed	•*Cottonseed oil/meal*
Seeds/sprouts	Grape seed oil	Sesame oil	Chestnut oil	Hazelnuts
Oils	Sunflower oil	Safflower oil	*Lard*	Walnuts
	Pine nuts	Tapioca	Pecans	Brazil nuts
	Canola oil	•Seitan	Palm kernel oil	*Fried foods*
	Spinach	Tofu	Green pea	Soybean
Beans	Fava beans	Pinto beans	Peanut	Carob
Vegetables	Kidney beans	White beans	Snow pea	
Legume	String/wax	Navy/red	Legumes (other)	
Pulses		Azuki beans	Carrots	
Roots	Chutney	Lima beans	Chickpeas	
	Rhubarb	Chard		
Citrus fruits				
	Guava	Plum	Cranberry	
	•Pickled fruit	Prune	Pomegranate	
	Dry fruit	Tomatoes		
Fruits	Figs			
	Persimmon juice			
	•Cherimoya			
	Dates			

bowel aspirate and is more accurate. To perform the test, you drink either a lactulose or a glucose drink and collect breath samples. Hydrogen is produced when lactulose or glucose come in contact with the gut flora. A significant rise in hydrogen levels indicates small bowel overgrowth.

EAV TESTING

The electrical acupuncture voltage (EAV) test is widely used in Europe after much positive research. Although it has met with FDA resistance in the United States, there are many skillful professionals who use this test to successfully diagnose and determine appropriate therapies.

The test measures the electrical activity of your skin at designated acupuncture points. You hold a negative rod in one hand, the practitioner places a positively charged pointer on a variety of points on your skin, and a meter measures the voltage reading between the points. The test can determine which organs are strong or weak, which foods help or hurt you, which nutrients you need or have excessive levels of, and how old patterns are contributing to your health today. It is a fast, noninvasive screening test.

Part 4

THE DIGESTIVE WELLNESS PROGRAM:

You Can Change the Way You Feel!

Chapter 8

MOVING TOWARD A WELLNESS LIFESTYLE

"Health approaches seek to identify the causes (or potential causes) of disease and employ therapies designed to eliminate host susceptibility and hospitality to ill health. Health approaches give priority to therapies of minimum risk and high therapeutic gain, tailored to the individual's attitudes and circumstances."

RUSS JAFFE/WOMEN AND CHILDREN'S HEALTH UPDATE,
1994–5 SYLLABUS

HEALTH IS A continuum. At one end you have optimal health and at the other death.

Optimal Health   Death

Signs——Symptoms——Disease

Somewhere to the right of optimal health, you find you have less energy than you would like to have. Maybe you experience discomfort after eating. If at this point you contact your physician, he/she will probably tell you to chew your food more thoroughly and take an over-the-counter medication for discomfort. You may find over time the problem disappears. The body's own innate healing balance has restored itself without much help from you. On the other hand, you may find that the discomfort is getting worse. Now you also experience bloating and gas. Again, your physician is likely to recommend a simple medication. And over time, the problem may go away. If it continues to get worse, your physician will be able to make a "diagnosis" and give a clinical name to your problem—yes, you have diverticulitis or irritable bowel syndrome.

In a wellness scenario, the time to tackle the problem is when you have the first small signs. Paying attention to what your body is trying to tell you is the first principle of wellness. Indigestion is not caused by a Rolaids deficiency. Listening to your body can help you make healthful changes in your lifestyle that will affect not only your tummy, but your entire well-being. For example, if your indigestion happens when your stress level is high, then you can focus on building stress management tools. If your indigestion happens after you eat milk products, then the solution may be the elimination of dairy products. If your indigestion is worse when you are out of shape, then an exercise program may be in order.

Most of us make short-lived attempts toward wellness. We begin a new diet each Monday, we make New Year's resolutions that we've forgotten by Valentine's Day, and other plans get washed away by daily responsibilities. It's not that we aren't trying; we are. But in order to implement long-lasting changes in lifestyle we need a plan.

The following exercise is a great way to discover and prioritize which areas of your life need attention. You may feel that your relationships have little or nothing to do with the fact that you have chronic diarrhea, but until you balance your relationships, you can't know for sure. The mind is not separate from the body. It is well-documented that the thoughts we have influence our physical condition. All domains of wellness affect our sense of well-being.

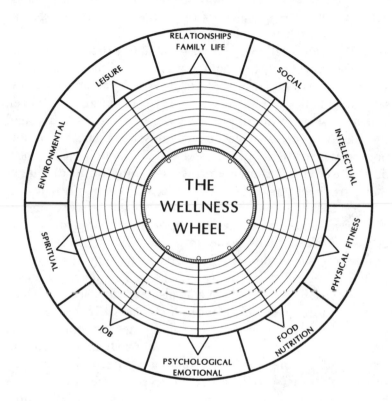

WELLNESS WHEEL

How satisfied are you today in each of these areas of your life? Rate them on a scale from 1 to 10, with 1 being the most dissatisfied to 10 being the most satisfied.

Now look at your wellness wheel. Would it roll? Which

spokes are the shortest? The short spokes are the areas you've paid less attention to recently, so they offer the greatest areas of discovery and opportunity. They help you prioritize which areas you need to pay attention to the most today.

Next, study the overall look of your wheel. Are you generally satisfied or dissatisfied with your life? People with 8s, 9s, and 10s generally feel pretty good about themselves; their lives are moving in the right direction. People with 0s, 1s, 2s, and 3s may be feeling a lack of confidence and have low self-esteem. If you have lots of short spokes on your wheel, you may want to boost your support systems. Find a friend to talk to or get a professional counselor to help you sort out your priorities. My wellness wheel changes each time I do this exercise, depending on what's going on in my life at that particular time. It is a dynamic, ever-changing wheel.

Now that you have looked at the spokes, choose one or two areas where you see an opportunity for growth and change. Make a small, achievable goal—like "I will only eat dessert one time this week" or "I will call my sister whom I haven't spoken to in twenty years." Be reasonable and easy on yourself. Small, attainable goals lead to success, which leads to more goal-setting and more success. If you've never exercised, begin by walking or biking twenty minutes once or twice a week. If you'd like to cut out coffee, you can quit or cut back. Some people find they only "need" the first cup of the day; other people switch to decaf. Remember that the journey toward wellness is as important as the destination. Don't worry about "getting there"; just enjoy the scenery!

When you work consistently on a wellness lifestyle, you expect to be healthier in ten years than you are today. Of course, we do age and we may meet with an unexpected illness, but in general, people who pay attention to how they feel have a greater sense of well-being. They also feel more responsible and in control of their lives.

In our culture, we approach aging as a "going-downhill" process. We expect to spend the last twenty to thirty years of our lives adapting to loss of function. But we all have friends who lead active, healthy lives until ripe old age. I have a friend who is ninety-six years old, works as a stock broker four days a week, and spends a long weekend at his country home. His health isn't perfect, but his life is full and his mind is interested and busy. His body is aging, but his spirit is youthful. Anyone who wants to can change their expectations and set goals of greater healthspan and well-being.

Wellness is more than the absence of illness. Wellness is having the energy to do the things you dream of. Wellness is the belief that your body wants to heal itself and that you can improve your health over time, rather than stand by and watch it deteriorate. Does that mean you won't age? No, all people age. But we can build a strong house, so that we age gracefully. Having a healthy body prevents chronic, degenerative illnesses that are primarily products of our lifestyle. Wellness demands that we take responsibility for our own health and make changes in the way we live in order to help our body function more optimally. We are required to ask questions, rather than just accept the cultural norm.

Complimentary medicine is rapidly becoming integrated into American culture and into conventional care. Recently, 125 medical schools were polled about their alternative medicine curricula. Of the 117 schools that responded, 64 percent indicated that they offer either complete courses on alternative medicine, or sections on alternative medicine in other courses. Between 1990 and 1997, Americans have increased their use of complimentary medicine. In 1990, 36.3 percent of people polled used alternative therapies; by 1997 the number had risen to 46.3 percent. The therapies most used included herbal medicine, massage, megavitamins, self-help groups, folk remedies, energy healing, and homeopathy. People sought out alternative medicine mainly for chronic health problems such as back problems and headaches. When the results of this poll were extrapolated, total out-of-pocket expenditures for complimentary and alternative therapies were estimated to be about $27 billion, which compares to the projected expenses for all U.S. physician services.

Although it will probably take at least another decade for complimentary practices to be fully integrated into current standard medical practice, the changes are happening rapidly. Complimentary medicine is cost-effective; honors the feelings, wisdom, and knowledge of the patient; and empowers each person to be active in her own care. It puts the soul and spirit back into medicine, and this is what we are all embracing. (But obviously, you know this—you have this book in your hands!)

In the following chapters, you will be given a wellness prescription which includes general guidelines, followed by specific guidelines. Because you are unique, you need to tailor these plans to suit your current needs and lifestyle. You would benefit from a consultation with a certified clinical nutritionist (CCN), a certified nutrition specialist (CNS), or a physician who specializes in nutritional medicine. These professionals can help you determine the essentials of your program, its duration, and how to work with it over time. But remember, you are the boss. You're the only one who knows exactly how you feel.

When you find a health professional whom you like, trust, respect, and are attuned with, listen to his or her advice. When you agree on a plan of action, follow through. You can only really tell what the results will be if you follow the plan over a period of time. If you feel that a given therapy isn't helping after a set amount of time, it may not be the correct one for you. If you have a bad feeling about a therapy or about the person you are working with, do something about it. Be bold, ask questions, educate yourself, and direct your own care.

Many people "shop around" for therapeutics and practitioners and never really complete any given program. You aren't doing yourself a favor if you don't make a commitment. If you want to add another therapy or modality to your program, talk it over with the health professional you are working with. Team efforts often give the best results, but only with commitment and communication.

Here are some people you may want to put on your wellness team: medical doctor, chiropractor, naturopathic physician, energetic healer, clinical nutritionist, physical therapist, acupuncture practitioner, herbalist, homeopath, psychologist counselor, colon therapist, massage therapist, or body worker. Each of these professionals can guide you toward health from their own perspective. There are many roads to wellness. If you find yourself at a dead end, turn around and take another road.

Chapter 9

FIRST THINGS FIRST: DETOXIFICATION

"It can be strongly said that the health of an individual is largely determined by the ability of the body to detoxify."

JOSEPH PIZZORNO, MICHAEL MURRAY, N.D.s,
ENCYCLOPEDIA OF NATURAL HEALTH,
PRIMA PUBLICATIONS, 1991

CLEANSING AND FASTING are integral to holistic healing. The basic tenets of functional medicine are clean the body, remove any irritants, whether they be food, medicine, or microbes, provide the proper nutrients for the body to use as building materials, replace missing intestinal flora, enzymes, and hydrochloric acid, and give the body time to heal itself.

We are exposed to toxins everywhere—from the air we breathe to the foods we eat, even as a result of metabolism. These toxins cause irritation and inflammation throughout our bodies. People have always been exposed to toxic substances, but today's exposure to contaminants far exceeds that of previous times. Each week approximately 6,000 new chemicals are listed in the Chemical Society's *Chemical Abstracts*, which adds up to over 300,000 new chemicals each year. On average we consume 14 pounds each year of food additives, including colorings, preservatives, flavorings, emulsifiers, humectants, and antimicrobioals. In 1990, the EPA estimated there were 70,000 chemicals commonly used in pesticides, foods, and drugs. In 1992, the National Research Council published a report which suggested that environmental toxins play a role in neurological illnesses like Parkinson's disease, Alzheimer's disease, and amyotrophic lateral sclerosis. The link between breast cancer and pesticide usage is becoming stronger and stronger. It is estimated that up to 25 percent of the U.S. population has heavy metal poisoning.

Our body normally produces toxins as a by-product of metabolism. We call these toxins endotoxins, which means they come from within us. If not eliminated, these endotoxins can irritate and inflame our tissues, blocking normal functions. Endotoxins formed by bacteria and yeasts can be absorbed into the bloodstream. Antibodies formed to protect us against the harmful effects of these endotoxins often trigger a systemic effect, causing an autoimmune reaction, so our body begins fighting itself.

By assisting your body in removal of stored toxins through detoxification programs, your body can more easily heal itself. Although cleansing is important for healthy people, it is essential for people who don't feel as well as they would like to.

One of the many functions of the liver is to act as a filter, to let nutrients pass, if possible to "humanize" other substances, and to transform toxins into safe substances that can be eliminated in urine and stools. When the liver enzymes fail to break down these toxins, they are stored in the liver and fatty tissue throughout our bodies. Common medications can inhibit the liver's ability to adequately process toxins. Acetaminophen (Tylenol) causes liver damage when used in combination with alcoholic beverages. Cimetidine, an ulcer medication, limits the liver's ability to detoxify foreign substances. A thorough cleansing program works systemically, cleansing all the cells in your body of harmful toxins.

Throughout time and in various cultures, people have seen the need for periodic internal cleansing. Native Americans and Mexicans use sweat lodges. Ancient Roman bath houses had rooms for bathing in steam, warm water, and cold water. Jewish women have used ritual mikva baths to cleanse both body and spirit. Most Swedish people have home saunas, and our own health clubs have saunas, streambaths, and Jacuzzis. People "take the waters" in Europe and parts of the United States. Hawaiians use steam and a form of massage, called *lomilomi*, where they scrub people clean with the red Hawaiian dirt and sea salt. In fact, mud and clay have been used worldwide to draw toxins from the body while simultaneously providing essential nutrients.

Fasting is an important part of many religious holidays and customs. Both Jesus and John the Baptist fasted to gain mental and spiritual clarity. During Ramadan, an important Muslim holiday, people fast during daylight hours for a month. Jewish people fast on Yom Kippur. Indigenous people of many cultures use fasting as a way to clarify thought and provoke vision.

Removal of waste material—detoxification—is essential to the healthy functioning of our bodies. This is shown in the many different ways the body cleanses itself. Skin is our body's largest organ. In addition to being a protective organ, it is also an organ of elimination through perspiration. Sneezes clear our sinuses. Lungs breathe out carbon dioxide, and even the breath allows for removal of some wastes. Kidneys filter wastes from the bloodstream. Stool is the residue from the digestive process. The liver filters the substances that are absorbed through the digestive barrier into the bloodstream. White blood cells gobble up bacteria and foreign substances, and the lymphatic system clears the debris from circulation. During a cleansing program, your body more rapidly recycles materials to build new cells, take apart aged cells, and repair damaged cells.

Most detoxification programs focus on the liver (or colon). The liver is, in my opinion, the most overworked organ of the body. It has responsibility for manufacturing 13,000 different enzymes, producing cholesterol, breaking down estrogen, regulating blood sugar, filtering blood, manufacturing bile, breaking down old red blood cells, and detoxifying harmful substances. When the liver loses its ability to easily perform these functions, we begin to feel poorly, with many systems out of balance.

The liver acts as a filter for nearly everything that enters the bloodstream and changes toxic substances by converting them from a fat-soluble form into a mycellized form that the kidneys can excrete. This process occurs in the cytochrome P450 pathway, also known as phase I deconjugation. The CP450 pathway is where most drugs and petrochemicals are metabolized. When this pathway becomes overloaded, the liver loses its conversion capacity and substances get stored in the liver and in fat cells throughout the body. This is especially important with petrochemicals and fat-soluble residues. In phase I/CP450 pathways, fat-soluble substances are pulled out of storage so they can be effectively eliminated from the body. In phase II, the body converts these substances to a water-soluble form by adding molecules onto them. They can then be excreted in the urine and stool. These two phases require specific nutrients to work properly. The average American diet often fails to meet these needs. (Functional liver testing can actually show how well your phase I and phase II detoxification pathways are working.) These toxins affect how we feel, contributing to poor immune function, low energy levels, lack of digestive wellness, poor functioning of heart and respiratory systems, and overall lowered health status. Removal of these toxins can be transforming on many levels, providing an increase in energy and creativity.

It is best if you follow a detoxification program under the supervision of a medical or health professional. Toxins released too quickly can make you feel worse than when you began and can aggravate your symptoms. For instance, a detox program may provoke temporary symptoms of fatigue, headaches, diarrhea, constipation, irritability, and lightheadedness, which usually subside within the first few days. A professional can guide you gently through the process so that you get the maximum benefits for both mind and body with minimum discomfort.

DETOXIFICATION PROGRAMS

There are many different detoxification programs. Fasting, modified fasting, metabolic cleansing, colonic irrigation, steaming, mud packs, saunas, herbal detoxification programs, and hot tubs all have therapeutic detoxification benefits. When choosing a detoxification program, it must meet specific criteria: It needs to (1) work with your life and your values, (2) be thorough, and (3) be gentle and nurturing to your body.

Over the past several years, I have personally and professionally relied on three main detoxification programs that are effective and gentle: fruit and vegetable cleansing, metabolic cleansing, and low-temperature steams and saunas. I also recommend vitamin C flushes between cleansings. Other professionals may prefer fasting programs or colonic irrigation, which in the right hands can be powerful tools for healing. Because there are many fine books on fasting and colonic irrigation, I have not included information about them here.

Fruit and Vegetable Cleansing

This gentle cleansing method is outlined in chapter 6 as the elimination portion of the elimination provocation challenge.

You eat all you want of fruits, vegetables, and rice and use olive and canola oils as condiments for seven to ten days. Fresh fruit and vegetables juices are an excellent source of easily assimilated nutrients and alkalizing minerals and can enhance the detoxification pathways. It's important to eat every two to three hours to keep your blood sugar levels normal. The major benefit of this detox method is that you can do this on your own without professional supervision. Of course, if you are under a doctor's care or taking medication of any kind, you'll need to let your physician know of your plans. The first few days may require mental and physical adjustments to your new regimen, but most people feel a sense of general well-being. You may notice that many of your outstanding symptoms have disappeared or become less aggravated.

You may also experience some discomfort during the first three or four days. Headaches are fairly common and may be the result of withdrawal from caffeine, sugar, alcohol, or other substances. They are an indicator that toxins are being flushed out or that your body is going through withdrawal. To facilitate this, drink a lot of water, diluted juices, and all herbal teas except those containing caffeine. Some people develop rashes or pimples as the skin works hard to eliminate toxins. Saunas, steambathing, and massaging your skin with a soft, dry brush or loofa can help your skin. If you are constipated, make sure you eat enough fiber-rich fruits and vegetables (apples, broccoli, pears, sweet potatoes, peas, brussel sprouts, corn, potatoes, carrots, greens, blackberries, bananas, strawberries, raspberries, and spinach). If you are constipated, toxins may be reabsorbed into your bloodstream, causing symptoms such as headaches and nausea. So add a fiber supplement; psyllium seeds or psyllium seed husks work well. Begin with 1 teaspoon in water, and drink up quickly before it turns into a gel. Aloe vera juice may also help regulate your bowels.

Metabolic Cleansing

Metabolic cleansing is a gentle yet deep method of detoxification, and it is the best, most thorough program I have used. The foundation of this program is a hypoallergenic/sensitive rice-based protein and nutrient drink. The first week you eat only the drink and all you want of rice, all fruits except citrus, all vegetables except nightshade-family foods, and small amounts of oils. Citrus fruits are excluded because many people are sensitive to them. Nightshade vegetables—potatoes, tomatoes, eggplant, green peppers, and chili peppers—are excluded because 10 to 15 percent of people with joint pain become painfree when these vegetables are removed from the diet. If you know that you are sensitive to bananas, melons, or other foods that are allowed on the plan, then avoid them as well. It is possible for people to continue their normal daily routine while on this program, whereas juice fasting requires nearly total rest and relaxation.

This program is administered only through health professionals who can monitor your progress, determine when you should quit, and help you adjust if you have any difficulties. This program may be inappropriate or may need modification for people in poor health or on specific medications, and must be supervised by someone who is familiar with its effects. People who score over 50, or 10 or more in any one section on the Metabolic Screening Questionnaire below, may want to begin with repair and do a detoxification later. A different protein drink or supplement can help heal your digestive tract and can be used over time to strengthen your system before the detox.

During a metabolic cleansing, most people find a dramatic alleviation of symptoms and a distinct improvement in energy levels. The high levels of nutrients found in the rice protein drink and in the fruits and vegetables help the liver activate its detoxification pathways and move unwanted materials out of the body. The intention here is to allow your digestive system to rest, relax, and heal itself.

Once you have completed the cleansing, it is important to slowly reintroduce foods back into your diet. This is an ideal time to screen yourself for food sensitivities, as described in chapter 6. Being a food sleuth takes a lot of patience; it's not always apparent which foods cause adverse symptoms. But with persistent detective work you can discover many of them. Keep a running record of everything you eat and of your symptoms. Food sensitivities often display delayed reactions, so it may take up to forty-eight hours to feel the effect of a newly introduced food.

You may want to have testing done for food allergies and sensitivities at this time. If you have uncovered a problem, these tests can further pinpoint which foods and substances are making you ill.

Metabolic Screening Questionnaire

Use this questionnaire to chart your health and progress. Rate each of the following symptoms based on your health profile for the past thirty days.

POINT SCALE: ⎯⎯⎯⎯⎯⎯⎯⎯⎯⎯⎯⎯⎯⎯⎯

   0 = **Never or almost never have the symptom.**
   1 = **Occasionally have it; effect is not severe.**
   2 = **Occasionally have it; effect is severe.**
   3 = **Frequently have it; effect is not severe.**
   4 = **Frequently have it; effect is severe.**

DIGESTIVE TRACT	____ Nausea or vomiting	**Total** ____
	____ Diarrhea	
	____ Constipation	
	____ Bloated feeling	
	____ Belching or passing gas	
	____ Heartburn	

EARS	____ Itchy ears	Total ____
	____ Earaches, ear infections	
	____ Drainage from ear	
	____ Ringing in ears, hearing loss	
EMOTIONS	____ Mood swings	Total ____
	____ Anxiety, fear, or nervousness	
	____ Anger, irritability, or aggressiveness	
ENERGY/ ACTIVITY	____ Fatigue, sluggishness	Total ____
	____ Apathy, lethargy	
	____ Hyperactivity	
	____ Restlessness	
EYES	____ Watery or itchy eyes	Total ____
	____ Swollen, reddened, or sticky eyelids	
	____ Bags or dark circles under eyes	
	____ Blurred or tunnel vision (Does not include near- or far sightedness)	
HEAD	____ Headaches	Total ____
	____ Faintness	
	____ Dizziness	
	____ Insomnia	
HEART	____ Irregular or skipped heartbeat	Total ____

_____ Rapid or pounding
heartbeat

_____ Chest pain

JOINTS/   _____ Pain or aches in joints   **Total** _____
MUSCLES
                 _____ Arthritis

                 _____ Stiffness or limitation of
                 movement

                 _____ Pain or aches in muscles

                 _____ Feeling of weakness or
                 tiredness

LUNGS   _____ Chest congestion   **Total** _____

                 _____ Asthma, bronchitis

                 _____ Shortness of breath

MIND   _____ Poor memory   **Total** _____

                 _____ Confusion, poor
                 comprehension

                 _____ Poor concentration

                 _____ Difficulty in making
                 decisions

                 _____ Stuttering or stammering

                 _____ Slurred speech

                 _____ Learning disabilities

MOUTH/   _____ Chronic coughing   **Total** _____
THROAT
                 _____ Gagging, frequent need to
                 clear throat

                 _____ Sore throat, hoarseness,
                 loss of voice

	___ Swollen or discolored tongue, gums, lips	
	___ Canker sores	
NOSE	___ Stuffy nose	**Total** ___
	___ Sinus problems	
	___ Hay fever	
	___ Sneezing attacks	
	___ Excessive mucus formation	
SKIN	___ Acne	**Total** ___
	___ Hives, rashes, or dry skin	
	___ Hair loss	
	___ Flushing or hot flashes	
	___ Excessive sweating	
WEIGHT	___ Binge eating/drinking	**Total** ___
	___ Craving certain foods	
	___ Excessive weight	
	___ Compulsive eating	
	___ Water retention	
	___ Underweight	
OTHER	___ Frequent illness	**Total** ___
	___ Frequent or urgent urination	
	___ Genital itch or discharge	

Vitamin C Flush

Vitamin C is necessary for maintenance of the cytochrome P-450 detoxification pathways in the liver. It is used by physicians intravenously to help remove toxins from the body during chelation therapy. Vitamin C has been well researched for its ability to help detoxify bacterial toxins, drugs, environmental toxins, and heavy metals from our bodies. Its gentle and potent detoxification counteracts and neutralizes the harmful effects of manufactured poisons.

High levels of vitamin C help detoxify the body, rebalance intestinal flora, and strengthen the immune system. The vitamin C flush can be used between metabolic cleansing therapies or at the first sign of a cold or infection. If your immune system is weak or you've been exposed to a lot of toxins, you may want to do a vitamin C flush once a week for a month or two. On days when you are not doing a vitamin C flush, take a minimum of 2,000 to 3,000 milligrams. Humans are one of the only animals that do not produce their own vitamin C, so we need to replenish our supply daily.

To do a vitamin C flush, you take vitamin C to the level of tissue saturation. You'll know you've reached it because you will have watery diarrhea. You'll need to purchase powdered mineral ascorbate C, which is more easily tolerated by most people because it doesn't change your pH balance. The amount you take varies depending on your personal needs that day. Many of us require about 5,000 milligrams; others need fifteen or twenty times as much. For instance, if you're coming down with a cold, have chronic fatigue syndrome, or are under excessive stress, you'll probably need a lot more.

Instructions for a vitamin C flush: Take 2 or 3 teaspoons of vitamin C powder, mix with water or fruit juice, and drink. Half an hour later, repeat. If you don't have diarrhea thirty minutes after the second dose, do it again. If you haven't gotten diarrhea after three doses, begin to take 2 to 3 tea-spoons of vitamin C powder every fifteen minutes. If you still haven't experienced diarrhea after another hour, increase the dosage. Do not stop with just gas. Adding vitamin C rapidly helps prevent bloating and cramping. Stop once you get diarrhea. Keep track of how much vitamin C you take. This will help you determine your optimal dosage—it's three-quarters of the amount it takes to produce a daily vitamin C flush—and how much vitamin C to take the next time you do a flush.

Low-Temperature Saunas and Steams

Low-temperature saunas or steambaths are useful to elimi-nate fat-soluble chemicals from our systems. They are com-monly used to help detoxify people who have had high exposure to pesticides, solvents, pharmaceutical drugs, and petrochemicals. Slow, steady sweat encourages the release of fat-soluble toxins through the skin from their storage sites in our tissues. Most saunas and steambaths are set at temper-atures too high to accomplish this, so be sure the dry sauna is set between 110 and 120 degrees Fahrenheit and the steambath is at 110 degrees Fahrenheit so you can stay in for at least forty-five minutes without getting too hot or chilled. It is best to spend thirty to sixty minutes in a sauna/steam at least three to five times a week. Releasing toxins cannot be accomplished with higher heat or shorter amounts of time. After you are done sweating, you must shower im-mediately afterward using a glycerin based soap such as Neu-trogena. It will wash away the toxins and keep you from reabsorbing them.

You can perform this detoxification in a variety of ways. To use the sauna at your local health club, make sure you can use it first thing in the morning so that you can control the temperature without disrupting other people who want it hotter. Or purchase a sauna. A home sauna can be made in almost any closet with professional services or kits. I recently had the opportunity to sit in a far-infrared sauna. From the first instant, I felt the difference. The heat went deep yet felt really soft. It reminded me of the difference between heating one's house with a wood stove and heating with electric heat. This heat felt really wonderful, penetrating, and calming. The unit was fully portable. During the summer, you could probably accomplish the same detox by spending an hour lying in the sun or by sitting in a hot car— just not too hot! No research studies have been done on these home methods, but they would probably work if used consistently. The object is to sweat slowly and steadily.

If you have extreme toxicity to environmental chemicals, you'll need to detox under the supervision of a physician. The temporary release of toxins into your circulation can be quite severe and debilitating. Some clinics specialize in using saunas for medical detoxification. In her excellent book, *Poisoning Our Children*, Nancy Sokol Green describes her experience in a detox clinic in depth: "On the fourteenth day of detox, I started experiencing allergic symptoms, such as eyelid swelling, while I was in the sauna! . . . I was actually beginning to reek of the pesticides that had been sprayed in my home. . . . Several of the patients at the clinic who were sensitive to pesticides had to stay away from me as I triggered adverse reactions in them."

As Russell Jaffe says, "There is an equation of health. In its elegant simplicity it may seem too simple. However, the validity of this equation is shown both in the practical utility of its application and in the absence of any scientific evidence against it.

Health = (Nutritional + Behavioral Competence) − (Distress + Toxic Load)."

Personally, I do a detox at least twice a year. The latest research on pesticide and petrochemical residues shows endocrine and immune disruption at the low levels we are exposed to daily. For prevention, I prefer to expel them from my body on a regular basis.

Chapter 10

DIET MEANS "WAY OF LIFE"

"We are what we repeatedly do. Excellent, then, is not an act, but a habit."

ARISTOTLE

EATING IS OUR most intimate contact with our environment. We eat pounds of food each day, putting food inside of our bodies and turning it into us! This is truly an amazing process. But how much attention do we really put into what goes into our mouths? And how much do we really understand about nutrition? I often find that my clients have many misunderstandings about nutrition and food—one of the most common of which is that fats are bad for you. There are also many misunderstandings about cholesterol. Your challenge is to find a way of eating and living that suits your emotional and physical needs.

The word *diet* comes from Greek and means "a manner of living" or "way of life." The Latin root means "a day's journey." The key is to make real changes—changes you can live with successfully on a long-term basis—in the way you approach food, fitness, and the challenges and opportunities of living.

In this chapter I will outline a plan that can help you take charge of your health and feel good on every level. Because I don't know you and your specific needs, you will have to modify these general recommendations. If you have a specific digestive condition—candidiasis, chronic fatigue, migraines, ulcers—look at the reference material for that condition and incorporate those ideas into this plan. For instance, if you have Crohn's disease, you'll probably want to avoid grain and dairy products totally. If you have arthritis, you may find that tomatoes, peppers, eggplant, and potatoes aggravate your condition. Integration of your specific needs with a general life plan will give you the best results.

There are many healthful ways to eat. Last year, I put on a seminar in which one speaker spoke on low-carbohydrate diets, another on macrobiotics, another on the vegan diet (which is a total vegetarian diet), another on the blood-type diet, and another on Ayurvedic eating. I planned this seminar to show people how different diets work for different people. You need to find one that works for you and your lifestyle. What is common to all of these ways of eating is that they all rely on natural, home-cooked, genuine-food meals; they are devoid of artificial colors and flavors, trans fatty acids, and sugar; and they are loaded with phytonutrients, fiber, and good-quality fats.

The world of nutrition is certainly confusing, but it is important to find what works best for you.

CLEANING OUT THE PANTRY

Go into your cabinets, refrigerator, and freezer and toss out any foods that contain hydrogenated vegetable oil, vegetable shortening, or partially hydrogenated vegetable oils. If you read labels, you'll find them in margarine, cookies, crackers, cereals, frozen foods, packaged foods, breads, snack foods, salad dressings, mayonnaise, and so on. Because they are used so widely, your pantry may end up looking like Old Mother Hubbard's.

Why am I asking you to throw out food? Hydrogenated oils are used in foods because they are cheap, have a long shelf-life, and give a buttery texture to foods. While this enables manufacturers to use inexpensive materials to reap high profits, these oils are extremely unhealthy for your body.

Liquid oils are turned into solid vegetable shortenings by the hydrogenation process. Hydrogenation converts the naturally occurring "cis" form of fat molecules into a "trans" form. When our body tries to use trans fats, they block normal biochemistry, inhibiting the function of enzymes that are involved in the synthesis of cholesterol and fatty acids. In an analogy, trans fats are like using the wrong key to open a lock and then having the key break in the lock. The trans fats jam the position so the cis fats don't fit. Trans fatty acids are found nowhere in nature and have been associated with hardening of the arteries (atherosclerosis), some types of cancer, and all inflammatory illnesses—like arthritis, eczema, irritable bowel syndrome, and more. Recent research indicates that these fats play at least as large a role in heart disease as do saturated fats.

Trans fatty acids also affect our body's electrical circuitry. European research has shown that essential fatty acids found in the cis formation are necessary for electrical and energy exchanges that involve sulfur-containing proteins, oxygen, and light. Trans fatty acids are not suitable in these processes and jam the "plug" for the cis fats. These electrical currents are responsible for all body functions, from the way our minds work to heartbeat, cell division, muscle coordination, and energy levels.

Trans fats are stickier than cis fats, says Udo Erasmus, "increasing the likelihood of a clot in a small blood vessel causing strokes, heart attacks, or circulatory occlusions in

other organs, such as lungs, extremities, and sense organs."
Our hearts use fatty acids as their main fuel. Trans fats are
less easily broken down by enzymes and have slower use as
an energy source, which could have serious consequences in
a high-stress situation. Trans fatty acids also interfere with
our liver detoxification pathways.

Each cell in our bodies has a fatty membrane around it.
Cell membranes that incorporate hydrogenated fats lose their
flexibility and become more rigid, because trans fats are fairly
solid at body temperature. This interferes with normal cellular function. Trans fats also change the permeability of the
cell membranes, which allows substances to enter where they
don't belong. If we eat hydrogenated oils, and the average
American consumes 6 to 8 percent of his or her total daily
calories in them, then our body fat is comprised of these
fatty acids.

While you're cleaning out your kitchen, toss out the following foods: high-sugar foods, highly processed foods including white flour products and enriched foods, foods that
contain a lot of food additives and colorings, and foods that
have a shelf life that extends into the next millennium. If
you feel guilty about tossing out these foods, donate them
to a soup kitchen. If you feel angry, write to the manufacturers and tell them to improve the quality of the foods they
produce. It's a bit more expensive to eat healthful foods, but
we are worth it! We can spend money on excellent foods or
we can spend it on medications and medical bills!

REPLACE YOUR PANTRY

Now you're ready to go shopping. It's important to read
food labels carefully. It will take you longer the first few
times you go shopping, but soon you'll be zipping through
the store with your new food recognition. The foods that
you bring into your home need to provide excellent nourish-

ment. If you're careful about what you eat at home, the treats you eat at parties and restaurants will be indulgences you can feel good about. The idea isn't to be perfect, but to make progress and build good health habits slowly.

There are great treasures waiting to be uncovered in your local market and health food store that add flavor, fun, and variety to your foods. If you've never been to a health food store, the salespeople will be happy to show you around and steer you to products that meet your specific needs.

RULES FOR EATING, COOKING, AND SHOPPING

1. Eat local foods in season, when possible.
2. The life in foods gives us life.
3. Plan ahead. Carry food with you.
4. Eat small, frequent meals to sustain even energy levels.
5. Eat when you are hungry; stop when you are satisfied.
6. Relax while eating.
7. Choose organically grown foods whenever possible.
8. Eat as many fruits and vegetables as possible.
9. Eat lean protein.
10. Drink clean water.
11. Respect your own biochemical uniqueness.
12. Increase high-fiber foods.
13. Eat high EPA/DHA fish one to two times a week.

1. Eat local foods in season. Local foods are fresh and have the highest levels of nutrients. They also have the largest energy fields and the greatest enzyme activity. Ask the produce manager at your supermarket to purchase locally grown products whenever possible. Make it part of your routine to shop at local farm stands and farmer's markets. Eating local foods in season is the concept behind macrobiotics. Because Japanese people brought macrobiotics to this country, we think of it as "eating Japanese foods," but that isn't the original intention.

Eating foods in season also helps cut down on the amount of pesticides and herbicides we consume. Foods that are flown in from outside the country—grapes from Chile, coffee from South America, bananas from Mexico—are not regulated by the same pesticide standards as foods grown in the United States. Often we get back on imported produce the very pesticides that we banned. Eating local foods also helps the local economy and the environment by cutting down transportation costs and reducing consumption of fossil fuels. Think locally, act globally!

2. The life in foods gives us life. Food is fuel. Food gives us energy. Because we really *are* what we eat, if we eat foods that have little enzyme activity, they don't "spark" our body to work correctly. Enzymes are to our body what spark plugs are to the engine of our car. Without those sparks, the car doesn't run right. So if a food isn't biologically useful, who needs it? Not only do high-sugar foods not provide any nutritional benefit except calories, but sugar takes nutrients like chromium and B-complex vitamins to metabolize it. When we eat a sugar-laden diet, we continually take nutrients from our "bank account," so over time our reserves become depleted.

3. Plan ahead. Carry food with you. I've found that planning ahead and carrying food with me are two of the greatest tools for healthful eating. If you carry a bag lunch, you know it'll be healthful because you made it at home where you have only healthful foods. Just put in some leftovers or a quick sandwich with a salad and/or a piece of fruit. Add a beverage and you've got lunch. Special containers and zip-loc bags simplify the process. Planning meals ahead of time also helps you consolidate shopping trips and ultimately conserves time.

4. Eat small, frequent meals to sustain energy levels. Snacking is the best trick I know for boosting energy levels. People in Europe, South America, and Japan stop in the middle of the afternoon to have tea. Our children rush home from school and eat us out of house and home. Only American adults are too busy to stop. If you find that from 3 to 6 P.M. it's difficult to concentrate, try this simple trick: Have something to eat in the middle of the afternoon and again just before you leave work. Here are a few quick snack ideas: Eat half a sandwich you saved from lunch plus a piece of fruit, a bagel and cream cheese with tomatoes, a rice cake with peanut butter and apples, a cup of soup and several pretzels, or a handful of nuts and raisins. You'll find your energy level will stay more constant throughout the day.

5. Eat when you are hungry; stop when you are satisfied. This sounds like a simple statement, but often we eat when we aren't hungry because we're lonely, angry, depressed, bored, or because we're at a social event and everyone else is eating. Before you eat anything, ask yourself the simple question: Am I hungry? If you are, then eat. If you aren't, divert your attention to other activities. Eating when you're not hungry contributes to poor digestion. Let your body use what it has before you put more into it.

6. Relax while eating. Many times we don't even stop long enough to sit down when we eat. Yet eating is a time of rejuvenation of body and spirit. Take a few extra minutes to enjoy and relish the food that you eat. Take a few moments to reflect on your day and your life. Doing this can help keep your whole day in balance.

One way I've found to encourage peace of mind during meals is to say grace. It puts me in touch with the bounty of the earth we live on, makes me pay attention to the people I am with and be grateful for their presence in my life, helps me thank the people who produced the food, and reminds me that we all depend upon each other and on community.

7. Choose organically grown foods whenever possible. Organic foods generally have higher levels of nutrients because organic farmers pay more attention to their animals' health and to their soils. Animals raised on organic farms are given foods that nature intended. We benefit because we don't get extra doses of hormones added to our foods. Organic farmers add more nutrients to the soil because they know that healthy plants can better fend off pests and that those nutrients end up in the foods. Bob Smith, from Doctor's Data, has released a study which analyzed organic versus commercially grown apples, pears, potatoes, wheat, and wheat berries. He found that mineral levels in organically grown foods were twice as high on average as commercially grown foods.

8. Eat as many fruits and vegetables as possible. The available research is overwhelming about the positive benefits of eating fruits and vegetables. They are chock full of vitamins, minerals, fiber, and phytochemicals (plant chemicals) that protect us from heart disease, cancer, and probably everything else. Research on phytochemicals is in its infancy, yet very promising. Citrus fruits, garlic, onions, chives, tomatoes, grapes, soybeans and other legumes, fruits, green tea, and cabbage family foods which include broccoli, kale, kohlrabi, cauliflower, collards, mustard greens, rutabaga, turnips, brussel sprouts, and bok choy—all contain phytochemicals that protect us from developing degenerative diseases. High-fiber diets also protect our colons; they reduce the incidence of polyps and bowel diseases and the risk of developing colon cancer. It's best to eat at least five half-cup servings a day, but more is better—up to nine or eleven.

9. Eat lean protein, and eat high EPA/DHA fish one to two times a week. On average, Americans eat too much protein, and this excess can tax the kidneys. The saturated fats found in beef, pork, and the skin of poultry are artery-clogging and ought to be limited or avoided altogether. Focus instead on lean protein sources such as legumes, skinless poultry, and fish. Other protein sources may be higher in good fats and are also recommended; these include cold-water fish, tofu, nuts, and seeds. Cold-water fish are an excellent source of EPA and DHA fatty acids. These essential fats are critical to the eyes (over 60 percent of the retina is composed of DHA), brain, thought processes, nervous system, and heart. Studies show that people who eat cold-water fish at least twice a week have a reduced incidence of heart disease. Although many of us can make DHA from other fats, others lack the enzymes and nutrients essential for this conversion to occur. The most beneficial sources of DHA are salmon, mackerel, sardines, halibut, tuna, and herring. It's best to eat these fish at least twice each week. Finally, algae and sea vegetables also contain some DHA and EPA.

10. Drink clean water. Our bodies are 70 percent water. If we don't adequately hydrate the cells with this essential substance, they cannot function properly. Moreover, the water we drink and consume in food is a carrier, bringing nutrients to cells and taking away wastes. Making sure that you get plenty of high-quality water every day is one of the most promising routes to digestive wellness. F. Batmanghelidj, M.D., has written a book called *Your Body's Many Cries for Water*, which documents the many fantastic roles that water can play. Clean water and good hydration can help prevent many health conditions, from gout to asthma. He even believes water is the best cure for ulcers.

The issue for many then becomes the quality of water. Director of the Hawaii Board of Health, Dr. Bruce Anderson, has noted that if a chemical is used in our culture, it will show up in the water supply. We can now detect these chemicals in parts per trillion! The significance of such low amounts of these chemicals is unknown, as only 0.5 percent of our tap water becomes drinking or cooking water. The rest is used for bathing, washing our cars and clothes, watering lawns, or flushing toilets. So does it really make sense to spend the money to make our tap water as pure as filtered or bottled water? Is it even possible, considering the quantity of water we use?

Unfortunately, many cities fail to provide excellent water. The sources are often groundwater that is easily contaminated by runoff. The EPA estimates that 1.5 trillion gallons of pollutants leak into the ground each year, with the highest incidence of contaminants from lead, radon, and nitrates (from fertilizers). Over 700 chemicals have been found in tap water, but testing is done on less than 200 of these.

There isn't one correct answer about where to get the best drinking water. If you have a well, have the water tested for bacterial content and pollutants. Find out about your local drinking water, where it originally comes from, how it's processed, and if it has fluoride added to it. Ask your water department for an analysis, and if it pleases you, drink tap water. There is much controversy today about the use of chlorine in tap water. The levels of chlorine needed to kill bacteria are rising due to increasing bacterial resistance, but chlorine has been strongly associated with elevated cancer risks. A simple water filter can efficiently remove chlorine from tap water. Activated charcoal filters are inexpensive and can remove many pollutants from tap water. Distilled water systems and reverse osmosis are recommended by many health experts. However, the water distillation process removes all minerals from water, and because minerals are generally transported through the body through diffusion, the regular consumption of distilled water leads to leaching of minerals from the body. So although distilled water may be wonderful while detoxing, I cannot recommend its regular usage.

The reverse osmosis process is a sophisticated water filtering process and it is widely used in dialysis units, which need highly purified water. Reverse osmosis alone does not always kill microbes, and the recommendations in dialysis units is to combine reverse osmosis with deionization techniques to insure water purity. If you are concerned about bacterial contamination, reverse osmosis alone may not be protective.

The latest water system on the market is called the "ionizer plus." This water appears to have other water systems beat on all levels. The water is put through micro-filters and then exposed to ultraviolet light, which kills all microbes. In addition, the water clusters are made into smaller microclusters which change the surface tension of the water. This makes it easier for the water to be absorbed into cells, carrying nutrients and removing waste products. The machine can also alkalize water which makes more electrons available to prevent free radical damage. It is believed that drinking this alkalized water helps change the biological terrain of the individual, which ultimately makes it less possible for them to become or stay ill. People with digestive disorders and other health conditions often see changes in how they feel in days. This may actually be the simplest and most direct route to true digestive wellness because it can help normalize pH, dysbiosis, and *Candida*, as well as keep your body easily alkalized.

Bottled water isn't necessarily any better than tap water. Often it's local, city tap water which has just been carefully filtered. And if you are buying spring water, you'll want to know about the water source and its purity. If you are buying water in plastic bottles, you may also be ingesting small amounts of plastic, and some plastics have known hormone-disrupting effects. If you do regularly buy bottled water, ask the manufacturer for information on water source, type of plastics used, mineral content per glass, and a report on levels of toxic substances in the water. In European countries, bottled water is preferred because of its high mineral content, and this can be an excellent source of essential minerals.

Willard Water is a patented water product that was the first microclustered water product. In a special process, minerals and special castor oil are added to water to decrease surface tension and water cluster size. Willard Water is more easily carried inside cells and has antioxidant properties beyond that of regular water. It can be purchased in health food stores.

11. Respect your own biochemical uniqueness. Remember the foods that are best for you are foods that agree with your body and your unique biochemistry. In practice, about half the people I work with do best on a high–complex carbohydrate, high-fiber, natural-foods diet. The other half seem to do best on a low-carbohydrate, relatively high-protein diet high in fruits and vegetables. Many people with digestive problems do best avoiding all grains and dairy. It's important to experiment with your own diet to find out what works best for you specifically. There are many eating plans publicized by books and other media. Whether you try the zone diet, the blood-type diet, macrobiotics, a vegan diet, Ayurvedic eating plans, natural hygeine/food combining, or some other program, what is imporant is how it makes you feel and whether you can live with it over the long term. A proper diet ought to make you feel energetic and ought to keep your immune system strong. It's always fun to experiment with eating plans, but please make sure that whatever you try is well balanced. The eating programs listed above have this in common: they are all based on real, natural food. None contain sugars, processed foods, alcohol, high levels of saturated fats, or other harmful food components. The body was designed to run on real foods; a natural foods diet is the ultimate direction in eating for all of us, no matter exactly how we shape it. The rest of your family may have little or no problem eating wheat products, dairy products, or any other food, but if you do, it's best to avoid them. If you really want to get well and stay well, you and your needs must come first. Your family will understand if you eat something different. If you are invited to someone's home, call several days ahead of time and let the host know you are on a restricted eating program. With advance notice, you may be able to eat nearly everything. If not, have a snack before you go and eat what you can. Perhaps you can bring a dish that suits your needs. Remember that restaurants are there to cater to you. Tell the food server if you need a menu item prepared a special way. Restaurants are becoming more used to accommodating people who have specific dietary needs.

12. Increase high-fiber foods. The connection of diet to constipation is well substantiated. Dr. Dennis Burkitt was the first researcher to connect a high-fiber diet with better health. He noticed that people eating a traditional African diet in rural areas had almost no diabetes, irritable bowel syndrome, constipation, diverticular disease, colon cancer, or heart disease. In comparison, Africans consuming a Western diet had the expected incidence of these problems. In India he found a hospital where the incidence of appendicitis was only 2 percent of that in a similar American hospital. At the same hospital there was virtually no hiatal hernia, which affects nearly 30 percent of Americans over the age of fifty. After looking at many factors, Dr. Burkitt concluded that the high amount of fiber in traditional diets was necessary for maintaining good health.

Known as the father of the fiber hypothesis, Dr. Burkitt made his discoveries in the 1970s. Since then, we have learned much more about fiber and how it contributes to health. For instance, we now know low-fiber diets lead to digestive disorders found in one out of four Americans. Improvement in bowel function can help prevent diverticulosis, appendicitis, colon polyps, colon cancer, hemorrhoids, and varicose veins. Diets high in soluble fiber are helpful to people with irritable bowel syndrome, Crohn's disease, hiatal hernia, and peptic ulcer. Dietary fiber also helps prevent obesity by slowing down digestion and the release of glucose and insulin. Fiber has been shown to normalize serum cholesterol levels. High-fiber diets reduce the risk of heart disease, high blood pressure, and certain types of cancer.

Americans eat 12 grams of fiber on average a day. The National Cancer Institute recommends that we consume 20 to 30 grams of fiber daily, the same amount that Americans ate in 1850. So we are really trying to replace the fiber that was eliminated from our diet over the past 150 years! The foods that are the richest sources of fiber are whole grains (brown rice, whole wheat, bulghur, millet, buckwheat, rye, barley, spelt, oats), legumes (all beans except green beans), vegetables, and fruits. These foods comprise the bulk of a healthy food plan, with nuts, seeds, protein foods, and oils used as condiments. Although soluble and insoluble fibers work differently inside the body, it's important to remember that these fibers are mixed in foods. If you eat a wide variety of high-fiber foods, you will get both types of fiber without counting and measuring grams of soluble and insoluble fiber.

HEALTH BENEFITS OF DIETARY FIBER

Effect	Soluble Fiber	Insoluble Fiber
Reduce serum cholesterol	Strong	Mild
Longer full feeling	Strong	None
Sated appetite	Strong	Strong
Stabilized blood sugar	Strong	None
Reduce bacterial toxins	Strong	Strong
Speed bile acid excretion	Strong	Mild
Speed elimination	Mild	Strong
Absorb toxins	Mild	Strong
Soften stools	Mild	Strong
Improve bowel disorders	Mild	Strong
Produce gas	Strong	Mild
Block mineral absorption	None	Strong

Prepared by Martin Lee, Ph.D., *Putting the Pieces Together*, Manual for Conference, Great Smokies Diagnostic Laboratories, Asheville, N.C.

FOODS

Before I give you a shopping list, I want to discuss food basics. We eat several times each day, but few of us have studied nutrition. Most of our nutritional information has probably come from our mothers, a "health" class in high school, or the media. If we believe media reports, we'll be more confused about what to eat than ever. By learning more about the foods you eat, you can begin to make a healthful food plan that will allow you to enjoy eating and feel better. Once you make a decision to rely on natural foods, your body and mind will adjust so that natural foods taste more delicious than manufactured derivatives. Once your sugar and salt taste buds calm down, fruit will taste sweet and you won't need that salt shaker as much. What I said back in 1980 holds true today: "90 percent of your food should be excellent for your body, and 10 percent excellent for your soul."

Cereals

Cereals are an excellent way to increase your fiber intake. Unfortunately, the bulk of breakfast cereals contain too much sugar, hydrogenated oils, and other unhealthful ingredients, though some low-sugar, low-sodium cereals are sold in health food stores. Read package labels carefully. Check for the amount of sugar (4 grams = 1 teaspoon) and for the amount of fiber. If you have gluten or other grain sensitivities, you will be able to find many nongluten breakfast cereals in natural food stores. Healthy cereals are made with the whole grain, so be sure to buy those with brown rice instead of white rice or whole corn instead of degermed corn. You can also choose cereals with organically grown ingredients like oatmeal and bulghur. There are also many delicious grain blends, like seven-grain cereal, bear mush, and homemade granola.

Eggs

Eggs have been given a bad rap because they've been linked to cholesterol. In fact, eggs have high amounts of phospholipids that are integral to our cell membranes. They are a precursor to acetylcholine, an important neurotransmitter.

Many researchers now believe that eating eggs has little or no effect on the serum cholesterol levels of people who have normal serum cholesterol. Recent studies found no significant change after six weeks in the cholesterol levels of the healthy people after eating two hard-boiled eggs daily. Other studies have concurred that eating eggs can actually raise the "good" HDL cholesterol. Current thinking is that if your cholesterol levels are normal, it's fine to eat egg yolks that have not been oxidized (exposed to oxygen)—eggs that are hard-boiled, soft-boiled, or poached—since oxidized cholesterol can damage arteries and raise blood pressure. It's probably more healthful than harmful.

Studies linking high blood cholesterol levels to heart disease have proven to be only *one* accurate indicator of risk for developing heart disease. Only 25 percent of our cholesterol comes from the foods we eat. We manufacture the rest in our liver. Guided by a self-regulating mechanism, a healthy liver makes more cholesterol if we eat less and less if we eat more. From a holistic viewpoint, high serum cholesterol levels are indicative of liver distress. Eating a low-cholesterol diet may help, but if your liver is overproducing cholesterol, it usually isn't enough to correct the problem. Indeed, the link between dietary cholesterol and serum cholesterol levels has never been adequately demonstrated.

Cutting out hydrogenated oils and saturated fat can have more far-reaching effects on serum cholesterol than counting eggs. Eating fish like salmon and mackerel that are high in omega-3 fatty acids a few times a week can lower cholesterol levels. And a whole foods diet generally contains more trace nutrients which stabilize blood fats. Learning to meditate or fully relax can also significantly lower serum cholesterol, and a regular exercise program and weight loss help normalize both LDL and HDL cholesterol.

Because egg production in this country is big business, it's best to buy eggs from naturally raised chickens at your local natural foods store, from local farmers, and at farmer's markets. Commercially raised chickens live in unnatural settings, never seeing the light of day, never touching the earth beneath their cages, pumped with hormones to stimulate growth, and antibiotics to prevent disease. If you believe that the quality of a seed determines the health and vibrancy of the plant it produces, then by the same token if a chicken is artificially manipulated to produce eggs, how good is the quality of those eggs? For more information on this subject, the best resource is *The New American Diet* by John Robbins.

Fish and Seafood

Fish have easily digestible protein, many trace nutrients, high quality essential fatty acids, low cholesterol levels, and low saturated fat levels. This makes them a nearly ideal source of dietary protein. Fish that contain high omega-3 fatty acids are essential to our good health. EPA (eicosapentaenoic acid) and DHA (docosahexaenoic acid), the omega-3 fatty acids found in cold-water fish, are found in all the cells of our body. They are especially abundant in brain cells, nerve synapses, retina, adrenal glands, and sex glands. If we are healthy, we can make EPA and DHA oils from omega-3 oils found in foods. But many of us have decreased ability to make this conversion, especially people who are aging or who have a chronic illness or degenerative condition. Eating fish gives us these necessary fatty acids directly. The fish richest in this oil are salmon, halibut, tuna, mackerel, trout, sardines, eel, and herring. Low-fat fish or fish from tropical waters are still healthful to eat, but they do not have any significant levels of EPA/DHA oils. Marine algae also has significant amounts of EPA and DHA.

Studies show that people who eat high-fat fish twice a week have reduced risk of heart disease and stroke. Other studies have found these fish oils are protective or therapeutic for high serum cholesterol levels, angina, high blood pressure, rheumatoid arthritis, psoriasis, eczema, multiple sclerosis, asthma, lupus, allergies, inflammatory disorders, migraine headaches, and the prevention and treatment of cancer. Although supplementation with fish oil capsules is beneficial, the best way to get these oils is by eating the fish itself.

It's important when selecting fish to know where the fish came from. Do not eat fish found in polluted or questionable waters. Fish and shellfish found close to shore, in rivers, or in lakes may be environmentally contaminated. Because the fish we eat are high on the food chain, they have the ability to concentrate environmental toxins. Mollusks that filter water, like oysters, clams, mussels, and scallops, can concentrate pesticides up to 70,000 times the concentration of seawater. The FDA has set limits for pregnant women in eating certain fish, like bluefish and red snapper, because they cause birth defects. Half the world's fish catch is fed to livestock, further concentrating and passing on environmental contaminants. Farm-raised fish have fats that resemble the foods they are raised on. Because omega-3 fatty acids tend to go rancid, other types of oils are used in fish feed, lowering the amount of beneficial oils found in these fish.

Seaweeds, also called sea vegetables, are nutritious foods that are often neglected in American cuisine, though we have been exposed to them through macrobiotics and Japanese culture. Because we evolved from the sea, sea vegetables and weeds contain nutrients that are nearly identical in ratio and quality to those we use best. Many people find that eating sea vegetables gives them a tremendous energy boost, probably because the seaweed is filling some minute nutrient need.

Meat and Poultry

Meat and poultry are nutritious and delicious, but they are generally high in fat, contain unwanted dietary cholesterol, and contribute to the development of chronic degenerative diseases. It is well recognized that vegetarians are statistically healthier than meat-eaters.

Since writing the first edition of *Digestive Wellness*, I have softened my opinion on proteins in general. A significant portion of the American population has a condition called *insulin sensitivity*, which makes protein foods more attractive as a basis for their diets. People with insulin sensitivity often have hypoglycemia or diabetes; are apple-shaped rather than pear-shaped; and may have ovarian cysts, heart disease symptoms, or be diagnosed as "Syndrome X." If you find that you crave carbohydrates and sugars, and keep getting fatter and fatter, you may ask your doctor to run a glucose/insulin tolerance test for you. If you have insulin sensitivity, eating proteins and non-starchy fruits and vegetables as the basis for your diet makes sense.

When eating meats, make sure to choose lean cuts and to remove the skin from poultry. The skin in poultry contains most of the fat and half of the calories, so by removing it you can eat twice as much and stay within the same calorie count. Pork is marketed as "the other white meat," but the only truly low-fat cut of pork is the tenderloin.

Environmentally, food animals are a disaster. Most water pollution comes from runoff from animal farming. The antibiotics they are given go into our rivers and streams, fields, crops, and our bodies. The hormones they are fed affect us after we eat their meat. This doesn't even touch on the inhumane conditions in which these animals are raised and slaughtered.

It takes 16 pounds of grain to produce 1 pound of beef, which is an extremely wasteful use of our global natural resources. If we as a nation would consume just 10 percent less meat, there would be additional stores of grain to feed 60 million people each year. Countries that switch from a grain-based to a meat-based economy become poorer, have more hunger and starvation, and strip their land of natural resources.

By changing the foods you eat, you have an opportunity to help the world become a better, gentler place. For more information on this subject, read *Diet for a Small Planet* and *Food First* by Francis Moore Lappe, and *May All Be Fed* and *Diet for a New America* by John Robbins.

Oils, Nuts, and Seeds

When purchasing oils, it is essential to find ones that have been expeller pressed, cold pressed, or are extra virgin (for olive oil). These oils have undergone a simple process of warming and pressing unlike most grocery store oils which have been chemically treated with solvents, heated to temperatures which destroy all natural antioxidants, deodorized, bleached, refined, degumed, defoamed, and preserved. One should also avoid all products that contain hydrogenated oil, partially hydrogenated oil, margarine, or vegetable shortening. There are new margarines which contain no "trans" fats; yet when I read the ingredients, they don't really fit my definition of a "food!"

Extra virgin olive oil is widely available in grocery stores. It retains many of the original benefits of the olives themselves: betasitosterols, which balance serum cholesterol, and beta-carotene, components that help the liver, gallbladder, pancreas, brain, and blood. Olive oil is mostly monounsaturated. Both mono- and polyunsaturated fats help prevent heart disease, but monounsaturated fats don't have the damaging effects of large amounts of polyunsaturated fats.

Other oils are found at health food stores and some gourmet food shops. Keep all oils except olive oil in the refrigerator so they don't go rancid. Good quality oils vary in flavor and color—walnut oil tastes different from corn oil. You'll find it's best to use less of the stronger flavored oils.

Though the fat in nuts and seeds provides minerals and essential fats, use them sparingly. Too much can harm you and put on unwanted pounds. A cup of nuts contains between 800 and 1,200 calories, most of which come from fat. Chestnuts, which are delicious steamed or roasted, are an exception to this rule. A teaspoon as a garnish on salads or vegetables can add a lot of flavor and nutrients without adding too much fat. Buy raw or roasted nuts that have not been seasoned, dry roasted, or coated with sugar and/or salt. These are available in the baking section of most stores and in health food stores. Store nuts and seeds in the refrigerator or freezer to keep them fresh.

Peanuts are in the bean family and grow underground rather than on trees. Some peanuts have a mold, called aflatoxin, which is toxic and can cause cancer. Aflatoxin is tasteless, so it's impossible to tell if it's on your peanuts or peanut butter. A healthy person should be able to handle any aflatoxin they're exposed to, but a sick person may have a difficult time. Be sure to buy only the old-fashioned kind—ground up peanuts and salt. Almond butter, cashew butter, and sesame tahini are good alternatives.

SHOPPING LIST

Here is a shopping list of healthful foods. It includes some brand names I know, but hundreds more are equally fine. Because "natural" and organic foods are often less available and sometimes more expensive than other foods, many people have banded together to form informal food co-ops. Together, they can order from wholesale distributors of natural foods, and buy foods in bulk or by the case. Buying foods in bulk saves time and money, and most grocery and health food stores are happy to give a discount when you buy cases.

HEALTHY FOOD CHOICES

FRUITS & VEGETABLES

Eat at least five to nine servings a day of all fruits and vegetables. They are rich in nutrients and fiber, contain no cholesterol, and are low in fat. Olives and avocados are rich in essential fatty acids (oils), which also makes them high in calories, so if you're watching your weight, go easy!

LEGUMES (BEANS AND PEAS)

Use all types freely and often.

Black beans	Fava beans	White beans
Great northern beans	Kidney beans	Garbanzo (chickpeas)
Split peas, green and yellow	Pinto beans	Soybeans: tofu, tempeh, miso, flour, grits
Lima beans	Lentils: green, yellow, orange	

WHOLE GRAINS

Many people with digestive illness have difficulty handling grains of any type. If so, you may need to limit or eliminate this food group from your diet for a period of time or permanently.

*Denotes a grain that contains gluten.

Brown rice	Wild rice	Millet
Whole wheat:* whole wheat flour,* wheat berries,* cracked wheat,* bulghur,* wheat bran,* couscous*	Buckwheat Barley* Rye* Oats*: oatmeal,* whole oats,* oat bran*	Spelt* Quinoa Kamut Corn: flour, meal, bran, polenta, pop corn Amaranth

WHOLE GRAIN BREADS

Found in some grocery stores, bakeries, and natural food stores. Look for "whole wheat" or "stone ground wheat" on the label. If it says "wheat flour" or "enriched" flour, it's white flour. Dense, heavy breads usually contain the most nutrients and fiber.

GLUTEN-FREE BREADS AND PASTAS

Many stores are now carrying breads and pastas made with gluten-free flours like quinoa, rice, millet, and soy. These products are terrific for people with celiac disease, wheat, or gluten sensitivities.

Breads: whole grain
Pasta: whole wheat, corn, quinoa, semolina, Jerusalem artichoke, rice, soba, udon, cellophane noodles

Crackers: Akmak, Health Valley, Hain, Finn crisp, plain Ry-Krisp, Barbara's pretzels and breadsticks, Wasa (rye only), whole wheat matzoh

Tortillas, corn/wheat, English muffins, pita bread, rice cakes, whole grain muffins, pancakes, waffles

CEREALS

Health Valley
Barbara's Bakery
Kashi
Perky's

Nature's Path
Shredded wheat with bran
New Morning
Uncle Sam's cereal
McCann's Oatmeal

Nutrigrain
All Bran
Erewhon
Oatmeal
7-grain cereal

DAIRY PRODUCTS AND EGGS

Many people with digestive problems need to eliminate dairy products from their diet, so use only if you are able to digest them easily. Use low-fat products as a rule. Cheese is best used as a condiment. Try some grated parmesan or other types of cheese to zip up a dish, rather than eating hunks of cheese as a snack food.

Low- or non-fat yogurt
Low-fat cottage cheese
Goat's milk and cheese
Eggs: chicken, duck

Skim milk
Buttermilk
Parmesan
Butter and ghee in small quantities

Skim milk ricotta
Kefir
Yogurt cheese

FISH AND SEAFOOD

When possible, choose fish that are highest in Omega 3 fatty acids. All other fish and shellfish are good low-fat protein choices, but will not give the protective benefits of high Omega 3 fish.

Salmon: all types
Tuna: albacore, bluefin
Herring
Lake trout
All other fish and shellfish

Mackerel
Atlantic sturgeon
Anchovy
Eel
Seaweed and sea vegetables

Bluefish (sparingly)
Sablefish
Sardines

MEATS AND POULTRY

Choose low-fat cuts of meat and take the skin off poultry.

Lean hamburger and beef
Pork tenderloin
Chicken, without skin

Ground turkey
Venison
Turkey, light meat, no skin

Leg of lamb
Buffalo

BEVERAGES

Water is the most healthful beverage. Make certain your drinking water is uncontaminated. Fresh juices made from organic produce offer a delicious and healthful option, and buy organic juices and teas whenever possible. Check labels carefully for sugars added to juice drinks; only 100-percent pure juices can be labeled "juice."

Pure water	Grain coffee	Fruit juices
Vegetable juices	Pure carbonated waters	Green tea
	Herbal teas	

OILS, NUTS, AND SEEDS

Use only extra virgin or expeller pressed oils, organic oils whenever possible, and olive oil, except for stir frying or baking.

Oils:

Olive oil	Sesame oil	Canola oil
Sunflower oil	Safflower oil	Corn oil
Walnut oil	Almond oil	Soybean oil
Peanut oil	Rice bran oil	Macadamia nut oil

Nuts and Seeds:

Pistachio	Macadamia	Cashews
Almond	Chestnut	Pecans
Walnuts	Peanuts	Sunflower seeds
Pumpkin seeds	Sesame seeds	
Coconut, unsweetened		Pine nuts

CONDIMENTS

Condiments add great flavor to foods, with few calories or grams of fat. Read labels carefully; many sauces are salty, fatty, sugar laden, or filled with food chemicals. Homemade salad dressings are best.

Mustard	Horseradish	Salsa
Worcester-shire sauce	Tamari or shoyu sauce	Vinegars: balsamic, rice, fruit
Herbs and spices	Pepper: white or black	Olives: black and green
Anchovy paste	Pickles	Seaweed flakes
Sun dried tomatoes	Gomasio	Sauerkraut
Herbal blends in shakers	Capers	

Chapter II

SKILLS FOR DEVELOPING EMOTIONAL HARDINESS: STRESS MANAGEMENT

"Things which matter most must never be at the mercy of things which matter least."

GOETHE

RECENT DISCOVERIES HAVE proven beyond a doubt that our brains and immune systems are interlinked. Our thoughts affect us on a cellular level. The field of psychoneuroimmunology is a blossoming discipline which studies the mind-body connection. More fatal heart attacks occur on Monday than any other day of the week. Could this have something to do with our attitude about Mondays? Researchers believe it does.

We experience stress on four levels: physical, environmental, mental/emotional, and spiritual. In preceding chapters we've talked a lot about physical and environmental stress,

183

so here we will focus on the mental, emotional, and spiritual aspects. All our lives have stressful periods. We can't eliminate them, but we can learn to flow with them more easily. It is often the meaning we attach to our experiences that makes them stressful or stress-free.

Stress and emotions play a major role in many digestive problems. Anyone who has ever had diarrhea from "nerves" can attest to that. The butterflies that people feel in their stomach when they're nervous happen to all of us. There are more nerve endings in the digestive system than in the spine. If you can experience an aching back due to stress, why not an "aching" immune system? For those of us who have a digestive Achilles' heel, stress affects us as diarrhea, gas, bloating, or pain.

The digestive system has its own nervous system, which can function entirely on its own without the brain's help. In fact, before ulcer medications revolutionized the treatment of ulcer pain, surgeons cut the vagus nerve from the brain to the stomach, and the digestive system continued to operate completely! In this second nervous system, we find every neurotransmitter that is found in the brain. In fact, we secrete more seratonin in the GI than in the brain! When we say that we feel stress in our guts, we really mean it! Continued stress in our body, mind, or meanings affects the body's ability to heal and perform. If the body is using most of its energy to put out fires, it has less time for maintenance and repair. Because the digestive tract repairs and replaces itself every few days, it is one of the first places where our bodies alert us that all is not well. People who have digestive-related problems can benefit from stress management tools.

Though we mainly think of stress as a negative thing, it does have a positive side. The stress of going to college, getting married, having children, or getting a promotion provides opportunities and challenges that force us to change, grow, and strive to fulfill our potential.

Stress = Opportunity

But even positive stress can overwhelm us, causing distress.

When we bite off more than we can chew, we feel stressed out. In many instances, we have little control over stressors like illness, loss of a job, financial worries, and death. But even in these circumstances we can have control over our thoughts and behavior. This is where stress management offers many benefits. Studies have shown that people who have emotional hardiness handle distress more easily than people with less resilience. Hardy people take on a challenge, make a commitment, take control, and see what happens. If success comes their way, it encourages them to try new things. If they fail, they pick themselves up and try again, recognizing that experience gained from "failure" adds to life's perspective. Fortunately, it's possible for anyone to learn hardiness skills.

Mental stress is one of the greatest challenges to our immune systems, putting pressure on nearly every organ and system in the body. When we feel stressed out, our bodies react with an increased heartbeat, shallow and rapid breathing, a release of adrenaline, and raised blood sugar levels and oxygen rates. Our muscles tense so we can move quickly. An increased blood supply is sent to our brain and major muscles, with decreased blood flow to our extremities. Even our pupils dilate and we sweat more. Our bodies react this way because our minds tell us there is a dangerous situation that requires quick thinking and movement. Historically, this might have been a bear on our path, a forest fire, or the exhilaration of the hunt. Today, it can be anything from a near car collision, three phone lines ringing at once, to burnt toast! Because our first reaction is to unconsciously hold our breath and breathe shallowly, deep breathing exercises are an excellent stress management tool. Breathing deeply brings more oxygen to our tissues while waste products are excreted. It slows us down, so we feel more balanced and centered and can make clearer decisions. Deep abdominal breathing is something you can do anywhere, and no one can tell!

ABDOMINAL BREATHING EXERCISE

Take ten deep breaths through your nose. As you inhale, feel your belly expand; feel the inhalation spread until it fills your lungs to the top. Exhale by letting your lungs deflate gently. Remember that there aren't any awards for how big your lungs get or how many seconds you can hold your breath! Notice how you feel. If you're calmer, remember this tool and use it as needed.

How do you know when you're under too much stress? Your body will usually tell you before your mind does. You may get a neckache, backache, or headache, a sick feeling in your stomach, hives, fatigue, or a myriad of other symptoms. But even though your body is telling you to stop, you keep on going. Our culture rewards this type of behavior. But we owe it to ourselves to listen to our own needs more carefully and to respond to them in kind. Pain and discomfort is our body's way of asking us to pay attention, now!

SIGNALS OF STRESS

Emotional	Physical	Behavioral
Moodiness	Muscle tension	Overuse of
Worry	Aches and pains	drugs/alcohol
Irritability	Fatigue	Overeating
Hostility/anger	Sleep disturbances	Forgetfulness
Bad dreams	Diarrhea	Clumsiness
Lassitude	Digestive symptoms	Depression
Defensiveness	Headaches	Tension
Difficulty		Poor eating
concentrating		

We can tune into these signals, or we can choose to ignore the messages and carry on with our activities. If we ignore them, the symptoms may go away, or they may blast louder and louder until we are forced to pay attention, or our bodies break down. Being attentive to small signals allows us to gently get back on track without experiencing major upheavals in our lives.

The most important component of a good stress management program is to have a plan with reasonable and realistic goals. If you need to, get a buddy or professional who will support you. Think of the ways in which you might slip or lose your way and prepare for them. Once your goals and support system are in place, you can forge into action.

SELF-RENEWAL

The best stress management tool is exercise. Exercise makes us stronger and more flexible and increases our sense of balance, which helps keep us injury free. Regular exercise helps control blood sugar levels so our energy is more sustained, and being fit lowers the risk of heart disease. While exercise alone won't make you thin, a consistent exercise program can help you move toward your ideal body weight. In addition, our bodies release endorphins, morphinelike molecules, in the brain which make us feel happy! When I ask people to describe the benefits of their exercise program, they tell me they have more energy, have higher self-esteem, and feel more relaxed.

Positive thinking is an important part of stress management. If you could tape the conversation in your brain for an hour or two, you might find you had a lot of self-criticism or self-doubts. With practice we can easily learn to "flip" these negative images and turn criticism into a positive thought or plan of action. When we catch ourselves playing a negative tape, we need to eject it and put in a new tape. Instead of thinking "My ulcerative colitis will get worse and worse until I need surgery," you can flip the image and say, "So far I haven't licked this problem, but if I am persistent, I can improve my health."

PLAY THE HIT SIDE OF THE TAPE EXERCISE

Close your eyes for a minute, and think of all your most wonderful attributes. Compliment yourself freely. Take some time to appreciate your good points and achievements. Think about times in your life when you helped others, fell in love, and really felt good about yourself. Make a mental list of the nicest things you can say about yourself. It's okay if you repeat yourself. Think of five things for which you are grateful today.

After you finish, see how you feel, and repeat this exercise as often as you like. If you want, write your ideas down, and put them somewhere so you'll be reminded of how terrific you are and how many blessings fill your life. Liking ourselves also helps our view of others and the world around us.

Most of us invest a lot of energy in our work, home, family, and friends. But stress management means you need to make time to be nice to yourself. Take an hour every day to recharge your batteries. It's not important what you do. Each of us will find renewal in different things. Here are some ideas: read something for fun, play a musical instrument, listen to music, garden, exercise, be outdoors, have a date with a friend, write a letter, keep a journal, enjoy a hobby, take a class, go to church/temple, meditate. Vacations are an important way to put our lives in perspective, to value what is truly important. Learn to nurture yourself.

Prioritizing helps us find the balance point in our lives. Balance is hard to achieve and maintain, but it is an honorable goal. Like many people, if something really interests me, I take on new responsibilities and enjoyable events until I become overwhelmed. Then I make a list of all of my commitments and prioritize them to see what I can let go of responsibly. Soon my life is back in balance—until the next exciting possibility comes along and I'm overcommitted again. Be assertive: Learn to say no!

On the other hand, many people never grab for the ring, and they watch the world go by because they're worried about taking a risk. For these people, it's important to find a spark of interest and act on it. Doing nothing because we're fearful of failure can be as stressful as overachieving.

The demands placed upon us in this fast-paced world are unrealistically high. We are expected to play many roles perfectly—mate, son/daughter, mother/father, businessperson, athlete, spiritual being, and public citizen, both locally and globally. After all, the Greek and Roman gods and goddesses were excellent at only one thing. So why do we put such unreasonable and unrealistic demands on ourselves? A Buddhist saying is: "Expectation is the root of all suffering." If we can be easier on ourselves and in our relationships, we can find more love, contentment, and peace.

Compartmentalizing thoughts is a useful tool. Since we can only think about or act upon one responsibility at a time, it helps to put each one in a "compartment." The pearl here is to be able to be 100 percent present and focused on each task while you are doing it. This frees the mind and calms the spirit.

COMPARTMENTALIZATION EXERCISE

Imagine you are sitting before a rolltop desk with pigeonholes in it. In each hole is a scroll tied neatly with a ribbon. See yourself opening one scroll at a time, examining it, putting it back in its proper place, selecting another, and repeating the process. Do this for several minutes. Find a way to use these pigeonholes in your daily life to help you accomplish tasks step-by-step. Practice this exercise to help you create closure between tasks and events in your life.

QUICK IDEAS FOR STRESS MANAGEMENT

Eat healthy foods.
Develop better communication skills; learn to really listen.

Exercise regularly.
Spend time outdoors.
Make time for yourself each day for pleasure or relaxation.
Meditate or learn self-hypnosis or visualization techniques.
Realize that you don't have to be perfect.
Think creatively.
Go at your own pace.
Think of solutions, not problems.
Prioritize.
Keep journals.
Live one day at a time.
Play and laugh.
Spend time with friends and family.
Be flexible.
View your problems as an opportunity for growth.
Plan for chaos in your daily schedule.
Set clear priorities and stick to them.
Breathe deeply.
Plan ahead: wake up fifteen minutes earlier each morning, keep your car in good working order, put a duplicate car key in your wallet, and so on.
Learn to say "No!"
Unplug your phone or let your answering machine pick up the calls.
Take a bath, shower, steam, or Jacuzzi.
Make lists. Keep a calendar or appointment book.
Drive 10 mph slower.
Take one day a week to relax. Honor the Sabbath.
Believe that people have good intentions and are doing the best job they can.
See the world through a "loving" filter.

Part 5

A Functional
Approach to
Therapeutics/
Self-Care

Chapter 12

Natural Therapies for Common Digestive Problems

"Disease bias means that we take health for granted, waiting to act when health is gone and disease emerges. Once we make this assumption, we can soon become so preoccupied that our horizon is filled with diseases to combat. Because disease looms so large, our sight is obscured to the possibilities of health."

RUSSELL JAFFE, M.D.

THIS CHAPTER PROVIDES a comprehensive list of self-care ideas for the most common digestive problems. The remedies are mostly nutritional and herbal because those are the fields I know best; I have included other modalities whenever possible. The most important ones are listed first. Read each section that applies to you, find the remedies for your symptoms, look especially for repetitive ones, and try those first. Also try the remedies that make the most sense intuitively.

193

Each herb or nutrient is listed separately, but often they can be found in combination supplements. You'll notice that specific recommendations are repeated for many problems. Although each health condition has its own unique properties, many have similar characteristics that respond to similar treatment programs. You may want to work with a health professional to tailor a program that will best suit your needs.

Health care is both a science and an art. You may need the science in the form of lab-testing, diagnosis, and evaluation of your needs. (Your doctor will order the customary lab work. I have included information about functional lab tests which are most likely to reveal new information; these tests will probably be unfamiliar to your physician. The Directory will help you connect with the appropriate labs.) The art of healing comes into play when determining which paths to follow, which ideas have the most merit, and which dosages are appropriate. Healing often happens in layers. Sometimes you try the right thing at the wrong time. Later, you try it again with great results because the initial obstacle had been removed. If the first program you try doesn't work or only works partially, try another. You can feel better if you are persistent and patient.

This chapter contains classic digestive problems. We start our journey at the mouth and move south. Some of the following ideas alleviate symptoms, while others work to help your body heal the underlying cause. You can begin your program by taking a multivitamin and mineral supplement. Be sure to purchase one that is hypoallergenic.

Multivitamin with minerals: Think of a multivitamin with minerals as inexpensive health insurance, and arm yourself with an excellent supplement. Your diet is likely to be deficient in several nutrients which it can provide. Because minerals are bulky, you'll find yourself taking anywhere from four to nine pills daily. Look for a supplement which contains the following: 1,000 milligrams of calcium, 500 milligrams of magnesium, no more than 400 IU of vitamin D, a minimum of 100 IU of vitamin E, a minimum of 250 milligrams of vitamin C, 200 micrograms of chromium, 200 micrograms of selenium, 5–10 milligrams of manganese, at least 15 milligrams of zinc, and at least 25 milligrams of each B-vitamin. If you do this, the rest of the nutrients will be in line.

MOUTH

The mouth is the first digestive organ, after the brain (see chapter 3). The health of our teeth, tongue, and gums is integral to the health of the rest of the digestive tract. Digestive enzymes in saliva begin the process of carbohydrate digestion, and chewing sends signals to the brain, which in turn sends signals to the stomach that food is on the way. Thorough chewing of food can help with indigestion.

Irritation and inflammation in the mouth can be signs of food or chemical sensitivities or allergies. The mouth is our first contact with ingested allergens. Careful investigation of the mouth area can give information about a person's nutritional status. Cracks down the center of the tongue are an indication of the need for increased B-complex vitamins. Bleeding gums indicate the need for vitamin C and bioflavonoids. Receding gums indicate bone loss, so bone nutrients are needed. Deep pockets in gums indicate the need for vitamin C, bioflavonoids, and CoQ10.

Bad Breath/Halitosis

Yes, bad breath can be digestive in origin. It can be caused by low HCl levels in the stomach, poor flora, and/or constipation. But, first, consult a dentist to see if it is caused by poor dental hygiene, periodontal disease, or tooth infections. If so, follow your dentist's advice, and also look in the section on gum and tooth health which follows. If your gums and teeth are healthy, look to your digestive capacities. Using mouthwash is like putting a Band-Aid on a broken leg.

Healing Options

Eliminate constipation: See section on stool transit time in chapter 3 and do the self-test. Make sure you are getting plenty of fiber and liquids and are having one to two bowel movements each day. Magnesium is essential for normal peristalsis. Dosage: 400–800 milligrams magnesium daily.

Probiotic supplement: Take one or two capsules of acidophillus and bifidus between meals.

Lactose intolerance: Lactose intolerance can cause bad breath, other digestive symptoms, and headaches. The simplest way to discover if you have lactose intolerance is to avoid all dairy products and dairy-containing food for two weeks, then see if your symptoms have improved.

If the problem persists: This may be a sign that you are fermenting rather than digesting your foods. (1) To check out your HCl levels, try 1 teaspoon vinegar in a glass of water with meals or betaine HCl tablets. If the HCl causes burning, you probably don't need HCl. You can neutralize the acid with milk or baking soda. (2) Ask your doctor to run a comprehensive digestive and stool analysis with parasitology evaluation. You may have dysbiosis, parasites, or a *Helicobacter* infection (the bacteria implicated in ulcers). A CDSA can help you find out what's amiss.

Cracks in the Corners of the Mouth and Lips

Our skin is continuously replacing itself, and the places where our skin folds need to be replaced even more often. B-complex vitamins, particularly vitamins B_2 (riboflavin) and B_6 (pyridoxine), assist in formation of new skin. Cracks at the corners of our lips, called cheilosis, are most often associated with these nutrient deficiencies. They can easily become infected by yeast (*Candida albicans*). If they do not respond to nutritional therapy, have a physician look for other causes.

HEALING OPTIONS

B-complex vitamins: Dosage: 50–100 milligrams one to three times daily in trial for four weeks.

Gingivitis and Periodontal Disease

Gingivitis is an inflammation of the gums which, if left alone, often progresses to periodontitis, an inflammation of the bone around the teeth. Periodontal disease increases with plaque build-up, age, long-term use of steroid medications, in diabetics, people with systemic disease, and smokers. The presence of silver fillings, which contain 50 percent mercury, has also been found to predispose people to periodontal disease. One study showed that when silver fillings were removed, 86 percent of the 125 oral cavity symptoms were eliminated or improved.

Gingivitis and periodontitis are complex problems which have complex solutions. Periodontal disease will affect nine out of ten Americans during their lifetimes, and four out of ten will lose all their teeth. Regular dental care is essential. Follow your dentist's advice and practice consistent oral hygiene: brush and floss daily.

Nutrition plays a critical role in dental health. One recent study looked at gingivitis, plaque adhesion, and calculus deposit with regard to the eating habits of teenagers. They concluded that teenagers with diets adequate in nutrients had better oral health than teenagers with diets that contained fewer nutrients.

Teeth are made of bone material and need the same nutrients for rebuilding as other bones. It has long been considered that receding and inflamed gums were a sign that people brushed too hard, causing damage to the gums, but new theories propose that gums recede because bone throughout the body, including the teeth, is demineralizing. If other bones need seventeen nutrients to remineralize, the same goes for teeth. Calcium alone cannot reverse the problem. Stress and fast-paced living can cause bone loss by making the body more acidic. To compensate, the body takes alkaline materials from bones and teeth.

Vitamin C deficiency causes bleeding gums and loose teeth and contributes to gingivitis. One symptom of scurvy, a vitamin C deficiency disease, is bleeding gums. We rarely see outright scurvy in our population, but we often see people with bleeding gums. Vitamin C is also important for bone formation and collagen synthesis and is essential for gum repair. Vitamin A is also necessary for collagen synthesis and formation of gum tissue.

Other researchers look to zinc deficiency or a low zinc to copper ratio as the culprit in gum disease. Zinc is integral to maintenance and repair of gum tissue, inhibits plaque formation and reduces inflammation by inhibiting mast cell release of histamine. It also plays a role in immune function.

Vitamin E has been used clinically for periodontal disease. Bacterial plaque, long known to be a culprit in tooth decay and gingivitis, produces compounds which weaken and irritate the gum tissue. They include endotoxins and exotoxins, free radicals, connective tissue-destroying enzymes, white blood cell poisons, antigens, waste products and toxins.

Antioxidant nutrients and coenzyme Q10 have been associated with improved gum health, reduced periodontal pocket depth and less tooth movement. Bioflavonoids make the tissues stronger, reduce inflammation and cross-link with collagen fibers, making them stronger. Because bioflavonoids work synergistically with vitamin C, bleeding gums often respond to vitamin C and bioflavonoid supplementation.

Folic acid, a B-complex vitamin, is important for maintenance and repair of mucous membranes. The need for extra folic acid was first noted for pregnant women, while subsequent studies have shown that it plays an important role for gingival health in all people.

HEALING OPTIONS

Improved diet: Focus on fresh fruits, vegetables, whole grains and beans. Foods rich in flavonoids are beneficial: blueberries, blackberries, purple grapes.

Multivitamin with minerals: Since you are depleted in many nutrients, arm yourself with an excellent multivitamin with minerals. Because minerals are bulky, you'll probably take anywhere from four to nine pills daily. Look for a supplement which contains the following: 1,000 milligrams calcium, 500 milligrams magnesium, no more than 400 IU vitamin D, 100–200 micrograms chromium, 100–200 micrograms selenium, 5–10 milligrams manganese, at least 15 milligrams zinc, and at least 25 milligrams of each B-vitamin.

Coenzyme Q10: Dosage: 75 milligrams daily for a trial period of three months.

Antioxidants: Vitamins C and E, selenium, glutathione, N-acetylcysteine, superoxide dismutase (SOD), beta-carotene, and other antioxidant nutrients are depleted in diseased gum tissues. Supplementation can facilitate repair. For ease of use, purchase an antioxidant supplement which contains many antioxidants. Dosage: Use as directed for three months.

Vitamin C: Dosage: 500–1,000 milligrams one to three times daily.

Bioflavonoids: Use quercitin, bilberry (blueberry), grapeseed extract, or pycnogenol for their antioxidant and anti-inflammatory effects.

Myrrh: Myrrh has been used since biblical times. It has soothing and antiseptic properties for mucous membranes.

Folic acid mouthwash: Use of a 0.1 percent folic acid mouthwash can be quite effective. Be sure to have your blood tested for pernicious anemia first, because folate supplementation can cause nerve damage in people with vitamin B_{12} deficiencies.

Fish oil capsules: In a controlled placebo trial, it was found that MaxEPA fish oil capsules significantly reduced gingival bleeding and reduced inflammatory factors. Dosage: 2 grams EPA/DHA daily.

Mouth Ulcers/Canker Sores

Mouth sores are common. Most of us have experienced mouth ulcers, canker sores, or cold sores, but some people have chronic problems with them. Usually found inside the mouth, canker sores, called *aphthous stomatitis*, or aphthous ulcers, are the result of poor intestinal flora, food sensitivities/allergies, stress, hormonal changes, and nutritional deficiencies. High-sugar foods and high-acid foods, like pineapples, citrus, and tomatoes, sometimes trigger canker sores.

If you have recurring canker sores, thoroughly investigate the possibility of food sensitivities. Also, make sure your toothpaste, mouthwash, and floss aren't causing the problem. A study showed that use of Piroxicam, an NSAID, caused mouth ulcers which resolved when the patient was taken off the medication. If you have canker sores that don't resolve after several weeks, let your doctor or dentist examine you.

HEALING OPTIONS

Allergies and sensitivities: Cigarettes, toothpaste, mouthwash, and flavored dental floss can cause irritation. Make sure they are not the source of your problem. Food sensitivities often are. Rule them out carefully with the elimination/provocation diet and/or food allergy/sensitivity blood testing.

Probiotics: *Lactobacillus acidophillus* is often beneficial in prevention and treatment of canker sores. Dosage: one to two capsules or ¼ to ½ teaspoon of the powder three times daily; take between meals.

B-complex vitamins: Deficiencies in vitamin B_1, B_2, B_6, B_{12}, and folic acid have been associated with recurrent canker sores. People with B-complex deficiencies showed significant improvement of mouth ulcers during three months of supplementation with B-complex vitamins.

Gluten sensitivity: Gluten is a protein fraction found in wheat, rye, spelt, oats, and barley. A considerable amount of research has been done on the connection between gluten intolerance and mouth ulcers because people with celiac disease (sprue) often have recurring mouth sores. About 25 percent of people with chronic canker sores have elevated antibodies to gluten, which indicates a specific sensitivity. When they avoid gluten-containing grains, their mouth sores go away.

Iron deficiency anemia: Iron deficiency is associated with canker sores. If you get recurrent canker sores and are anemic, you may respond to iron supplementation. People who are not anemic will not benefit. Ask your physician to test you for anemia. Dosage: 30–75 milligrams elemental iron daily. Because iron tends to be constipating, a slow-release iron, like Feosol or generic equivalents, may be helpful. Floradix, an herbal iron supplement, is gentle and works well. Cooking in cast iron pots and pans is another way to gain iron from your diet.

Stress management: Ask yourself if stress plays a significant role in your canker sores. If so, consider yourself lucky and use the information discussed in chapter 11 to make changes in your lifestyle that will benefit all of you, not just your mouth!

Zinc: Zinc deficiencies have been linked to mouth ulcers. Zinc plays an important role in healing wounds and immune system function. In one study, zinc supplementation helped heal canker sores 81 percent of the time in people with low zinc levels or a low zinc to copper ratio.

TOPICAL REMEDIES

Ice: Ice compresses dry up canker sores quickly. Apply ice directly to the sore for either forty-five minutes once a day or several times a day for five minutes each. You'll still have a scab that needs to heal, but the sores won't be painful.

Licorice root: Licorice root is soothing to the mucous membranes of the digestive tract, and chewable licorice can help reduce inflammation and pain from mouth ulcers. Licorice promotes healing of mucous membranes by stimulating production of healing prostaglandins. Just be sure to buy DGL licorice which has had the glycyrrhizins removed. Glycyrrhizins can raise blood pressure and lower serum potassium levels. Chew two licorice tablets between meals as needed up to four times daily, or eat real licorice, such as Panda brand. Most licorice is made with anise, not licorice.

Myrrh: Myrrh is an herb that has been used since biblical times to soothe mucous membranes. It has antiseptic properties and can be used in a variety of ways. Chewing gum with myrrh can be temporarily soothing, and a glycerin tincture can be used topically to soothe the sores. It can be combined with the herb goldenseal in tea, paste, or tincture.

Goldenseal: Goldenseal is soothing to mucous membranes and also has antiseptic properties. It can be taken internally, dabbed directly on the sores, or drunk as a tea.

Castor oil: An old Edgar Cayce remedy is to soak a cotton swab in castor oil and apply to the canker sore.

Thrush

Thrush is a yeast infection in the mouth and throat. It has a white, cottage cheesy look and is common after use of antibiotics. Thrush can be treated with either prescription or natural medicines. If it persists, you must treat yourself systemically. It is of primary importance to use probiotic supplements of acidophillus and bifidus to reestablish normal mouth/throat flora. Natural remedies such as garlic, grapefruit seed extract, pau d'arco, and mathake tea, along with dietary changes, can make your body inhospitable to *Candida*. Follow the protocols for *Candida* infections. In one study, one-third of people with thrush were found to have folic acid, vitamin B_6 or vitamin B_{12} anemias, so it's worth having your doctor check you for anemias and B vitamin status.

Tongue Problems

Glossitis is an inflammation of the tongue, which can be extremely red and smooth. People may also develop other symptoms; the most common is called "geographic tongue" where the center of your tongue looks like a miniature Grand Canyon. Look in a mirror, look at your friend's and family's tongues, and you'll probably find one. People may also have scalloping on the edges of their tongues.

Tongue problems can arise from systemic illness, so celiac, diabetes, anemia, and syphilis should be ruled out by your physician. More often tongue problems are indicators of nutritional needs or mouth irritants, like smoking or other chemicals. Studies have found that glossitis is a sign of protein-calorie malnourishment, nutritional deficiencies, or marginal nutritional deficiencies of several vitamins and minerals. It affects 5 percent of our elderly. It most often signals the need for increased B-complex vitamins and iron. You will often find a reddened tongue with pellagra, which is caused by a deficiency of niacin (vitamin B_3). Therapeutics for glossitis are almost identical to those for canker sores.

HEALING OPTIONS

B-complex vitamins: The most important B vitamins for tongue health are riboflavin (B_2), niacin (B_3), vitamin B_{12} and folic acid. Choline is found in B-complex vitamins and also plays a vital role in tongue health. Dosage: 50–100 milligrams one to three times daily for a trial period of four to six weeks.

Iron deficiency anemia: This can also cause a sore and inflamed tongue. Have your physician check to make sure your iron status is normal.

Zinc: Zinc is important for healing. Dosage: 25–50 milligrams daily.

Food sensitivities: Check for food sensitivities.

Vitamin E: One study of elderly people with glossitis found that they had lower serum levels of vitamin E. It is not known if vitamin E is just a marker or if it will help therapeutically, but vitamin E has low toxicity and is worth trying.

ESOPHAGUS

The most common problems in the esophageal area are belching, medically called "eructation," and heartburn, also called gastric reflux.

Belching/Eructation

Belching is a symptom of gas in the upper part of the digestive tract. It is a release of trapped air from the stomach and usually comes from swallowed air. Just as a baby needs to be burped if he/she swallows air, we also burp if we swallow air—it's normal. Other than being culturally embarrassing, it's usually without problem. In fact, in China it's considered polite to belch after a meal—it means you really enjoyed it!

Foods and drink that contain air contribute to belching. Without fail if I have a carbonated drink, I burp. Whipped cream and egg whites can have the same effect. Gulping drinks and food causes us to take in more air, while eating slowly prevents us from swallowing air. People also swallow air during exercise and while chewing gum, and sucking on pipes or cigarettes. If you are overweight, you are more likely to belch from exercise.

Be thankful that you belch; air trapped in the stomach can be painful and belching is a safety valve which relieves the pressure. If you have a problem with the amount of belching you do, here are some suggestions.

Healing Options

Eat slowly. Chew your food well.

Avoid carbonated beverages.

Stop smoking: If you smoke, stop. Be glad you have such a benign reason to stop.

Reach and maintain ideal body weight: If you are significantly overweight, lose some weight.

Stop chewing gum or sucking on candy.

Check your supplements. Some can cause belching, such as fish oils.

Heartburn/Gastric Reflux and Hiatal Hernia

Heartburn is caused by stomach acid backing up into your esophagus. The esophageal sphincter is supposed to keep the stomach contents in place, but if the sphincter relaxes, acid can push up into the esophagus. The most common symptoms are a burning sensation above the stomach, excessive salivation, belching, regurgitation, and a sour taste in the mouth. One-third of the people in America experience frequent heartburn, and 3 to 7 percent suffer from esophageal illness caused from the acid reflux which causes scarring, constriction of the esophagus, and swallowing disorders. Some drugs can cause heartburn, including birth control pills, diazepam, nicotine, nitroglycerine, progesterone, provera, and theophylline.

Four to five million Americans seek medical advice each year for heartburn and hiatal hernia. Heartburn is common among pregnant women whose organs are squashed in a most peculiar way. For most people, heartburn is a mild, self-limiting problem, yet for 20 percent of the people affected, it becomes a serious health problem. Stress plays some part in it. Other things that trigger heartburn include wearing tight fitting clothes, lying down, bending over, and eating large meals or specific foods. If you experience heartburn in the middle of the night, be sure to eat at least four hours before going to bed.

Hiatal hernia occurs when a portion of the stomach gets pushed through the diaphragm and into the thoracic cavity where it doesn't belong. Hiatal hernias may or may not cause symptoms, the most common of which is heartburn. It's found in about 20 percent of all middle-aged Americans. Dr. Dennis Burkitt hypothesized that hiatal hernia was a contemporary problem and the result of a modernized diet. Gastric reflux and hiatal hernia have been on the rise over the past twenty years and occur most often in people of Caucasian descent. These problems are rarely seen in people eating high-fiber diets. Dr. Burkitt felt that the pressure of straining with bowel movements pushed the upper part of the stomach out of place. Chiropractic adjustment can gently put the stomach back in place, and in many cases only a single adjustment is necessary.

People commonly take antacids for temporary relief of heartburn. Initially, use of antacids causes the body to produce more hydrochloric acid that helps digest food. Parietal cells respond by making more acid. Eventually the parietal cells get exhausted, so over the long term, antacids cause the parietel cells to make less hydrochloric acid. Hans Selye, father of modern theories about stress, devised the model that before an organ breaks down, it overworks. There are other repercussions of taking antacids. A recent study looked at 155 healthy people who had been using antacids for heartburn/reflux over long periods of time. The study found that 47 percent had erosion of the esophagus and 6 percent had Barrett's esophagus, a more serious condition. Most bacteria can't live in a high-acid environment and are killed in the stomach. Low stomach acid predisposes people to dysbiosis. Antacids also decrease your stomach's ability to digest protein by reducing the effectiveness of protease enzymes. H2 blockers, such a Tagamet and Zantac, and protein-pump inhibitors, such as Prilosec, are the most common prescription medications used for acid reflux. These medications are effective while you take them, but once you discontinue their use, your problem often recurs.

HEALING OPTIONS

Osteopathic care and chiropractic adjustment: Seek chiropractic care for hiatal hernia. Cranial-sacral adjustments can often correct gastric reflux, especially in children. Chiropractic or osteopathic adjustment is often all the therapy you need for these problems.

Dietary: Eat healthy foods. Increase fruits, vegetables, grains, beans, and high-fiber foods. Drinks and foods that are more acidic, like tomatoes and citrus, are more likely to cause heartburn. Dairy products have been shown to trigger symptoms, but more symptoms were provoked with milk with higher fat contents, suggesting that fat was the culprit, rather than the milk. Alcoholic beverages, coffee, and to a lesser extent, tea provoked heartburn, as well as high-fat, fried and spicy foods, onions, and chocolate. Trigger foods are individual—you need to discover what yours are.

If you are overweight, lose weight.

Place a 6-inch beam under the head of your bed: If you suffer from nighttime heartburn, raising the head of your bed can alleviate symptoms. Although you might think that raising your bed would feel strange, the difference is barely noticeable, and the heartburn improves.

Possible *Helicobacter pylori* infection: *Helicobacter pylori* is a bacteria which has been implicated in gastric and duodenal ulcers. In some cases, it is also involved in gastric reflux. Treatment with antibiotics and bismuth-containing supplements or drugs can cure *H. pylori*.

Hydrochloric acid: Heartburn has traditionally been treated with antacid therapy, but often it responds well to supplementation with hydrochloric acid pills. Often the symptoms of excess stomach acid and decreased stomach acid are the same. To test yourself, dilute a tablespoon of apple cider vinegar with water and drink with meals. If the vinegar is not strong enough to show results, take one to two HCl tablets with meals. If you do not need the HCl, you will feel a burning sensation which can be neutralized with milk or baking soda. If you need it, you'll feel relief of symptoms.

Cabbage juice: Cabbage juice has been a long-standing folk remedy for heartburn. Its high glutamine content is probably the key to its success. Cabbage juice has a strong flavor, so dilute with other vegetable juices.

Glutamine: Although I was unable to find any references for use of glutamine for heartburn, it makes theoretical sense. The digestive tract uses glutamine as a fuel source and for healing. It is effective for healing stomach ulcers, irritable bowel syndrome, and ulcerative bowel diseases, and it makes sense that it would be useful in the upper GI as well. Dosage: Begin with 8 grams daily.

Slippery elm bark: Slippery elm bark has demulcent properties, and it's gentle and soothing to mucous membranes. It has been a folk remedy for both heartburn and ulcers in European and Native American cultures and was used as a food by Native Americans. It can be used in large amounts without harm. Drink as a tea, or chew on the bark. Recipe for tea: Take 1 teaspoon of slippery elm bark in two cups of water. Simmer for twenty minutes and strain. Sweeten if you want, and drink freely. You can also purchase slippery elm lozenges at health food stores and some drug stores.

Lobelia: Massage tincture of lobelia externally onto the painful area and take two to three drops internally. This is a remedy recommended by Dr. Christopher, one of the greatest American herbalists of our times.

Ginger: This herb can provide temporary relief in a tea. Steep ½ teaspoon of powdered ginger or 1½ teaspoons of fresh ginger per cup of boiled water for ten minutes and drink. If you like, sweeten it with honey. Use freely.

Meadowsweet herb: Also a demulcent, meadowsweet soothes inflamed mucous membranes. To make a tea, steep 1 to 2 teaspoons of the dried herb in one cup of boiled water for ten minutes. Sweeten with honey if you like. Drink three cups daily.

STOMACH

Gastric Hypofunction/Hypochlorhydria

Hypochlorhydria has been associated with many common health problems. Not all of them are considered "digestive" problems, but they are. As we age, the parietal cells in the stomach lining produce less hydrochloric acid. In fact, half of people over the age of sixty have hypochlorhydria (low stomach acid), and by age eighty-five, 80 percent of the healthy people tested had low stomach acid. Overconsumption of fatty foods increases the secretion of HCl, contributing to GERD and heartburn. Medications are given to block HCl production, when a dietary change is what may actually be needed.

The balance of stomach acidity is vital to the health of the stomach and to our overall health. Hydrochloric acid (HCl) is our body's first line of defense against disease-causing microbes. Low HCl levels open us to the possibility of food poisoning and dysbiosis along the digestive tract. Overgrowth of bacteria in the intestinal tract occurs in 20 percent of people aged sixty to eighty and in 40 percent of people over age eighty. Adequate HCl is necessary for the absorption of vitamin B_{12} from food. B_{12} deficiency causes weakness, fatigue, and nervous system problems. Several minerals require an acidic environment for absorption, including iron, calcium, magnesium, zinc, and copper, and most B-complex vitamins require normal levels of stomach acid. Vitamin C

Low Gastric Acidity

Common symptoms of low gastric acidity
Bloating, belching, burning, and flatulence immediately after meals
A sense of fullness after eating
Indigestion, diarrhea, or constipation
Multiple food allergies
Nausea after taking supplements
Itching around the rectum
Weak, peeling, and cracked fingernails
Dilated blood vessels in the cheeks and nose (in nonalcoholics)
Acne
Iron deficiency
Chronic intestinal parasites or abnormal flora
Undigested food in stool
Chronic *Candida* infections
Upper digestive tract gassiness

Diseases associated with low gastric acidity

Addison's disease	Chronic hives
Asthma	Lupus erythematosis
Celiac disease	Myasthenia gravis
Dermatitis herpetiformis	Osteoporosis
(herpes)	Pernicious anemia
Diabetes	Psoriasis
Eczema	Rheumatoid arthritis
Gall bladder disease	Rosacea
Graves disease	Sjögren's syndrome
Chronic autoimmune	Thyrotoxicosis
disorders	Hyper- and hypothyroidism
Hepatitis	Vitiligo

Used with permission from *Encyclopedia of Natural Medicine*. Copyright 1991 by Michael Murray, N.D. and Joseph Pizzorno, N.D., by Prima Publishing, 1991, Rocklin, Calif. To order this book, call (916) 632-4400.

levels are also low in people with poor stomach acid. Acid is critical for the breakdown of protein bonds in the stomach. Poor acid content in the stomach causes indigestion. The symptoms of hypoacidity often mimic those of hyperacidity.

FUNCTIONAL LABORATORY TESTING

Heidleburg Capsule Test: This test measures your ability to produce hydrochloric acid when challenged with alkaline substances. See chapter 7 for complete details.

HEALING OPTIONS

Betaine HCl: Dosage: Begin with one 10 milligram capsule of betaine HCl with meals. If you do not respond, build slowly to a maximum of 5 capsules with each meal. If you experience burning, immediately neutralize the acid with 1 tsp baking soda in water or milk. That indicates that you now have too much HCl and are irritating your stomach lining. Cut back your dosage to a comfortable level.

Vinegar: You can increase stomach acidity with vinegar. Dilute 1 teaspoon of vinegar in water and drink with each meal. Gradually increase the amount of vinegar, up to 10 teaspoons. If you experience burning, immediately neutralize the acid by drinking a glass of milk or taking a teaspoon of baking soda in water.

Vitamin B$_{12}$ deficiency: Have your physician test your serum B$_{12}$ levels. If your levels are in the high-normal range, you don't have a deficiency. If your levels are low-normal, you may still be deficient in vitamin B$_{12}$. More sensitive tests of vitamin B$_{12}$ status are methylmalonic acid and homocysteine levels, but these tests are not widely available and are fairly expensive. A more expedient and less expensive route is to ask your physician to give you 1,000 micrograms of vitamin B$_{12}$ by injection weekly for four weeks. Then you and your doctor can evaluate the benefits. You may use sublingual vitamin B$_{12}$ lozenges to prolong the effects of the vitamin B$_{12}$ shots.

Multivitamin with minerals: Adequate HCl is necessary for absorption of vitamins and minerals. Since you are depleted in many nutrients, arm yourself with an excellent multivitamin with minerals. Because minerals are bulky, you'll probably find yourself taking anywhere from four to nine pills daily. Look for a supplement which contains the following: 1,000 milligrams calcium, 500 milligrams magnesium, no more than 400 IU vitamin D, 100–200 micrograms chromium, 100–200 micrograms selenium, 5–10 milligrams manganese, at least 15 milligrams zinc, and at least 25 milligrams of each B-vitamin.

Digestive enzymes: I recommend plant-derived enzymes because they are able to work in the low pH of the stomach and in the neutral environment of the intestines. They provide protease and lipase for the stomach and serve your enzyme needs throughout the digestive tract. Dosage: one to two with meals for a trial period of four weeks.

Swedish bitters: Bitters are a long-standing remedy for poor digestion in Europe. They stimulate production of hydrochloric acid. Take bitters either in tablet or liquid form as needed.

Chew food thoroughly.

Eat small meals frequently: Small meals are easier to digest.

Avoid drinking liquids with meals: Fluids dilute stomach acid.

Gastric Ulcers and Gastritis

A 1994 National Institutes of Health statement reports that "Peptic ulcer disease is a chronic inflammatory condition of the stomach and duodenum that affects as many as 10 percent of people in the United States at some time in their lives. The disease has relatively low mortality, but it results in substantial human suffering and high economic costs."

Gastric ulcers occur in the stomach and the duodenum (the first section of the small intestine) where gastric juice has burned a hole in your lining. It hurts! Gastric juice, which has a 0.5 percent concentration of hydrochloric acid, would burn your hand if you spilled some on it. A mucus layer protects the stomach tissue from being eaten away by the protein-splitting enzyme, pepsin, and gastric juices. Secretions of bicarbonate (baking soda) from the stomach lining are mixed into the mucus, buffering the acid. This makes an effective barrier to keep the stomach lining from harm. Pepsin, the real villain in this story, slowly digests this mucus layer, and if the mucus isn't replaced, gastric juices come into contact with the stomach lining and ulcers occur.

Until recently it was believed that ulcers were the result of high stomach acidity and high stress levels. Stress does play a significant role in ulcers and gastritis. While low-grade stress probably won't cause an ulcer, severe stress has been shown to cause ulcers in both animal and human studies. Psychological stress increases stomach acid and causes the mucus to become more fragile, making it easier for ulcers to form.

In the 1970s, receptor sites on the stomach lining were found which regulate secretion of hydrochloric acid, and drugs were developed to block these receptor sites. These drugs, called H2 blockers, have been effective in healing ulcers but not in preventing recurrence.

About 10 percent of stomach and duodenal ulcers are caused by the use of NSAIDs, such as aspirin, Tylenol, Motrin, and prescription pain relievers. Continued use of these therapies has been widely shown to cause ulcers and hospitalizations. It has been estimated that 107,000 people are hospitalized each year due to NSAID complications, and at least 16,500 NSAID-related deaths occur each year among arthritis patients alone. More recently, a new class of drugs called *protein-pump inhibitors* has been used, the most common of which is Prilosec. These drugs absolutely block stomach acid production. They appear to be safe, although approximately 2.5 percent of people may experience severe side effects. Protein pump inhibitors are metabolized in the liver via the

CP450 pathways. It may be a good idea to do a liver cleanse/detox before going onto these drugs in order to increase their effectiveness.

In 1982, Australian physician Barry Marshall discovered the presence of a bacteria, Helicobacter pylori (H. pylori), between the stomach lining and the mucous membrane. This bacteria is found in 80 percent of people with duodenal and stomach ulcers and with gastritis. H. pylori is found in about 30 percent of people, but only 10 percent will experience ulcers. This poses curious questions: Why do some people have Helicobacter infection, yet no GI upset? Do some people have a genetic predisposition to ulcers when exposed to Helicobacter? Will the others be candidates for ulcers and gastritis later on? We don't know yet.

Ten percent of people with ulcers and gastritis do not have Helicobacter pylori infection, nor have they used NSAID medications. For these people, the cause of ulcers and gastritis is still a mystery. Looking at stress, diet, and lifestyle in these people may yield important clues.

What is known is that when H. pylori is eradicated, ulcers heal and don't recur. It's important to treat diagnosed Helicobacter infections; long-term infection increases the risk of duodenal or gastric ulcers, asymptomatic chronic gastritis, chronic indigestion, and stomach cancer. The most common therapies used by physicians are called triple therapies, and consist of the use of an antibiotic or antiparasitic drug, an H2 blocker or protein-pump inhibitor, and bismuth. Your doctor will choose the specific medications that will be most effective and most cost-effective. These short-term therapies are quite effective at eradicating Helicobacter pylori infections. Despite treatment, 20 percent of people have a relapse of their ulcer within six months without aggravation from NSAID medications. Bismuth is an elemental mineral which protects the stomach lining by protecting the mucous membrane from being dissolved by pepsin. Although this treatment has minor side effects, the overall outcome shows improved quality of living and less psychological stress after therapy.

Because ulcers have been experienced throughout history, people have found effective natural therapies. Most physicians are not aware of these therapies, but nutritionally oriented physicians have been using them with promising results. For example, Leo Galland, M.D., has been using a combination of antibiotic therapy and bismuth, with DGL licorice, citrus seed extract, goldenseal, activated charcoal, and aloe vera. Dietary recommendations for people with ulcers may be useful. Low-fiber diets may contribute significantly to ulcers. A South African physician, G. Borok, studied over a thousand patients with ulcers, and concluded that elimination of refined sugars, white-flour products, milled maize, chocolate, fries, soft drinks, and desserts will reduce gastric irritation. He also suggests avoiding tea and coffee. A recent study on the diet of people with duodenal ulcers found that people who had good vitamin A intake, followed a high-fiber diet, and ate seven or more servings of fruits and vegetables per day, rather than three servings or less, reduced risks of developing ulcers by 54 percent, 45 percent, and 33 percent, respectively. Again, this shows that a great diet can reduce your risk of all sorts of health problems.

Gastritis: Gastritis is a stomach inflammation without an ulcer or sore. It's usually caused by medications, including corticosteroids, NSAIDs, cancer drugs, and antibiotics; drinking alcoholic beverages; organ failure; and severe stress or trauma. Common symptoms of gastritis include hiccups, loss of appetite, indigestion, nausea, vomiting, vomiting of blood, and dark stools. It is common in the elderly, affecting 20 percent of people between the ages of sixty and sixty-nine, and 40 percent of people over age eighty. The lack of hydrochloric acid secretion in the elderly allows for bacterial growth, such as *H. pylori*; however, when treated with antibiotics, symptoms improve.

Long-term effects of gastritis include poor vitamin B_{12}

status in all people. Signs of B_{12} deficiency often mimic those of senility. Many people have B_{12} deficiencies with normal serum B_{12} levels. More sophisticated tests of B_{12} status are available, such as homocysteine and methylmalonic acid.

Atropic gastritis is usually treated with H2 blockers or protein-pump inhibitors. Looking at triggers, such as stress, medications, and poor HCl production is also important for prevention.

One new therapy to watch is the use of lactoferrin, or cow's colostrum, for eradication of *H. pylori*. Research is unclear at this point, but it appears that lactoferrin is effective at killing *H. pylori* bacteria but also that people with high levels of gastritis and *Helicobacter* also have high levels of lactoferrin in their stomach. Is the lactoferrin helping the *H. pylori* gain a foothold and helping it gain necessary iron for its metabolism? Or is the lactoferrin called in by the body's immune system to help rid us of the bacteria? At this point, I'm not sure, but soon the research will lead us to an answer.

FUNCTIONAL LABORATORY TESTING

Helicobacter pylori test.

HEALING OPTIONS

Water: One very simple remedy for ulcers and gastritis is to drink huge amounts of water. Drink four to six glasses of water during the pain, and the pain may magically disappear. A fascinating book on this subject is *Your Body's Many Cries for Water*, by F. Batmanghelidj, M.D. Drink at least eight to ten glasses of water each day.

Licorice: DGL (deglycyrrhized) licorice helps heal the stomach mucus lining by increasing healing prostaglandins that promote mucus secretion and cell proliferation. Licorice enhances the blood flow and health of intestinal tract cells. It's important to use DGL licorice to avoid side effects caused by whole licorice. Dosage: Chew two to four tablets three times daily.

Aloe vera: Aloe vera is a folk remedy for ulcers and has been approved by the FDA for use in oral ulcers. It is soothing and healing to mucous membranes.

Gamma-oryzanol: Gamma-oryzanol, a compound found in rice bran oil, is a useful therapeutic tool in gastritis, ulcers, and irritable bowel syndrome. It acts on the autonomic nervous system to normalize production of gastric juice and has also been shown to be effective in normalizing serum triglycerides and cholesterol, symptoms of menopause, and depressive disorders. Studies involving 375 hospitals in Japan indicate that gamma-oryzanol was effective in reducing symptoms from 80 to 90 percent, with over half of the participants experiencing total or marked improvement. Typical dosage was 100 milligrams three times daily for three weeks. Occasionally the dosage was doubled, and often the therapy was used longer. Minimal side effects were experienced by 0.4 percent of the people.

Rice bran oil is widely used in Asia as a cooking and salad oil and is available in the United States at some gourmet stores. Dosage: 100 milligrams of gamma-oryzanol three times daily for a trial period of three to six weeks.

Cabbage juice: Cabbage juice is a long-standing folk remedy for heartburn. Dosage: Drink 1 quart of cabbage juice daily for a trial period of two weeks.

Glutamine: Glutamine is the most popular antiulcer drug in Asia today. The digestive tract uses glutamine as a fuel source and for healing. It is effective for healing stomach ulcers, irritable bowel syndrome, and ulcerative bowel diseases. Dosage: Begin with 8 grams daily for a trial period of four weeks.

Grapefruit or citrus seed extract: Citrus seed extract has widely effective antiparasitic, antiviral, and antibiotic properties. Dosage: 75–250 milligrams three times daily.

Goldenseal: Goldenseal is soothing to mucus membranes, enhances immune function, and has antibiotic and antifungal properties.

Sano-Gastril: Sano-Gastril is a chewable tablet which buffers the acidity of the stomach. (Sano-Gastril is marketed in this country by Nutri-Cology/Allergy Research Group; this is not an endorsement, but the only product of its type.) Sano-Gastril is composed of an extract called glycine-max and a specific strain of *Lactobacillus acidophillus* plus vitamin C and other nutrients. A study using two tablets three times daily was done on ninety-three people with ulcers and gastritis. After one month each participant was X-rayed to see progress. At that time twelve out of twenty-two people with gastric ulcer, twenty-five out of fifty-eight people with duodenal ulcer, and four out of twelve people with gastritis were completely healed. Two tablets of Sano-Gastril three times daily before meals relieved heartburn completely within five to ten minutes in 76 percent of 158 people.

Slippery elm bark: Slippery elm bark has demulcent properties and has been a folk remedy for both heartburn and ulcers. It can be used in large amounts without harm. Drink as a tea, chew on the bark, or take in capsules. Recipe for tea: Simmer 1 teaspoon of slippery elm bark in two cups of water for twenty minutes and strain. Sweeten if you want, and drink freely. Dosage: two to four capsules three times daily for a trial period of three weeks.

Evening primrose oil: Evening primrose oil increases the levels of prostaglandin E2 series, which promotes healing and repair. Dosage: 1,000–2,000 milligrams three times a day for a trial period of four weeks.

Flax: Low dietary intake of the essential fatty acid linoleic acid has been associated with duodenal ulcers. Flaxseeds and oil are excellent sources of linoleic acid. A benefit to using ground flaxseeds rather than the oil is that the mucous portion of the flaxseed buffers excess acid, which makes it ideal for inflammation in the stomach and throughout the gastrointestinal tract. Linoleic acid is also found in pumpkin seeds, tofu, walnuts, safflower oil, sunflower seeds and oil, and sesame seeds and oil. Dosage: 2 to 3 teaspoons Flaxseed oil goes rancid in a matter of weeks. Store it in the freezer to keep it fresh.

Zinc: Zinc increases the rate of healing and can prevent damage to the stomach lining. Dosage: 50–100 milligrams daily.

Vitamin A: Vitamin A is protective and promotes healing of gastric ulcers. Dosage: 10,000–25,000 IU daily. Daily short-term treatment dosage may be 50,000–75,000 IU for up to three weeks. Pregnant women should not exceed 10,000 IU vitamin A.

Other important nutrients: Copper, 2 milligrams daily; vitamin E, 400 IU daily; B-comlex; N-acetylcysteine.

PANCREAS

The pancreas has three main functions in the body: to neutralize stomach acid, to produce digestive enzymes, and to produce insulin to regulate blood-sugar levels. When food passes from the stomach to the duodenum, the pancreas secretes bicarbonates. This is essentially baking soda which neutralizes the acidity of chyme so that it won't burn the internal tissues of the intestines. The pancreas also secretes enzymes which digest carbohydrates, protein, and fats. Proteins are broken down by these molecules into single amino acids. When protease enzymes are doing their job, they also protect us from allergic reactions caused by protein particles being absorbed into the bloodstream which trigger an antigenic response. Poor production of pancreatic juice is called pancreatic insufficiency.

The signs of pancreatic insufficiency include gas, indigestion, bloating, discomfort, undigested food in our stools, undigested fat in our stools, and food sensitivities. It is common in people with candidiasis or parasite infections and is an underlying cause of hypoglycemia. Pancreatic insufficiency also increases as we age. People with pancreatitis and cystic fibrosis have pancreatic insufficiency. Stool testing by complete digestive stool analysis provides an indirect measure of pancreatic function by measuring chymotrypsin, a pancreatic enzyme for digestion of protein, and by measuring how well you are able to digest meats and vegetables. The Chymex test is also a measure of pancreatic activity.

Causes of pancreatic insufficiency are stress (mental and physical), nutritional deficiencies, poor diet, eating only cooked foods, exposure to radiation or toxins, hereditary weaknesses, drugs, and infections.

FUNCTIONAL LABORATORY TESTING

1. Comprehensive digestive stool analysis (CDSA).
2. Chymex testing for pancreatic function.
3. Food allergies—IgE.; food sensitivities—IgG or IgG4.

HEALING OPTIONS

Eat in a relaxed manner.

Chew your food thoroughly.

Limit beverage intake with meals: Drinking liquids at meals dilutes the gastric juices in the stomach and pancreatic juice in the small intestines.

Pancreatic enzyme supplements: Clinical experience shows that pancreatic enzymes work well as a digestive aid. Glandular-based supplements, like pancreatic enzyme preparations, are directed to specific tissues, helping to initiate repair. Pancreatic enzymes also help restore the balance of GI flora. In studies done on monkeys, it was shown that pancreatic enzymes were able to kill *Clostridium*, *Bacteroides*,

Pseudomonaceae, Enterobacter, E. coli, and *Klebsiella.* Continued use of pancreatic enzymes can help with repair and maintenance of pancreatic tissue.

Pancreatic tissue from pigs has been widely used over the past fifty years to supply missing pancreatic enzymes. You can purchase products from health food stores or ask your physician to prescribe them. The United States Pharmacopoeia (USP) regulates the strength of pancreatic enzymes. For best results use a preparation that is 4x to 10x. Dosage: one to two tablets/capsules at the beginning of meals.

Vegetable enzymes: For people who would rather have a vegetarian alternative to pancreatic enzymes, vegetable enzymes are a suitable option. These enzymes are derived from a fungus called *Aspergillus oryzae* which is used to ferment soy sauce, tamari, and miso.

These enzymes work in a much wider range of pH than pancreatic enzymes, enhancing digestion in the stomach as well as in the intestines. Because they are not broken down by stomach acid, the required dosage is much smaller than that for pancreatic enzymes. Vegetable enzymes are also less likely to cause food allergy reactions. Some companies include probiotic bacteria in daily supplements. Dosage: one to two capsules at the beginning of meals.

GALLBLADDER

The gallbladder, a pear-shaped organ that lies just below the liver, holds bile for the liver, which produces it. The gallbladder's function is to store and concentrate bile which emulsifies fats, cholesterol, and fat-soluble vitamins by breaking them into tiny globules. These create a greater surface area for the fat-splitting enzymes (lipase) to act on for digestion. Between meals the gallbladder concentrates bile.

Gallbladder problems usually indicate poor liver function.

The liver is the most complex organ in the body. Unlike the heart which has one major function—to beat—the liver has a multitude of functions which include regulation of blood sugar levels, making 13,000 different enzymes, "humanizing" food by acting as a filter, breaking down toxins, manufacturing cholesterol and bile, breaking down hormones, and more. Because of its complexity and the 10,000 pounds of toxins it must filter over a lifetime, the liver can easily become overwhelmed.

When we eat a meal that contains fat, the liver and gallbladder are stimulated to release bile, which contains bicarbonates (baking soda) that alkalize stomach acid in the duodenum. Each day the liver secretes about a quart of bile, which is absorbed into the body from the ileum and colon and returned to the liver to be used again. Drugs and other toxins are eliminated from the liver through bile. The brown color of stool comes from the yellow color of bilirubin in bile. When you eat food containing fat, bile is released from the liver and concentrated bile is released from the gallbladder. However, people who have had their gallbladders removed don't get this burst of bile. In order to reproduce this infusion of bile, it is recommended that they take bile salts with fatty meals.

Gallstones

The most common digestive problem associated with the gallbladder is gallstones. One in five Americans over the age of sixty-five has gallstones, and half a million surgeries are performed each year for removal of the gallbladder. Women are two to four times more likely to be affected by gallstones than men. However, most people who have gallstones are never bothered by them, and doctors only treat them if they are causing problems. An inflammation of the gallbladder can lead to pain and discomfort. Symptoms can range from abdominal discomfort, bloating, belching, and food intolerances. When you have more than one stone, you may experience a sharp pain or a spasm under the ribs on the right side. Occasionally the pain will be felt under your right shoulder blade. These pains are often strongest after eating a high-fat meal.

Diet plays an important role in prevention of gallbladder disease. Low-fat, low-meat, and vegetarian diets are recommended, as is a low-sugar, high-fiber intake. In fact, a recent study of over 1,100 people found that none of the forty-eight vegetarians in the group had any gallstones at all. There was an increase in gallstones in people who were heavy coffee drinkers. Dennis Burkitt, a British M.D. who lived and worked in Africa for twenty years, found that he performed only two surgeries for gallbladder removal among Africans eating an indigenous diet.

If you are overweight, losing weight will reduce your risk of developing gallstones. Just be careful because several studies have shown that fasting and *extremely* low-fat, low-calorie diets increase your risk of developing gallstones. Fasting for more than fourteen hours raises the risk of problems due to gallstones. So easy does it while dieting; always eat breakfast.

Exercise is also important for the prevention of gallstones. It has been postulated that thirty minutes of exercise five times each week could reduce the risk of gallstones by 34 percent. In a 1998 study, men who watched less than six hours of television per week had a gallstone rate less than that of men who watched more than forty hours of television per week; this study suggests that 34 percent of the cases of symptomatic gallstone disease in men could be prevented by increasing exercise to thirty minutes of an endurance-type training, five times per week.

Medical treatment for gallstones consists of an injection of a drug that dissolves the gallstones, oral medication to dissolve stones, lithotripsy which breaks stones with sound waves, or surgical removal of the gallbladder.

Physicians familiar with natural therapies have favorable results treating gallstones without use of drugs or surgery by having their patients detoxify the liver and strengthen liver function. Metabolic cleansing or other detoxification programs are a critical first step in treatment. Food sensitivities also play an important role in the development of gallstones—most patients with gallbladder disease have them and they must be identified.

FUNCTIONAL LABORATORY TESTING

1. Liver function profile.
2. Home test for bowel transit time.
3. IaG or IgG4 testing for food sensitivities and IgE testing for food allergies.
4. Heidleburg capsule test for levels of hydrochloric acid production.

HEALING OPTIONS

Low-fat diet: Low-fat diets help prevent gallstones and also reduce pain and inflammation associated with gallstones. Saturated fats found in dairy products, meats, coconut oil, palm oil, hydrogenated oils, and vegetable shortening stimulate concentration of bile. While a low-fat diet is optimal, essential fatty acids are vital to gallbladder function and overall health. Make sure you get 1–2 tablespoons of uncooked expeller pressed oils or extra virgin olive oil each day—the easiest way is in salad dressing.

Low-sugar diet: Several studies have indicated that people who consume a lot of sweets are more likely to develop gallstones.

Decrease coffee intake: Coffee may trigger gallbladder attacks in susceptible people. Use of either regular or decaffeinated coffee raised levels of cholecystokinin and caused gallbladder contractions. Stop drinking coffee and see what effect this produces. Some people get horrible headaches or flulike symptoms when they withdraw from caffeine. If you do, wean yourself gradually.

Vegetarian diets: Vegetarian diets have been found to be helpful in reducing the incidence of gallbladder disease.

Eat breakfast: Fasting for more than fourteen hours raises your risk of problems due to gallstones.

Reduce bowel transit time: People with gallstones have significantly slower transit times than healthy people. Eat more high-fiber foods and drink more fluids.

Drink six to eight glasses of water every day!

Rule out food sensitivities: In 1968, Breneman found that food sensitivities play a role in gallbladder disease. He put sixty-nine patients on an elimination diet consisting of beef, rye, soy, rice, cherry, peach, apricot, beet, and spinach. After three to five days, all people were symptom-free. With a slow reintroduction of foods they were sensitive to, symptoms returned. The most common food offenders were eggs (3 percent), pork (64 percent), and onions (52 percent). What's interesting about this study is that beef and soy are often trigger foods for food sensitivity reactions.

Rule out deficient levels of hydrochloric acid: In a *Lancet* study, about half of the people with gallstones had insufficient levels of hydrochloric acid. A Heidleburg capsule test can determine if you have sufficient levels of hydrochloric acid. You can also take HCl supplements with meals. Begin with one 500 milligrams capsule of HCl with 150 milligrams of pepsin. If you don't need the HCl, you'll experience a burning or warm sensation. If this is uncomfortable, you can drink some milk or a teaspoon of baking soda in water to neutralize the acid. Many people with low-acid secretion need several HCl tablets per meal; increase the dosage slowly to find the correct one for you. Too much will cause a warmth or burning sensation.

Milk thistle/silymarin (*Silybum marianum*): Extracts of the herb milk thistle have been used historically since the fifteenth century for ailments of the liver and gallbladder. It helps normalize liver function, detoxify the liver, which it does gently and thoroughly, and improves the solubility of bile. Silymarin promotes the flow of bile and helps tone the spleen, gallbladder, and liver. Dosage: Three to six 175 milligram capsules daily of standardized 80 percent milk thistle extract with water before meals.

Lipotrophic supplement: Lipotrophic supplements contain substances which help normalize liver and gallbladder functions. They may contain dandelion root, milk thistle, lecithin, or phosphatidyl choline, methionine, choline, inositol, vitamin C, black radish, beet greens, artichoke leaves (*Cynara sclymus*), turmeric, boldo (*Peumus boldo*), fringe tree (*Chioanthus virginicus*), greater celandine, and ox bile. Lipotrophics may also contain magnesium and B-complex vitamins (B_6, B_{12}, and folate) to enhance their function. Dosage: Use as directed on the label. Use 1,000 milligrams each of methionine and choline daily.

Lecithin: Phosphatidyl choline, the most biologically active form of lecithin, and lecithin have been shown to make cholesterol more soluble, which reduces formation of gallstones. Studies have shown that as little as 100 milligrams of lecithin three times daily will increase lecithin concentration in bile. Dosage: 500 milligrams daily.

Vitamin C: Vitamin C has been shown to prevent formation of gallstones. Vitamin C is required for the enzymatic conversion of cholesterol to bile salts. People with high risk to developing gallstones have low ascorbic acid levels. Dosage: 1–3 grams daily.

Liver/gallbladder flush: Anecdotal stories about people showing up at their doctor's office with a jar full of stones after a gallbladder flush are abundant, but there is little documentation to validate whether what they passed are really gallstones or just congealed olive oil. Nonetheless many people testify to the benefits of the gallbladder flush. Do this procedure at home *only* under the supervision of a physician.

From Monday through Saturday, drink as much natural apple juice as possible. Continue to eat normally and take your usual medications or supplements. On Saturday eat a normal lunch at noon. Three hours later (3 P.M.) dissolve 1 tablespoon of Epsom salts (magnesium sulphate) in ¼ cup of warm water and drink it. This is a laxative and helps peristalsis move the stones through your digestive system. It doesn't taste great so you may want to follow it with some orange or grapefruit juice. Two hours later (5 P.M.) repeat the Epsom salts and orange or grapefruit juice. For dinner eat citrus fruits or drink citrus juices. At bedtime, drink ½ cup of warm extra virgin olive oil blended with ½ cup of lemon juice. Go to bed immediately and lie on your right side with your knees pulled up close to your chest for half an hour. On Sunday morning take 1 tablespoon of Epsom salts in ¼ cup of warm water an hour before breakfast. If you have gallstones, you will find dark green to light green stones in your bowel movement on Sunday morning. They are irregular in shape and size, varying from small like kiwi seeds to large like cherry pits. If you have chronic gallbladder problems, you may want to repeat this again in two weeks. This can be repeated every three to six months if you continue to form stones.

Bile salts: These are useful for people who have already had their gallbladders removed. Dosage: one to two with fatty meals.

SMALL INTESTINE

The most common symptoms of small intestinal problems are gas and bloating. When you are having digestive discomfort, it is important to rule out candidiasis, food sensitivities, pancreatic insufficiency, parasites, and small bowel bacterial overgrowth, which may be underlying causes of gas and bloating. Use of digestive supplements and beneficial flora can also be helpful.

Flatulence/Intestinal Gas

Everyone has gas. It's normal. In fact, we "pass gas" an average of ten to fifteen times a day. Most of our gas comes from swallowed air. Chewing gum, drinking carbonated drinks, and whipped foods like egg whites and whipped cream all contribute to swallowed air. The gas we pass is mainly nitrogen (up to 90 percent), carbon dioxide, and oxygen, which are odorless. Gas and bloating are also a product of the fermentation of small pieces of undigested foods by the bacteria in our intestines. Fermentation produces stinky gases like methane and hydrogen sulfide, which has the odor of rotten eggs. Other substances, like butyric acid, cadaverine, and putrescine are present in tiny amounts, but they are noted for the mighty fragrance they give to gas.

Some of us experience excessive amounts of gas, which can be not only embarrassing but also an uncomfortable sign that something is out of balance. Millions of people have bloating and discomfort associated with gas. If you've ever made wine, you'll recall putting a balloon on the top during the fermentation process that allowed for expansion of the gasses produced. Our bellies act like a balloon, expanding to contain the gas produced by fermentation.

Foods from the cabbage family, dried and sulfured fruits, and beans all contain sulfur which gives gas a rotten egg odor, but sulfur also has critical usage throughout our bodies. Cucumbers, celery, apples, carrots, onions, and garlic are all commonly known to cause gas. People with lactose intolerance experience gas when they eat dairy products. Eating a high fiber diet is healthful, but your intestinal flora need to adjust gradually to these dietary changes. You may have insufficient levels of hydrochloric acid, intestinal flora, pancreatic enzymes, or a dysbiosis which is causing your problems. Food sensitivities, especially to wheat and grains, can also cause excessive gas.

Functional Laboratory Testing

1. Small bowel bacterial overgrowth test.
2. Complete digestive and stool analysis with parasitology.
3. IgE and IgG allergy testing.
4. Lactose breath test.

Healing Options

Chew your food well and eat slowly: These simple activities can have far reaching effects on healthy digestive processes and gas reduction.

High-fiber diet: Most of us need to dramatically increase the amount of dietary fiber we eat, but raising these levels too quickly can cause a lot of gas and discomfort. Our flora go wild with sudden increases in dietary fiber, and the fermentation of these fibers causes gas. Increasing your fiber intake more slowly will solve this problem. High-fiber foods include whole grains, beans, and many fruits and vegetables.

Cooking beans: Beans are an excellent source of vegetarian protein, containing both soluble and insoluble fibers, and sitosterols that help normalize cholesterol levels. However, beans are notorious for their gas-producing effects. They contain substances which are difficult for us to digest. For instance, beans, grains, and seeds hold their nutrients with phytic acid. Soaking or sprouting releases the nutrients so that we can absorb more of them. First, soak the beans for four to twelve hours, then drain off the water, replace with new water, and simmer for several hours until they are soft. Some people find that putting a pinch or two of baking soda in the water helps reduce gas. Others add kombu, a Japanese sea vegetable, or ginger. Beano is an enzyme product that contains the enzymes necessary for digestion of beans. Place a drop or two on your food; it really helps reduce flatulence. Beano is sold widely in drug and health food stores.

We produce digestive enzymes for foods we commonly eat. If you eat beans rarely, start by eating a tablespoon or two of beans each day. Your body may begin to produce the enzymes necessary for their digestion.

Lactose intolerance: The inability to digest lactose, the sugar in milk, is a frequent cause of gas. Eliminate all dairy products for at least two weeks and see if there is improvement. Make sure to eliminate all hidden dairy products found in foods. These are listed in the section on lactose intolerance in chapter 7.

Food sensitivities: Although lactose intolerance is the most common food sensitivity, people can be sensitive to nearly any other food. The most likely culprits are sugars and grains. Careful charting of your foods and flatulence levels can help you detect which foods are giving you the most trouble.

Food sensitivities don't usually exist by themselves. If you have a number of food sensitivities, check for *Candida* infection and dysbiosis.

Fermentation dysbiosis: An imbalance of intestinal flora often causes excessive gas. *Candida* fungi cause fermentation of sugars, fruits, and starches which we feel as gas and bloating. A comprehensive digestive and stool analysis, or small bowel bacterial overgrowth test, can determine whether or not you have a *Candida* infection or other dysbiotic imbalance.

Digestive insufficiencies/intestinal flora and enzyme supplementation: Many people find that supplementation with digestive enzymes at meals, either vegetable or pancreatic enzymes, plus probiotic supplements containing acidophillus and bifidobacteria, really help prevent gas. Dosage: one to two digestive enzymes with meals.

Acidophilus and bifidobacteria: Use of beneficial bacteria supplementally can make a tremendous difference in your ability to digest foods. Beneficial flora can help reestablish the normal microbial balance in your intestinal tract. Dosage: one to two capsules or ¼ to ½ teaspoon powder two to three times daily on an empty stomach. Mix powdered supplement with a cool or cold beverage; hot drinks kill the flora.

Avoid Sorbitol and Xylitol: Sorbitol and xylitol are undigestible sugars found in most sugarless candy and gum. They are used by diabetics and dieters because these sugars are sweet but don't affect blood sugar levels. Large amounts of sorbitol and xylitol cause gas, but even small amounts can cause a problem in people who are sensitive.

Parasites: Parasites often cause gas and bloating. If you have explored more obvious causes, you may want to have a stool test for parasites.

Chlorophyll: Chlorophyll liquid or tablets can help prevent gas. Take two to three times daily with meals.

Ginger, fennel, and anise: Most of us have at least one of these spices in our kitchen, and they are valuable tools for reducing gas. Put a few slices of fresh ginger or ½ teaspoon of dried ginger in a cup of boiling water and steep until cool enough to drink. It will soon begin to dispel your gas from both ends, and you'll be much more comfortable. Fennel and anise can be used in tea or simply chew on the seeds to relieve gas. In Indian restaurants, you find small bowls of these seeds. They also cleanse the palate with their sweet pungency.

Herbs and herbal teas: Traditionally herbs and spices were added to foods to aid digestion. Nearly all our common kitchen herbs and spices have a beneficial effect, including basil, oregano, marjoram, parsley, thyme, celery seed, peppermint, spearmint, fennel, bayberries, caraway seed, cardamom seed, catnip, cloves, coriander, lemon balm, and sarsaparilla. You can find many digestive herbal tea blends in health food stores.

Parasites

Some symptoms of parasites appear to be like any other digestive problem. Chronic diarrhea is often a sign of a parasitic infection. Other symptoms include pain, constipation, bloating, gas, unexplained weight loss, fatigue, unexplained fever, coughing, itching, rashes, bloody stools, abdominal cramping, joint and muscle aches, irritable bowel syndrome, anemia, allergy, granulomas, nervousness, teeth grinding, chronic fatigue, poor immune response, and sleep disturbances. These symptoms can come and go due to the life cycles of the specific parasite involved.

If your anus itches at night, you may have pinworms. They are most commonly found in children and parents of small children. It's fairly simple to determine whether or not you have pinworms: When you feel the itching, put a piece of cellophane tape on your anus, and examine the tape for small white wiggly worms that look like white pieces of thread that move! Or you can simply put your finger into your anus and see if you pull out any worms. With children, you can use tape or just look.

Recently there have been references in the scientific literature which suggest that parasites may be the primary cause of allergies. Parasites cause damage to the lining of the digestive tract which allows large molecules to enter the bloodstream. This provokes an antigenic response. This theory is revolutionary and additional research needs to be done to determine just how large a role parasites play in allergies.

PARASITE TESTING

Many physicians request parasitology testing on random stool samples, but this type of testing is not very accurate. Even with repeated samples, accurate results are found only 85 to 90 percent of the time. Many parasites, like Giardia, live farther up the digestive tract so that many labs now give an oral laxative to induce diarrhea when testing for parasites. This type of sample is called a stool purge.

Other parasites are found by using a rectal swab rather than a stool sample. Because some parasites generally live in the mucous membranes that line the intestinal tract rather than in the feces, a rectal swab enables a physician to collect a sample of the mucus. Stool purge tests and rectal swabs used with random stool samples give a much more accurate picture of colon health than single or multiple random stool samples. Many labs collect a random stool sample, a purge stool sample or two, and a rectal swab. The most accurate stool testing is usually done by labs that specialize in parasitology testing. Due to the high volume of samples, high-tech microscopes, and slow pace, their staff have become experts in detection and recognition of parasites.

HEALING OPTIONS

Prescription medication may be the most efficient treatment for most parasite infections. Within a week or two you are parasite-free. However, these medications can be hard on the liver and disruptive to the intestinal flora. After using them, it's wise to take acidophilus and bifidobacteria to replace and rebalance the intestinal flora.

Natural options work more slowly—about a month—but are highly effective. They generally contain garlic, wormwood (artemesia), goldenseal, black walnut, and/or grapefruit seed extract. Acidophillus and bifidobacteria should be replaced after therapy is finished.

Garlic: Historically, garlic has been used for pinworms; it has antiviral, antibacterial, and antifungal properties. Allicin, the active component in garlic, has been shown to be effective against *Entamoeba histolytica* and *Giardia lambia*. *Entamoeba histolytica* is an amoeba which has been used to evaluate the value of antiamoeba drugs.

Goldenseal: Goldenseal has been used historically to balance infections of mucous membranes throughout the body. It is also effective with *Candida* infections. Berberine sulfate, an active ingredient in goldenseal, has been shown to be effective against amoebas and giardia parasites.

Artemisia annua/wormwood: Wormwood has been used for centuries in China and Europe for worms and parasites.

It contains sesquiterpene lactone which works like peroxide. It is believed to affect the parasite membranes, weakening them so our natural defense system kicks in. Artemisia also contains an ingredient which is effective against malaria even when it is resistant to quinine drugs. Tea of wormwood has been successfully used for pinworms and roundworms by Dr. Christopher, one of America's foremost herbalists. Caution: Artemisia is safe when used in a tea or capsule, but pure wormwood oil is poisonous. Dosage: ¼ to ½ teaspoon powdered wormwood once or twice daily or make a tea using 2 teaspoons of fresh leaves or tops in 1 cup water. Drink ½ cup a day, one teaspoon at a time.

Black walnut: The juice of unripe, green hulls of black walnuts has been traditionally used for treatment of parasites and fungal infections. Black walnut is a folk remedy for ringworm, athlete's foot, and healing cracks in the palms and feet.

Dichroea febrifuga (Saxifragaceae): Dichroea is a Chinese herb called Changshan which is effective against malaria, amoebas, and giardia.

Jerusalem oak/American wormseed/chenopodium anthelminticum: A folk medicine used throughout the Americas, the Jerusalem Oak expels roundworms, hookworms, and tapeworms, and is especially useful for children. More scientific studies need to be done to confirm the historical usage of this herb.

Pumpkin seeds: Pumpkin seeds have also been used historically as a folk medicine for tapeworms and roundworms. In order to be really effective, enormous amounts must be eaten: 7–14 ounces for children and up to 25 ounces for adults. Mash them and mix with juice. Two or three hours afterward, take castor oil to clear your bowels.

Celiac Disease/Sprue/Gluten Intolerance

Celiac disease, also called celiac sprue or gluten sensitive enteropathy, is caused by an inability to properly digest foods containing gluten. It is a permanent condition. Gluten is found in many grains including wheat, oats, rye, barley, and spelt. The gliadin fraction in the gluten is believed to be the cause of the problem. In susceptible people, gluten-containing grains damage the lining of the small intestine. Because people with celiac disease do not absorb nutrients well, they are likely to become malnourished. Celiac disease is chronic, has a genetic component, and may affect several family members. It occurs about twice as often in women as in men and mainly affects people of northwestern European ancestry. It rarely occurs among people of African, Jewish, Mediterranean, or Asian descent.

Some people have celiac disease without symptoms, while others can be very ill. Symptoms are characterized by recurring attacks of diarrhea or constipation, abdominal cramping, gas, weakness, and steatorrhea (gray or tan fatty stools). Less common symptoms are arthritis, fatigue, brain-fog, bone pain, schizophrenia, fibromyalgia, depression, and epilepsy. Celiac disease is usually recognized early in childhood, but may disappear in adolescence and reappear later in adulthood. Anemia is common in people with celiac disease. A recent pediatric study showed that half of the people tested were anemic, and a small percentage of children with anemia really had undiagnosed celiac disease. Other long term consequences of celiac disease can be diminished calcium reserves and poor fat-soluble vitamin status, which includes vitamins A, D, E, and K.

About half of all people with celiac disease are also lactose intolerant at the time of their diagnosis (see page 210 on lactose intolerance). Lactase, the enzyme required to split lactose, is manufactured at the tips of the villi. Because these villi are damaged in people with untreated celiac disease, their bodies can't manufacture the lactase. Once people have gone onto a gluten-free diet and the intestinal lining is repaired, a few will be able to tolerate dairy products. Remember that about 70 percent of us are lactose intolerant, so many people with controlled celiac disease will still be affected by dairy products.

Therapeutics consist of avoiding grains which contain gluten; that stops the irritation to the gut and allows it to heal.

Many people find quick relief in three to four days, although complete healing of the intestines will take longer. Nutritional therapies may help you heal faster. If you don't feel better in four to six weeks, you need to investigate other possibilities that may be delaying your healing. Because of the malnourishment that celiac can cause, supplementation of nutrients is necessary.

It's not easy to completely change your diet to avoid all gluten-containing foods. Americans depend on a wheat-based diet and many other foods that have gluten-containing grains. In addition to obvious sources of gluten, many products have hidden sources. Salad dressings, some hot dogs, ice cream, bouillon cubes, chocolate, and foods containing hydrolyzed vegetable protein may contain gluten. Fortunately, because of the many people who are intolerant of gluten, more gluten-free products are being introduced into the marketplace. Excellent breads, pastas, crackers, pancake mixes, cereals, and cookies are now available. A new home test kit may soon be on the market which can help you determine which foods contain gluten. People with celiac disease are often lactose intolerant as well and should avoid dairy products, but this is usually temporary and resolves as they heal.

While celiac disease was previously thought to be rare, new studies indicate that many people without obvious symptoms have subclinical celiac disease. According to analysis of IgG and IgA blood testing, an estimated 1 person in 258 may have celiac disease. Other studies place its incidence at 1 person in 1,000 to 5,000. What makes these figures so different? It appears that there are several types of gluten sensitivity: celiac disease, tropical sprue (caused by an infection or toxin and treated with antibiotics), and gluten sensitivity (caused by leaky gut syndrome). While symptoms may be similar for these problems, the treatments vary considerably. People with celiac disease must avoid gluten-containing foods for life. People with tropical sprue are generally treated with antibiotics and over time are able to use gluten-containing grains without further problems. People with wheat and/or gluten sensitivity often find that after avoidance of those foods for four to six months and a nutritional program that supports healing and friendly flora, they can then begin eating grain products without further problems.

FUNCTIONAL LABORATORY TESTING

1. Antigliadin antibody test and the rectal gluten challenge test: Diagnosis is usually made by excluding other possibilities and then performing an intestinal biopsy. New tests, such as the antigliadin antibody test (AGA) that determines celiac disease and the rectal gluten challenge test that determines gluten sensitivity, are useful without being invasive. Italian research has also found two additional tests to be accurate: the antijejunum antibody test (JAB) and the antiendomysium test (EMA). Both blood tests are not yet available in the United States.

2. Food allergy/sensitivity screening: Test for wheat, oats, rye, barley, gluten, and gliadin; IgE and IgG antibody testing are all required. Gluten antibodies are positive in people with celiac disease and gluten intolerance. IgA levels are also higher in people with celiac disease, but a negative test does not always rule it out. Additional food sensitivities are likely.

3. Intestinal permeability screening: Test for leaky gut/intestinal hyperpermeability.

4. Iron status/nutrient status: Celiac disease causes malabsorption of nutrients. Many people with celiac disease have iron deficiency anemia, low vitamin A, D, E, and K, poor fat absorption, and other mineral deficiencies. Several labs have tests which help determine which nutrients need supplementation.

5. Comprehensive digestive and stool analysis with parasitology: This test can be used to determine if there is an unidentified underlying cause of the celiac disease.

6. Rule out lactose intolerance: The lactose breath test determines lactose intolerance. Elimination of dairy products from your diet also helps determine if dairy products are contributing to your problem.

HEALING OPTIONS

Diet: Avoid all gluten-containing grains and products that contain them, even in small amounts. Gluten-containing grains include wheat, rye, barley, oats, millet, and spelt. It is essential to read all labels carefully and become an expert at reading between the lines.

FOODS WHICH MAY CONTAIN HIDDEN GLIADIN

Texturized vegetable protein: It may contain *wheat* along with soy or corn.

Barley malt.

Starch (when listed in the ingredient list): If it doesn't say "corn-starch," it may contain gluten.

Desserts: Ice cream cones, ice cream which contains gluten stabilizers, most cakes, cookies, and muffins.

Meats: Luncheon meats, hot-dogs, and sausages may contain grains. Self-basting turkeys contain hydrolyzed vegetable protein which may contain gluten.

Cheese and dairy: Some processed cheeses contain wheat flour and/or oat gum.

Pasta: Most pasta is wheat. Semolina is a type of wheat which contains a high level of gluten. You can find gluten-free pasta at gourmet and health food stores.

Miscellaneous (some brands contain gliadin): Curry powder, most white pepper, dry seasoning mixes, gravy mixes and extracts, meat condiments, catsup, chewing gum, pie fillings, baked beans, baking powders, salad dressings, sandwich spreads, museli, cereals, instant coffee, breadcrumbs, vanilla and flavorings made with alcohol, and most dips.

Digestive enzymes: Either pancreatic or vegetable enzymes can be used to enhance digestive function. Dosage: one to two with each meal. Specific amylase enzymes can be of particular benefit.

Acidophilus/bifidobacteria: Probiotic flora enhance digestive function.

Gut-healing nutrients: Glutamine, gamma-oryzanol, and N-acetyl-D-glucosamine are all healing to the intestinal lining. While no specific testing has been done on therapeutic use of these nutrients in people with celiac disease, clinical experience with celiac and other diarrheal illnesses indicates their usefulness.

Multivitamin with minerals: Zinc, selenium, folic acid, iron, and vitamins A, B_6, D, E, and K have all been shown to be deficient in people with celiac disease. Get a good quality multiple vitamin with minerals. Look for a supplement that is hypoallergenic and contains no grains or dairy.

COLON/LARGE INTESTINE

Common problems in the large intestine, also called the colon, include constipation, diarrhea, diverticular disease, irritable bowel syndrome, inflammatory bowel disease, ulcerative colitis, Crohn's disease, hemorrhoids, polyps, and colon cancer. Proper functioning of the colon requires a high-fiber diet. The colon is home to trillions of beneficial bifidobacteria and other flora that ferment dietary fiber which, in turn, produces short-chained fatty acids, butyric acid, valerate, propionic acid, and acetic acid. These short-chained fatty acids are the primary fuel of the colonic cells. Without adequate fiber, we starve the colonic cells and weaken the integrity of the colon. Butyric acid has been shown to stop the growth of colon cancer cells in vitro and is used clinically to heal inflamed bowel tissue.

The colon's main function is the reabsorption of nutrients and water into our bodies and the elimination of toxic wastes. Adequate intake of liquids is essential for good colon health. Water, juices, herbal teas, and fresh fruits contain liquids that are hydrating to the stool. Coffee, alcohol, and soft drinks are more diuretic, which increases our need for healthful fluids.

Constipation

Constipation affects 4 million Americans each year. Physicians write more than a million prescriptions for constipation annually, and we spend $725 million a year on laxatives. Constipation is a big problem! People are constipated when they strain to have a bowel movement, have hard stools, infrequent or incomplete bowel movements, discomfort, or a perception that bowel habits are different from usual. Some people feel fatigue, achiness, and mental sluggishness from constipation; others get headachy. Constipation affects women twice as often as men and is more common in people over age sixty-five. Although aging is commonly listed as a cause of constipation, it is due more to the results of lifestyle. Elderly people often eat low-fiber foods, rely on packaged and prepared foods, take medications that interfere with normal bowel function, and have decreased mobility. Each of these factors by itself increases the risk of chronic constipation and is not necessarily a progression of aging.

Many other factors can be the underlying cause of constipation. Hormones play a role. Women often notice that their bowel habits change at various times in their menstrual cycles. Pregnancy is a common, but temporary, cause of constipation, which can also be caused by an underactive thyroid. Some diseases can affect the body's ability to have bowel movements. Parkinson's disease, scleroderma, lupus, diabetes, kidney disease, and certain neurological or muscular diseases like multiple sclerosis can cause constipation. Colon cancer can also cause it. Neurological problems such as injuries to the spinal column, tumors that sit on nerves, nerve disorders of the bowel, and certain brain disorders are other causes.

Bowel movements should be painless. If you experience pain, see your physician. You may have a structural abnormality, fissure, hemorrhoid, or more serious problem. Pain during bowel movements can cause a muscle spasm in the sphincter which can delay a stool. Magnesium helps relieve and prevent muscle spasms.

Bowel transit time is a newer parameter of constipation that is widely used in preventive health care. Bowel transit time is the amount of time it takes for food to go from the mouth, through the digestive system, and out in stool. Reports from the National Institutes of Health suggest that a "normal" range of bowel movements is from three to twenty-one each week. While this may show what is "average," it is not a good indicator of what is "normal." It is normal to have one to three soft bowel movements each day. Optimal bowel transit time is twelve to eighteen hours, so if you are only having three bowel movements each week, you have a transit time of fifty-six hours, which is way too long. Slow bowel transit times raise the risk of colon diseases and contribute to other health problems due to the reabsorption of toxins back into the body. A recent study showed an increased risk of colon cancer in people who are chronically constipated. This makes sense in light of current theories about fecal transit time. If you haven't done the transit time self-test, now would be a good time!

Dennis Burkitt, M.D., studied bowel habits of Africans living in small towns and large cities. He found that people who ate indigenous local foods had an average of a pound of feces each day, with twelve-hour transit times. He found that people living in cities on Western diets only excreted 5 ½ ounces of stool each day, with average transit times of forty-eight to seventy-two hours. People on native diets had extremely low incidences of diseases common to Western civilization, such as appendicitis, diabetes, diverticulitis, gallstones, coronary heart disease, hiatal hernia, varicose veins, hemorrhoids, colon cancer, and obesity. When these people moved into cities and ate a Westernized diet, they too developed these diseases. Dr. Burkitt attributed much of this disease to poor dietary fiber intake in a modernized diet.

For most people, a diet high in fiber and fluids solves the problem. Be sure to drink six to eight glasses of water, juices, or herbal teas and eat at least five servings of fruits and vegetables each day. Brussels sprouts, asparagus, cabbage, cauliflower, corn, peas, kale, parsnips, and potatoes contain high amounts of fiber. Make whole grains the rule and processed grains the exception. The addition of high-fiber cereals at breakfast can make a big difference. Legumes, like kidney, navy, pinto, and lima beans, have a large amount of dietary fiber.

Make these dietary changes slowly. A quick change to a high-fiber diet can cause gas pains. As your body gets used to this new way of eating, it will adapt. Remember that the requirements for most of us are to double our daily fiber intake. Cut back on low-fiber foods, including meats, dairy products, pastries, candy, soft drinks, and white bread.

Exercise helps relieve constipation by massaging the intestines. Many of my clients have found that regular exercise keeps their bowels regular.

Overuse of laxatives is common and contributes to your problems. Chronic use of laxatives, even herbal laxatives, causes the bowels to become lazy, and the muscles become dependent on laxatives to constrict. People often find they need more and more laxatives to have the same effect. Some laxatives can cause damage to the nerve cells in the wall of the colon. If you have used laxatives, you need to retrain your body to have bowel movements on its own. Try sitting on the toilet each morning for twenty minutes and relax. Over time your body will remember how to relax and function normally.

A recent study compared the use of psyllium seeds with the use of docusate sodium, a common stool softener. The psyllium was more effective at relieving constipation than the stool softener. So use psyllium and eat more fiber!

Pay attention to your body's needs. When your body gives you the signals that it's time to defecate, stop what you are doing and go to the bathroom. When you ignore your body's urges, the rectum gets used to being stretched and fails to respond normally. Feces back up into the colon, causing discomfort. If you dislike having a bowel movement at work, school, or in a public restroom, readjust your attitude and get used to the idea. Everybody's doing it!

HEALING OPTIONS

Double your fiber intake: Fresh produce, organically grown if possible, gives life to our cells. Eat a minimum of five fruits and vegetables every day. More is better. They are rich in fiber, vitamins, minerals, trace nutrients, fluids, and vitality. Eat whole grains like whole wheat berries, oatmeal, millet, amaranth, quinoa, rye berries, and brown rice. Eat bran *or* whole grain cereals at breakfast; they can significantly boost your fiber intake in just one meal. Beans and peas are also loaded with healthful fibers. They are a low-fat protein source, and their soluble fiber and sitosterols help normalize cholesterol levels.

Psyllium seed husks: Psyllium seeds add bulk and water to stool, which allows for easy passage. Though not a laxative, psyllium seeds do regulate bowel function, are beneficial for both diarrhea and constipation, and do not cause harmful dependencies. Build up gradually to one teaspoon of psyllium with each meal to avoid gas and cramping from sudden introduction of fiber. As your dietary fiber increases, you will probably find that you no longer need psyllium seeds.

Wheat bran/corn bran: Wheat and corn bran can be used in the same way as psyllium seeds. They add bulk and moisture to stool, which allow them to pass more easily. Use 1 teaspoon with meals.

Increase fluids: Drink at least six to eight glasses of water, fruit juice, or herbal teas each day. Coffee, alcoholic beverages, and soft drinks have a dehydrating effect on the body.

Improve bowel habits: Ignoring your body's natural urge to defecate can cause constipation. Take time each morning to have a bowel movement. If you go when nature calls, it takes just a minute or two.

Stop using laxatives and enemas.

Improve bowel flora: Poor bowel flora causes the digestive system to move sluggishly. Use of antibiotics, hormones, and steroid drugs, high stress levels, and poor diet can also cause an imbalance of intestinal flora. Bifidobacteria help regulate peristalsis. Dosage: Acidophillus and bifidobacteria two to three times daily. If you are able to digest yogurt, it has a normalizing effect on the bowels and can be helpful for either constipation or diarrhea.

Magnesium: Magnesium helps keep peristalsis—rhythmic muscle relaxation and contraction—working by proper relaxation of muscles. Americans have widespread magnesium deficiency that contributes to constipation. According to recent studies, 75 percent of magnesium is lost during food processing, and 40 percent of Americans fail to meet the RDA levels for daily magnesium intake. When magnesium deficiency or a calcium/magnesium imbalance is present, poor bowel tone can occur. On the other hand, too much magnesium can cause diarrhea. Dosage: 400–500 milligrams daily.

Lactose intolerance: People with lactose intolerance sometimes become constipated from dairy products. Avoid milk and dairy-containing foods for two to three weeks and see if there is a change. Read the section on lactose intolerance in chapter 7 to find hidden sources of lactose. Take the lactose breath test to determine if you are intolerant.

Medications: Many medications can cause constipation: pain relievers, antacids that contain aluminum, antispasmodic drugs, antidepressants, tranquilizers, iron supplements, anti-convulsants, diuretics, anesthetics, anticholinergics, blood pressure medication, bismuth salts, and laxatives. If you noticed that constipation occurred suddenly after you began to take a new medication, discuss it with your doctor.

Begin an exercise or movement program.

Food sensitivities, dysbiosis, leaky gut syndrome: People with chronic constipation who do not respond to diet, fiber, liquids, and exercise should have digestive testing to see if dysbiosis, food allergies, or parasites are the underlying problem.

Vitamin C: Vitamin C can help soften stool. The amount varies depending on individual needs. Use a vitamin C flush to determine your daily needs.

Biofeedback: Biofeedback has been used successfully to treat constipation in people who have problems relaxing the pelvic floor muscles.

Diarrhea

Diarrhea is a symptom, not a disease. If you have chronic diarrhea, it's important to find the underlying cause. Chronic diarrhea can be the result of drugs, diverticular disease, foods or beverages that disagree with your system, infections—bacterial, fungal, viral, or parasitic—inflammatory bowel disease, irritable bowel syndrome, malabsorption of fats, lactose intolerance, laxative use and abuse, malabsorption, contaminated water supply, or cancer. People with gallbladder problems often experience diarrhea after a fatty meal. With careful questioning and laboratory testing, your physician will be able to find the cause. Once you have a diagnosis, you can decide how to approach the problem.

Diarrhea occurs when you have a bowel transit time that is too fast. Feces don't sit in the colon long enough for water to be absorbed back into your body so the stool comes out runny. (It's truly amazing how much water is usually absorbed through the colon—2 gallons every day.) If you have chronic diarrhea, you aren't getting the maximum benefit from foods because you aren't absorbing all the nutrients. Loss of fluids and electrolyte minerals can make us disoriented and weak. In infants, small children, and the elderly, dehydration can be dangerous and can happen suddenly. It's important to replace lost fluids to prevent dehydration. Drink eight to ten glasses of water, fruit and vegetable juices, or broths each day. Infants can be given a fleet enema, which is easily purchased at drug stores. Follow the directions in the package.

Most diarrhea is self-limiting. It is nature's way of getting rid of something quickly from your body. So for acute diarrhea, just let it flow and keep drinking plenty of water. If you have severe abdominal or rectal pain, fever of at least 102 degrees Fahrenheit, blood in your stool, signs of dehydration—dry mouth, anxiety, restlessness, excessive thirst, little or no urination, severe weakness, dizziness or light-headedness—or your diarrhea lasts more than three days, call your doctor. Be more cautious with small children, people who are already ill, and the elderly.

Diarrhea is the body's way of getting rid of something disagreeable—food, microbes, or toxins. You usually aren't very hungry when you have acute diarrhea. Many foods "feed" the bugs and you instinctively stop eating. The diet recommended for people with diarrhea is called the BRAT diet, which stands for bananas, rice, apples, and toast. These foods are bland and binding. Soda crackers, chicken, and eggs can also be eaten. You can make a pretty tasty rice pudding with apples, rice, eggs, and cinnamon, which is also binding.

Many other substances can cause diarrhea, including an excess of vitamin C and magnesium. For instance, antacids which contain magnesium salts can cause diarrhea. Sorbitol, mannitol, and xylitol are sugars found in dietetic candies and sweets that cause diarrhea. Even in small amounts, they can cause diarrhea in people sensitive to them. Some people have the same reaction to fructose or lactose.

FUNCTIONAL LABORATORY TESTING

Prolonged diarrhea is a symptom that warrants thorough investigation. These are a few of the tests that may give you information about what's causing your problem.

1. Complete digestive and stool analysis with parasitology.
2. Hydrogen breath test for small bowel overgrowth.
3. Lactose breath test.
4. Food allergy and sensitivity testing IgG and IgE.

HEALING OPTIONS

Healing options depend on the cause of the diarrhea. See the appropriate sections for complete healing options.

Eliminate dairy products: Lactose intolerance is a common source of diarrhea. Avoid milk and dairy-containing foods for two or three weeks to see if the diarrhea stops.

Acidophilus and bifidobacteria: These beneficial bacteria help normalize bowel function. They ferment fiber which produces short-chained fatty acids to fuel the colonic tissue. You can also take probiotic supplements to help prevent traveler's diarrhea.

Handwashing: The simple act of washing hands with soap can help reduce the incidence of ongoing diarrhea. In a study done with mothers of children with prolonged diarrhea, the mothers were simply asked to wash their own hands with soap and water before preparing food and eating and to wash their children's hands before eating and as soon as possible after a bowel movement. There was an 89 percent reduction in diarrhea in the handwashing mom's group in comparison with the control group.

Food allergies and sensitivities: Diarrhea is a common symptom of food sensitivities and allergies. Blood testing can help you determine which foods you are reacting to. Or you can go on an elimination diet for one week and slowly reintroduce foods. Although a painstaking process, you can find most food sensitivities and allergies this way. For more complete instructions, see food sensitivities and the elimination/provocation diet in chapter 7.

Goldenseal: This herb is highly effective for treatment of acute diarrhea caused by microbial infection. Be sure to use goldenseal in recommended dosages as it may also cause diarrhea if used in excessive amounts.

Saccharomyces boulardii: This friendly yeast has been used successfully to prevent and treat diarrhea caused by antibiotics. It boosts levels of secretory IgA, which is a protective part of the immune system. Saccharomyces is often found in supplements that contain acidophillus and bifidobacteria.

Yogurt: Yogurt is a folk remedy for diarrhea. It contains active bacteria, *L. thermophilus* and *L. bulgaricus*, which help prevent and stop diarrhea.

Diverticular Disease

Diverticula are pea-sized pouches that have blown out of the intestinal wall, primarily in the colon. The underlying cause of diverticula formation is constipation. Soft, bulky stools easily pass through the colon and respond to peristaltic waves; hard, dehydrated stools are harder to push along, and the bowel wall has to work harder. As a result, the muscles in the colon thicken to help this abnormal situation, which results in greatly increased pressures within the bowel. Over time, this prolonged pressure can blow out portions of the bowel wall, causing diverticular pouches.

Psyllium: Adding psyllium fiber as a daily supplement can help solidify stools. Begin with 1–2 teaspoons in at least 8 ounces of water.

Avoid sorbitol: Sorbitol, manitol, and xylitol are nondigestible sugars found in sugar-free candy. They can easily cause diarrhea, gas, and bloating.

Zinc: Much research has been done on zinc and diarrhea in children. It shortens the duration of acute diarrhea by boosting the body's immune system. Dosage: 20 milligrams daily in children, 50 milligrams daily in adults, for up to two weeks.

Thirty to forty percent of all people over the age of sixty have diverticular disease, which occurs more commonly in women than in men and with increasing frequency with age. Eighty-five percent of the people who have diverticula are symptom-free, and it's not a problem unless the pouches become inflamed or rupture. They usually heal on their own, but sometimes require surgery. When they become infected, causing diverticulitis, there is pain and often a fever. It is usually at this point that a physician will order tests to discover diverticulitis and diverticulosis. These infections are treated with antibiotics and a soft-fiber diet. Once the inflammation resolves, a high-fiber diet is recommended. Diverticular pouches don't go away, but a high-fiber diet will prevent most further attacks. Repeated episodes of diverticulitis may require surgery. A disease of Western civilization, diverticular disease occurs rarely in people who consume a high-fiber diet.

Healing Options

High-fiber diet: A high-fiber diet is of first and foremost importance for preventing the development and recurrence of diverticular disease. If you are recovering from a flareup of diverticulitis, begin with a soft-fiber diet. Cook vegetables until fairly soft, eat cooked fruits, use easy to digest grains like oatmeal, and make vegetable soups with tofu. Foods with seeds (like strawberries, poppy seeds, sesame seeds, pumpkin seeds) can catch in your diverticula and cause irritation. Until healed, avoid seed foods.

Once you are feeling well, establish a high-fiber diet as a normal part of your life. Focus on fruits, vegetables, whole grains, and legumes. Meat, poultry, fish, and dairy products contain zero fiber and need to be eaten in moderation. Psyllium seeds are a good fiber supplement choice because they are nonirritating. Studies have shown that people eating a high-fiber, low-fat diet lower their risks of diverticular disease significantly. (Men who eat a high-red meat, low-fiber diet have even higher incidences.) It may take you some time to get accustomed to a high-fiber, low-fat diet, but it will be worth the effort. The benefits reach further than your digestive tract, lowering your risk factors for cancer, heart disease, and diabetes. Be certain to drink plenty of water and other healthy beverages.

Acidophilus/bifidobacteria: Friendly flora can help fight the infection while it's active and protect you from future infection. Dosage: one capsule two to three times daily for prevention; two capsules three times daily during flareup.

Gamma-oryzanol: While studies of gamma-oryzanol, a compound in rice bran oil, were not directly involved with diverticulitis, gamma-oryzanol is known to have a healing effect on the colon (see discussion under Gastric Ulcers and Gastritis above). Rice bran oil is available in the United States at some gourmet stores. Dosage: 100 milligrams three times daily for a trial period of three to six weeks.

Glutamine: The digestive tract uses glutamine, the most abundant amino acid in the body, as a fuel source and for healing. Studies have not been done with diverticulitis, but glutamine is regenerative for the colon in general. Dosage: Begin with 8 grams daily for four to eight weeks.

Evening primrose oil: Evening primrose oil increases the levels of prostaglandin E2 series, which promote healing and repair. Dosage: 1,000–2,000 milligrams three times a day.

Aloe vera: Aloe vera, which contains vitamins, minerals, and amino acids, has been used by many cultures to heal the digestive tract. Its anti-inflammatory properties are soothing to mucous membranes, and it has been shown to reduce pain. It also stimulates the immune system, increasing white blood cell activity and formation of T-cells, and contains enzymes that help break down dead cells and toxins. It also reduces bleeding time, which is important with ruptured diverticula.

Slippery elm bark: Slippery elm bark has demulcent properties and is gentle, soothing, and nourishing to mucous membranes. Drink as a tea, chew on the bark, or take in capsules. Recipe for tea: Simmer 1 teaspoon of slippery elm bark in two cups of water for twenty minutes and strain. Sweeten if you want and drink freely; it can be used in large amounts without harm. Dosage: two to four capsules three times daily.

Multivitamin with minerals: Take a good supplement.

Irritable Bowel Syndrome

Irritable bowel syndrome (IBS) affects 10 to 20 percent of all American adults and is the most common gastrointestinal complaint, although most people who have it never seek a physician's help. Over the years, IBS has had a variety of names: spastic colon, spastic bowel, mucous colitis, colitis, and functional bowel disease. Associated symptoms are abdominal pain and spasms, bloating, gas, and abnormal bowel movements. Diarrhea alternating with constipation is the most common pattern. Bowel movements usually relieve the discomfort. People with irritable bowel syndrome do not have any obvious changes in bowel structure or other serious complications and rarely require hospitalization. Nonetheless, IBS can significantly restrict one's lifestyle. Twice as many women as men seek medical help for IBS, and it often appears in the teen years or early adulthood.

Women may experience a flareup in their symptoms around their menstrual period. The most common symptom associated with menstruation is pain. Because chronic pelvic pain can lead to hysterectomy, physicians need to be clear that IBS is not causing the pain. When IBS is the culprit, hysterectomy won't eliminate it.

Anemia, weight loss, rectal bleeding, and fever are not symptoms of irritable bowel syndrome. Bowel changes accompanied by these symptoms need to be checked out by a physician to discover the cause.

The causes of irritable bowel syndrome are multifactorial. Many studies are flawed because they only test one factor at a time and generalize about results. For instance, some people with IBS improve when they eliminate wheat from their diets, while the majority won't notice any benefit. Unfortunately, there's no single cause for IBS, but hopefully we can find the causes for each person and work with them individually in response to their biochemical uniqueness.

Low-fat, high-fiber diets are best. Eat small meals, and chew food well. Dietary recommendations need to be tailored to your personal reactions. It is commonly advised to avoid alcohol and monitor sugar intake, coffee, beans, and cabbage family foods (broccoli, Brussels sprouts, cauliflower) because they can be difficult to digest. You need only avoid those foods if they bother you.

Food allergies and intolerances, medication, stress, hormone changes, low fiber diets, and infection all play a role in IBS. Food sensitivities are found in half to two-thirds of people with IBS and are more prevalent in people who have allergies or come from allergic families. The most common foods that trigger IBS are wheat, corn, dairy products, coffee, tea, citrus fruits, and chocolate. In one study in which people were put on a food-elimination diet for a year, bloating and distension was relieved by 88 percent, colic pain was reduced by 90 percent, diarrhea was reduced 85 percent, and constipation improved in 54 percent. Also, 79 percent of people who had other symptoms, such as hay fever, asthma, eczema, and hives, saw these symptoms improve.

Undiagnosed lactose insufficiency is often the cause of IBS. In a recent study of 242 people, it was found that 43 percent had total remission of IBS when they excluded dairy products from their diet, and another 41 percent had partial improvement. Taking the lactose hydrogen breath test is a valuable way to discover who would benefit from a lactose-free diet. You can also discover this by avoiding all dairy foods and products which contain dairy foods for at least two weeks to see how you feel. If you have only moderate improvement, other foods may also be playing a role in your symptoms.

Lactose is not the only sugar to cause problems. Our cells use single sugar molecules (monosaccharides), but many foods contain two-molecule sugars (disaccharides) which must be split. New research suggests that many people are unable to split mannitol, sucrose, sorbitol, fructose, and other disaccharides, and a high percentage of people with IBS are intolerant of one or more of these sugars. The result is diarrhea, gas, and bloating. These people find that fruit, especially citrus fruit, aggravates their symptoms. Hydrogen breath tests are being used experimentally to diagnose this, but are not on the market at the present. You can do a self-test by avoiding all fruit and sugar for at least ten days. Be sure to read labels carefully and avoid any product which contains glucose, sucrose, malt, maltose, corn syrup, fructose, brown sugar, honey, maple syrup, molasses, and lactose. You'll find that sugar is everywhere, but if disaccharides are the cause of your IBS, it is worth the time and trouble. If sugars and fruits make you feel worse, do the self-test and a blood or stool test for *Candida* infection. People with *Candida* often feel worse after eating sugars and fruits.

Recent technology has provided new insight into the causes of IBS. High levels of methane shown in hydrogen breath tests are associated with IBS and indicate an infection in the small intestine, most commonly *Clostridium difficile.* (See more on lab testing in chap. 7.) *Clostridium* often responds to *Saccharomyces boulardii* supplementation.

Parasites and *Candida* overgrowth are overlooked causes of irritable bowel syndrome. One study showed that 18 percent of the study participants had treatable parasitic infections, while another found *Giardia* in 9 percent and parasites in 15 percent of the study population. Leo Galland, M.D., has found that Giardia was responsible for problems in nearly half of his patients with IBS. Even benign pinworms can cause severe colonic cramping at a certain stage of their life-cycle. Ask your doctor to order a comprehensive digestive and stool analysis with parasitology to determine if parasites or *Candida* are making you sick.

Antibiotics are well-known causes of temporary diarrhea and GI problems. Steroid medications can also affect the balance of flora. The good flora are eliminated, especially in people who are on repeated doses of antibiotics, which allows other microbes to dominate the intestinal tract. *Acidophillus, Bifidobacteria,* and *Saccharomyces boulardii* supplements can help restore intestinal balance.

Irritable bowel syndrome has also been treated as a psychosomatic illness—"it's all in your head"—because there appears to be no other obvious reason for it. People with IBS often have reason to feel stressed-out, nervous, and depressed about their condition. Although stressful situations often trigger IBS symptoms, stress itself doesn't cause IBS, and people with IBS have no greater incidence of depression than other people with chronic health problems. IBS can cause social embarrassment and is the second most common cause for missing work, after the common cold.

FUNCTIONAL LABORATORY TESTING

1. Comprehensive digestive and stool analysis with parasitology.
2. Lactose breath test.
3. Hydrogen breath test for methane levels.
4. Food allergy and sensitivity testing: IgE and IgG or IgG4.
5. Intestinal permeability screening.

HEALING OPTIONS

Fiber: Fiber and high-fiber diets are recommended for people with IBS. Focus on eating a minimum of five daily servings of fresh fruits and vegetables, plus whole grains, beans, and peas. You can use high-fiber cereals to boost fiber content, but recent research indicates that wheat bran made the problem worse in 55 percent of cases, whereas it only improved symptoms in 10 percent of patients. This is not surprising because a significant number of people with IBS have a hypersensitivity to wheat products.

If you want to add a fiber supplement, use psyllium seeds. Psyllium seeds were found to be more effective than wheat bran overall. They caused a decrease in abdominal bloating, whereas wheat bran increased bloating. In one study in which psyllium was given to people with IBS, it improved several parameters by increasing the number of bowel movements per week, enlarging stool weight, and speeding up transit times. No negative side effects were reported.

Lactose intolerance: Lactose intolerance is often the underlying cause of IBS. Take the hydrogen breath test or eliminate all dairy products and products containing dairy from your diet for at least two weeks to help you determine whether lactose intolerance is contributing to your problem.

Gamma-oryzanol: Gamma-oryzanol, a compound found in rice bran oil, is a useful therapeutic tool for IBS. It acts on the autonomic nervous system to normalize production of gastric juice (see discussion under Gastric Ulcers and Gastritis above). Dosage: 100 milligrams three times daily for a trial period of three to six weeks.

Glutamine: Glutamine, the most abundant amino acid in the body, is used by the digestive tract as a fuel source and for healing IBS. Dosage: 8 grams daily for a trial period of four weeks.

EPA/DHA fish oil: Fish oils inhibit the formation of inflammatory prostaglandins and leukotrienes. They may be effective in reducing the pain and inflammation associated with IBS. Dosage: 1,000–2,000 milligrams daily in fish oil capsules, or 300 milligrams daily of Neuromins.

Peppermint oil: Peppermint oil is a muscle relaxant that is widely used in England for IBS. To get the oil into the intestines intact, use enteric coated peppermint oil. (The coating prevents it from dissolving in the stomach.) Dosage: one to two capsules daily between meals. During a spasm, you can rub a drop or two of the oil inside your anus with a finger.

Herbs: Chamomile, melissa (balm), rosemary, and valerian all have antispasmodic properties. They help relieve and expel gas, strengthen and tone the stomach, and soothe pain. Valerian, hops, skullcap, and passion flower are all calming herbs, which can be found in a combination product. Antidepressant medication is often used by physicians for IBS; these gentle, effective calmatives may give you similar results. Use these herbs in capsules, tinctures, and teas.

Ginger: Ginger, either fresh or powdered, helps relieve gas pains. It can be added to foods or used in tea. Within twenty to thirty minutes you'll be belching and/or passing gas which will relieve the discomfort. To make tea: take two or three slices of fresh ginger or ½ teaspoon dried ginger in one cup of boiled water. Combine it with other herbs, like peppermint or chamomile, to enhance the effect.

Multivitamin with minerals: Take a good supplement.

Calcium/magnesium citrate: Anecdotally, many people have found that calcium/magnesium supplements prevent or alleviate the muscle spasms associated with IBS, as these minerals have powerful antispasmodic effects. Dosage: 500–1,000 milligrams calcium, 300–750 milligrams magnesium. *Caution:* too much magnesium will cause diarrhea.

Behavioral therapies: Biofeedback, self-hypnosis, and other relaxation techniques are widely used to help people with IBS. Stress often triggers bowel symptoms, and learning stress modification techniques can alter our reactions. If we don't react with alarm to a situation, our body doesn't sense it as stressful.

Inflammatory Bowel Disease, Crohn's Disease, and Ulcerative Colitis

Inflammatory bowel diseases (IBD) share many of the symptoms of IBS, but they are very different problems. IBD involves inflammation of the digestive tract, which can occur anywhere from the mouth to the rectum. Symptoms include abdominal pain, cramping, and diarrhea, which may be accompanied by fever, rectal bleeding, abdominal tenderness, abscesses, constipation, weight loss, awakening during the night with diarrhea, and a failure to thrive in children. Symptoms come and go and can go into remission for months or years, and about half of the people with IBD have only mild symptoms. People with IBD often develop complications, which include inflammation of the eyes or skin, arthritis, liver disease, kidney stones, and colon cancer. Of people with ulcerative colitis, 20 to 25 percent eventually require surgery due to massive bleeding, chronic illness, perforation of the colon, or risk of colon cancer. Though the risk of developing colon cancer for people with widespread IBD is much higher than in the general population, it doesn't rise when only the rectum and distal end of the colon are involved.

The two most common types of IBD are ulcerative colitis and Crohn's disease. Most cases are diagnosed before age forty. IBD tends to run in families and is more prevalent among people of Jewish descent. IBD affects half a million Americans. Ulcerative colitis and Crohn's disease are similar but have different characteristics.

Ulcerative colitis is a continuous inflammation of the mucosal lining of the colon and/or rectum. In the descending colon it is sometimes called "left-sided disease," and in the rectum, it is called distal disease, ulcerative proctitis, or proctosigmoiditis. If sores are present, they are shallow, and it is generally milder and easier to treat in the rectum.

Crohn's disease can occur anywhere along the digestive tract, from mouth to rectum, but is most common in the colon and ileum near the ileocecal valve. It is sometimes called "right-sided disease." Frequent symptoms are fevers that last twenty-four to forty-eight hours, canker sores in the mouth, clubbed fingernails, and a thickening of the GI lining which may cause constrictions and blockage. Inflammation develops in a skip pattern, a little here and a little there, and goes more deeply into the tissues than with ulcerative colitis. In later stages, it can form abscesses and fistulas, little canals that lead to other organs or form tiny caves. If you require surgery for Crohn's disease, it is important to know which part of the intestines were removed and which nutrients may have inadequate uptake (see the absorption chart in chapter 7).

IBD is considered an autoimmune disease (your body begins attacking itself). The causes are multifactoral and have produced much debate. Four theories are that IBD is caused by an infection, a hypersensitivity to antigens in the gut wall, an inflammation of the blood vessels which causes ischemia (a lack of blood supply to the tissues), and food sensitivities. These causes are interconnected and may all be present to some extent in everyone with Crohn's disease.

Medical treatment for IBD consists of anti-inflammatory drugs, steroids, and sometimes antibiotics. While these medications can often relieve symptoms of IBD, they carry their own risks. Some specific drug side effects include bone loss due to use of steroid medications, and folic acid deficiency from use of sulphasalazine (Asulfadine). Medications are often necessary, but use of complimentary therapies can reduce the need, so that when you really need medication during a flareup it works appropriately. The good news is that effective natural therapies address each of the four theories, reduce the need for prescription medications, and heal the bowel. Among the hundreds of patients with IBD that Drs. Jonathan Wright and Alan Gaby have seen, most have improved, many dramatically. The key to success appears to be getting people into remission. Once a flareup has died down, dietary therapies are highly successful in preventing a recurrence.

Diet plays an important role in IBD. The incidence of IBD is growing rapidly in Western countries, but is rare in cultures where people eat a native diet. People who eat a high amount of sugars and low-fiber diets have a higher incidence of IBD, and there are correlations of IBD with cigarette smoking and eating fast foods.

Food sensitivities play a significant role in IBD. About half of Dr. Wright and Dr. Gaby's patients report significant improvement with use of an elimination diet over a three-week period. After this, they gradually add foods back into their diet to see which ones provoke bloating, pain, diarrhea, bleeding, or other symptoms. One study found that 13 percent of children with IBD were allergic to cow's milk during infancy. It is essential to check for food allergies and food sensitivities. Studies have shown reduction in symptoms and inflammation in people who adhere to a hypoallergenic diet. People with bowel disease are especially sensitive to most grains. Chemicals from some foods are irritating to the bowels. Truly, nearly any food can cause irritation and inflammation. In various studies, citrus, pineapple, dairy, coffee, tomatoes, cheese, bananas, sugar, additives, preservatives, spices, beverages other than water, bread, and so forth have been implicated. You'll need to be tested for both IgE and IgG antibodies.

There is no one diet that helps all people with IBD, although the Elemental Diet and Haas Specific Carbohydrate Diet (details of the Haas program are discussed in the Healing Options) work especially well for people with Crohn's disease. The Elemental Diet is comprised of synthetic foods you drink or are given through a tube. The Elemental Diet, which has resulted in a reduction of intestinal permeability as well as its symptoms, has been found to be as good as steroids in reducing inflammation in a flareup of Crohn's disease. But there are problems with use of the Elemental Diet. It is unpalatable to many people and they won't drink it. Newer products which are tastier are coming on the market.

The Specific Carbohydrate Diet eliminates all simple sugars. As discussed under IBS, many people are unable to split disaccharide sugars (lactose, sucrose, maltose, and isomaltose) into single molecule sugars. This may explain, in part, why the diet is so successful. The Specific Carbohydrate Diet also eliminates grains, which generally cause inflammation of the intestines in people with IBD. The Specific Carbohydrate Diet works especially well for people with Crohn's disease.

A new dietary twist on ulcerative colitis and Crohn's is a low-sulfur diet. Studies have shown an increase in sulfur-eating bacteria in people with bowel disease in comparison with other people. In one study, people were advised to avoid high-sulfur foods including eggs, cheese, whole milk, ice cream, mayonnaise, soy milk, mineral water, sulfited drinks (including wine), nuts, and cruciferous vegetables (e.g., broccoli, cabbage, cauliflower, brussels sprouts, etc.), and to reintroduce red meats. They were advised to get protein from milk, fish, and chicken. The researchers found significant changes—people had no relapses or attacks while on the diet, and there were no adverse effects from the diet itself. The expected relapse rate had been 22.6 percent. Of the four people in the study, one was able to stop taking steroid medication and had been attack-free for eighteen months, compared to the four attacks experienced in the eighteen months before the dietary changes. The other three showed microscopic improvement of inflammation. The number of daily bowel movements in all four was reduced from six to one and one-half.

Leaky gut syndrome (increased intestinal permeability) is prevalent in IBD. Often an infectious or parasitic condition underlies it. A flareup of symptoms commonly occurs with infections. The most common microbes involved are *E. coli*, staphylococcus, streptococcus, Proteus, *Mycoplasma pneumoniae*, *Clamydia psittaci*, *Clostridium difficile toxin*, and *Coxiella burnetii.* Bacterial infections occurred in one-quarter of all reoccurrence of IBD in these studies. Research from England implicates measles as a possible cause of Crohn's disease. They found measles virus in diseased parts of the colon. Swedish researchers find a high incidence of IBD in people who were exposed to measles in utero. A British study showed that people who had received live measles vaccines had a threefold increase of Chrohn's disease, while ulcerative colitis rose by two-and-a-half times. This study did not prove that the bowel disease was actually caused by the disease, only that there was a correlation. Mold sensitivity, and allergies to *Candida* and other types of fungus have also proven to provoke IBD symptoms. Although there is not much research on the yeast connection and IBD, clinicians have often found antifungal therapies to be useful. Friendly flora have been found to be dramatically out of balance in people with IBD, so use of probiotic supplements is highly recommended. Use of the comprehensive digestive and stool analysis with parasitology screening and intestinal permeability tests will uncover many of these problems.

Some people with Crohn's disease have flare-ups in a seasonal cycle which suggests an allergy component to the illness. While studies have shown that allergy is a factor in a small number of people, a survey of members of the National Foundation of Ileitis and Colitis showed that 70 percent of people with IBD listed other symptoms which were probably allergic. This led one researcher to say "inflammatory bowel disease is just another possible facet of allergy."

IBD is not caused by emotional illness or psychiatric disorder, though the condition may cause emotional problems due to its chronic nature, painful episodes, and lifestyle limitations. Prolonged treatment with steroid medications can cause side effects of depression, mania or euphoria, and bone loss.

Because of bleeding and continued irritation, malabsorption of nutrients is often found in people with IBD. These same nutrients are often vital for repair, so the cycle worsens. Low serum levels of zinc, an important nutrient for wound repair, are often found in people with IBD. Folic acid helps repair tissue and prevents diarrhea. Prolonged bleeding can cause deficiencies of copper, zinc, iron, folic acid, and vitamin B_{12}.

Many studies have shown an increased need for antioxidant nutrients such as vitamin A, vitamin E, selenium, glutathione, and superoxide dismutse. People with IBD have an increased level of leukotrienes, produced by neutrophils, which increase pain and inflammation. Many natural substances can modulate these effects. For instance, omega-3 fatty acids, found in cold-water fish, can reduce inflammation caused by leukotrienes and the arachidonic acid cascade.

There is a higher incidence of IBD in women who take oral contraceptives. Women with a history of IBD or with a family history of IBD may want to choose a different form of birth control.

Several studies have shown bone loss in people with Crohn's disease and ulcerative colitis. While incidence of loss in some studies is correlated with use of steroid medications, in others it appears to be independent. It is advisable to do at least a baseline bone density study to see if you are at risk. If so, increasing all bone nutrients would be advised. A study on low-impact exercise in people with Crohn's disease found that bone density was significantly increased. So get out there and exercise regularly. Exercise is not optional for any of us!

Functional Laboratory Testing

1. Comprehensive digestive and stool analysis with parasitology.
2. Lactose breath test.
3. Elisa food and environmental sensitivity testing.
4. Intestinal permeability screening.
5. Nutritional analysis of blood and/or hair.
6. Antioxidant analysis.
7. Bone density testing.

HEALING OPTIONS

Dietary: Eliminate simple sugars and fast foods (flareups occur more frequently when fast foods are eaten). Grains and dairy products often aggravate the condition.

Specific carbohydrate diet: Many people have found relief from using the Specific Carbohydrate Diet outlined in Elaine Gottschall's book *Food and the Gut Reaction* (reissued as *Breaking the Vicious Cycle*). Foods which are allowed are beef, lamb, pork, poultry, fish, eggs, natural cheeses, homemade yogurt, fruits, nuts, pure fruit juices, weak coffee, weak tea, and peppermint and spearmint teas. Also allowed are corn, soy, safflower, sunflower, and olive oils. No grains, dairy products, legumes, potatoes, yams, or parsnips are allowed on the diet. No sugars or alcoholic beverages are consumed. For delicious recipes and more detail, read the book.

This diet is beneficial because it eliminates most foods that cause sensitivities—grains and dairy products. Similar to the *Candida* diet, it helps restore intestinal balance. While going on the diet alone may be effective, it is most effective after laboratory testing has determined your unique biochemistry. For example, if you find that you are not sensitive to grains or dairy products, you'll be able to include them in your food plan. Most foods can be added back into your diet within six months, while fixed sensitivities must be avoided long-term.

Lactose intolerance: Hydrogen breath testing or elimination of all dairy products and foods containing dairy from your diet for at least two weeks can help determine whether lactose intolerance is contributing to your problem. Definitely eliminate dairy during a flare-up of your illness.

Food sensitivities: Food sensitivities play a significant role in ulcerative colitis and Crohn's disease, occurring approximately half the time. The most common offenders are dairy products, grains, and yeast, followed in frequency by egg, potato, rye, coffee, apples, mushrooms, oats, and chocolate. Some people are sensitive to more than one food. Going on an elimination diet/cleansing diet is a simple way to eat foods which are less likely to trigger symptoms. The slow addition of new foods in the challenge/provocation stage will give you an idea of which foods make you feel worse. You can also do a blood test for food sensitivities.

Glutamine: Glutamine is the first nutrient I recommend for bowel and intestinal health. It is the most abundant amino acid in our bodies. The digestive tract uses glutamine as the primary nutrient for the intestinal cells, and it is effective for healing stomach ulcers, irritable bowel syndrome, and ulcerative bowel diseases. Douglas Wilmore, M.D. has been using high doses of glutamine to heal digestive tracts in people with IBD who have had surgery in which part of the colon was removed. When only a short portion of the colon remains, people develop chronic diarrhea, a condition called short bowel syndrome. With a high-fiber, high-glutamine diet, and short-term use of growth hormones, Dr. Wilmore is able to help normalize bowel function. Studies have shown reduced glutathione levels specifically in colon cells. Glutathione levels are low in both inflamed and normal bowel tissue. Glutathione is also synthesized from glutamine. Another way to raise glutathione levels is to supplement with N-acetylcystiene. Dosage: Begin with 8–20 grams daily for a trial period of four weeks.

Folic acid: One of folic acid's main functions is to help with the repair and maintenance of epithelial cells, such as those in the bowel. The drug asulfadine causes a 30 percent loss of folic acid. Even those who don't take asulfadine may benefit greatly from folic acid supplementation. One study of twenty-four people with bowel disease were given either a placebo or 15 milligrams of folic acid daily. Beneficial changes to the cells were observed in those receiving the folic acid. In my own clinical experience, I have found that a combination of glutamine and folic acid can often rapidly reduce inflammation and irritation in bowel disease.

Omega-3 fatty acids: Omega-3 fatty acids are found in cold water fish and have been used to reduce inflammation in rheumatoid arthritis, psoriasis, and ulcerative colitis by reducing the production of leukotrienes. Salmon, mackerel, herring, tuna, sardines, and halibut are all excellent sources of EPA/DHA oils. Eating these fish several times a week can supply your body with these essential fats. Brown and red seaweeds also provide generous amounts of omega-3 oils, but carrageenan, an extract from seaweed, may increase the inflammation in the colon. While carrageenan is used in animals to produce IBD, in humans the research is not yet clear. To be on the safe side, avoid red and brown seaweeds.

You can also take one to three capsules of EPA/DHA oils or 300 milligrams of neuromins daily. In a recent study, it was found that use of Max/EPA decreased disease activity by 58 percent over a period of eight months. No patient worsened, and eight out of eleven were able to reduce or discontinue use of medication. The dosage was fifteen capsules of Max/EPA, which contained 2.7 grams of EPA and 1.8 grams of DHA, per day. Many other studies also show the benefit of fish oils.

Quercetin: Quercetin, the most effective anti-inflammatory bioflavonoid, can be used to reduce pain and inflammatory responses and control allergies. Dosage: 500 to 1,000 milligrams three to four times daily.

Acidophilus/Bifidobacteria/Saccharomyces boulardii: Imbalance of friendly flora allows for proliferation of pathogenic microbes, such as *Candida*, *Bacteroides*, *Citrobacter*, and more. It is believed that dysbiosis is a primary cause of IBD in many cases. Use of probiotic supplements can help restore balance of intestinal flora. Dosage: one to two capsules three times daily one-half hour before meals.

Gamma-oryzanol: Gamma-oryzanol, a compound found in rice bran oil, is a useful therapeutic tool for gastritis, ulcers, and irritable bowel syndrome (see discussion under Gastric ulcers and Gastritis above). Dosage: 100 milligrams three times daily for a trial period of three to six weeks.

Butyrate enemas: Butyrate is the preferred fuel of the colonic cells. It is produced when fiber in the colon is fermented by intestinal flora, predominantly bifidobacteria. A few studies have shown that butyrate enemas, taken twice daily, helped heal active distal ulcerative colitis.

Herbs: Demulcent herbs—marshmallow, slippery elm, acacia, chickweed, comfrey, mullein, and plantain—are beneficial and soothing to the intestinal membranes and help stimulate mucus production. All are gentle enough to be used at will; try them in capsule or tea form. Other herbs used by people with bowel disease include wild indigo, purple cornflower, echinacea, American cranesbill, goldenseal, cabbage powder, wild yam, bayberry, agrimony, neem, aloe vera, chamomile, feverfew, ginger, ginko biloba, St. John's wort, milk thistle, valerian, peppermint, hawthorne, and La Pacho.

Multivitamin with minerals and antioxidant nutrients: Due to general malabsorption and poor dietary habits in people with Crohn's disease and ulcerative colitis, it is wise to add a good-quality multivitamin with minerals to your daily routine. Deficiencies of many nutrients have been found in people with IBD: calcium/magnesium, folic acid, iron, selenium, vitamins A, B_1, B_2, B_6, C, D, E, and zinc. Because some researchers feel that oxidative damage plays a significant role in IBD, the supplement should contain adequate amounts of antioxidant nutrients: at least 10,000 IU beta-carotene or other carotenoids, 400 IU vitamin E, 250 milligrams vitamin C, 200 micrograms selenium, 5 milligrams zinc, plus other nutrients. It may also contain CoQ10, glutathione, NAC, pycnogenol, superoxide dismutase (SOD), and other antioxidants. It is best to buy a supplement that is free of foods, herbs, and common allergens.

Bovine cartilage: Bovine cartilage is shown to have anti-inflammatory and wound-healing properties. Its benefit has been documented in many illnesses, including ulcerative colitis, hemorrhoids and fissures, rheumatoid arthritis, and osteoarthritis.

Hemorrhoids

About half of Americans over the age of fifty have hemorrhoids. They are not life-threatening or dangerous, just unpleasant. They occur when blood vessels in and around the anus get swollen and stretch under pressure, similar to varicose veins in the legs. They are found either inside the anus (internal hemorrhoids) or under the skin around the anus (external hemorrhoids). Internal hemorrhoids may become so swollen that they push through the anus. When they become irritated, inflamed, and painful, they are called protruding hemorrhoids.

Straining during bowel movements is a common cause of hemorrhoids. The most common symptom is bright red blood with a bowel movement. Hemorrhoids are also common but temporary during pregnancy. Hormonal changes cause the blood vessels to expand. During childbirth, extreme pressure is put on the anus. Hemorrhoids also occur in people with chronic constipation or diarrhea. Sitting for long periods, heavy lifting, and genetics are other influential factors. In most cases, hemorrhoids go away in a few days. If you have bleeding that lasts longer, have your doctor examine you to rule out a more serious problem.

A high-fiber diet with plenty of fluids—water, fruit juices, and herbal teas helps prevent hemorrhoids since fiber and fluids soften stool so they pass through easily. No straining with bowel movements means less pressure on the blood vessels near your anus. So increase your intake of fruits, whole grains, legumes, and vegetables, especially those containing the most fiber: asparagus, brussels sprouts, cabbage, carrots, cauliflower, corn, peas, kale, and parsnips. Eating a high-fiber breakfast cereal significantly increases your fiber intake.

Hemorrhoids generally don't itch. If your anus itches mainly at night, you might have pinworms. The best time to check for them is at night while you itch. Place a piece of tape around your finger, sticky side out. Put the tape on your anus, pull it off and check for worms, which look like moving white threads. If you are checking one of your children, you can use the tape method or just look. Another cause of rectal itching is called pruritus ani which can be caused by food sensitivities, contact with irritating substances (laundry detergent or toilet paper), fungi, bacterial infection, parasites, antibiotics, poor hygiene, or tight clothing. If you have hemorrhoids, you might find relief from the following suggestions.

PREVENTION

Diet: A high-fiber diet usually prevents hemorrhoids and allows them to heal. Increase your intake of fruits, vegetables, whole grains and legumes, and drink plenty of fluids, including water, fruit juices, and herbal teas.

Psyllium seed husks: Psyllium seeds add bulk and water to stool, which allows for easy passage. They regulate bowel function and can be beneficial for both diarrhea and constipation. Because they are not a laxative, they do not cause harmful dependency. Gradually build up to 1 teaspoon of psyllium with each meal to avoid gas and cramping from the sudden introduction of fiber. As your dietary fiber increases, you will probably find you no longer need to take psyllium seeds.

Wheat bran/corn bran: Wheat and corn bran can be used in the same way as psyllium seeds to add bulk and moisture to stool, allowing them to pass more easily. Take 1 teaspoon with meals or eat a high-fiber breakfast cereal. Be sure to add fiber to your diet slowly to prevent any gas or discomfort.

Acidophilus/bifidobacteria: Poor bowel flora causes the digestive system to move sluggishly. Use of antibiotics, hormones or steroid drugs, high-stress levels, and poor diet can cause an imbalance of intestinal flora. Take *Acidophilus* and *Bifidobacteria* two to three times daily to help regulate peristalsis. If you are able to digest yogurt, it also has a normalizing effect on the bowel and can be helpful for either constipation or diarrhea.

Magnesium deficiency: Americans have widespread magnesium deficiency that contributes to constipation. According to recent studies, we lose 75 percent of magnesium during food processing, and 40 percent of Americans fail to meet the RDA levels for daily magnesium intake. One of the many functions of magnesium is the proper relaxation of muscles, and peristalsis is comprised of rhythmic muscle relaxation and contraction. When magnesium deficiency or a calcium/magnesium imbalance is present, poor bowel tone can occur. On the other hand, too much magnesium can cause diarrhea. Dosage: 400–500 milligrams daily.

Lactose intolerance: People with lactose intolerance can become constipated from dairy products (see discussion in chapter 7).

Hormone changes: Women often notice that their bowel habits change at various times in their menstrual cycle. Pregnancy is a common but temporary cause of constipation and hemorrhoids. An underactive thyroid can also cause constipation.

Vitamin C: Vitamin C can be used to help soften stool. The amount needed depends on your individual needs. Use a vitamin C flush to determine your daily need for vitamin C (see chapter 9).

HEALING OPTIONS

Change your bathroom habits: In many countries, people squat to relieve themselves. A squatting position on the toilet takes pressure off the rectum and can help during a flare-up of hemorrhoids. (You may feel a little silly, but who's watching!) Also wipe gently with soft toilet paper. It may help to wash your anal area with warm water after each bowel movement, or if you have a bidet, now is the time to use it.

Salves: Salves can soothe inflamed tissues. Spread vitamin E oil, comfrey, calendula ointment, or goldenseal salve gently on the anus with your fingers. Witch hazel is also soothing to hemorrhoidal tissue. Put some on a cotton ball and press gently. Repeat treatments several times daily.

Sitz baths: Sitz baths are an old-fashioned remedy for hemorrhoids that are still in favor with the medical profession.

Place 3 to 4 inches of warm water in the bathtub and sit in it for ten minutes several times daily. You can improve the results by adding ¼ cup Epsom salts or healing herbs— chamomile, chickweed, comfrey, mullein, plantain, witch hazel, and yarrow are all healing and soothing to mucous membranes. Most of these are weeds and may even be growing in your yard. (Comfrey is a very easy herb to grow; just put it in a place where it can spread. It helps with wound healing of any sort and is also soothing for colds and lung problems.) Bring a large pot of water to a boil. Steep 1 to 2 cups of fresh herbs or ½ cup of dried herbs until cool, strain and add to bathwater.

Horse chestnut: Horse chestnuts, also called buckeye, help tone blood vessels, improve their elasticity, and reduce inflammation. They can also be used in a sitz bath. Chop up 2 cups of horse chestnuts, add to boiled water, strain, and add infusion to bathwater. Sit in bath twice daily for ten to fifteen minutes. You can also take 500 milligrams of the bark orally three times daily. Horse chestnut salves are also available.

Butcher's broom: Butcher's broom helps strengthen blood vessels and improves circulation. Dosage: 100 milligrams extract three times daily.

Vitamin E: Vitamin E helps bring oxygen to the tissues and promotes healing. You can use it topically or take it internally. Dosage: 400–800 IU of d-alpha tocopherol and mixed tocopherols daily.

Vitamin C and bioflavonoids: Vitamin C and bioflavonoids increase capillary and blood vessel strength so that they don't rupture easily. Bioflavonoids are also essential to collagen formation and elasticity of blood vessels. Berries of all types and cherries have high amounts of protective bioflavonoids. Dosage: 500–2,000 milligrams daily plus 100–1000 milligrams bioflavonoids, which can usually be purchased in a single supplement.

DMSO: In the literature, there is one anecdotal study in which a physician used DMSO topically for hemorrhoids. By his report, a 70-percent solution of DMSO will dissolve blood-engorged hemorrhoids almost overnight. It may be worth trying.

Chapter 13

NATURAL THERAPIES FOR THE DIVERSE CONSEQUENCES OF FAULTY DIGESTION

"When one comes into a city to which he is a stranger, he ought to consider its situation, how it lies as to the winds and the rising of the sun; for its influence is not the same whether it lies to the north or to the south, to the rising or to the setting sun. . . . From these things he must proceed to investigate everything else. For if one knows all these things well, or at least the greater part of them, he cannot miss knowing, when he comes into a strange city, either the diseases peculiar to the place, or the particular nature of the common diseases. . . ."

HIPPOCRATES, *ON AIRS, WATERS, AND PLACES*, c. 400 B.C.

THIS CHAPTER DISCUSSES functional approaches to arthritis, eczema, psoriasis, migraines, fibromyalgia, scleroderma, chronic fatigue syndrome, asthma, autism, and food and

271

environmental sensitivities. All these seemingly diverse medical problems are rooted in digestive conditions like leaky gut syndrome, parasites, and dysbiosis. When the intestinal lining heals and intestinal flora regain balance, these conditions often improve dramatically.

For each health condition I have provided general information about the disease, recommendations for functional laboratory testing, and healing options, with the most important ones discussed first. With careful investigation and patience, you may find the underlying conditions that influence how you feel. You won't need to follow every remedy, but many of them can be found in combination products. You will note that although these health conditions are different, many of the healing options are the same.

Of course, you'll need to clean up your diet, correct any nutrient imbalances, get regular exercise, and find time to nurture yourself. If at first you don't find major improvement, keep working at it. You may not have found the best remedy or combination of therapies on the first try. Patience and perseverance bring the best results. It takes time to resolve chronic illnesses.

ARTHRITIS

Arthritis refers to over a hundred diseases that cause inflammation of the joints. The old-fashioned term for arthritis is rheumatism, and today physicians who specialize in arthritis are called "rheumatologists." Arthritis affects 40 million Americans and accounts for 46 million medical visits per year. The two most common types of arthritis are osteoarthritis and rheumatoid arthritis. Other common types include psoriatic arthritis, ankylosing spondylitis, gout, Lyme disease, and Sjögren's syndrome. Each of these diseases has its own characteristics, but they all share the symptoms of pain and inflammation in joints. There are many causes for arthritis:

genetic, infections, physical injury, nutritional deficiencies, allergies, metabolic and immune disorders, stress, and environmental pollutants and toxins. Several types of arthritis have well-documented associations with faulty digestive function, and osteoarthritis responds well to dietary changes. Rheumatoid arthritis, ankylosing spondylitis, lupus, Sjögren's disease, and Reiter's syndrome may be caused by a combination of genetics, dysbiosis, food or environmental sensitivities, and leaky gut syndrome.

The current drugs of choice for arthritis pain are nonsteroidal anti-inflammatories (NSAIDs). However, NSAIDs block the production of prostaglandins which stimulate repair of the digestive lining. This causes increased leaky gut syndrome. Use of NSAIDs in children with rheumatoid arthritis showed that 75 percent had gastrointestinal problems caused by the drugs. And the more NSAIDs people take, the leakier the gut wall becomes, the more pain and inflammation follows, which sets up a continuously escalating problem. To make matters worse, many NSAIDs also have a negative effect on the ability of cartilage to repair itself. They block our body's ability to regenerate cartilage tissue by lowering the amounts of healing prostaglandins, glucosaminoglycans, and hyaluronan, and by raising leukotriene levels.

Other drugs commonly used to ameliorate the symptoms of arthritis also have well-known side effects. Natural therapies for arthritis reduce the need for such medications and their accompanying side effects. These natural therapies can be astonishingly effective.

The dietary connection between rheumatoid arthritis and food sensitivities was first noted by Michael Zeller in 1949 in *Annals of Allergy*. He found a direct cause and effect by adding and eliminating foods from the diet. He joined forces with Drs. Herbert Rinkel and Theron Randolph to publish a book called *Food Allergy* in 1951. Theron Randolph, M.D. is the father of a field of medicine called clinical ecology, which studies how our environment affects health. He found that people with rheumatoid arthritis who were not reacting to foods had at least one sensitivity to an environmental chemical.

Randolph sent questionnaires to over 200 of his patients with osteoarthritis and rheumatoid arthritis to assess how well treatments were working. Their responses showed that when they avoided food and environmental allergens, there was a significant reduction in arthritic symptoms. Randolph also felt that other types of arthritis, including Reiter's syndrome, ankylosing spondylitis, and psoriatic arthritis, have an ecological basis.

Since then other studies have been done on the relationship between food sensitivities and arthritis. In a study of forty-three people with arthritis of the hands, a water fast of three days brought improvement in tenderness, swelling, strength of grip, pain, joint circumference, function, and SED rate (a simple blood test that determines a breakdown of tissue somewhere in the body). When some of these people were tested with single foods, symptoms reoccurred in twenty-two out of twenty-seven people. In other studies, the foods most likely to provoke symptoms after an elimination diet were, in order of most to least: corn, wheat, bacon/pork, oranges, milk, oats, rye, eggs, beef, coffee, malt, cheese, grapefruit, tomato, peanuts, sugar, butter, lamb, lemon, and soy. Cereals were the most common food, with wheat and corn causing problems in over 50 percent of the people. In another study, it was found that forty-four out of ninety-three people with rheumatoid arthritis had elevated levels of IgG to gliadin. Among these forty-four people, 86 percent had positive RA factors. In yet another study, fifteen out of twenty-four people had raised levels of IgA, rheumatoid factor, and wheat protein IgG with a biopsy of the jejunum. Six of the wheat-positive people and one of the wheat-negative people had damage to the brush borders of their intestines. The researchers felt that the intestines play an important role in the progression of rheumatoid arthritis. Increased intestinal permeability allows more food particles to cross the intestinal mucosa, which triggers a greater sensitivity response.

The concept of food sensitivity and increased intestinal

permeability is gaining acceptance as more physicians see the clinical changes in their patients when they use this approach. Testing for food and environmental sensitivities, parasites, toxic metals, candidiasis, intestinal permeability, and comprehensive digestive and stool analysis often provides an understanding of an underlying cause of the disease.

Candidiasis frequently plays a role in arthritis and is a possible aggravator in rheumatoid arthritis. Yeast in the gastrointestinal system may be the result of antibiotics, oral contraceptives, steroid medications, increased use of alcohol or sugar, or a stressed immune system. Treatment of *Candida* infections in the digestive system has improved rheumatoid symptoms in many cases. To find out if it complicates your symptoms, do the self-test in this book as well as a blood or stool test.

Infection can trigger arthritis and joint inflammation. Why they move to the joints or cause joint pain is unknown at this time. But the phenomenon is well documented. If *Candida*, Lyme's disease, chlamydia, *Klebsiella*, *Salmonella*, or another infection is present, your physician can recommend a variety of therapeutics, including both natural and pharmaceutical remedies. If you have increased intestinal permeability, nutrients such as glutamine, quercetin, gamma-oryzanol and beneficial flora can help heal the leaky cells. An elimination diet or fasting can significantly reduce joint inflammation, pain, and stiffness, and increase mobility. By careful addition of foods over the course of three months you can see which foods cause symptoms to recur. Blood testing can significantly aid in this process because you have a much clearer idea of which foods you are sensitive to. No blood test is 100 percent accurate, so you still need to go through the dietary regimen. After a period of four to six months, you will be able to tolerate most of the troublesome foods. Repeat blood testing at that time is advised.

After that, many people will be pain-free, while others may still have some arthritic symptoms. There is documentation in the literature about arthritis and deficiencies of nearly every known nutrient. When the needed nutrients are supplied, the body can begin to balance itself. Though there are many additional nutritional and herbal products that help people with arthritis, no one thing works for everyone, so persist until you find the therapies that work best for you. Give each one at least a three-month trial before giving up on it. I remember Abraham Hoffer, M.D. telling about a patient at a conference many years ago. He had recommended the man take 1,000 milligrams of vitamin C daily for his arthritis. The man took the vitamin C faithfully each day without any improvement. After a whole year, he suddenly became pain-free!

People with arthritis are often too acidic. To buffer this acidity, the body pulls alkaline minerals out of the bones. These minerals are sometimes deposited in joints throughout the body. Use of litmus paper to test the first morning urine can determine whether an acid/alkaline imbalance is contributing to arthritis. See the table "Food and Chemical Effects on Acid/Alkaline Body Chemical Balance" in chapter 7.

Specific recommendations for various types of arthritis—osteoarthritis, rheumatoid arthritis, psoriatic arthritis, and ankylosing spondylitis—follow.

Osteoarthritis

Osteoarthritis is the most common type of arthritis. It's the kind we associate with aging, although nutritionally oriented physicians believe it has more to do with poor dietary habits and biochemical imbalances. Pain is usually the first symptom. The main characteristics are stiffness, achiness, and painful joints that creak and crack. Stiffness may be worse in the morning and after exercise. Osteoarthritis begins gradually and usually affects one or a few joints, most commonly in the knee, hip, fingers, ankles, and feet. As joints enlarge, cartilage degenerates. Eventually, hardening leads to bone spurs. You lose flexibility, strength, and the ability to grasp, accompanied with pain. Risk of osteoarthritis, especially arthritis in the knee, increases if you are overweight; losing weight helps.

FUNCTIONAL LABORATORY TESTING

1. Elisa allergy testing for foods.
2. Comprehensive digestive and stool analysis.
3. Intestinal permeability screening.
4. *Candida* testing, either separately or in CDSA.

HEALING OPTIONS

Some of these suggestions will significantly help your arthritis; others may not help at all. You can look for products which combine these substances. Be patient and give whatever you try time to work. Try one or two at a time until you find a program that suits your body's unique needs and lifestyle.

Elimination/provocation diet: Follow the directions outlined in chapter 7. For best results, work with a nutritionist or physician who is familiar with food sensitivity protocols.

Nightshade diet: In the 1970s, Norman Childers, a horticulturist, popularized the Nightshade Diet. Elimination of nightshade family foods helps only a small percentage of people with arthritis, but people who respond are usually helped a great deal. The nightshade foods are potatoes, tomatoes, eggplant, and peppers (red, green, yellow, chile). An elimination diet of one week followed by a reintroduction of these foods provides a good test. Blood testing also picks up these sensitivities.

Multivitamin with minerals: People with arthritis are often deficient in many nutrients. Aging, poor diet, medications, malabsorption, and illness all contribute to poor nutritional status. At least seventeen nutrients are essential for formation of bone and cartilage, so it's important to find a supplement that supports these needs. Look for a supplement which contains 800–1,000 milligrams calcium, 400–500 milligrams magnesium, 15–45 milligrams zinc, 1–2 milligrams copper, 10,000 IU vitamin A, 200 micrograms selenium, 50 milligrams vitamin B₆, and 5–10 milligrams manganese in addition to other nutrients. Follow dosage on bottle to get nutrients in the appropriate amounts.

Vitamin E: Twenty-nine people with osteoarthritis were given 600 IU of vitamin E or a placebo daily. Out of fifteen who received vitamin E, 52 percent reported improvement. Another study showed no improvement in those with osteoarthritis who were given vitamin E supplementation of 1,200 IU daily. Dosage: Try 800 IU for two to three months. It is very safe and may help some people. Just be sure to buy d-alpha tocopherol, which is the natural and active form of vitamin E.

Vitamin C: Vitamin C is an essential nutrient for every anti-arthritis program. Vitamin C is vital for formation of cartilage and collagen, a fibrous protein that forms strong connective tissue necessary for bone strength. Vitamin C also plays a role in immune response, helping protect us from disease-producing microbes. Many types of arthritis are caused by microbes, which vitamin C helps combat. It also inhibits formation of inflammatory prostaglandins, helping to reduce pain, inflammation, and swelling. Vitamin C is also an antioxidant and free-radical scavenger; free-radical formation has been noted in arthritic conditions. Dosage: 1–3 grams daily in an ascorbate or ester form.

Glucosamine sulfate and chondroitin sulfate: Glycosamine sulfate and chondroitin sulfate are nutrients used therapeutically to help repair cartilage, reduce inflammation, and increase mobility. Green-lipped mussels are a rich source of glycosaminoglycans. Use of glycosamine sulfate has no associated side effects although anecdotally it *may* raise serum cholesterol levels. It either works or it doesn't. Give it a three-month trial. Dosage: 500 milligrams three times daily either with or without chondroitin sulfate.

Alfalfa: Alfalfa is a tried and true folk remedy for arthritis. Many people attest to its benefits, but more research is needed on it. Alfalfa is an abundantly nutritious food, high in minerals, vitamins, antioxidants, and protein. Alfalfa may help because of its saponin content or its high nutrient and trace mineral content. It is widely used as a nutritional supplement in animal feed.

Dosage: fourteen to twenty-four tablets in two or three dosages daily or grind up alfalfa seeds and take three tablespoons of ground seeds each day. You can mix them with applesauce, cottage cheese, oatmeal, or sprinkle on salads. Another method is to cook 1 ounce of alfalfa seeds in 3 cups of water. Do not boil them, but cook gently in a glass or enamel pan for thirty minutes, and strain. Toss away the seeds and keep the tea. Dilute the tea with an equal amount of water. Add honey if you like. Use it all within twenty-four hours. Yet another method is to soak 1 ounce of alfalfa seeds in 3 cups of water for twelve to twenty-four hours. Strain and drink the liquid throughout the day.

Yucca: Yucca has been used by Native Americans of the Southwest to alleviate symptoms of arthritis and improve digestion. It's a rich source of saponins with anti-inflammatory effects. Studies have been done with both rheumatoid and osteoarthritis with significant improvement in 56 to 66 percent of the people who tried it. People taking yucca over one and a half years also had the additional advantage of improved triglyceride and cholesterol levels and reduction in high blood pressure, with no negative side effects. Dosage: two to eight tablets daily.

Omega-3 fatty acids/fish oils: Fish oils come from cold water fish and contain eicosapentaenoic acid (EPA) and dicosahexaenoic acid (DHA). The fish with the highest levels are salmon, mackerel, halibut, sardines, tuna, and herring. These omega-3 fatty acids are essential because we cannot synthesize them and must obtain them from our foods. Fish oils inhibit production of inflammatory prostaglandin E2 series, inhibit cylcooxygenase and thromboxane A2, all of which come from arachidonic acid. Fish oils shift the production to thromboxane A3, which causes less constriction of blood vessels and platelet stickiness than thromboxane A2.

Research has shown fish oils are really helpful for some people with arthritis. Fish oil capsules reduce morning stiffness and joint tenderness. They produce moderate, but definite improvement in arthritic diseases at dosages from eight to twenty capsules daily. Similar results can be obtained by eating fish with high EPA/DHA two to four times a week. Because fish oils increase blood clotting time, they should not be used by people who have hemophilia or who take anticoagulant medicines or aspirin regularly. Dosage: It's easiest for most people to eat fish two to four times each week. High dosages in capsule form should be monitored by a physician. Neuromins is a patented algae-derived DHA which can be taken in smaller doses of about 2 grams daily.

Ginger: Ginger is an old Ayurvedic remedy that was given to people with rheumatoid and osteoarthritis. It reduced pain and swelling in various amounts in 75 percent of the people tested, with no reported side effects over three months to two and a half years. Ginger can be used as an ingredient in food and tea or taken as a supplement. Dosage: 2 ounce fresh ginger daily or 3,000–7,000 milligrams powdered ginger.

Cetyl myristoleate: Cetyl myristoleate (CM) was discovered by Harry Diehl, a researcher at the National Institute of Health. He found that mice did not develop arthritis when CM was given. When he himself developed arthritis, Diehl took CM and his arthritis resolved. Jonathan Wright, M.D., has found CM to be clinically valuable in about half of his patients. CM appears to actually "cure" arthritis in many instances. I was able to find two studies on CM; both had astounding results. CM was found to be best used in combination with glucosamine sulfate, sea cucumber, and MSM preparations. Recommended duration of use is two to four weeks. Carbonated beverages, caffeine, chocolate, and cigarettes are not allowed while taking CM and its associated supplements.

Superoxide dismutase: Superoxide dismutase (SOD) plays an important role in reducing inflammation and has been used alone, with copper, manganese or copper, and zinc for various arthritic conditions. Oral SOD doesn't seem to work as well, except when used in a copper/zinc preparation. Some physicians are using SOD in injections. Wheat grass extracts of SOD can be purchased at health food stores. Most people who try them experience benefits, but there is little scientific research to date. Some veterinarians are using wheat grass SOD with arthritic animals with excellent results.

Methylsulfonylmethane: Methylsulfonylmethane (MSM), a naturally occurring derivative of DMSO, is now being used as a supplement. Although DMSO has a distinct odor that prevents many people from using it, MSM is odorless. MSM is found in unprocessed, fresh foods and is also manufactured by our bodies. MSM helps reduce pain and inflammation, and gives the body the sulfur compounds necessary to build cartilage and collagen. It is also useful in allergies, blood sugar control, and asthma. Dosage: 1,000–5,000 milligrams daily. Best taken with 1,000–5,000 milligrams of vitamin C for absorption.

S-adenosylmethionine: A recent player on the scene is S-adenosylmethionine (SAMe), a synthetic version of a chemical that is naturally made in our bodies from methione. Research on SAMe shows it to have powerful antidepressant effects without the side effects of pharmaceutical antidepressant medications. SAMe has also been shown to be as potent an anti-inflammatory drug as indomethacin without the negative side effects in people with arthritis.

Bromelain: Bromelain is an enzyme derived from pineapple that acts as an anti-inflammatory in much the same way that evening primrose, fish, and borage oils do. It interferes with production of arachidonic acid, shifting to prostaglandin production of the less inflammatory type. It also prevents platelet aggregation and interferes with the growth of malignant cells. Bromelain can be taken with meals as a digestive aid, but as an anti-inflammatory it must be taken between meals. Dosage: 500–1,000 milligrams two to three times daily between meals.

Quercetin: Quercetin is the most effective bioflovonoid in its anti-inflammatory effects; others include bromelain, curcumin, and rutin. Bioflavonoids help maintain collagen tissue by decreasing membrane permeability and cross-linking collagen fibers, making them stronger. Quercetin can be used to reduce pain and inflammatory responses and for control of allergies. Dosage: 500–2,000 milligrams daily. It appears to reduce inflammatory cytokines.

Boswellia: *Boswellia serrata,* an Ayurvedic remedy that has been traditionally used for arthritis, pain, and inflammation, has been shown to moderate inflammatory markers such as nitric oxide and 5-lipoxygenase. Western studies are promising, but more needs to be done. In the meantime, Boswellia is nontoxic and may be useful.

Tumeric/curcumin: Tumeric has powerful anti-inflammatory properties. Some of the mechanisms involved include its ability to block leukotrienes and arachadonic acid, both of which cause inflammation and pain. An effective dosage of tumeric is 10–60 grams daily. Curcumin, the active pain-relieving ingredient, can be taken in much smaller doses of 500 milligrams three times daily. For those lucky enough to live in warm areas where tumeric can be grown and used fresh, it can be juiced, grated, used in stir-fry, and eaten freely. Tumeric also is a lovely flowering garden plant.

Folic acid plus vitamin B$_{12}$: In a recent study, people with osteoarthritis in their hands were given 20 micrograms vitamin B$_{12}$ plus 6,400 micrograms folic acid daily, and they reported a significant reduction in symptoms. This is a tiny amount of vitamin B$_{12}$ and a large amount of folic acid, which is nontoxic even at these high levels.

Devil's claw: Devil's claw (*Harpagophytum procumbens*) is a South African root that is commonly used as an arthritis remedy. It reduces pain and inflammation. Several studies have shown it to work as well as phenylbutazone, a common NSAID medication. It is commonly used in low-potency homeopathic dilutions of 2X in Germany.

Black cohosh: Black cohosh (*Cimcifuga racemosa*) has long been used by European and American herbalists to reduce muscle spasm, pain, and inflammation. It can be used as either a tincture or in capsules.

Cider vinegar: Jarvis, in his book, *Vermont Folk Medicine,* popularized the use of apple cider vinegar and honey for the relief of arthritis. Vinegar and honey are alkalizing to the body, which helps dissolve calcification in the joints. Many people have found relief on this program, although there has been no scientific documentation.

Pulse electromagnetic fields: A small study was done on twenty-seven people with osteoarthritis using low-pulsed electromagnetic fields at an extremely low frequency during eighteen half-hour sessions. Halfway through the study 34 percent improved; at the end of treatment 36 percent improved; and one month later 47 percent had improved. This was significantly different than the control group—8, 10, and 14 percent. This treatment has no known negative effects and is certainly worth trying.

Rheumatoid Arthritis

Rheumatoid arthritis is characterized by inflammation of joints most often in the hands, feet, wrists, elbows, and ankles with symmetrical involvement. It can start in virtually any joint. The onset may be sudden, with pain in multiple joints, or may come on gradually, with more and more joints becoming involved. Joints become swollen and feel tender and can degenerate and become misshapen. They are often stiffest in the mornings and also feel worse after movement. The rheumatoid factor (RF) is a blood test that will become elevated in most cases of rheumatoid arthritis. While it may get better or worse, once established it is nearly always present to some extent. Standard treatment is aspirin or NSAIDs, and steroid medications.

Rheumatoid arthritis has a genetic component, often running in families. The gene marker HLA-DR4 is present in 50 to 75 percent of people with rheumatoid arthritis. *Proteus mirabilis*, a bacteria commonly found in the digestive tract, typically doesn't cause illness, but when present in a person who is HLA-DR4 positive, it may trigger an autoimmune response which leads to rheumatoid arthritis. Some researchers believe that rheumatoid arthritis is the result of repeated episodes of *Proteus* infection. *Proteus mirabilis* antibodies are generally found in people with RA. Vegetarian diets have long been shown to be of benefit in rheumatoid arthritis. In one unique study, a decrease in antibodies to *Proteus mirabilis* was observed in subjects on the diet. Proteus infections can be treated with either natural or pharmaceutical therapy.

Food and environmental sensitivities, malabsorption, parasites, *Candida*, and leaky gut syndrome also play a role in rheumatoid arthritis. Any food may trigger a reaction, but the most common aggravators, in descending order, are corn, wheat, bacon/pork, oranges, milk, oats, rye, eggs, beef, coffee, malt, cheese, grapefruit, tomato, peanuts, sugar cane, butter, lamb, lemons, and soy. Some people with it are gliadin sensitive (sensitive to grain; see Celiac disease). It's hard to generalize or predict which of these factors will be found in each person, but usually one or more is present. Each of them needs to be investigated. Leaky gut is probably not a primary cause of rheumatoid arthritis, but long-term use of NSAID medication often makes it a factor.

FUNCTIONAL LABORATORY TESTING

1. Elisa allergy testing for foods.
2. Comprehensive digestive and stool analysis.
3. Intestinal permeability screening. Stop use of NSAIDs

for three weeks prior to test. You can also use the IP test to monitor your progress.

4. Heidelberg capsule testing for HCl status.
5. Methane breath test for small bowel bacterial overgrowth.
6. Liver function testing. People with rheumatoid arthritis are also shown to have reduced function in the detoxification pathways.

HEALING OPTIONS

Try one or two of these suggestions at a time, and you'll gradually find a program that suits your unique needs and lifestyle. You may find combination supplements for arthritis that includes many of these substances.

Food and environmental sensitivities: Explore the relationship between your arthritis and food and environmental sensitivities through laboratory testing and the elimination/provocation diet.

Elimination/provocation diet: Follow directions in chapter 7. For best results, work with a nutritionist or physician who is familiar with food sensitivity protocols.

Hypochlorhydria/low HCl levels: Low levels of hydrochloric acid (HCl) were found in 32 percent of people tested with rheumatoid arthritis. Half of these people had small bowel bacterial overgrowth. Thirty-five percent of patients with normal levels of HCl had small bowel bacterial overgrowth compared with none of the normal controls. Small bowel overgrowth was found most in people with active arthritic symptoms.

Dosage: Varies from person to person. To find the optimal amount for you, begin by taking one HCl tablet with each meal for one day. The next day, take two tablets with each meal, gradually increasing the dosage. At some point you will feel a warm, burning sensation in your stomach; your optimal dose is one tablet less than this. If the burning sensation is uncomfortable, quickly drink a glass of milk or water with a teaspoon of baking soda.

Nightshade diet: Elimination of nightshade family foods helps only a small percentage of people with arthritis, but people who respond are usually helped a great deal. A one-week elimination diet with a gradual reintroduction of nightshade family foods offers a good test. Blood testing also picks up these sensitivities.

Multivitamin with minerals: People with arthritis are often deficient in many nutrients. So it's important to find a supplement that supplies at least seventeen nutrients essential for formation of bone and cartilage. Look for a supplement which contains 800–1,000 milligrams calcium, 400–500 milligrams magnesium, 400–800 IU vitamin D, 15–45 milligrams zinc, 1–2 milligrams copper, 10,000 IU vitamin A, 200 micrograms selenium, 50 milligrams vitamin B_6, and 5–10 milligrams manganese in addition to other nutrients. Follow dosage on bottle to get nutrients in the appropriate amounts.

Vitamin E: In a study with vitamin E supplementation of 1,200 IU daily, there was a decrease in pain in people with rheumatoid arthritis. (For dosage, see discussion under Osteoarthritis.)

Vitamin C: Vitamin C is an essential nutrient for every anti-arthritis program. (For more on vitamin C, see discussion under Osteoarthritis.) Dosage: Take 1–3 grams daily in an ascorbate or ester form.

Alfalfa: Alfalfa is a tried and true folk remedy for arthritis, but more research is needed on it. Dosage: Take fourteen to twenty-four tablets in two or three dosages daily or prepare alfalfa seeds as discussed under Osteoarthritis.

Yucca: Yucca has been used by Native Americans of the Southwest to alleviate symptoms of arthritis and improve digestion. (For more on yucca, see discussion under Osteoarthritis.) Dosage: two to eight tablets daily.

Gamma linolenic acid: Patients with rheumatoid arthritis were given 1.4 grams daily of gamma linolenic acid (GLA) from borage oil. It significantly reduced their symptoms: swollen joints by 36 percent, tenderness by 45 percent, swollen joint count by 28 percent, and swollen joint score by 41 percent (some people responded in more than one area). Use of oil of evening primrose in the study group and olive oil for the control group showed that both oils helped reduce pain and morning stiffness. Several people were able to reduce use of NSAIDs, but none were able to stop the medication. The modest results in this study were probably due to the use of NSAIDs with the oil of evening primrose. The same results could be obtained by use of evening primrose or borage oil alone. Dosage: 1,400 milligrams.

Omega-3 fatty acids/fish oils: Research has shown that some people with rheumatoid arthritis have found it very helpful to eat fish high in omega-3 fatty acids—salmon, mackerel, halibut, sardines, tuna, and herring—or take fish oil supplements. (For more on omega-3 fatty acids/fish oils, see discussion under Osteoarthritis.) Dosage: It's easiest for most people to eat fish two to four times each week. High dosages in capsule form should be monitored by a physician.

Cetyl myritoleate: See page 280.

Glucosamine sulfate: Glycosamine sulfate is used therapeutically to help repair cartilage, reduce swelling and inflammation, and restore joint function. (For more on glycosamine sulfate, see discussion under Osteoarthritis.) Dosage: 500 milligrams two to four times daily.

Ginger: Ginger is an old Ayurvedic remedy that was given to people with rheumatoid and osteoarthritis. (For more on ginger, see discussion under Osteoarthritis.) Dosage: 2 ounces fresh ginger daily in food or tea or 3,000–7,000 milligrams powdered ginger.

Superoxide dismutase: Superoxide dismutase plays an important role in reducing inflammation and has been used alone, with copper, manganese, or copper and zinc for various arthritic conditions. (For more on superoxide dismutase, see discussion under Osteoarthritis.)

Methylsulfonylmethane: See page 281.

S-adenosylmethionine: See page 281.

Bromelain: Bromelain acts as an anti-inflammatory in much the same way that evening primrose, fish, and borage oils do. (For more on bromelain, see discussion under Osteoarthritis.) Dosage: 500–1,000 milligrams two to three times daily between meals.

Quercetin: Quercetin is the most effective bioflavonoid in its anti-inflammatory effects. (For more on quercetin, see discussion under Osteoarthritis.) Dosage: 500–1,000 milligrams two to four times daily.

Boswellia: *Boswellia serrata* is an Ayurvedic remedy that has traditionally been used for arthritis, pain, and inflammation. Boswellia has been shown to moderate inflammatory markers such as nitric oxide and 5-lipoxygenase. A specific preparation of Boswellia called H-15 was given to 260 people and found to be effective in treating rheumatoid arthritis: 50–60 percent of the subjects had good results. Boswellia is taken over the long term as a treatment for rheumatoid arthritis, not specifically for immediate pain. Dosage: 1,200 milligrams two or three times daily.

Devil's Claw: See page 282.

Black cohosh: Black cohosh, *Cimcifuga racemosa*, has long been used by European and American herbalists to reduce muscle spasm, pain, and inflammation. It is especially useful in rheumatoid arthritis and fibromyalgia. It can be used either as a tincture or in capsules.

Capsicum/cayenne pepper: Cayenne has been well studied for its temporary relief of arthritis pain. Creams with capsicum are used topically to relieve pain. (These creams may burn when first applied.) They work by blocking leukotrienes and arachadonic acid, which ultimately blocks substance P, which causes pain. Eighty percent of people who have used the topical cream experience pain relief.

Tumeric/curcumin: See page 282.

DL phenylalanine: DL phenylalanine is an amino acid that is used therapeutically for pain and depression. It is effective for treating rheumatoid arthritis, osteoarthritis, low back pain, and migraines. "D" is the naturally found form, and "L" is its synthetic mirror. The combination of DL slows down the release of the phenylalanine. It appears to inhibit the breakdown of endorphins, our body's natural pain relievers. Dosage: 400–500 milligrams three times daily.

Copper: Copper is involved in collagen formation, tissue repair, and anti-inflammatory processes. People with rheumatoid arthritis often have marginal copper levels. Traditionally, copper bracelets have been worn to help reduce arthritic symptoms. W. Ray Walker, Ph.D. tested people who had benefited from copper bracelets by having them wear copper-colored aluminum bracelets for two months: fourteen out of forty participants deteriorated so much they couldn't finish the two months. More than half reported that their arthritis had worsened. Dr. Walker found that 13 milligrams of copper per month was dissolved by sweat, and presumably much of that was absorbed through the skin. Supplementation with copper increases levels of SOD. Dosage: Wear copper bracelet or supplement with 1–2 milligrams daily in a multivitamin preparation. If you are working with a physician, you may temporarily add a supplement of copper salicylate or copper sebacate until copper levels return to normal.

Niacinamide: Most of the B-complex vitamins have been shown to reduce inflammation and swelling associated with arthritis. Dr. Kaufman recommends using niacinamide at a rather high dosage with excellent results. It doesn't cure the arthritis but really helps while you take it. If you are going to try this, do so with your physician's supervision. High levels of niacinamide can be liver toxic. Dosage: 500–2,000 milligrams daily.

Cider vinegar: Although there is no scientific documentation about apple cider vinegar and honey, many people report relief. Because vinegar and honey are alkaline, they may help dissolve calcification in the joints.

Breast implants: Silicone breast implants may cause rheuma-toidlike symptoms in some women, although research is divided. If you have rheumatoid arthritis and silicone or saline breast implants, it would be smart to be tested for silicone antibodies/allergies on an annual basis. Many women feel remarkably better once breast implants have been removed.

Psoriatic Arthritis

Psoriatic arthritis affects 5 to 7 percent of people with psoriasis who have joint pain as well as the more common skin and nail symptoms. There is not yet agreement on whether this is an advanced stage of psoriasis or a completely separate but similar disease. The arthritic condition closely resembles that of rheumatoid arthritis, although people with psoriatic arthritis usually have a negative rheumatoid factor. Fingers, toes, and the lower back are the most likely joints to be affected. Skin and joint symptoms may flare up or improve simultaneously. This disease can be mild, but it can also be severely deforming and disabling.

No one really knows what causes psoriatic arthritis, although it appears to have genetic, environmental, and immunologic origins. The gene marker HLA-B27 is present in most people with this disease. Some researchers have concluded that chronic exposure to bacteria in the gut, tonsils, and skin results in inflammation throughout the body, particularly in the skin and joints. The interaction of these bacteria with a specific gene type may cause an autoimmune reaction, which causes the early symptoms.

Inflammation of psoriatic arthritis is involved with arachidonic acid pathways. A healthful diet plus essential fatty acids help reduce and prevent further inflammation. Evening primrose, borage, and fish oils, tumeric, curcumin, bromelain, and quercetin all work on these pathways.

HEALING OPTIONS

See Rheumatoid Arthritis and Psoriasis.

Ankylosing Spondylitis

Ankylosing spondylitis is characterized by a progressive fusion of joints in and around the spine. It affects Caucasian men 90 percent of the time and typically becomes evident between the ages of ten to thirty. It starts off as a low backache, which is often worse in the mornings. Symptoms get progressively worse and spread from the lower back to the mid-back and up to the neck. The spine gradually becomes fused. Later, shoulders, hips, and knees may be affected. Symptoms flare and subside. Secretory IgA levels are usually elevated in people with ankylosing spondylitis.

The role of dysbiosis in ankylosing spondylitis is the most researched and best understood of all the arthritic diseases. An infection in the intestines, usually of a bacteria called *Klebsiella*, causes a local immune reaction. The antibodies for *Klebsiella* fit the gene HLA-B27. While *Klebsiella* is normally not a disease-producing microbe, it appears in people with the HLA-B27 gene marker as if the antibodies produced to kill it attach to the HLA-B27 cells and destroy them, causing joint pain and inflammation. This concept of autoimmune disease may explain why some people get certain illnesses and others don't. It's the presence not only of a specific gene, but also of a microbe that activates destruction of the cells.

What begins as a local infection triggers an autoimmune disease. As the latest research shows, in M. Leirisalo-Repo's words, "An association between inflammatory bowel disease and enteroarthritis and the spondyloarthropathies has been known for awhile . . . and it now seems evident that chronic gut inflammation is either associated with or is even the cause of chronicity of peripheral arthritis and the development of ankylosing spondylitis."

While the gene marker HLA-B27 is present in 96 percent of people with ankylosing spondylitis, not all people with this gene marker have the illness. This marker is also present in 10 to 15 percent of the general population. Research shows 70 to 80 percent of people with ankylosing spondylitis have the *Klebsiella* bacteria in their stools. *Yersinia, Shigella,* and *Salmonella* bacteria are also associated with this process and may contribute to the disease in people who are not infected with Klebsiella.

It is important to make an early diagnosis of ankylosing spondylitis so that progression of the disease can be slowed or halted. Because it usually appears as a low backache, many people seek chiropractic help or massage therapy or take anti-inflammatory medications. But such remedies can't correct dysbiosis in the intestinal tract. Because men commonly have low back pain, they often have irreversible damage before a correct diagnosis is made.

About half the people with ankylosing spondylitis experience dramatic improvement when they eliminate dairy products. Thirteen out of twenty-five people who were studied had good results, and another four had moderate improvements. Of the respondents whose results were good, eight were able to discontinue NSAID medication. Six patients kept dairy-free for over two years because they were so satisfied with the results. The elimination of dairy products is a simple and effective treatment to try. Although the mechanism for this improvement is unclear, it is suggested that a dairy-free diet modifies the bacterial ecosystem of the gut, which may have benefits. Another hypothesis is that milk allergy causes chronic irritation to the gut as well as gut permeability.

Leaky gut syndrome is present in people with ankylosing spondylitis. Unfortunately, NSAIDs are commonly used to treat ankylosing spondylitis, causing even greater intestinal permeability. This, in turn, causes more sensitivity to foods and environmental substances.

FUNCTIONAL LABORATORY TESTING

1. Secretory IgA.
2. Comprehensive digestive and stool analysis.

3. Elisa food and environmental sensitivity screening.
4. Intestinal permeability screening.

HEALING OPTIONS

Treat the infection: Your physician can prescribe an appropriate antibiotic to treat the underlying infection. If you are working with a physician who specializes in natural therapies, he or she may suggest the use of colloidal silver, goldenseal, and/or grapefruit seed extract.

Bifidobacteria and acidophilus: Because treatment for the infection will alter your intestinal flora, take probiotic supplements of supportive healthy bacteria to reestablish them. Dosage: one to two capsules two to three times daily or ¼ to ½ teaspoon powder mixed with a cool or room-temperature beverage taken between meals.

Eliminate all dairy products: Half of all people with ankylosing spondylitis respond to a milk-free diet. Do a home trial by eliminating all dairy products for eight weeks, including milk, yogurt, ice cream, creamed soups, frozen yogurt, powdered milk, and whipped cream. Also eliminate less obvious sources, such as bakery items, cookies, hot dogs, lunchmeats, milk chocolate, most nondairy creamers, pancakes, protein-powder drinks, ranch dressing, and anything that contains casein, caseinate, lactose, sodium caseinate, and whey.

Follow the recommendations for osteo- and rheumatoid arthritis: Once the underlying infection has been treated and flora have been reestablished, try other healing options for your remaining symptoms.

ASTHMA

Asthma affects about 5–8 percent of the U.S. population, more than 14 million people. It is more common in boys than in girls during childhood, but the incidence evens out between genders in adulthood. The incidence of asthma has been rising at an alarming rate: Between 1982 and 1992, there was a 42 percent increase, and age-adjusted deaths rose by 40 percent. These rates have continued to rise.

Symptoms of asthma include shortness of breath, wheezing, chest tightness, and coughing. Its more technical name is *reversible obstructive pulmonary disease*, or ROPD. Asthma can be a chronic or an occasional problem. Most people with asthma also have allergies. The causes of asthma are multifactoral and not well understood. Exposure to stress, poor air quality, grasses, molds, smoke, chemicals, bacterial infections, colds, viruses, pollens, dust, and sensitivity to cockroaches and pets can trigger asthma attacks. Increasing ozone levels are directly correlated with an increase in hospital admissions for asthma. Anyone can be sensitive to these events, but people with asthma are much more sensitive. During an attack, changes take place in your lungs that make breathing difficult: Your lungs begin to produce more mucous than normal. It's very thick and sticky, and tends to clog up the tubes. The air tubes become inflamed and swell. This causes the air tubes to narrow, and breathing becomes labored. Oxygen supply to the rest of the body is limited, carbon dioxide builds up, and the body becomes more acidic.

Asthma attacks can come on suddenly or build over several hours or days. Medical treatment consists of medications, inhalers, allergy shots, and peak flow meter machines, which help you breathe. Reducing allergen exposure also helps. Excellent air filtration systems, efficient vacuum cleaners, laundering bedding in hot water, and keeping bedrooms scrupulously clean and uncluttered can be effective in preventing asthma attacks.

When exposed to allergens, people with asthma have inflammation in their digestive tract that causes a leaky gut. Although the symptoms are felt in the lungs, it is believed that people with asthma have mucous membrane problems in general. *Candida* and other fungal infections have been linked with asthma. One study found fungal infections in fifty-two out of sixty-four subjects. After two years of anti-sensitivity treatment, a good to excellent response was reported in 60 percent of the subjects. This may be due to steroid medications, such as inhalers and prednisone, which are well-known triggers of *Candida*. This doesn't account for the amount of fungus found. It may also be due to a deficiency of secretory IgA found in mucous membranes throughout the body as a consequence of asthma.

Asthma responds best to lifestyle changes and stress management techniques. Learning to develop emotional hardiness and a relaxed manner in stressful situations can greatly reduce the incidence and severity of asthma attacks. Exercise is usually beneficial for people with asthma, although there is one type of asthma that only occurs post-exercise. Cleaning up you diet is essential. Get rid of sugars, alcohol, processed foods, and food additives. Allergies and asthma are a problem with total load. If you can keep the total below the threshold, you stay symptom-free.

FUNCTIONAL LABORATORY TESTING

1. IgE and IgG food allergy testing.
2. Intestinal permeability testing.
3. *Candida* antibodies and sensitivity testing.

HEALING OPTIONS

Dietary changes: Eliminate sugar, alcohol, processed foods, and food additives from your diet. Focus on fresh fruits and vegetables and natural foods. Discover food allergens and avoid those foods for four to six months. Slowly reintroduce those foods.

Exercise: Research shows that twenty to thirty minutes of aerobic exercise four or five times each week will reduce use of medications and symptoms of asthma. It is important to go at your own pace and to not overdo—you don't want to cause exercise-induced asthma! If you are not already exercising, build up slowly and ask your doctor or a fitness instructor for a personalized program.

Focus on healing mucous membranes: People with asthma benefit from nutrients that promote healthful mucous membranes in the lungs and gut. Helpful nutrients include vitamin A, glutamine, N-acetyl glucosamine, N-acetyl cysteine (NAC), and folic acid.

Vitamin C: Vitamin C is well documented in the literature to be of use in asthma protection. It protects lung responsiveness and function and reduces asthma symptoms. Vitamin C has antioxidant, anti-allergy, antiviral, and antimicrobial properties. Dosage: 1000 milligrams and up, to bowel tolerance.

Magnesium: Magnesium deficiency is common in people with asthma. Magnesium is a powerful muscle relaxant and can help prevent and reduce the severity of asthma attacks. Dosage: 400–800 milligrams daily.

Fish Oils: The research on fish oils and asthmatics has been extensive and confused. Some people benefit tremendously, while others don't. It is well known that fish oils decrease inflammatory leukotrienes, cytokines, and arachadonic acid. Cod liver oil may be a good supplement because it also contains vitamin A, which is protective of the lung mucosa. Dosage: Eat fish high in EPA/DHA at least twice each week, 2,000–2,500 milligrams daily EPA/DHA fish oil, 300 milligrams Neuromins, or 2,000–2,500 milligrams cod liver oil.

Quercetin: Quercetin is a powerful and gentle mast cell inhibitor and antihistamine. Take at first sign of lung tightness and through the duration of the asthma attack. Dosage: 300–1,000 milligrams as needed. As far as I know, there is no toxic dose.

Arginine: Nitric oxide (NO) acts as a bronchodialator. Arginine is a precursor to NO release. Dosage: 250–1,500 milligrams daily.

Ginko biloba: One study on ginkgo showed improvement in symptoms, lung function, and reduced airway hyperreactivity. Ginkgo is a known free-radical scavenger, enhances circulation, protects nerves, and has an anti-inflammatory effect. Dosage: Ginkgo biloba standardized extract, 180–240 milligrams daily.

Multivitamin with antioxidants: Research documents the increased need for glutathione peroxidase, vitamin C, and vitamin E in people with asthma. Glutathione peroxidase is an enzyme that is dependent on both selenium and glutathione. Vitamin B_6 and B_{12} levels have also been found to be lower in asthmatics. Look for a multivitamin that contains at least 400 IU vitamin E, 1000 milligrams vitamin C, 200 micrograms selenium, reduced glutathione or NAC, and 5 or more milligrams of manganese. If you look for a multivitamin that has a dosage of three or more tablets you may also find 400–600 milligrams magnesium as well.

Traumeel S: Traumeel S is a homeopathic product that was used in a double-blind placebo-controlled study. Subjects continued to use their corticosteroid medications during the study. Over twenty weeks, the use of medications was reduced from 4.6 milligrams daily to 2.6 milligrams daily. Their general symptoms improved significantly, and serum IgE levels dropped substantially. Frequency of infection was decreased from three in four before Traumeel S to zero in one with it. Symptoms improved significantly and people had an increased sense of well-being. Dosage: one ampule given subcutaneously every five to seven days.

Coleus forskolin: This herb has been shown to have bronchodialating effects on the lungs and to be beneficial for asthma. It simulates the production of cyclic AMP. Impaired cyclic AMP production is believed to be an underlying cause of asthma.

Adrenal support: Asthma, like all allergies, responds to adrenal support. Corticosteroid drugs mimic the body's natural adrenal hormones. Anything you can do to enhance your body's own production of steroid hormones will be of benefit. Although literature is scant, animal studies with licorice hold promise. Use DGL licorice unless blood pressure is extremely low. Most licorice candy does not contain any licorice, but some gourmet licorice does. Be careful, as too much may raise your blood pressure. Adrenal glandulars, panthothenic acid (vitamin B_5), and Siberian ginseng may also be of use.

ATTENTION DEFICIT DISORDER

Attention deficit disorder (ADHD) affects 3–5 percent of all school-age children and an estimated 17 million Americans. It is characterized by patterns of inattention and/or hyperactivity and impulsive behavior. This behavior occurs both at home, socially, and in school settings. Problems also include failure to complete tasks, problems staying organized, difficulty keeping track of things, making careless mistakes, and becoming easily distracted. ADHD can show up as fidgetiness, excessive movement or talking, impatience, difficulty waiting or taking turns, or blurting out answers.

There are three main subtypes of ADHD: predominantly inattentive, predominantly hyperactive, and combined type. It is three to ten times more prevalent in boys than girls. The main symptom in girls with ADHD is usually inattentiveness, rather than the hyperactivity usually seen in boys. Children with inattentiveness may go undiagnosed. As children with ADHD become teenagers, the problems continue and the incidences of drug addiction, poor grades, dropping out of school, and crime increase. ADHD continues on through adulthood and the predominant features are failure to complete tasks, disorganization, difficulty paying attention, and difficulty beginning tasks. Understandably, these character traits can cause relationship problems. ADHD has been called a *reward deficiency syndrome*, because dopamine activity is reduced. Dopamine is associated with reward mechanisms

in the brain, and deficiencies are implicated in addictive be-
haviors, including alcohol abuse, drug abuse, smoking, food
addictions, gambling addiction, and sexual addiction. Our
prisons are filled primarily with people who have ADHD or
other learning disorders. There may also be deficits in other
neurotransmitters, such as acetylcholine and seratonin.

Standard treatments for ADHD rely on pharmaceutical
drugs that control symptomatic response. I have had the opportunity to see PET scans of children with ADHD without
medication, with medication, and with combined natural
therapies. Children on medication had reduction in symptoms, but their PET scans were highly abnormal. The natural therapies almost normalized the PET scans. The best
approach to ADHD is to find the underlying causes to base
treatment on. The difficulty with this approach is that it
takes more time and effort on the part of the child and
parents than does taking medications. The rewards can be
great if you can help normalize someone's biochemistry for
a lifetime.

The causes of ADHD are many. It is imperative that each
person is considered to be unique and that functional tests
are performed. The functional medicine approach looks at
the triggers of ADHD. These include environmental toxins,
use of antibiotics for recurrent infections, dysbiosis, nutritional insufficiencies, and a genetic predisposition. People
with ADHD often have impaired digestion and leaky gut.
The Institute for Functional Medicine found a 74 percent
incidence of increased intestinal permeability in a test of
sixty-six children. Food and environmental allergies are extremely common. Hyperactive children have histories of
more ear infections than do other children with learning
problems. Children with recurring ear infections usually have
some food allergies, most commonly to dairy products. Recurring ear infections have also been associated with an increased incidence of ADHD, with its severity increasing with
the number of ear infections. Ninety-four percent had three
or more infections, and 69 percent had more than ten

infections. Elimination diets have been found to be effective in many, but not all, people with ADHD.

Imbalanced essential fatty acid profiles are commonly found in ADHD, especially low arachadonic acid and DHA levels and high levels of undesirable trans fatty acids. Fatty acid testing can determine exactly which fatty acids to supplement or increase in the diet. The brain and central nervous system rely on fatty acids for proper function. DHA deficiencies results in increased brain permeability, which allows neurotoxins to have free access to the brain.

Other nutrients have been found to be altered in ADHD. Magnesium, iron, calcium, zinc, and vitamin B_1 levels are consistently low. Studies using multivitamins have been disappointing. In one study of thirty-one children, only two were able to avoid medication. Still, for those two children, the results were 100 percent beneficial. There is often altered blood sugar metabolism, for which people with ADHD compensate by eating a large amount of sugar and refined carbohydrates. Chromium, vanadium, B-complex vitamins, and eating small frequent meals can be helpful. Elimination of refined carbohydrates and emphasis on good quality protein and fats in the diet is also beneficial.

Plasma amino acid levels were tested in twenty-eight children with ADHD. In comparison with controls, they had significantly lower levels of phenylalanine, tyrosine, tryptophan, histidine, and isoleucine. These amino acids are all critical to healthy brain function and moods. Plasma or urinary amino acid testing can provide useful information.

A study at the Functional Medicine Institute in Gig Harbor, Washington found dysbiosis to be prevalent in ADHD. In stool samples, the incidence of *Candida* was 32 percent and protozoa 41 percent.

FUNCTIONAL LABORATORY TESTING

1. Hair mineral analysis, especially for heavy metals such as lead and mercury.

2. Fatty acid blood testing.
3. Spectracell functional nutrient and antioxidant testing.
4. Intestinal permeability testing.
5. IgE and IgG food allergy blood testing.
6. Comprehensive digestive stool analysis with parasitology.
7. Screening for environmental contaminants. Two good tests are the Elisa/Act test from Serammune Labs and urinary d-glucaric acid levels. The d-glucaric acid test is a general indicator of xenobiotic substances, while the Elisa/Act test shows a reaction to specific environmental substances.
8. Organic acid testing

HEALING OPTIONS

Normalize fatty acid deficiencies: Studies have documented low arachadonic acid and DHA levels in children with ADHD. There have not been good studies to see the results on fatty acid supplementation with fish oils or arachadonic acid. Base dietary and supplement recommendations on the fatty acid test results.

Elimination diet: Not all people with ADHD will have food allergies or sensitivities. For those who do, an elimination diet will show dramatic improvements in behavior and learning abilities. Of twenty-six children with ADHD tested, nineteen (73 percent) responded favorably with an elimination diet. These nineteen children reacted to many foods, dyes, and/or preservatives. Fifteen children with ADHD and food-induced ADHD had their brains mapped with EEG. There were changes in brain electrical activity when symptom-provoking foods were given.

Vitamin therapy: Forty-one children with ADHD were given a maximum of 3 grams niacin, 3 grams vitamin C, 1.2 grams calcium panthothenate (vitamin B_5), and 600 milligrams vitamin B_6. After three months, 29 percent showed significant improvement.

Probiotics: Acidophillus and bifidobacteria were found to be absent in 46 percent of the stool samples of sixty-three children with ADHD.

Chelate heavy metals: Scalp hair from 277 first-graders was examined. Teachers completed a questionnaire for rating ADHD. A striking relationship has been found in many studies between hair lead levels and behavior: the higher the lead, the worse the behavior. High hair manganese has been associated with violent behavior in children.

Magnesium: Magnesium deficiency symptoms look a lot like the symptoms of ADHD. In a trial, children were given 3 milligrams of magnesium per pound of body weight—for example, a 75-pound child would have received 225 milligrams per day. There were significant reductions in symptoms associated with ADHD over six months. In comparison, the controls worsened.

Ginkgo biloba: Ginkgo has been shown to have anti-anxiety effects and to improve memory function. Dosage for children: 60–120 milligrams standardized extract daily. Adult dosage: 180–240 milligrams daily.

American ginseng: American ginseng has been used successfully with ADHD. Dosage in children: 200 milligrams plus 60 milligrams ginkgo twice daily.

St. John's wort: Hypericum, more commonly known as St. John's wort, has been used primarily for depression, but it does have mood-stablizing affects. It has been found to be particularly effective when used with American ginseng and ginkgo. Dosage: 150–600 milligrams twice daily. High doses may cause itchy skin after exposure to sun.

Pycnogenol: Anecdotal evidence for the use of pycnogenol is widespread. Pycnogenol is a powerful and gentle antioxidant. The spread of information on the Internet has promoted its use, and many people have found it to be extremely useful for ADHD.

Laritone Jr.: This French product was introduced to me by a Canadian pharmacist. I have used this product with two children; one had terrific results. It is composed of pig-brain phospholipids!

Dimethyaminoethanol (DMAE): Dimethyaminoethanol has been studied for use in ADHD. Although more studies need to be done, it does appear to decrease behavior problems and aggression while improving attention span and learing ability.

AUTISM

Autism is a genetic mental ailment that usually manifests by age three. Half a million Americans are affected by autism, and four out of five of those affected are males. Autism is equally distributed among all races and economic strata. Most children with autism are normal at birth and then regress. The incidence of autism has doubled over the past twenty years, which suggests an environmental basis in addition to a genetic predisposition to the disease. According to Jerry Kopelson, M.D., "what happens after [children] are born when they get a vaccine or are treated with antiobiotics has everything to do with the immune dysfunction that spills over into the central nervous system. I believe a chronic inflammation of the intestinal tract begins to occur, which leads to intestinal leakage, which then leads to immune dysfunction. If it gets sufficiently severe, it leads to central nervous dysfunction that we place in the autistic spectrum."

The work of Bill Shaw, M.D., has been pivotal in changing the ideology and treatment of autism. He has found metabolites in the urine of those affected that are fungal in origin. Instead of being broken down, as they are in the bodies of those without autism, they become brain-toxic substances that resemble opiates. When treated with antifungal drugs, those affected improve significantly and their urine metabolites normalize. Those who do not respond to antifungal medications often respond to antiparasitic medications.

Autistic children have poor brain development for social interaction and communication skills. They have trouble relating to the outside world. While often docile, people with autism can be aggressive or can hurt themselves. Repeated body movements such as hand flapping and rocking are typical. They are prone to seizures.

An exciting new treatment for autism is sweeping the nation. Secretin has long been used by gastroenterologists to test for pancreatic function. Victoria Beck, mother of Peter, an autistic child, had him worked up for his chronic diarrhea. After the test, she and her husband noticed that Peter's diarrhea had stopped and his behavior had improved dramatically. Victoria investigated and found that the secretin used as part of the test had provided the benefit.

At this point, over two hundred children have been treated with secretin. In a recent study of only three children, secretin given over a five-week period was shown to improve gastrointestinal function and improve behavior. Positive changes were noted in eye contact, alertness, and expansion of language. Children with chronic diarrhea have had normal bowel movements within a few days after receiving the secretin. Parents have also reported better sleeping patterns.

A recent study did a provocative urine test that showed elevated heavy metal loads in 1,005 of 56 children tested. Ninety-four percent showed environmental sensitivities and 98 percent had impaired liver function testing.

The Autism Research Institute is a clearinghouse for autism literature and research. They are listed in the resource directory. Bill Shaw has also written a wonderful book on autism, *Biological Treatments for Autism and PDD*.

I was unable to find any literature on essential fatty acids and autism, but because the brain is 60 percent fatty acids, it makes sense to do fatty acid analysis. I'd also look for specific amino acid imbalances. Again, the literature on this topic is scant.

FUNCTIONAL LABORATORY TESTING

1. Organic acid testing.
2. Comprehensive digestive stool analysis.
3. Liver function profile, with caffeine, acetominophen, and aspirin challenge.
4. IgE and IgG food allergy blood testing.
5. Hair mineral analysis and urinary metal challenge testing
6. Gliaden and gluten antibody testing.
7. Essential fatty acids.
8. Urinary amino acid testing.

HEALING OPTIONS

Treat dysbiosis and *Candida*: Treat the underlying cause of the illness. You can either use prescription medications or natural products such as garlic, oil of oregano, capryllic acid, and grapefruit seed extract. Eliminate all refined carbohydrates and sugars from the diet.

Food allergies/sensitivities: It is common for people with autism to have sensitivities to gluten/gliaden, which are found in wheat, rye, spelt, amaaranth, oats, and barley. Diary products should be eliminated to see if there may be a true dairy allergy to the milk protein casein. Other foods may also trigger reactions. Do testing and an elimination diet.

Secretin: Secretin is a hormone produced in the first part of the small intestine, the duodenum. It stimulates the release of bile and pancreatic enzymes. Secretin works to heal the gut, and therefore the immune system, of autistic children. It has been found to be effective in 75 percent of the children within a few days of the first treatment. Secretin may need to be given every three to six weeks. Secretin is given by injection, and some physicians are experimenting with sublingual administration. The dosage is quite small, 2.0 and 3.5 CU/kg.

Di-methyl-glycine (DMG): DMG used to be called vitamin B_{15} or calcium pangamate. It was first developed by

Soviet scientists, and once it hit the American markets there was much controversy as to its exact chemical structure. In a recent three-month study, 80 percent of children improved. The most dramatic effects were dramatic improvements in speech. Other benefits include improvement in eating and normalization of bowel movements. During the first two weeks some children had difficulty sleeping, and some became more active. According to Bernard Rimland, M.D., the effects of DMG will usually be seen within a week, but give it at least a six-week try before you decide it didn't work.

Vitamin B_6 and magnesium: Vitamin B_6 alleviates the symptoms of autism. There have been eighteen studies that have shown it to have positive effects in behavior. There was marked improvement in 30–40 percent of the children tested. A few of the children showed minor side effects including irritability, sensitivity to noise, and bedwetting. These symptoms are all common to magnesium deficiency and cleared when additional magnesium was given. Most children with autism are magnesium deficient. Magnesium and vitamin B_6 do not cure autism, but do improve it significantly.

Dosage, vitamin B_6: 75–800 milligrams daily. Carl Pfeiffer, M.D., calculated vitamin B_6 needs based on dream recall—good dream recall indicates adequate B_6. I have tried this with many clients and found it to be true for them and for me personally. Too much B_6 and I dream continuously and feel like I never fell asleep!

Dosage, magnesium: 150–300 milligrams. Too much magnesium will cause diarrhea.

Glutamine: Glutamine is the main fuel for our small intestine. It increases immune and muscle strength, normalizes bowel movements, and heals gut mucosa. Give in generous doses: 5–15 grams daily. It can be mixed with water or juice.

Acidophillus/bifidobacteria: Replace beneficial flora. Give ¼ teaspoon two to three times daily. If the child is being breastfed, the mother can take the same dosage.

N-acetylcysteine and lipoic acid: NAC and lipoic acid are antioxidants that can help reduce free-radical inflammation. Selenium joins with the NAC to form an scavenger enzyme, glutathione peroxidase.

CHRONIC FATIGUE SYNDROME

Fatigue is one of the most common complaints that bring people into a physician's office. Fatigue can be caused by nearly every illness and is part of the natural healing process. Excessive fatigue that lasts and lasts may be a sign of illness or of chronic fatigue syndrome. Also called CFIDS, CFS, myalgic encephalomyclitis, chronic Epstein-Barr virus, and yuppie flu, chronic fatigue syndrome is a long-lasting, debilitating fatigue that is not associated with any particular illness. Although people have been fatigued for millennia, the term "chronic fatigue syndrome" was only coined in 1988. CFIDS affects about 3 people per 100,000, and symptoms last approximately two and a half years on average. Most people eventually return to normal health.

People with chronic fatigue syndrome have by definition been extremely tired for at least six months for no obvious reason. The Center for Disease Control has provided the following criteria for diagnosis of CFDIS: First, the fatigue is not eliminated by rest, and the fatigue substantially reduces the person's ability to function normally. Second, the diagnosis includes at least four of the following symptoms for a period of at least six months: loss in ability to concentrate or short-term memory function; sore throat; swollen and tender lymph nodes; muscle pain; multijoint pain without swelling or redness; headaches of a new type, pattern, or severity; sleep disturbances; and exercise-caused fatigue that lasts more than twenty-four hours. CFIDS often begins with an infectious disease, like a flu, accompanied by fevers that come and go. There is often accompanying joint stiffness and pain, sore throat, cough, sleep disturbances, light sensitivity, night sweats, and extreme exhaustion after the slightest exertion. It's common that a short walk or bit of exercise wipes out your energy for days afterward. People with CFIDS share many common symptoms, but not everyone has all the same ones. Some people have the Epstein-Barr virus, or Cytomegalovirus, but others don't. Sometimes healthy people have high blood titers for these viruses and have no symptoms of CFIDS. It's possible that these viruses trigger CFIDS, but it's also possible that the low immune function in people with CFIDS increases their chances of catching a wide variety of infectious illnesses.

Many people with CFIDS cannot hold down a job and many are depressed because the fatigue is so extreme. Those who do work come home exhausted and go immediately to bed so they can generate enough energy for work the next day. Because there isn't any apparent cause and no observable symptoms (like boils or measles), people with CFIDS are often confronted by people and doctors who just don't believe it's real.

COMMON SYMPTOMS OF CHRONIC FATIGUE SYNDROME

Symptom	Percentage affected
Fatigue	100
Mental sluggishness, foggy thinking, inability to concentrate	50–85
Depression	50–85
Pharyngitis	50–75
Exhaustion after minimal exertion that can last for days	50–60
Stiffness and muscle pain	50–60
Muscle weakness	40–70
Joint pain, arthritislike symptoms	40–50
Headache	35–85

In 1990, the Center for Disease Control in Atlanta began to keep records and study people with CFIDS in order to understand more about possible causes and therapies. We now know that CFIDS is multifactoral and affects many biochemical systems. There is an impairment in the ability of the mitochondria—the power plants in each of our cells—to produce energy. Cytokine production of interleukin 2 is low and causes poor immune function. Other immune parameters appear to be overstimulated. Although this seems paradoxical, it's probably not. According to Hans Selye, an expert on stress, our systems initially react to stress by overproducing. If working harder doesn't eventually solve the problem, they underproduce. Many people with CFIDS have exhausted adrenal glands and produce low amounts of cortisone and other adrenal hormones. Almost always they have dysbiosis, and most have *Candida* infections. There is usually leaky gut syndrome, accompanied by a host of food and environmental sensitivities. The liver is overburdened and overworked. The toxic by-products of life accumulate in tissues, and the cycle deepens.

Eventually, the mitochondria are affected. Mitochondria are the energy factories inside our cells, creating ATP energy from glucose in a complicated process called the citric acid cycle, or Kreb's cycle. Believed to have evolved from bacteria that had a symbiotic relationship with us, mitochondria create energy for us while we give them a home to live in—a win/win situation! We know this because the DNA in our mitochondria differs from the DNA in the rest of our cells, in that it resembles bacterial DNA. Mitochondrial function can be tested with an organic acid test, and this testing has provided evidence that mitochondrial DNA is damaged much more easily and is more susceptible to environmental toxins and other stressors. As chronic fatigue symptoms progress, the mitochondria often need nutritional support of their own. Many companies make products to facilitate this, including Mitochondrial Resuscitate and Kreb's Cycle Nutrients.

Using a tilt table, researchers have found that many people with CFIDS have low blood pressure with a test called the postural blood pressure test. Complimentary medicine physicians have long used reclining and standing blood pressures to detect poor adrenal function. Individuals with healthy adrenal function experience only a five-point rise in blood pressure when they move from a reclining to a standing position. In people with poor adrenal function, blood pressure remains the same or drops. So the real question is: Is the tilt-table hypotension the primary culprit behind or an indicator of poor adrenal function? In any case, some people with low blood pressure respond to an increase in salt intake to at least 1,000 milligrams daily, or by taking medication to increase blood pressure.

There aren't any panaceas for CFIDS, but there are therapies that can gradually help restore people to health. It's important to address detoxification, viral load, digestive function, dysbiosis (including *Candida* and parasites), mitochondrial function, intestinal flora, environmental contaminants, heavy metals, underlying allergies, and hormone imbalances (especially thyroid and adrenal), as well as to restore the immune system. If this seems daunting, it can be. The causes and specifics are different for each person. Careful partnership between practitioner and patient will give the very best results. CFIDS is one area in which conventional, mainstream medicine has little to offer. If you've tried everything that your doctor has recommended and still aren't any better, you need to broaden your approach.

Restoration of digestive competency and nutrition go a long way toward normalizing CFIDS. Work with a nutritionally oriented health professional to design a program that meets your specific needs. The first steps are discovering any underlying problems which aggravate and drive the condition using the tests listed below. It's important to check carefully for parasites; one study found *Giardia* in 28 percent of subjects with CFIDS. *Giardia* hangs out in the mucous membranes and is difficult to detect with random stool samples. A rectal swab is a more direct method to diagnose its presence. Then develop and follow a diet based upon foods that are healthful for you and a nutrient-rich program designed to boost immune, brain, and cellular function. When you are ready, add exercise—a little bit at a time.

The biological, rather than medical, approach to chronic fatigue saves money and works better. In one study of cost-effectiveness it was determined that a nutritional approach costs $2,000 compared with $10,000 for a medical approach. The patients on nutritional programs reported greater improvements in function and subjective well-being. They were able to significantly reduce the amount of medications they used.

The CFIDS Association in Charlotte, North Carolina, and the CFIDS and Fibromyalgia Health Resource in Santa Barbara, California offer a wealth of information for people with CFIDS. See Resources for specific address information. You can obtain information about medications, herbs, nutritional supplements, diet, exercise, and additional therapies. See listings in the Resources.

FUNCTIONAL LABORATORY TESTING

1. Comprehensive digestive and stool analysis with parasitology.
2. Elisa testing for food, airborne, and chemical sensitivities. Elisa-Act test is the most inclusive.
3. Liver function profile.
4. Intestinal permeability screening.
5. Organic acids.
6. Hair analysis or urine test for heavy metals.

HEALING OPTIONS

After testing, you'll have a better idea of any underlying problems. Look up related sections in this book to help you with the specifics. Then move on to the 4-R approach: Remove, Replace, Reinnoculate, and Repair.

Metabolic cleansing: Metabolic cleansing involves going on a hypoallergenic food plan for one to three weeks and taking a nutrient-rich protein powder designed to help restore your liver's detoxification capacities. For a thorough discussion of metabolic cleansing, see chapter 9.

Food and environmental sensitivities: Avoid all foods and chemicals that you are sensitive to from your diet for four to six months. Use shampoos, soaps, and toiletries that are hypoallergenic for your specific needs, and natural household cleaning products that are healthier for you, your family, and the environment. Some people are sensitive to their mattresses, gas stoves, carpeting, and upholstery. You may need to wear 100 percent cotton clothes and use 100 percent cotton sheets and blankets. Work with a health professional who can help you thread your way through the details.

Acidophilus and bifidobacteria: Supplemental use of beneficial bacteria can make a tremendous difference in your ability to digest foods. Beneficial flora can help reestablish the normal microbial balance in your intestinal tract. The supplements you purchase may have additional microbes, such as Saccharomyces. Dosage: one to two capsules or ¼ to ½ teaspoon powder two to three times daily. Mix powdered supplement with a cool beverage and take on an empty stomach.

Digestive enzymes: Pancreatic or vegetable enzymes supply the enzymes that your body needs to digest fats, proteins, and carbohydrates. Products differ. Some contain lactase, the milk digesting enzyme; others have additional hydrochloric acid to assist the stomach; and some contain ox bile to help with emulsification and digestion of fats. Dosage: one to two capsules with meals.

Multivitamin with minerals: Because people with CFIDS have difficulty with absorption and utilization of nutrients, a highly absorbable, hypoallergenic nutritional supplement is necessary. Although products that contain herbs, bee pollen, spirulina, and other additional food factors are good for many people, people with CFIDS often feel worse after taking food-based supplements. Make sure you buy the supplements that are herb and food free. Choose a supplement that contains the following nutrients: 25–50 milligrams zinc, 5,000–10,000 IU vitamin A, 10,000–25,000 IU carotenes, 200–400 IU vitamin E, 200 micrograms selenium, 200 micrograms chromium, at least 25 milligrams of most B-complex vitamins, 400–800 micrograms folic acid and 5–10 mg manganese.

Vitamin C: Vitamin C boosts immune function and helps detoxification pathways and has been shown to have antiviral effects. Clinicians have found it useful in people with CFIDS. Dosage: 3,000–5,000 milligrams daily. Do a vitamin C flush. See detailed instructions on pages 154–155.

Magnesium: Found in green leafy vegetables and whole grains, magnesium is involved in over three-hundred enzymatic reactions in the body. It is essential for energy production, nerve conduction, muscle function, and bone health. People with CFIDS are often deficient in magnesium. Supplemental magnesium can improve energy levels and emotional states, while decreasing pain. Most people improve with use of oral magnesium supplements, but some need intravenous injections. Physicians can give 1,000 milligrams magnesium sulfate by injection. In one study, magnesium injections improved function in twelve out of fifteen people, compared with only three receiving the placebo. Dosage: 500–1,000 milligrams magnesium citrate or magnesium/potassium aspartate (aspartic acid helps mobilize magnesium into the cells).

Coenzyme Q10: Coenzyme Q10 is necessary for energy production, immune function, and repair and maintenance of tissues. It also enhances cell function. CoQ10 is widely used in Japan for heart disease and has been researched as an anti-tumor substance. Dosage: 60–100 milligrams daily. Trial period: two months: 90–100 milligrams daily.

Essential fatty acids: Several studies have shown people with CFIDS to have fatty acid imbalances. In a recent study, a combination of evening primrose oil and fish oil or a placebo of olive oil was given to seventy people with CFIDS. Of the people taking fish and evening primrose oils, 74 percent showed improvement at five weeks, and 85 percent showed improvement at fifteen weeks. In comparison, the placebo group showed 23 percent improvement at five weeks and 17 percent at fifteen weeks. Another study of the use of supplemental fatty acids showed improvement in twenty-seven out of twenty-nine people with CFIDS over twelve to eighteen weeks. Twenty people who had previously been unable to work full-time for an average of over three years were able to go back to work full-time after an average of sixteen weeks. Sixteen months later twenty-seven out of twenty-eight remained improved, and twenty were still progressing. Dosage: Flax oil capsules 2–3 grams daily or EPA/DHA fish oil once or twice daily plus evening primrose or borage oil 1–2 grams daily. Because magnesium and vitamin B_6, as well as the proper genetics, are necessary to convert flaxseed oil into EPA and DHA, it is advisable to take at least some preformed DHA.

Methionine: Methionine, an essential sulfur-containing amino acid, is commonly deficient in people with CFIDS. It acts as a methyl donor for transmethylation reactions throughout the body, especially in the brain. It also helps sulfoxidation for liver detoxification pathways and is a precursor for other sulfur-containing amino acids such as cysteine and taurine. People with CFIDS probably have an increased need for methionine. Some people find improvement with a general amino acid supplement that supplies methionine, lysine, and carnitine simultaneously. Dosage: 500–1,000 milligrams.

A recent player on the scene is SAMe, a synthetic version of a chemical that is naturally made in our bodies from methionine. Research on SAMe shows it to have powerful antidepressant effects without the side effects of pharmaceutical antidepressant medications. SAMe has also been shown to be as potent an anti-inflammatory drug as indomethacin without the negative side-ffects in people with arthritis. A good article on SAMe appeared in the March 22, 1999 edition of *Newsweek*.

L-carnitine: The vast majority of people with CFIDS have low levels of acylcarnitine, although their levels of free carnitine are normal. Carnitine, vital for the conversion of fats into energy, also plays some role in detoxification and is believed to be essential for heart function. Finally, carnitine helps transport long-chain fatty acids into the mitochondria. Carnitine deficiencies result in muscle weakness, aches, and poor tone. When people were supplemented with 4 grams daily of acetyl-carnitine, half showed improvement in their symptoms. Dosage: 4 grams acetyl-carnitine daily.

Lysine: Often people with CFIDS also have herpes infections. Some people find good results with a general amino acid supplement, which supplies carnitine, lysine, and methionine as well as other amino acids. Dosage: 1–2 grams daily at the first sign of an outbreak; 500 milligrams daily for prevention.

Malic acid: Malic acid comes from apples and is important in energy production at a cellular level. Several physicians have found malic acid supplementation reduces fatigue and pain of fibromyalgia. Dosage: six to twelve tablets daily, decreasing dosage over time. Each tablet contains 300 milligrams malic acid/magnesium hydroxide.

Immune-stimulating herbs: Echinacea, goldenseal, astragalus, phytolacca (pokeweed), licorice, and lomatium all have immune-stimulating properties. They can also help prevent secondary infections while you are in a susceptible state. Take them preventively or therapeutically as directed.

Adrenal support: People with CFIDS often need adrenal support, such as adrenal glandular supplements or herbal supplements such as licorice and Siberian ginseng. Vitamin C and panthothenic acid (vitamin B_5) are also needed for proper adrenal function. If your blood pressure is low, you can use whole licorice; if not, use DGL, which will not affect aldosterone levels and blood pressure. It's best to take adrenal support in the morning and at lunch. If taken too late in the day, adrenal support can stimulate energy when you want to be winding down.

Nicotinamide adenine dinucleotide (NADH): In a study monitoring the effect of nicotinamide adenine dinucleotide (NADH) on people with CFIDS, twenty-six subjects were given the reduced form of NADH for four weeks and a placebo for an additional four weeks. Thirty-one percent showed improvement when on NADH, while only 8 percent improved when taking the placebo. Subjects were less fatigued and had improvement in quality of life. NADH is integral to the citric acid cycle of energy production. Once again, we are reminded that each person has unique needs. While most people did not benefit, NADH may be a useful treatment for those who did. More research needs to be done to see if 10 milligrams daily, the amount given in the study, is the proper dosage; if a longer treatment program would be of additional benefit; and what, if any, are the long-term benefits.

Exercise: People with CFIDS find exercise to be totally exhausting and draining. It is common for one period of exercise to be followed within six to twenty-four hours by two to fourteen days of exhaustion and muscle aches. Paradoxically, exercise is helpful for restoring function in people with CFIDS, and so it's advisable to begin with simple walking, swimming, or biking for five minutes daily. If you can, increase by one or two minutes a day each week. If you feel that you are at your maximum, maintain your present length of exercise time until your fatigue lessens. Don't push yourself hard. Slow and steady wins the race. Studies have shown that two-thirds of people with CFIDS benefit through exercise, although it is critical to not overdo.

Stress management: Development of strong support systems is vital. People with CFIDS often have the illness for a long time and can greatly benefit from support groups.

Exchange of information and dialogue with people who understand what you are going through can expedite recovery. Take time for yourself, rest, and relax.

There is a new hypothesis that people with CFIDS are functioning in an anaerobic state so light anaerobic exercise may be most beneficial. Working with light weights, leg lifts, and use of weight machines to your capacity without causing fatigue may be more beneficial than aerobic exercise. As you begin to feel better, incorporate aerobic exercise—walking, biking, swimming, and dancing. Prioritize so you have energy for what's most important. Be patient, kind, and loving to yourself.

ECZEMA/ATOPIC DERMATITIS

Eczema, or atopic dermatitis, is a catchall name for any inflammation of the skin. It is a chronic skin condition characterized by redness, itching, and sometimes oozing, crusting, and scaling. The itch makes us scratch, which causes redness and inflammation. Approximately ½ to 1 percent of us have eczema and it affects 10 percent of all children. It can first appear at any age, but most often during the first year of life. Babies can have ezcema on their faces, scalp, bottom, hands, and feet. In children and adults, it may be more localized. Eczema is on the rise in industrialized countries. The causes are multifactoral and include imbalanced intestinal flora, leaky gut, food allergies, environmental contaminants such as air pollution and tobacco smoke, and genetic predisposition. The red patches are itchy, scaly, and dry, which encourages people to use lotions and creams to which they are often allergic. This complicates the problem further. Eczema varies over time, flaring up and calming down, at times better and worse. Emotional stress, heat, increase in humidity, bacterial skin infections, sweat, pets, hormone fluctuations, dust, molds, pollens, toiletries, cosmetics, and wool clothing commonly aggravate eczema. As children age, they may continue to have eczema; it may disappear; or they may develop other allergies, including asthma. People with eczema have high levels of IgE, secretory IgA, and eosinophils, all allergy signs.

There are strong connections between eczema and food, microbial, and inhalant allergies. Food allergies diagnosed through IgE and skin testing is apparent in most children with eczema. In a study of 165 children between the ages of four months and twenty-two years, researchers found that 60 percent had at least one positive skin-prick test for food allergies. When they challenged these results with a double-blind placebo-controlled study, thirty-nine of sixty-four subjects had positive tests, with milk, egg, peanut, soy, wheat, codfish, catfish, and cashews accounting for 89 percent of the positive food-allergy challenges. Undoubtedly, many more would be borne out by IgG, IgA, and IgM testing. Studies of children with eczema have shown that eczema improved in forty-nine out of sixty-six children after elimination of the particular foods. Foods that aggravate eczema, in descending order, were: eggs, cow's milk, food coloring, tomatoes, fish, goat's milk, cheese, chocolate, and wheat.

A study was made of 122 children, aged four months to six years, with food intolerance. Of them, 52 children had eczema; the rest had chronic diarrhea. The allergies caused damage to the intestinal lining, and there was a decrease in the body's ability to defend itself due to lactose intolerance and dysbiosis, which caused leaky gut syndrome, which led to more food antigens and sensitivity. Children with eczema had more damage than those with chronic diarrhea.

Breast-feeding dramatically reduces a baby's risk of developing eczema and allergies in general. Babies with eczema, and probably most babies, should not be given cow's milk, milk products, eggs, or wheat before one year of age. As their digestive system matures, they can better handle these complex foods. Babies with eczema who drink formula should be tested by skin prick to determine which formulas are most suitable for them. Because babies are born without intestinal flora in their digestive tracts, giving supplemental flora to the baby (and the mother, if she's nursing) can quickly alleviate baby eczema. The best flora for infants is *Bifidobacteria infantis*. Natren makes a formula called Life-start, which works amazingly well. For older children, products designed for children are also useful.

Elimination of foods, stress, and allergens can significantly alter the course of the disease. Even though you cannot control all factors, controlling enough of them will allow you to stay under the symptom threshold. Jonathan Wright, M.D. had success in thirty-nine out of forty patients with eczema who followed this program: 50 milligrams zinc three times daily for six weeks, plus 2 milligrams copper daily, 5 grams omega-3 fatty acids (evening primrose or borage oil) twice a day for three months, and omega-6 fatty acids (EPA/DHA fish oils) 1–2 grams three times daily for four weeks.

The most common treatment for eczema is cortisone cream, which suppresses your body's normal immune function. However, there is often a rebound effect after you stop using the cream, and your symptoms return worse than before. Natural creams with chamomile, licorice, and comfrey root are very effective at soothing and healing eczema without negative side effects.

Exercise may be especially beneficial for people with eczema. A recent study indicated that exercise reduced the inflammation associated with eczema by stabilizing the hypothalamic-pituitary axis.

Another approach to reduce eczema is to vacuum fastidiously! One recent study attributed a reduction in eczema severity to a reduction in mattress dust and carpet mites by using a high-filtration vacuum cleaner and bed covers. So keep your bedroom clean and clutter-free.

FUNCTIONAL LABORATORY TESTING

1. Allergy testing for IgE, food, mold, dust, and inhalants.
2. Sensitivity testing; Elisa testing.

3. Complete digestive and stool analysis. Check to see if there is dysbiosis and how well the body is digesting. Some studies indicate a low level of hydrochloric acid in people with eczema, and the CDSA can give a general indication of HCl production.
4. Intestinal permeability screening. It will most likely be positive.
5. Heidelberg testing for adequacy of hydrochloric acid production.

HEALING OPTIONS

Food and environmental sensitivities: Follow the directions in chapter 9. An elimination/provocation diet (discussed in chap. 7) can significantly reduce eczema. Foods that you are sensitive to will generally make you itch. Often the itching starts soon after the meal, but it can be delayed up to forty-eight hours, which makes tracking down the foods a bit tricky. Food allergy and sensitivity testing can help you determine which foods to eliminate from your diet.

Avoidance: Eliminate all foods and chemicals that you are sensitive to for four to six months. Use natural household cleaning products and shampoos, and soaps and toiletries that are hypoallergenic. If you are sensitive to mattresses, gas stoves, carpeting, and upholstery, you may need to use cotton clothing and sheets that allow the skin to breathe naturally. Work with a health professional who knows how to help you meet your needs.

Lactobacillus and bifidobacteria: Restoring the normal balance of flora in your intestinal tract can help reduce eczema. Use of beneficial bacteria supplementally can make a tremendous difference in your ability to thoroughly digest foods. The supplement you purchase may have additional microbes, such as *Saccharomyces.* Dosage: one to two capsules two to three times daily, or ¼ to ½ teaspoon powder two to three times daily. Mix powdered supplement with a cool beverage. It works best on an empty stomach.

Babies and small children with eczema: Babies are born with sterile digestive tracts, and as soon as they are born they are exposed to microbes of all sorts. Dairy and soy products are difficult to digest until the baby's digestive system has mature flora. Supplementing with beneficial flora, *Bifidobacteria infantum* and others will help your baby digest food more easily and heal the eczema. Use probiotic formulas specifically designed for infants, toddlers, or small children. Dosage: ⅛ to ¼ teaspoon three times daily. If the mother is breast-feeding, she should also take ¼ teaspoon three times daily.

Check for *Candida* infection: Fungal infections are a common cause of eczema. In a study of 115 men and women with eczema, 85 were sensitive to fungus and after they were treated with fungal creams, oral ketakonazole, or a yeast-free diet, there was much improvement. Take the yeast self-test and do blood testing or complete digestive and stool analysis to determine if yeast is contributing to your eczema.

Natural eczema creams: Herbal creams can be as effective as cortisone creams in reducing eczema, and they don't have the negative side effects. Chamomile creams are widely used in Europe. Licorice root stimulates production of healing and anti-inflammatory prostaglandins. Comfrey root contains allantoin which promotes healing. Some products contain all three of these ingredients. Look in health food stores or ask your health professional to find a product that works for you.

Multivitamin with minerals: It is wise to add a good quality multivitamin with minerals to your daily routine. However, you probably cannot get all the nutrients you require from a single tablet or capsule. Look for a supplement that has *at least* 100 micrograms chromium, 100 milligrams selenium, 5–10 milligrams manganese, 500 milligrams calcium, 250 milligrams magnesium, 25–50 milligrams zinc, 1–2 milligrams copper, 10,000–25,000 IU vitamin A (not beta carotene; pregnant women should not exceed 10,000 IU daily), and 400 IU vitamin E. Zinc and vitamin A are essential for healthy skin and mucous membranes, and zinc is also necessary for production of anti-inflammatory prostaglandins and formation of hydrochloric acid. There are many anecdotal tales about the effectiveness of vitamin E and eczema, but no controlled studies.

It is best *not* to buy a supplement that contains many different foods and herbs because you may be unknowingly sensitive to one or more of the ingredients. Be sure to buy a supplement that is free of common allergens.

Quercetin: Quercetin, the most effective bioflavonoid for anti-inflammation, can be used to reduce pain and inflammatory responses and control allergies. Dosage: 500–1,000 milligrams three to four times daily.

Tumeric: For eczema, tumeric can be used in combination with Neem, an Ayurvedic remedy for parasites and infections.

Vitamin C: A study of ten young people with severe eczema showed that supplementation with vitamin C significantly improved eczema and immune function. They needed only half as many antibiotics for treating skin infections as the control group. Dosage: 1,000–3,000 milligrams mineral ascorbates or Ester-C daily. Do a vitamin C flush once a week.

Neutralizing reactions: There are many ways to minimize the effects of food sensitivities. Clinical ecologists can provide neutralization drops to counteract your reaction to particular foods. These drops work like allergy shots—a small amount of what you are sensitive to helps stimulate your body's natural immune response. Malic acid can also curtail sensitivity reactions.

Evening primrose oil and flaxseed oil: Studies show that people with eczema generally have low levels of both omega-3 and omega-6 fatty acids. The first step in metabolism of linoleic acid, which allows for the conversion into gamma-linolenic acid (GLA), is often impaired in people with eczema. Taking GLA directly in evening primrose, flax, or borage oil circumvents blockage. GLA has an anti-inflammatory effect and benefits immune function. Dosage: 1–2 grams three times daily. Trial period: four weeks.

Fish oils: One recent study on people with eczema showed a 30 percent improvement in a four-month trial of eight capsules of fish oil per day. Though the placebo group was given corn oil, which gave an improvement of 24 percent, results suggest that people with eczema have a generalized need for essential fatty acids.

Eating cold water fish—salmon, halibut, sardines, herring, tuna—two to four times each week can provide you with the omega-3 oils you need. If you use fish oil capsules, do so under the supervision of a physician. They cause a significant increase in clotting time and should not be used by people with hemophilia or those on aspirin or anticoagulant drugs.

Nickel-restricted diet: The relationship between nickel sensitivity and eczema has appeared recently in scientific literature. Nickel is an essential nutrient that is found in many enzymes. However, excess nickel is an irritant to the gastrointestinal lining. You can be tested for nickel sensitivity through skin testing or an oral challenge. Nickel is used as an alloy in jewelry, so if jewelry irritates your skin or turns it gray, you may be sensitive to nickel. If you are, it is recommended that a low-nickel diet be followed for a limited period of time. High-nickel foods are chocolate, nuts, dried beans and peas, and grains.

FIBROMYALGIA AND MYOFASCIAL PAIN SYNDROME

Fibromyalgia is characterized by long-term muscle pain and stiffness. It affects about 2 percent of the general population and 20 percent of people with arthritic disease. It used to be called "fibrositis," which implies an inflammation of fibrous and connective tissues like muscles, tendons, fascia, and ligaments. Myofascial pain syndrome is characterized by just a few painful and achy places, most often in the jaw, that are tender when trigger points are touched. Fibrositis is a non-specific term that identifies both fibromyalgia and myofascial pain syndrome.

Fibromyalgia is characterized by generalized aching, pain, and tenderness throughout the body. People complain of neck, shoulder, lower back and hip pain that seems to move around from place to place. People often report changes in sleep patterns and wake up often during the night with a feeling of achiness, stiffness, and fatigue. Other symptoms occur less frequently and include intolerance to cold or heat, bladder problems, Raynaud's phenomenon, nasal congestion, teeth grinding, abdominal pain, constipation or diarrhea, headaches, numbness or swelling in hands and/or feet, anxiety, and depression. People with fibromyalgia often report a traumatic event that triggered initial symptoms: emotional or physical stress, an accident, or a severe infectious illness. Though common, this doesn't occur in everyone.

Fibromyalgia occurs more in women than in men and has an incidence of 1 percent in people under sixty and 4 percent in people over sixty. Fibromyalgia shares many symptoms with chronic fatigue syndrome, though it is classified as its own disease. People with fibromyalgia, unlike those with chronic fatigue syndrome, usually do not have low acyl-carnitine levels or have a viral infection as a trigger. Recent studies indicate that myofascial pain, fibromyalgia, and CFIDS are on a continuum of the same disease path, with myofascial pain being the mildest, fibromyalgia moderate, and CFIDS the most severe.

People with fibromyalgia are often misdiagnosed and go from doctor to doctor in search of help. They are generally put on anti-inflammatory drugs and antidepressants. One study showed that 90 percent of people treated with anti-inflammatory drugs were still symptomatic after three years. Conventional medical therapies for fibromyalgia usually are unsuccessful. They fail to address possible underlying causes of the illness. Leo Galland, M.D. finds food and environmental sensitivities, *Candida*, or parasites to be causal factors in fibromyalgia. Doing a stool test may be useful in diagnosing the cause of fibromyalgia. When the underlying problem has been identified and treated, fibromyalgia resolves.

A very small but promising study was done with three people who had fibromyalgia for five to ten years. They were tested for food and environmental sensitivities with the Elisa/Act test and given dietary restrictions. They were put on a detoxification program and personalized nutritional therapies to meet their needs and stimulate repair of cells and tissues. The final component was stress management, with recommendations for relaxation training, exercise, and biofeedback. In six to twelve weeks, these people showed a reduction of 80 to 90 percent in their symptoms. They also showed a significant reduction in the number of foods and environmental sensitivities in repeated Elisa testing. More research needs to be done in this area.

Nutritional therapies have been successful in the reduction of symptoms. Fifty people with either CFIDS or fibromyalgia were given products made by Mannatech, a multilevel supplement company, including freeze-dried aloe, plant-derived saccharides with freeze-dried fruits and vegetables, and a wild yam product with multivitamins and minerals. Although all subjects in the study had previous unsuccessful medical treatment, there was a remarkable reduction in symptoms, with continued improvement over the nine-month test period. Although this was a small, preliminary study, it shows promise for the nutritional approach to fibromyalgia and CFIDS.

Use of a single supplement may bring some relief, but a total program is necessary to bring dramatic relief and true healing. Taking coenzyme Q10, vitamins B_1, B_6 and C, arginine, 5-HTP, SAMe, essential fatty acids, antioxidants, niacin, and magnesium malate (magnesium plus malic acid) in addition to a hypoallergenic diet has been shown to have positive effects. Acupuncture has been proven useful in treating fibromyalgia.

One unusual approach to fibromyalgia is the use of guaifenesin, a gout medication. Endocrinologist Dr. St. Amand believes that people with fibromyalgia have calcium phosphate deposits on muscles, tendons, and ligaments. Amand developed his theory after observing a high level of dental calculus (calcium phosphate deposits) among his fibromyalgia patients. His therapy (which includes a healing crisis, or a period of worsening of symptoms before improvement) begins with a dose of 300 milligrams of guaifenesin per day. He reports this working in 20 percent of his patients, but if no healing crisis occurs after two weeks, Amand increases the dose to 600 milligrams daily. At this level, another 50 percent of his patients improve, while the remaining 30 percent seem to require higher doses. In two months of treatment, one year of fibromyalgia can be reversed; however, the longer you've had the disease, the longer you need to stay on the medication. While doing this therapy, avoid all salicylates, because they negate the treatment. This would include aspirin; herbs such as willow bark and aloe; and some common products that may contain salicylates, such as Ben Gay, Listerine, eyeliner, and some herbal hair sprays. As guaifenesin is a weak antigout medication with few side effects, the therapy certainly seems worth trying.

Functional Laboratory Testing

1. Comprehensive digestive and stool analysis.
2. Liver function profile.
3. Elisa food and environmental sensitivity testing.
4. Intestinal permeability screening.
5. Oxidative stress evaluation.

Healing Options

Metabolic cleansing: Metabolic cleansing involves going on a hypoallergenic food plan taking a nutrient rich protein powder designed to help restore your liver's detoxification capacities. Use this protocol for one to three weeks. See chapter 9 on detoxification and metabolic cleansing.

Food and environmental sensitivities: Eliminate all foods and chemicals that you are sensitive to for four to six months (see discussion in chap. 7). Work with a health professional who can help you find your way through the details.

Acidophilus and bifidobacteria: Use of beneficial bacteria taken supplementally can help reestablish the normal microbial balance in your intestinal tract. The supplement you purchase may have additional microbes as well. Dosage: one to two capsules two to three times daily or ¼ to ½ teaspoon powder two to three times daily. Mix powdered supplement with a cool beverage and take on an empty stomach.

Digestive enzymes: Pancreatic or vegetable enzymes supply the enzymes your body needs to digest fats, proteins, and carbohydrates. Some products contain lactase, the milk-digesting enzyme, others have additional hydrochloric acid to assist the stomach, and some contain ox bile to help with emulsification and digestion of fats. Dosage: one to two with meals.

Multivitamin with minerals: A high-quality hypoallergic nutritional supplement is necessary. Although products that contain herbs, bee pollen, spirulina, and other additional food factors are good for many people, it's best to buy supplements that are herb- and food-free. Look for the following levels of specific nutrients: 50–100 milligrams vitamin B_1, 50–100 milligrams vitamin B_6, 200–400 IU vitamin E, 10,000 IU vitamin A, 10,000–25,000 IU carotenes, 200 micrograms selenium, 200 micrograms chromium, 5–10 milligrams manganese, glutathione, cysteine, or N-acetyl cysteine, plus additional nutrients. Antioxidant nutrients—carotenes, vitamins C and E, selenium, glutathione, CoQ10, cysteine, and NAC—have been shown to be needed in larger quantities in people with fibromyalgia. In a recent study, people with fibromyalgia had an increased pyruvate-to-lactate ratio, which may indicate the need for more vitamin B_1 and B_6.

Vitamin B_1: People with fibromyalgia have lower levels of red blood cell transketolase, which is a functional test for vitamin B_1 (thiamin) status. Researchers found that supplemental thiamin pyrophosphate worked better than other forms. This suggests a metabolic defect rather than a true deficiency. This may also reflect a magnesium deficiency because thiamin-dependent enzymes require magnesium.

Vitamin C: Vitamin C boosts immune function, helps detoxification pathways, and has antiviral effects. Dosage: 3,000 milligrams daily. Once a week, do a vitamin C flush. (See directions for C Flush, pages 154–155.)

Magnesium: It is very common for people with fibromyalgia to be deficient in magnesium. Serum magnesium levels are often normal, but if more sophisticated tests like red blood cell magnesium are done, magnesium levels are often low. Supplemental magnesium can improve energy levels and emotional states while decreasing pain. Most people improve by using oral magnesium supplements, but some need an intravenous injection of 1,000 milligrams magnesium sulfate by a physician (for more on magnesium, see discussion under Chronic Fatigue Syndrome). Choline citrate can greatly enhance oral magnesium utilization (available from Perque/Seraphim listed in Directory). Dosage: 500–1,000 milligrams magnesium citrate or magnesium/glucinate.

Malic acid: Malic acid found in apples is important in energy production at a cellular level. Several physicians have found malic acid supplementation reduces fatigue and the pain of fibromyalgia. Dosage: six to twelve tablets of 300 milligrams malic acid/magnesium hydroxide daily, decreasing dosage over time.

Coenzyme Q10: Coenzyme Q10 is necessary for energy production, immune function, repair and maintenance of tissues, and enhanced cell function. Dosage: 60–100 milligrams daily. Trial period: two months.

Quercetin: Quercetin is the most effective bioflavonoid in its anti-inflammatory effects and can be used to reduce pain and inflammatory responses and control allergies. (For more on quercetin, see discussion under Osteoarthritis.) Dosage: 500–1,000 milligrams three to four times daily.

Glucosamine sulfate: Glycosamine sulfate is used therapeutically to help repair cartilage, reduce swelling and inflammation, and restore joint function, with no reported side effects. Dosage: 500 milligrams two to four times daily.

Gamma-oryzanol: Although no specific studies have been done with fibromyalgia, gamma-oryzanol, a compound found in rice bran oil, heals damage to the intestinal tract and normalizes serum triglycerides, cholesterol, symptoms of menopause, and depressive disorders. Dosage: 100 milligrams three times daily for a trial period of three to six weeks.

Glutamine: Glutamine, the most abundant amino acid in our bodies, is used in the digestive tract as a fuel source and for healing stomach ulcers, irritable bowel syndrome, ulcerative bowel diseases, and leaky gut syndrome. Dosage: Begin with 8 grams daily. Trial period: four weeks.

Arginine: People with fibromyalgia have been shown to have lower levels of arginine than other people. Dosage: 500–1,000 milligrams or a mixed free amino acid supplement.

5-HTP: 5 Hydroxy-tryptophan: People with fibromyalgia have lower tryptophan levels than controls. Studies have shown 5-HTP to be of benefit in fibromyalgia. Tryptophan is a precursor to serotonin, a neurotransmitter that helps us sleep and prevents depression. Tryptophan itself is only available by prescription at a few pharmacies nationwide due to a contaminated batch several years ago. Fortunately, 5-HTP, the intermediary metabolite between tryptophan and serotonin, is available as a supplement. Passion flower, an herb with high levels of tryptophan, has been used historically for depression, anxiety, and insomnia, all of which are symptoms of fibromyalgia. Tryptophan is also found in cashews, cheddar cheese, eggs, halibut, peanuts, salmon, sardines, shrimp, turkey, and tuna. Dosage: 200–600 milligrams daily of 5-HTP, or 500–2,000 milligrams daily of tryptophan. Doses can be divided between morning and bedtime.

Cayenne/Capsaicin: The prescription drug Capsaicin, a cayenne pepper cream, was used in a study of forty-five people with fibromyalgia. It was found to improve grip strength and reduce pain over a two-week period. Capsaicin cream burns temporarily, but this diminishes over time.

S-adenosyl-L-methionine: A recent study of forty-seven people with fibromyalgia showed that injections and oral supplementation of S-adenosyl-L-methionine significantly reduced muscle tenderness and the number of tender points, lowered pain severity, and benefited depression and anxiety. S-adenosyl-L-methionine is produced in our bodies from methionine. It is the active methylating agent for many enzyme reactions throughout the body, especially in the brain. People with fibromyalgia can probably make this conversion, so oral methionine may be useful clinically. In the study, dosages were 200 milligrams given daily as intramuscular injection, plus 400 milligrams taken orally twice daily.

Electro-acupuncture: In a study of electro-acupuncture with people with fibromyalgia, half the people received acupuncture on four points; the other half received acupuncture 20 millimeters away from the actual point. Seven out of eight symptom parameters improved in the four-point electro-acupuncture treated group. None changed in the placebo group. In the electro-acupuncture group, a quarter had no improvement, half improved satisfactorily, and a quarter had their symptoms disappear completely. Although this study was done with electro-acupuncture, similar results would occur with classical acupuncture.

Food and Environmental Sensitivities

Food sensitivities are the result of leaky gut syndrome. It's important to discover the underlying cause, which may be parasites, *Candida* infection, bacterial or viral infection, pancreatic insufficiency, medications, or poor lifestyle habits. Two types of allergies cause reactions: acute or immediate hypersensitivity reactions (Type I) and delayed hypersensitivity reactions (Type II–IV).

True food allergies (Type I) are rare. They affect from 0.3 to 7.5 percent of children and 1 to 2 percent of adults. Type IgE antibodies bind to the offending food antigens and cause the release of cytokines and histamines which results in hives, skin rashes, closing of the throat, respiratory distress, runny nose, itching, and sometimes severe reactions of asthma and anaphylactic shock. These symptoms can occur within minutes to hours after the food is eaten. Foods which most often trigger these reactions are eggs, cow's milk, nuts, wheat, soy, white fish, and shellfish. Physicians diagnose food allergies through the use of patch skin tests and RAST blood testing, but these tests do not accurately determine food or environmental sensitivities.

Type II–IV reactions are the result of food or environmental factors and cause symptoms which are delayed, taking several hours to several days to appear. This makes tracking them down very difficult. They are more common than true food allergies, affecting 24 percent of American adults. Food sensitivities cause a wide number of symptoms resulting from a typical leaky gut reaction. (See chart listing common symptoms of food and environmental sensitivities in chapter 6.) Food molecules enter the bloodstream through damaged mucosal membranes, the body recognizes them as foreign substances (antigens) and triggers an immune reaction to get rid of them. Prolonged antibody response overwhelms the liver's ability to eliminate the antigens, so the toxins enter the bloodstream and trigger delayed hypersensitivity response, inflammation, cell damage, and disease. Almost any food can cause a reaction, although the foods that provoke 80 percent of food sensitivity reactions are wheat, beef, dairy products, egg, pork, and citrus.

Two types of food sensitivities are recognized by doctors

of preventive medicine and clinical ecology: cyclic and fixed. Cyclic account for 80 to 90 percent of food sensitivities. These reactions occur after a specific food has been eaten over and over, causing a reaction. If you avoid eating the food for four to six months, your body will most likely tolerate it again. However, you must correct the underlying leaky gut syndrome, or the problem will reoccur with that or other foods. With the fixed type, sensitivities don't go away, even if you have avoided eating the foods for periods of time. Occasionally, you can eat it after years of avoidance without provoking symptoms.

These reactions happen when antibodies are triggered in response to foods, chemicals, and bacterial toxins. They damage cells and inflammation occurs due to the damage. Many people are aware of which foods and chemicals bother them, but just as often the cause is hidden. With repeated exposure to these foods, our bodies slowly adapt to the irritants and the symptoms that are provoked.

Usually we learn to live with the symptoms. Remember your first cigarette or glass of beer? It was probably distasteful to you. You probably didn't like the feeling of the smoke in your throat and lungs, and didn't like the taste of beer. With continual use of beer or cigarettes, those initial reactions disappear, and eventually we like and even crave them. They still have a negative effect on our system, but our body has adapted to it. This model works for our relation to foods and chemicals as well. Habitual use dulls our ability to recognize their negative health effects. Because of this phenomenon, we can make use of the elimination/provocation challenge.

The idea behind the elimination/provocation challenge is simple—only eat foods that you are unlikely to be sensitive to for a week or two, and then add back the foods you normally eat to "challenge" your system. Removal of offending foods calms down symptoms. Challenging yourself with these foods allows you to determine which foods trigger symptoms. Careful addition of only one food each two days makes it easier to determine which foods caused the reaction.

While the elimination/provocation challenge sounds simple, the administration of it can be tricky. In general, people have no problem with the elimination part—a restricted food plan for a week can be accomplished with a bit of planning and discipline. Adding foods back into your diet slowly is more difficult. Symptoms are delayed and recipes contain a combination of foods, so that you can't easily tell which ones cause the reaction. Eating simple or single foods is helpful for determining which foods you may be sensitive to. You may feel badly after eating something, but not be certain which ingredient caused the distress. It then becomes necessary to remove all suspected foods for four days, and try them again one at a time. If you have the same reaction each time you add the food, you've found the culprit. If you have a food sensitivity to one food, you are often sensitive to all foods in the same food family. For example, some people who are sensitive to wheat are sensitive to all grains in the grass family. People who are sensitive to milk are often sensitive to cheese and whey. It is common to be sensitive to more than one food or food family.

Environmental illness, also called multiple chemical sensitivities, is becoming more and more common. In fact, two subspecialties of medicine are now devoted to it: environmental medicine and clinical ecology. Chronic exposure to food additives, household chemicals, building materials, re-circulating air, and impure water can so depress and weaken our immune systems that even a small amount of toxic exposure makes us ill.

To test for food allergies, run a RAST or modified RAST test, which checks for elevation of IgE antibodies. Elisa tests for food and environmental sensitivities check levels of IgG4 and sometimes IgM and IgA antibodies. You can also do an elimination/provocation test at home.

Though highly accurate, it can be frustrating. I prefer to use it along with a blood test, which helps reinforce and simplify the program.

If you have cyclic food or environmental sensitivities, you'll do best with a holistic approach. By avoiding substances you're sensitive to for a period of six months, your body will gradually stop reacting to most of them. It really helps the process if you also detoxify the body and the liver (see chapter 9). Natural foods, organically grown and nutrient rich, also help repair the body.

For people who are highly sensitive to foods, a four-day food rotation may be helpful in addition to complete avoidance of foods you are highly sensitive to. The theory behind the rotation diet is that when you eat a food, your body begins to produce antibodies against it. If you don't eat it again for several days, the antibodies are no longer present. When you eat the food on day five, the process begins again, but you never develop symptoms because the antibodies are never prepared at the correct moment. There are many good books on the four-day food rotation diet. My favorites are *If It's Tuesday, It Must Be Chicken* by Natalie Golos and Frances Golos Golbitrz. and *Dr. Sally's Allergy Recipes* by Sally Rockwell.

To set up the rotation, make four lists, dividing all foods into four groups, with a quarter of your fruits, vegetables, grains, proteins, oils, nuts, seeds and beverages in each group. Keep all foods from the same family in the same group. For example, all grains are in one family because of the similarity of their makeup. Follow these food lists in order and then begin again with the first list on the fifth day.

A comprehensive program of nutritional supplements will also help the cells regenerate and generally aid the healing process. As noted in the Elisa/Act patient handbook, "Persons suffering from immune system dysfunction and overload due to delayed hypersensitivity reactions often have a need for even greater supplementation because of poor functioning of the body's normal biochemical pathways." Exercise programs and stress management tools also play a part in recovery. If you follow a holistic program, you'll find that over time you will become less and less sensitive to foods and the environment.

FUNCTIONAL LABORATORY TESTING

1. Elisa Testing—IgG4 and possibly IgM and IgA.
2. RAST or modified RAST for IgE.
3. *Candida* testing, either serum or through CDSA.
4. Comprehensive digestive and stool analysis with parasite screening.
5. Intestinal permeability test (almost surely will be positive).

HEALING OPTIONS

Avoidance: Eliminate all foods and chemicals that you are sensitive to for four to six months. Health food stores specialize in wheat-free breads, rice noodles, and a plethora of foods for people with food allergies. If you are sensitive to chemicals, use natural household cleaning products. Some people are sensitive to mattresses, gas stoves, carpeting, and upholstery, which can make elimination tricky. Work with a health professional who can help you with the details.

Neutralizing reactions: There are many ways to help minimize the effects of food sensitivities. Clinical ecologists can provide neutralization drops to desensitize you to reactive foods. These drops work like allergy shots a small amount of what you are sensitive to stimulates your body's natural immune response. Malic acid is also useful to neutralize sensitivity reactions.

Supplements: There are combination products for leaky gut that contain combinations of many of the recommended supplements.

Quercetin: Quercetin, the most effective bioflavonoid thanks to its anti-inflammatory effects, can be used to reduce pain and inflammatory responses and control allergies. Dosage: 500–1,000 milligrams three to four times daily.

Tri-salts/malic acid: Alkalizing mineral salts that generally contain calcium, magnesium, and/or potassium bicarbonates help minimize reactions to foods. Alka-Seltzer Gold can be used in this capacity, since it contains sodium and potassium salts. Malic acid is also useful for stopping or slowing reactions to foods.

Gamma-oryzanol: Gamma-oryzanol, found in rice bran oil and products that help heal leaky gut syndrome, has been shown to be effective in normalizing serum triglycerides and cholesterol, symptoms of menopause, and depressive disorders. Dosage: 100 milligrams three times daily. Trial period: three to six weeks.

Glutamine: The most abundant amino acid in our bodies, glutamine is effective for healing the intestinal tract, including stomach ulcers, irritable bowel syndrome, and ulcerative bowel diseases. Dosage: 8 grams daily. Trial period: four weeks.

Digestive enzymes: If the pancreas cannot make or recirculate enough digestive enzymes, we don't digest foods sufficiently. Use of either vegetable or pancreatic enzymes helps you break down foods more completely. Dosage: one to two capsules/tablets with meals.

Multivitamin with minerals: To cure problems with leaky gut, it is wise to add a good quality, allergen-free multivitamin with minerals to a daily routine. Look for a supplement that has *at least* 100 micrograms chromium, 100 milligrams selenium, 5–10 milligrams manganese, 500 milligrams calcium, 250 milligrams magnesium, 15 milligrams zinc. It is best to buy a supplement that does not contain a lot of foods and herbs because you may be sensitive to one or more of the ingredients in the supplement itself.

Vitamin C: Vitamin C helps flush toxins from our bodies, so take extra vitamin C. Dosage: 1,000–3,000 milligrams mineral ascorbates or Ester-C daily. Vitamin C flush once every week or two.

N-acetylglucosamine: N-acetylglucosamine (NAG) helps promote good flora and protects against some microbes. NAG is high in mucopylysaccharides, which are critical to intestinal health.

MIGRAINE HEADACHES

Migraine headaches cause periodic disruption in the lives of 18 million Americans, affecting 6 percent of men and 18 to 17 percent of women every year. People with migraines have an increased risk of stroke. Migraines occur when blood vessels in the head contract and then dilate and swell. Migraines usually begin with a throbbing pain on one side of the head, which can spread to both sides. They are often preceded by a short period of mood changes, irritability, fatigue, numbness, or tingling on one side of the body, lack of appetite, changes in vision, or seeing bright spots. These symptoms may disappear when the headache appears or remain. Although symptoms vary from person to person, they have a consistent pattern in each individual. Migraine attacks may last from hours to days and may be accompanied by nausea, vomiting, and extreme sensitivity to light. Medications and other techniques work best if used at the beginning stages.

Migraines usually come on in response to a "trigger." Common triggers are foods and beverages, alcohol, stress, emotions, hormone changes, medications such as estrogen therapy, visual stimuli, or changes in routine. A recent study of 494 people with migraines cited the following triggers: stress in 62 percent, weather changes in 43 percent, missing a meal in 40 percent, and bright sunlight in 38 percent. Cigarettes, perfumes, and sexual activity also provoked migraines in some people. Other triggers are red wines, exhaustion, and monosodium glutamate (MSG).

Jean Munro, M.D., an English doctor who specializes in working with people with multiple chemical sensitivities, breaks migraines into four types. The first type is a classic migraine, which begins with a visual disturbance of some sort—flashing lights, blackening, or blurred vision. It usually involves one side of the head, and people often vomit. The migraine usually lasts one to three days and can be quite severe.

The second type is called a common migraine and is almost identical to the first except that there is no visual warning. It begins on one side, sometimes progressing to both, and there may be vomiting. The third type is called a basilar migraine, when the blood vessels at the base of the head dilate. It can be quite frightening and often causes a panicky feeling, accompanied by a sense of doom. A generalized headache is accompanied by a pins-and-needles sensation around the mouth, nausea, and tingling hands. The fourth type, called a motor migraine, is a variation on the basilar and may be quite severe. Half the body feels weak, head pain centers around the eye, and vision is distorted.

Of 282 patients with migraines whom Dr. Munro studied, 100 percent had food allergies or sensitivities. Over 200 of them were sensitive to wheat and/or dairy products. Other commom trigger foods were tea, oranges, apples, onions, pork, and beef. She found that foods eaten daily provoked more reactions than chocolate, alcohol, and cheese, which are thought to be the most common triggers. Dr. Munro also found that people who eliminated these foods from their diet and cleared their homes of environmental contaminants had the best results in prevention of migraines. Using mild household cleaners, getting rid of gas appliances, removing house plants with molds and fungus, frequent cleaning, and making a bedroom an oasis by removal of carpets and curtains resulted in fewer migraines. Although these people were still exposed to smoke, perfume, and other environmental triggers outside the home, changing the home environment and their diets lowered their threshold enough so that they became more tolerant. More recent studies show that IgG4 and anti-IgG antibodies increased after food challenges in people with migraines, which supports the food-sensitivity/allergy hypothesis. Other researchers have confirmed that many of the foods that Dr. Munro found also provoked symptoms. However, virtually any food can be a trigger.

John Diamond, M.D., has used the theory in his Diamond Headache Clinic in Chicago that foods high in amines also provoke migraines in some people. Dietary amines, which promote constriction of blood vessels, are normally broken down by enzymes, but some people with migraines have lower than normal amounts of the appropriate enzymes. The amines that provoke vasoconstriction are serotonin, tyramine, tryptamine, and dopamine. They are found in the greatest quantities in avocados, bananas, cabbage, eggplant, pineapple, plums, potatoes, tomatoes, cheese, canned fish, wine (especially red), beer, aged meats, and yeast extracts.

Some physicians give intravenous (IV) nutrients to people with migraines. An IV with 23 grams of magnesium sulfate, 200–300 milligrams of vitamin B_6, and 1,000 milligrams of arginine will often give migraine relief in just minutes. This injection must be given slowly to prevent a sudden drop in blood pressure.

Hormone fluctuations in women can worsen, improve, or trigger migraines. Many women only experience migraines at specific times in their menstrual cycle from ovulation through menstruation. Birth control pills and other estrogen containing medications are widely recognized to trigger migraines in susceptible women. When women stop taking the medications, their migraines typically disappear.

The truth is that migraines have many triggers that vary from person to person. Finding your triggers and the treatments that work best for you is key. You certainly won't need all the therapies listed below, but hopefully you'll find relief from some of them.

FUNCTIONAL LABORATORY TESTING

1. Intracellular magnesium, either RBC or lymptocytes.
2. IgG4 and IgE Elisa testing for food allergies/sensitivities.
3. Elisa testing for environmental sensitivities/allergies.
4. Intestinal permeability screening.
5. Comprehensive digestion and stool analysis with parasitology.
6. *Candida* antibodies or CDSA.

HEALING OPTIONS

Clean up your diet: Remove all sugars, alcohol, refined carbohydrates, and caffeine. One study found that a low-fat diet of less than 20 grams daily lowered the incidence of headache from nine each month to three each month. Headache intensity and the need for medications also dropped substantially. This information shows the importance of the diet and the quality of fats. In combination with good-quality omega-3 fatty acids, this could give great results for many people.

Food sensitivities and allergies: Avoid foods you are sensitive to. Make your home environmentally safe by using only natural cleaning supplies, removing gas appliances, cleaning out mold and mildew, using a dehumidifier, and making your bedroom into a safe harbor by removing unnecessary items, such as carpeting and drapery.

Riboflavin (vitamin B₂): Forty-nine people with recurrent migraines were given 400 milligrams of vitamin B_2 daily with breakfast for three months. The number of migraines declined by 67 percent and the severity diminished by 68 percent. Its maximum effect is reached after two or three months, so be patient and give it a good try. In another study, fifty-five people were given either a placebo or 400 milligrams of riboflavin daily. Over three months, 59 percent of the people on riboflavin improved by at least 50 percent. There were minor side effects in two people—one had diarrhea and the other had frequent urination. If you experience either of these side effects, decrease the dosage.

Candida: A recent study of the relationship between *Candida* and migraines found that thirteen out of seventeen migraine sufferers responded to a three-month program of diet and medication with fewer and less severe headaches. Blood testing showed a lowering of *Candida* antibodies as well. The four people who did not respond well didn't stick to the program! If you have migraines, take the home test for *Candida* infections and have your physician order additional testing.

Eat often: Low blood sugar levels often trigger migraines so don't skip meals. You may find that eating five to six small meals each day works better for you than three main meals.

Magnesium: Numerous studies have documented the relationship between low magnesium levels and migraine headaches. It is estimated that magnesium plays a role in at least half of all people with migraines. When magnesium is supplemented at levels of 600 milligrams daily, there is a significant decrease in the number of migraines. Alan Gaby, M.D., offers his patients magnesium injections (of B-complex, vitamin C, and calcium) which alleviate their migraine headaches within minutes. Dosage: Try 600 milligrams magnesium citrate or magnesium glycinate for at least three to four months.

Omega-3 fatty acids: Fish oil supplements contain high levels of DHA and EPA oils. They have been shown in many studies to reduce the severity, duration, and frequency of migraine headaches. Most of us can produce EPA and DHA by using flaxseed oil, borage oil, or evening primrose oil, or by taking alpha-linolenic acid (ALA) and gamma-linolenic acid (GLA) supplements. However, this conversion requires that we have not only the genetic ability to complete the conversion, but also adequate vitamin B_6 and magnesium. One study gave subjects 1,800 milligrams of FLA and ALA in six capsules daily, plus 3 milligrams of niacin, 20 milligrams of vitamin C, 25 milligrams of vitamin E, 20 milligrams of soy phosphidatides, 50 milligrams of magnesium, 1.3 milligrams of beta-carotene, and 0.3 milligrams of vitamin B_6. Of the 128 people who participated in the study, 86 percent had a reduction in the severity, frequency, and duration of their migraine headaches, 22 percent became migraine-free, and 90 percent had reduced nausea and vomiting. All of 14 percent of the subjects were able to reduce their medication to simple pain relievers. Stress reduction and relaxation are also recommended. Omega-3 fatty acids promote anti-inflammatory prostaglandins PG31 and the PGE3 series. High protein and omega-6 fatty acids promote inflammation and pain through the conversion of arachadonic acid to PGE2 and leukotrienes. Dosage: 1,800 milligrams GLA/ALA, 2,000–3,000 milligrams of fish oil, or 300–500 milligrams of neuromins daily.

Feverfew: Numerous studies have shown the herb feverfew (*Tanacetum parthenium*) to be effective in preventing and minimizing the severity of migraines. The active ingredient is believed to be sequiterpene lactone. Feverfew affects arachidonic acid metabolism, which inhibits the generation of leukotrienes and thromboxane that cause inflammation and pain. Feverfew also inhibits secretion of serotonin from platelets and has a dampening effect on substances that cause blood vessels to constrict. One classic study took people who had benefited from feverfew and put them on feverfew or a placebo. The people on the placebo had a significant increase in the number and intensity of headaches.

Feverfew needs to be taken on a daily basis as a prevention rather than as a medication. There is a difference between fresh and dried feverfew and between various samples. If you don't get relief from one type, try another. Fresh feverfew seems to work best. It is easy to grow, so you could just eat a few leaves each day. Tinctures are available and would best approximate fresh leaves. It also comes in a freeze-dried form that seems to be effective. Dosage: Twice daily fifteen to twenty drops tincture, one capsule or one to three fresh leaves.

Acupuncture: Acupuncture has been shown to reduce the incidence and severity of migraine headaches along with the drug metoprolol in controlled studies. Metoprolol was slightly more effective, but acupuncture produced fewer negative side effects.

Behavioral techniques: Biofeedback, hypnotherapy, and stress reduction techniques have all proven useful to some migraine sufferers. Behavioral techniques help us better understand stressors and how to cope more effectively.

Avoid monosodium glutamate: MSG can provoke migraine headaches, asthma, diarrhea, vomiting, and gastric symptoms. These problems can occur immediately after eating or may be delayed up to seventy-two hours, which makes their relationship to MSG more difficult to discover. Food product labels may be misleading, with MSG labeled "natural coloring"; some hydrolyzed vegetable protein contains MSG. You can challenge yourself with MSG to see if it brings on a migraine. The Elisa/Act blood test includes tests for MSG and glutamate sensitivity.

Quercetin: Quercetin, the most effective bioflavonoid due to its anti-inflammatory effects, can be used to reduce pain and inflammatory responses and control allergies. Dosage: 500–1,000 milligrams three to four times daily at onset of migraine; 500 milligrams daily as a preventive.

Chiropractic and massage: Chiropractic manipulation and massage can help blood and lymphatic supply and lessen muscle tension.

Caffeine: Caffeine plays a mixed role in migraines. For some people, it significantly reduces the number and severity of headaches; for others it triggers them.

Niacin: There have been reports of physicians who use niacin intravenously during a migraine to lessen severity and duration of headaches. The dose contains at least 100 milligrams niacin, which is infused slowly.

Antioxidants: Migraines are often triggered by substances that promote free radicals like cigarette smoke, perfume, hair spray, pollution, and household chemicals. One researcher found lower levels of superoxide dismutase in platelets of people with migraines than in people with tension headaches. More research needs to be done in this area, but taking adequate antioxidants in a multivitamin with minerals may help prevent migraines.

PSORIASIS

Psoriasis is a chronic skin rash characterized by scaling, patchy, silvery-looking skin. It can affect just knees, elbows, or scalp or can spread over most of the body. It often occurs at the site of a previous injury. Psoriasis often runs in families and usually develops gradually. It's believed that the thick scaling of psoriasis is due to overproduction of new skin and a rapid rate of skin breakdown. Psoriasis flares up due to stress, severe sunburn, irritation, skin creams, antimalarial therapy, or from withdrawal from cortisone, or it can be brought on by other triggers. Then it goes into remission. Arachadonic acid and leukotrienes are elevated in the urine of people with active psoriasis, which indicates that omega-3 fatty acids may be of benefit. Psoriasis affects about 1 percent of the American population as a whole, but 2 to 4 percent of Caucasians.

Psoriasis can also occur with joint inflammation as psoriatic arthritis (see discussion on arthritis) and is found in 5 to 7 percent of people with psoriasis. It isn't clear whether psoriasis and psoriatic arthritis are the same disease or two almost identical diseases.

Michael Murray, N.D., and Joe Pizzorno, N.D., have documented a number of factors that influence the progression of psoriasis, including incomplete digestion of protein, bowel toxemia, food sensitivities, poor liver function, reaction to alcoholic beverages, and eating high amounts of animal fats. Let's look at each of these factors.

When protein digestion is incomplete or proteins are poorly absorbed, bacteria can break down the proteins and produce toxic substances. One group of these toxins is called polyamines, which have been found to be higher in people with psoriasis than in the average population. Polyamines contribute to psoriasis by blocking production of cyclic-AMP. Vitamin A and an herb called goldenseal inhibit the formation of polyamines. Since protein digestion begins in the stomach, low levels of hydrochloric acid there can also cause incomplete protein digestion. Digestive enzymes and/or hydrochloric acid supplementation aid protein digestion.

Bowel toxemia plays an important role in psoriasis. A poor balance of intestinal flora due to stress, diet, medications, or other factors often leads to bacterial and fungal infection. In fact, many people with psoriasis have colonization of fungus in their digestive system and on their skin. In a recent study, twenty-one out of thirty-four people with psoriasis were found to have *Candida albicans* in the spaces between their fingers or toes, and the majority were also affected by fungi from the Tinea family. Other research found a 56 percent increase in nail fungus in people with psoriasis. Another study looked at stool samples of people with psoriasis and other skin disorders. Researchers found a high number of disease-producing microbes, predominantly yeasts, in the colon. This may not be the cause of psoriasis, but rather an indication of poor gut ecology. Treatment for yeast infection corresponded with a decrease in skin inflammation.

Elimination diets and hypersensitivity testing have also produced profound results. People with psoriasis have high levels of IgE antibodies, which indicate an allergic component. Intestinal dysbiosis predisposes people to food and environmental sensitivities, so people with hypersensitivities need to heal the intestinal lining by taking appropriate bacterial supplements.

Poor liver function may contribute as well. Liver function profile tests and the metabolic screening questionnaire can help you determine liver function, and the metabolic screening questionnaire can also be used to follow your progress. Incorporate a detoxification program with an elimination/ provocation diet to determine which foods may trigger your psoriasis (see chapter 9).

Alcohol consumption contributes to psoriasis, since alcohol contains many toxic substances, which stress an overburdened liver. *Candida albicans* (yeast) thrive when beer and wine are consumed. Even one glass can provoke symptoms. Alcohol also increases intestinal permeability.

The causes and treatment of psoriasis are complex. Successful treatment must encompass several approaches reflecting its complexity. Look for underlying causes and develop a personal program based on your needs.

FUNCTIONAL LABORATORY TESTING

1. Food and environmental sensitivity testing, IgE and IgG4 testing.
2. *Candida* testing (either blood or stool).
3. Liver function profile.
4. Intestinal permeability testing.
5. Blood testing for vitamin and mineral status.

HEALING OPTIONS

Elimination/provocation diet: Explore the relationship between your psoriasis and food and environmental sensitivities through laboratory testing and the elimination/provocation diet (see discussion in chap. 7). For best results work with a nutritionist or physician who is familiar with food sensitivity protocols.

Multivitamin with minerals: Take a good quality multivitamin with minerals every day. Look for a supplement that contains at least 25,000 IU vitamin A, 400 IU vitamin D, 400

IU vitamin E, 800 micrograms folic acid, 200 micrograms selenium, 200 micrograms chromium and 25–50 milligrams zinc. Each of these nutrients has been shown to be deficient in people with psoriasis. There are several vitamin A topical creams used by dermatologists for psoriasis. Vitamin A is a critical nutrient for healthy skin.

Stress management: Flare-ups of psoriasis often occur after a stressful event. Because stress has to do with our own internalization of an event, even a mildly stressful situation can trigger psoriasis. Learning stress modification techniques can change your attitudes about stressful situations, allowing you to let them roll by more easily. In a recent study, four out of eleven people showed significant improvement in psoriatic symptoms with meditation and guided imagery. Hypnotherapy, biofeedback, and walks in nature are other effective tools. Regular aerobic exercise is a powerful stress reducer.

Fish oils/EPA/DHA: The research on fish oils is mixed. Too much can be toxic; be especially careful during pregnancy and lactation. Eating fish or taking fish oils has been shown to have an anti-inflammatory effect on psoriasis for some people. Fatty acids contribute to healthy skin, hair, and nails, and fish oils promote production of anti-inflammatory prostaglandins. It is also possible that fish oils potentiate the activity of vitamin D and sunlight. Dosage: Eat cold water fish—salmon, halibut, mackerel, sardines, tuna, and herring—two to four times per week or take EPA/DHA capsules. Fish oils increase blood clotting time so use them carefully.

Sunlight and vitamin D: Sunlight stimulates our bodies to manufacture vitamin D, which has been shown to be an effective treatment for psoriasis. A good multivitamin usually has 400 IU vitamin D. An additional 400 IU could be beneficial or getting thirty minutes of sun each day. In general, slow tanning improves psoriasis, with sunshine and sunlamps prescribed as part of standard therapy. A recent study, done in Israel at the Dead Sea, long renowned for its treatment of psoriasis, showed that natural sunlight stimulated significant improvement in disease activity. One group was just given sunlight therapy, and the other received additional therapy in mud packs and sulfur baths. Both groups showed significant improvement in skin symptoms and with psoriatic arthritis, where present.

Aloe vera cream: A placebo-controlled study of sixty people with psoriasis found that a 0.5 percent aloe vera cream cured 86 percent of the subjects. Each person used the aloe vera cream three times each day for a period of one year, and the researchers concluded that aloe vera cream is a safe and effective cure for psoriasis.

Glucosamine: A new hypothesis is that glucosamine, a component of connective tissue widely used for arthritic conditions, may benefit people with psoriasis. Glucosamine plus fish oil can limit amphilregulin and transforming growth factor, which enhance psoriasis. There is no human research as yet, but glucosamine has little risk.

Milk thistle/silymarin: Extracts of the herb milk thistle have been used since the fifteenth century for ailments of the liver and gallbladder. Milk thistle, also known as silymarin, contains anti-inflammatory flavonoid complexes that promote the flow of bile and help tone the spleen, gallbladder, and liver. An excellent liver detoxifier, milk thistle has also been shown to have a positive effect on psoriasis. Dosage: three to six capsules of 175 milligrams standardized 80 percent milk thistle extract daily with water before meals.

Zinc: Zinc is necessary for maintenance and repair of skin, immune function, and healing. Copper and zinc compete for the same receptor sites during absorption. When zinc is deficient, copper is usually elevated. This is true for people with psoriasis.

Many studies have determined that people with psoriasis have lower levels of zinc than people in control groups. However, studies using oral zinc supplementation haven't always shown a clear improvement in psoriasis, though such studies have been of short duration—only six to ten weeks. Even though they didn't show improvement in the skin, they did show improvement in immune function and dramatic improvement in joint symptoms. It's possible that either zinc needs to be used along with other nutrients, or the timeframe of these studies was too brief to see improvement. Dosage: 50 milligrams zinc picolinate (an easily absorbed form of zinc) daily.

Selenium: Many studies have shown that people with psoriasis are deficient in selenium. Selenium is part of a molecule called glutathione peroxidase which protects against oxidative damage (free radicals). Giving supplemental selenium to people with psoriasis showed an increase in glutathione peroxidase levels and improvement in immune function, though not an improvement in skin condition. However, they were studies of short duration with selenium the only supplement. This underscores the concepts of patience when using natural therapies and of using more than one nutrient or approach at a time. Dosage: 200 micrograms daily, which you can get in a good multivitamin. Selenium can be toxic, so more is not necessarily better.

Saccharomyces boulardii: *Saccharomyces boulardii* is a cousin to baker's yeast. It has been shown to raise levels of secretory IgA, which are low in psoriatic arthritis and psoriasis. Dosage: one acidophillus/bifidus supplement containing *Saccharomyces boulardii*.

Topical creams: Many topical creams, oils, and ointments help psoriasis. Capsaicin, a cayenne pepper cream, helped 66 to 70 percent of the people who used it in a recent trial. The main side effect was that of a burning feeling associated with chili peppers, which quickly subsided. Vitamins A and E have also been used topically with success; one physician alternates them, one each day. Creams containing zinc are also effective, as are salves containing sarsaparilla. Goldenseal ointment or oral supplements can also be helpful.

Honduran sarsaparilla: Sarsaparilla, a flavoring in root beers and confections, has proven to be effective in psoriasis, especially the more chronic, large-plaque forming type. Sarsaparilla binds bacterial endotoxins. Dosage: 2–4 teaspoons liquid extract (1:1) daily; 250–500 milligrams solid extract (4:1) daily.

Lecithin/phosphatidylcholine: Lecithin was used in a ten-year study from 1940 to 1950. People consumed 4–8 tablespoons of lecithin daily, along with small amounts of vitamins A, B_1, B_2, B_5, B_6, D, thyroid and liver preparations, and creams. Out of 155 patients, 118 people responded positively. Lecithin-rich foods include soybeans, wheat germ, nuts, seeds, whole grains, eggs, and oils from soy, nuts, and seeds. Lecithin granules can be purchased in health food stores and added to foods as a cooking ingredient. Lecithin can also be purchased in capsule form, as can the active ingredient in lecithin, phosphatidylcholine. Dosage: 4–8 tablespoons daily or one to four capsules of phosphatidylcholine.

Propolis: Bees collect a resin from tree buds and convert it into a highly concentrated substance called propolis, which a Cuban study found to have anti-inflammatory properties. The research is preliminary, but the overall benefits of propolis are many and the risks are low.

Folic acid: There is much research on folate deficiency caused by the drug methotrexate, which is a folate antagonist medication often used for psoriasis. This seems ironic, because folic acid is one of the primary nutrients needed for proper skin formation. Jonathan Wright recommends high-dose folic acid therapy for psoriais—50–100 milligrams daily. Although I have never used dosages in those ranges, a dose of 10 milligrams daily is considered safe. However, if folic acid is taken by someone with a vitamin B_{12} deficiency, nerve damage can go undetected, so if you are going to use high levels of folic acid, have your doctor test your vitamin B_{12} status.

SCHIZOPHRENIA

Schizophrenia is a catchall diagnosis for people who are experiencing altered realities, including hallucinations, delusions, and thought confusion, which return periodically. During acute periods, people with schizophrenia experience a loss of energy, of sense of humor, and of interest in living. Because this illness varies so much in cause and nature, it is imperative to treat each person on an individual functional level. Specific testing of amino acids, food sensitivities, fatty acids, and gut health will reveal information relevant to each person. Often, studies of schizophrenia using nutritional models have been disappointing because all patients are lumped into one group. When groups are broken into sub-types or patients are seen individually, improvements are seen. Many therapies based on the pioneering work of Carl Pfeiffer, M.D., are still being used at molecular-based clinics worldwide. His book *Mental and Elemental Nutrients* is still a classic in the field.

Schizophrenics are found to have high levels of interleukin II, an inflammatory substance known to have the potential to cause symptoms similar to schizophrenia. Fish oils can help reduce levels of interleukin II and cytokines. Schizophrenics have shown altered fatty acid panels. Arachadonic acid, the omega-3 fatty acids, EPA, and DHA levels are often low. Doing a fatty acid test would make sense.

One subtype of schizophrenics respond well to gut-healing protocols and elimination of wheat products. Wheat sensitivity can cause chemicals in the brain that resemble opiates and cause hallucinations and behavior disturbances. Other classic food offenders in schizophrenia include dairy products, food additives, and chocolate, although nearly any food can cause problems.

People with schizophrenia have an increased need for anti-oxidant nutrients. Uric acid levels have been found to be low. Uric acid has antioxidant effects. Other antioxidants have also been found to be deficient. Poor free-radical protection can damage fat-dependent membranes, the nervous system, and the brain.

Schizophrenia appears to have an autoimmune component, which may be a result of the disease itself. Many studies have shown a correlation between a mother getting the flu while pregnant and an increase in schizophrenia in the children. Antibody levels are increased, and there are increased abnormal white blood cells, a decrease in C4 helper cells, and a decrease in T-cell response and formation.

FUNCTIONAL LABORATORY TESTING

1. Essential fatty acids.
2. Spectracell functional nutrient, oxidative, and cardiovascular profiles.
3. IgE and IgG food allergy testing.
4. Hair mineral analysis, for detection of heavy metals.
5. Urinary amino acids.

HEALING OPTIONS

Niacin: Abraham Hoffer, M.D., has long used niacin therapy for schizophrenia. It is believed that there is faulty niacin metabolism in this condition, because people with schizophrenia often do not experience the intense flushing that usually occurs with niacin ingestion.

Tryptophan/5-Hydroxy tryptophan (5-HTP): In fourteen patients tested, dietary restriction of tryptophan worsened their symptoms. Tryptophan can easily be converted to niacin, which may be one reason why it is of benefit. Tryptophan is also a precursor to seratonin, which affects mood, behavior, sleep, and carbohydrate cravings. Dosage: 1,000–2,500 milligrams tryptophan daily (only available by prescription) or 300–600 milligrams 5-HTP (available over the counter).

EPA/DHA fish oil: Schizophrenics have been well documented to have low omega-3 fatty acid levels. Twenty hospitalized patients were given ten grams of MaxEPA daily. There were significant improvements in psychological symptoms, behavior, and tardive dyskinesia after six weeks.

Serine: Much research has been done showing that high dose glycine is beneficial for schizophrenia. Concern has been posted as to the possible long-term neurological effects of high glycine supplementation. The mechanism of the response was believed to be the effect on NMDA receptor sites. NMDA function is low in people with schizophrenia. Newer research on serine shows that the positive effects of enhancing NMDA function can be achieved without the risks of high-dose glycine.

Folic acid: Folic acid levels are often lower in schizophrenia, while homocysteine levels are often higher, suggesting a defect in methylation. Thirty-three percent of patients with acute psychiatric disorders were given 15 milligrams of folic acid daily for six months in addition to standard treatment. The difference between the folic acid–treated group and the control group increased over time. Folic acid does not cause the diseas,e but correlates with its severity, flare-ups, and use of medications. Folic acid is also required by our bodies for the synthesis of serine, which has also been shown to have positive effect in schizophrenia. High levels of homocysteine due to a folate metabolism error have also been found consistently in people with schizophrenia. Dosage: The amount of folic acid is limited because it can mask a vitamin B_{12} deficiency. If you do not have a vitamin B_{12} anemia, you can take 15 milligrams daily.

Magnesium: Magnesium deficiency can produce depression, agitation, confusion, and disorientation. Twenty schizophrenic patients were evaluated for serum magnesium levels. Twenty-five percent were found to be magnesium deficient. Serum magnesium is not a sensitive test of magnesium deficiency, so if red blood cell magnesium were analyzed, the results would probably have been much higher. Half of the magnesium-deficient patients were exhibiting psychotic behavior, including hallucinations. In drug-treated schizophrenics, magnesium levels have been found to be consistently low. Supplementing with magnesium does not always show improvement in symptoms. Magnesium injections may be necessary at first to "prime the pump." Because so many enzymes are dependent on magnesium, a deficiency could affect other nutrients including vitamins B_1, B_6, E, and C and minerals such as zinc, copper, and selenium.

SCLERODERMA

Scleroderma is a connective tissue disease characterized by a thickening and loss of elasticity in the skin, joints, digestive tract (especially in the esophagus), lungs, thyroid, heart, and kidney. Mild or severe, it can flare up and subside in intensity. There are two forms of the disease: localized to one or two locations or generalized throughout the body. The most common initial complaint is loss of circulation in toes or fingers (Raynaud's syndrome), characterized by swelling and a thickening of skin.

Joint pain is an early symptom. As the disease progresses, the skin becomes taut and shiny, with the face becoming masklike. There may be red blotches on the skin where capillaries have broken. Small calcifications occur under the skin on the fingers. People become malnourished and may need supplemental foods or total parenteral feeding (tube feeding).

Scleroderma has definite digestive components. The esophagus is usually inflamed. The esophageal sphincter becomes stiff and loses elasticity which causes gastric juices to go up into the esophagus, burning the lining. People who have been on antacid medications are likely to have a yeast infection in their esophagus. Malabsorption leads to poor movement, dysbiosis, and semiobstructions in the small intestines. Small bowel bacterial overgrowth is common due to a loss of peristaltic function in the intestines. Use of steroid medications increases the likelihood of yeast infections in the digestive tract. Treatment with fluconazole will cure the infection temporarily but doesn't change the fact that there is a loss of movement in the area. Small bowel overgrowth must be routinely monitored and treated if an infection is present.

There is no single known cause of scleroderma. An evaluation was made of 178 people with scleroderma, in comparison with 200 controls. People with scleroderma were more likely to have higher concentrations of and levels of exposure to solvents, especially tricholoethylene.

There is evidence that prolonged exposure to silica, silicone, and chemical solvents significantly increases the risk of developing scleroderma. (Another possible association is in workers with repetitive hand and arm vibration.) In a small study, forty-four women and six men went through extensive testing and examination to see if there was a relationship between their work and autoimmune disease. They had been working in a factory for six years on average that produced scouring powder with a high silica content. Thirty-two, or 64 percent, showed symptoms of a systemic illness, six with Sjögren's syndrome, five with scleroderma, three with systemic lupus, five with a combination syndrome, and thirteen who didn't fit into any definite pattern of disease. Seventy-two percent had elevated ANA, an indicator of autoimmune connective tissue diseases. The conclusion was that workers who are continually exposed to silica have a high probability of developing an autoimmune problem. The research on breast implants is mixed. Silicone breast implants may also significantly raise the risk of developing scleroderma.

Natural therapies can work along with medical therapies for scleroderma. Infections must be treated, and beneficial flora given. Nutrients that help with collagen maintenance and repair are essential to help prevent loss of elasticity in skin and organs. Foods and supplements which help reduce production of arachidonic acid will reduce inflammation and pain. Good quality oils, fish, nuts, and seeds work in this way. It's also important to increase circulation and oxygen supply to the tissues. Finally, a nutrient-dense food plan must be developed that works to offset the problems of malnutrition which are common.

FUNCTIONAL LABORATORY TESTING

1. Methane breath test for small bowel bacterial overgrowth.
2. Elisa IgE and IgG testing for food and environmental sensitivities.
3. Free-DHEA/cortisol saliva test.
4. *Candida* testing.
5. Comprehensive digestive and stool analysis.
6. Liver function profile.
7. Testing for silicone sensitivity should be done on an annual basis for women with breast implants. Saline implants have a silicone casing which may also cause problems.

HEALING OPTIONS

Treat infections: Small bowel infections, esophageal *Candida* and other infections are likely to recur. No specific research has been done to show that use of supplementation with flora and other natural therapies can help with recurrence, but they do help to boost the immune system. You may be able to keep the infection at bay with use of colloidal silver, grapefruit seed extract, or garlic capsules. Each of these substances has wide antimicrobial properties, low toxicity, and a low incidence of negative side effects. Your physician will probably use antibiotics.

Detoxification: A liver function panel can determine whether your phase I and phase II liver detoxification pathways are working normally. Because the risk of scleroderma increases with solvent exposure, a liver detoxification program may be of significant benefit. In the few people I've worked with who have scleroderma, this has proven to be an effective starting point.

DHEA: DHEA is an adrenal hormone that has been found to be beneficial for people with scleroderma. Because DHEA is a powerful hormone, I recommend that you have a free-DHEA/cortisol test to determine if you actually need DHEA supplementation, and to monitor your dosage levels. Dosages will vary, depending on your personal needs.

Acidophilus **and** *bifidobacteria*: These help rebalance normal digestive flora. Dosage: one to two capsules or ¼ to ½ teaspoon two or three times daily.

Saccharomyces boulardii: *Saccharomyces boulardii* is a cousin to baker's yeast, which has been shown to raise levels of secretory IgA. Saccharomyces has also been shown to be effective in combating small bowel infections caused by *Clostridium difficile*, the main bacteria to be found in small bowel overgrowth. If your methane breath test shows a small bowel infection, you'll want to take supplements of *S. boulardii*. Dosage: one to two capsules three times daily between meals.

Elimination/provocation diet: Be certain to explore the relationship between your scleroderma and food and environmental sensitivities through laboratory testing and the elimination/provocation diet. Follow directions in chapter 7. For best results, work with a nutritionist or physician who is familiar with food sensitivity protocols.

Diet: People with scleroderma are usually malnourished. So eat at least five servings daily of fruits and vegetables and as many organic and natural foods as possible. You may want to supplement your diet with nutrient-rich protein powder drinks available at health food stores. To eliminate all foods that don't contribute to your nutritional well-being, reread chapter 8 and use the food chart. Make changes gradually.

Multivitamin with minerals: Poor diet, loss of movement in the digestive tract, loss of elasticity of the organs, infections, and medications all contribute to the malabsorption of nutrients. Selenium and vitamin C deficiencies are common in people with scleroderma. At least seventeen nutrients are essential for formation of bone and cartilage, so it's important to find a supplement that supports these needs. Look for a supplement that contains 10,000 IU vitamin A, 800–1,000 milligrams calcium, 400–500 milligrams magnesium, 400 IU vitamin E, at least 250 milligrams vitamin C, 50 milligrams vitamin B_6, 15–50 milligrams zinc, 5–10 milligrams manganese, 1–2 milligrams copper, and 200 micrograms selenium in addition to other nutrients. Follow the dosage on the bottle to get nutrients in appropriate amounts.

Vitamin C: Vitamin C is vital for formation of cartilage and collagen, which is a fibrous protein that forms strong connective tissue necessary for bone strength. Vitamin C also plays an important role in immune response, helping protect us from disease-producing microbes. Vitamin C also inhibits formation of inflammatory prostaglandins, helping to reduce pain, inflammation, and swelling. If you have *Candida* or bacterial overgrowth, vitamin C can boost your body's ability to defend itself. Vitamin C is also an antioxidant, needed to counter free-radical formation noted in sclerotic conditions. Dosage: 1–3 grams daily in an ascorbate or ester form.

Glycosamine sulfate: Glycosamine sulfate is used therapeutically to help repair cartilage, reduce swelling and inflammation, and restore joint function. Green-lipped mussels are a rich source of glycosaminoglycans. Use of glycosamine sulfate has no associated side effects. Dosage: 500 milligrams two to four times daily.

Licorice: DGL (deglycyrrhized) licorice helps heal mucous membranes by increasing healing prostaglandins that promote mucus secretion and cell proliferation. Licorice also enhances the blood flow and health of intestinal tract cells. Be sure to use DGL licorice to avoid side effects caused by whole licorice. Dosage: Chew two tablets three to four times daily.

Slippery elm bark: Slippery elm bark has demulcent properties so it's gentle and soothing to mucous membranes. It has been a folk remedy for both heartburn and ulcers in European and Native American cultures and was used as a food by Native Americans. Slippery elm bark can be used in large amounts without harm. Drink as a tea or chew on the bark. Recipe for tea: Simmer 1 teaspoon of slippery elm bark in two cups of water for twenty minutes and strain. Sweeten if you wish, and drink freely. You can also purchase slippery elm lozenges at health food stores and some drug stores.

Glutamine: Although I was unable to find any references for use of glutamine to heal the esophagus, it makes theoretical sense. The digestive tract uses glutamine as a fuel source and for healing. It is effective for healing stomach ulcers, irritable bowel syndrome, and ulcerative bowel diseases, and it is likely to be useful in the upper GI tract as well. Dosage: Begin a one-month trial with 8 grams daily in divided doses. If it's helpful, continue.

Ginger: Ginger can provide temporary relief, it has some anti-inflammatory properties, and it can help expel gas. Ginger can be used as an ingredient in food or taken as a supplement. Make a tea with ½ teaspoon of powdered ginger or 1½ teaspoon of fresh ginger per cup of boiled water. Steep for ten minutes and drink. If you'd like, sweeten it with honey. Cook with ginger and use it freely.

Meadowsweet herb: Also a demulcent, meadowsweet soothes inflamed mucous membranes. To use as a tea, take 1–2 teaspoons of the dried herb in one cup of boiled water. Steep for ten minutes, and sweeten with honey if you like. Drink 3 cups daily.

Gamma linolenic acid: One gram of evening primrose oil was given to four women with scleroderma three times daily for one year. They experienced a reduction in pain, improved skin texture, and healing of sores; red patches on skin due to broken capillaries were much improved. The researchers suggest that 6 grams daily may be of greater benefit. Dosage: 3–6 grams of evening primrose oil, borage oil, or flaxseed oil daily.

Omega-3 fatty acids/fish oils: Fish oil capsules reduce morning stiffness and joint tenderness. Similar results can be obtained by eating fish high in EPA/DHA—salmon, mackerel, halibut, tuna, sardines, and herring—two to four times a week. (For more on omega-3 fatty acids/fish oils, see discussion under Osteoarthritis.) Fish oils increase blood clotting time and should not be used by people with hemophilia or those who take anticoagulant medicines or aspirin regularly. Dosage: It's easiest for most people to eat fish two to four times each week. High dosages in capsule form should be monitored by a physician.

Bromelain: Bromelain is an enzyme from pineapple that acts as an anti-inflammatory in much the same way that evening primrose oil, fish oils, and borage oils do. It interferes with production of arachidonic acid, which reduces inflammation. It also prevents platelet aggregation and interferes with growth of malignant cells. Bromelain can be taken with meals as a digestive aid, but as an anti-inflammatory it must be taken between meals. Dosage: 500–1,000 milligrams two to three times daily between meals.

Quercetin: Quercetin is the most effective bioflavonoid in its anti-inflammatory effects. It can be used to reduce pain and inflammatory responses and for control of allergies. Dosage: 500–1,000 milligrams two to four times daily.

Coenzyme Q10: CoQ10 is an enzyme that works to enhance cell function. It is necessary for energy production, immune function, and repair and maintenance of tissues. Widely used in Japan for heart disease, it has been researched as an antitumor substance. Dosage: 60–100 milligrams daily. Trial period: two months.

Part 6

RESOURCES

DIRECTORY

PROFESSIONAL REFERRALS

If you would like a referral for a physician or nutritionist in your area, call one of the professional organizations. They all usually have referral lists on their web-sites or at their offices. Great Smokies Diagnostic Lab also has a referral list.

PROFESSIONAL ORGANIZATIONS

American Academy of Environmental Medicine (AAEM)
American Financial Center
7701 E. Kellogg, Suite 625
Wichita, KS 67207
(316) 684-5500

American College of Advancement in Medicine
P.O. Box 3427
Laguna Hills, CA
1-800-532-3688
(949) 583-7666
www.acam.org

American Chiropractic Association
1701 Clarendon Blvd.
Arlington, VA 22209
(703) 276-8800
www.amerchiro.org

American Holistic Medical Association
4101 Lake Boone Trail, Suite 201
Raleigh, NC 27607
(703) 556-9245

American Association of Naturopathic Physicians
601 Valley Street, Suite 105
Seattle, WA 98109
(206) 298-0126
Fax: (206) 298-0129
www.naturopathic.org

Association for Network Chiropractic
Innate Intelligence, Inc.
444 N. Main Street
Longmont, CO 80501
(303) 678-8086
www.networkchiropractic.org

Functional Medicine Institute
P.O. Box 1729
Gig Harbor, WA 98335
1-800-228-0622
www.fxmed.com

Clinical Nutritionists

International and American Associations of Clinical
   Nutritionists
5200 Keller Springs Road, Suite 410
Dallas, TX 75248
(972) 407-9089
Fax: (972) 250-0233
www.iaacn.org

Clinical Nutrition Certification Board
5200 Keller Springs Road, Suite 410

Dallas, TX 75248
(972) 250-2829
Fax: (972) 250-0233
www.cncb.org

Herbalists

American Botanical Council
P.O. Box 144345
Austin, TX 78714
(512) 331-8868
www.herbalgram.org

American Herbalists Guild
P.O. Box 70
Roosevelt, UT 84066
(435) 722-8434
Fax: (435) 722-8452
www.healthworld.com/associations/pa/herbalmedicine

LABORATORIES

The tests described earlier in this book are all performed by the laboratories listed below, which also offer a wide variety of other useful functional tests. The tests listed here are not the ordinary tests you will find in your local medical lab or hospital, although many tests that were originally only performed by these laboratories have found their way into local and national labs. Unless your physician is nutritionally oriented, she may be unfamiliar with many of these tests. Don't let that deter you from asking your physician to order any tests you feel may be appropriate for you and your condition. Your physician can call these labs for complete information packages and test kits. These labs also provide competent staff to assist your doctor with interpretation of the results.

Diagnos-Techs, Inc.
Clinical and Research Laboratory
6620 South 192nd Place J
Kent, WA 98032
1-800-878-3787
(425) 251-0596
www.Diagnostechs.com

Provides many laboratory tests including adrenal stress profile, DHEA, male and female salivary hormones, parasitology testing, Candida, Helicobacter, *digestion efficiency, secretory IgA, gastric pH, and liver function testing.*

Doctor's Data Inc. & Reference Laboratory
P.O. Box 111
30W101 Roosevelt Road
West Chicago, IL 60185
(708) 231-3649
1-800-323-2784
Fax: (708) 231-9190
www.doctorsdata.com

Provides many laboratory tests, including hair mineral testing, blood mineral analysis, urine and blood complete amino acid testing, mercapturic acid testing, D-glucaric acid, functional folic acid result, methylmalonic acid (B_{12} status), and diet analysis.

Great Smokies Diagnostic Laboratory
63 Zillicoa Street
Asheville, NC 28806
(828) 253-0621
1-800-522-4762
www.greatsmokies.lab.com

Provides many laboratory tests, including CDSA, lactose, and small bowel breath tests, liver detoxification profiles, intestinal per-

meability, Heliobacter pylori, *vitamin analysis, hair analysis, male and female hormone testing, DHEA/cortisol, secretory IgA, essential fatty acids, bone resorption, and homocysteine.*

Immuno Laboratories Inc.
1620 West Oakland Park Boulevard
Ft. Lauderdale, FL 33311
(305) 486-4500
1-800-231-9197
Fax: (305) 739-6563
www.betterhealthusa.com

Provides IgE, IgG4, and IgG1 food sensitivity assay, Candida albicans *assay, Epstein Barr virus profile,* Heliobacter pylori *testing, and more.*

Immunosciences Lab., Inc.
8730 Wilshire Boulevard
Suite 305
Beverly Hills, CA 90211
1-800-950-4686
(310) 657-1077
Fax: (310) 657-1053
www.immuno-sci-lab.com

Provides tests designed to detect immunological injury and environmental and genetic disposition. Tests include comprehensive immune function testing, lymphocyte immune testing, natural killer cell activity, immunotoxicology, silicone-related immune panels, chronic fatigue panels, gastrointestinal evaluation, viral antibodies, parasite antibodies, Candida *antibodies, bacterial antibodies, and secretory IgA.*

Meridian Valley Clinical Laboratory
515 West Harrison Street
Kent, WA 98032
(253) 859-8700

Provides a wide variety of tests including DHEA screening, cortisol, IgE, and IgG food allergies, essential amino acids, adrenal

*steroids, parasitology, CDSA, essential fatty acids, and fraction-
ated estrogens.*

Meta Metrix Medical Laboratory
5000 Peachtree Industrial Boulevard
Suite 110
Norcross, GA 30071
1-800-221-4640
(770) 446-5483
Fax: (770) 441-2237
www.metametrix.com

*Provides a wide variety of tests, including amino acid analysis, fatty
acid analysis, lipid peroxides, antioxidant vitamin status, minerals in
blood, urine, and hair, whole blood reduced carnitine, organic acids,
glutathione, ATP, IgG, and IgE food allergies, inhalant allergy testing, functional liver detoxification, intestinal permeability, plasma homocysteine, cysteine, total glutathione, and bone resorption.*

Pacific Toxicology Laboratories
6160 Variel Avenue
Woodland Hills, CA 91367
1-800-32TOXIC
(818) 598-3110
Fax: (818) 598-3116

*Provides testing for environmental pollutants and contaminants,
including panels for solvents and metabolites, pesticides, herbicides,
polychlorinated and polybrominated biiphenyls, PCBs, and heavy
metals, as well as OSHA compliance panels.*

Serammune Physicians Laboratory
14 Pidgeon Hill Drive
Suite 300
Sterling, VA 20165
1-800-553-5472
(703) 450-2980
Fax: (703) 450-2981

Provides comprehensive food and environmental blood testing through the Elisa/Act Test, which measures over 300 foods, environmental chemicals, preservatives, mercury sensitivity, and three major classes of yeasts. Comprehensive physician and patient guides provide lifestyle support for the lab results.

SpectraCell Laboratories, Inc.
515 Post Oak Boulevard
Suite 830
Houston, TX 77027
1-800-227-5227
(713) 621-3101

Provides functional vitamin, mineral, and antioxidant panels, as well as the most comprehensive functional cardiovascular profiles.

NUTRITIONAL AND HERBAL PRODUCTS

Listed below are companies that sell various health-related products. This list is short and cannot include the many wonderful companies that exist. This listing does not constitute an endorsement of any one company over another. Some companies sell to both professionals and stores, although not all products may be available in stores. Other companies sell only to health professionals; such companies are indicated with an *.

Advanced Medical
  Nutrition (AMNI)
2247 National Avenue
Hayward, CA 94545
1-800-437-8888
(510) 783-6969
Nutritional and herbal
  products

Allergy Research/
  Nutricology
30806 Santana Street
Hayward, CA 94544
1-800-545-9960
(510) 487-8526
www.nutricology.com
Nutritional and herbal
  products

Apothecure Pharmacy*
13720 Midway Road
Suite 109
Dallas, TX 75244
1-800-969-6601
(972) 960-6601
Compounding pharmacy

Biotics Research
  Corporation
P.O. Box 36888
Houston, TX 77236
1-800-231-5777
www.bioticresearch.com
Nutritional and health
  products

Cambridge Nutraceuticals
294 Washington Street
Suite 602
Boston, MA 02108
1-800-265-2202
(617) 695-1255
www.cambridgenutra.com
Primarily offers glutamine
  products

College Pharmacy
833 N. Tejon Street
Colorado Springs, CO
  80903
1-800-888-9358
Fax: (719) 634-4513 or
1-800-556-5893
e-mail: collegep@rmi.net

DNA Pacifica*
730 Summersong Lane
Encinitas, CA 92024
1-800-632-5382
(619) 632-5382
Nutritional and herbal
  products

Douglas Laboratories*
600 Boyce Road
Pittsburgh, PA 15205
1-888-792-5230
(412) 494-0122
Fax: (412) 494-0155
www.douglaslabs.com
A wide variety of nutri-
  tional products

Ecclectic Institute
14385 SE Lusted Road
Sandy, OR 97055
1-800-332-4372
(503) 668-4120
www.eccleticherb.com
Herbal products

Emerson Ecologics
18 Lomar Park
Pepperell, MA 01463
1-800-654-4432
Fax: 1-800-718-7238
Nutrional and herbal products and books; distrib-
  utor for many product
  lines

Homeopathic Educational
Services
2124 Kittredge Avenue
Berkeley, CA 94704
1-800-359-9051
(550) 649-0294
Homeopathic products and
books

HVS Labs*
P.O. Box 82246
Naples, FL 33941
1-800-521-7722
(941) 643-4636
www.hvslabs.com
Homeopathic products

Karuna*
42 Digital Drive
Suite 7
Novato, CA 94949
1-800-826-7225
(415) 382-0147
Nutritional and herbal
products

The Key Company*
1313 W. Essex
P.O. Box 3707
St. Louis, MO 63122
1-800-325-9592
or 1-800-392-9039
(Missouri)
Nutritional and herbal
products; hard-to-find
products

Metagenics*/Ethical Nutrients
971 Calle Negocio
San Clemente, CA 92673
1-800-692-9400
(714) 366-0818
www.metagenics.com
Nutritional and herbal
products; UltraClear
products

Metabolic Maintenance
P.O. Box 3600
Sisters, OR 97759
1-800-772-7873
Fax: (541) 549-3299
Nutritional and herbal
products

Natren
3105 Willow Lane
Westlake Village, CA
91361
1-800-992-3323
(805) 371-4737
www.natren.com
Nutritional and herbal
products

Neo-Life
Image Awareness
Corporation
1271 High Street
Auburn, CA 95603
(530) 823-7092
e-mail: jmcaphee@jps.net
Nutritional and herbal
products

Perque/Seraphim, Inc.*
14 Pidgeon Hill Road
Sterling, VA 20165
1-800-525-7372
(703) 450-2990
Nutritional and hypoallergenic products

Prima
1010 Crenshaw Boulevard
Suite 170
Torrance, CA 90501
(310) 320-1132
Nutritional and herbal
products

Professional Botanicals*
P.O. Box 988
Eden, UT 94409
1-800-824-8181
(801) 621-3450
Herbal products

Progressive Laboratories,
Inc.
1701 Walnut Hill Lane
Irving, TX 75038
1-800-527-9512
(214) 518-9660
Nutritional and herbal
products

Systemic Formulas*
P.O. Box 1516
Ogden, UT
1-800-445-4647
(801) 621-8840
Fax: (801) 521-8801
Nutritional and herbal
products

Thermal Life
High Tech Health, Inc.
1-800-794-5355
Fax: (303) 449-9640
Far infrared saunas

Thorne Research Inc.*
P.O. Box 25
Dover, ID 83825
1-800-228-1966
(208) 263-1337
Nutritional and herbal
products

Transitions for Health
621 SW Alder Street
Suite 900
Portland, OR 97205
1-800-228-1966
(503) 226-1010
www.transitions-for-
women.com
Progest cream; other
products

Tyler Encapsulations*
2204-8 NW Birdsdale
Gresham, OR 97030
1-800-869-9705
(503) 661-5401
Nutritional and herbal
  products

Vital Nutrients*
50 Silver Street
Middletown, CT 06457
1-888-328-992
Nutritional and herbal
  products

Werum Enterprises, Inc.*
P.O. Box 903
Shingle Springs, CA 95682
1-800-822-6193
(916) 677-1988
Nutritional and herbal
  products; books

Supplement Manufacturers

Phyto Pharmica*
825 Challenger Drive
Green Bay, WI 54311
1-800-553-2370
(920) 469-9099
Fax: 1-888-377-5657
www.phytopharmica.com

Enzymatic Therapy
825 Challenger Drive
Green Bay, WI 54311
1-800-553-2370
(920) 469-9099
Fax: 1-888-399-7680
www.enzymatictherapy.com

ASSOCIATIONS FOR SPECIFIC ILLNESSES

American Celiac Society
58 Musano Court
West Orange, NJ 07062
(973) 325-8837

American Liver Foundation
75 Maiden Lane, Suite 603
New York, NY 10038
1-800-GO LIVER (465-4837)
http://gi.ucsf.edu/alf.html

Celiac Sprue Associaton
P.O. Box 31700
Omaha, NE 68131
(402) 558-0600

CFIDS Buyer's Club
1187 Coast Village Road
  #1-280
Santa Barbara, CA 93108
1-800-366-6056

Chronic Fatigue Syndrome
Association
P.O. Box 220398
Charlotte NC 28222
1-800-442-3437
(704) 362-2343
www.cfids.@cfids.org

Crohn's & Colitis Foundation of America
386 Park Avenue South
New York, NY 10016
1-800-932-2423
(212) 685-3440
www.ccfa.org

Digestive Disease National
Coalition
407 Capitol Court NE
Suite 200
Washington, DC 20002
(202) 546-7497
Fax: (202) 546-7105

International Foundation
for Functional Gastrointestinal Disorders
P.O. Box 17864
Milwaukee, IL 53217
(414) 964-1799

Intestinal Disease Foundation, Inc.
1323 Forbes Avenue
Suite 200
Pittsburgh, PA 14219
(412) 261-5888

National Chronic Fatigue
Syndrome and Fibromyalgia Association
P.O. Box 18426
Kansas City, MO 64133
(816) 313-2000
Fax: (816) 524-6782
www.cfids.org

National Digestive Diseases
Information
Clearinghouse
P.O. Box NDDIC
2 Information Way
Bethesda, MD 20892
1-888-964-2001
www.niddic.nih.gov

National Headache
Foundation
428 W. St. James Place
Chicago, IL 60614
1-888-NHF-5552

Reach Out for Youth with
Ileitis and Colitis, Inc.
15 Chemung Place
Jerico, NY 11753
(516) 293-3102

Rheumatoid Disease
Foundation
7111 Sweetgum Drive SW
Suite A
Fairview, TN 37062
(615) 799-1002

Pediatric Crohn's & Colitis
  Association Inc.
P.O. Box 188
Newton, MA 02168
(781) 290-0902
www.cfids.org

Suggested Reading List

Bacteria/Antibiotics/Parasites

Chaitow, Leon. *Candida Albicans: Could Yeast Be Your Problem?* Healing Arts Publishing, 1998.

Crook, William. *The Yeast Connection.* Jackson, Tenn.: Professional Books, 1985.

———. *The Yeast Connection and the Woman.* Jackson, Tenn.: Professional Books, 1995.

Garrett, Laurie. *The Coming Plague.* New York: Farrar, Straus & Giroux, 1994.

Gittleman, Ann Louise. *Guess What Came to Dinner? Parasites & Your Health.* Garden City Park, N.Y.: Avery Publishing, 1993.

Schmidt, Michael, Keith Sehnert, and Lendon Smith. *Beyond Antibiotics.* Berkeley, Calif.: North Atlantic Books, 1993.

Trenev, Natasha. *Probiotics: Nature's Internal Healers.* Garden City Park, N.Y.: Avery Publishing, 1999.

Trenev, Natasha, and Leon Chaitow. *Probiotics.* London: Thorsens, 1990.

Detoxification

Baker, Sidney. *Detoxification and Healing.* Los Angeles: Keats Publishing, 1997.

Bennett, Peter, and Stephen Barrie. *7-Day Detox Miracle.* Prima Health Publishing, 1999.

Bland, Jeffrey. *20-Day Detoxification Diet.* Los Angeles: Keats Publishing, 1998.

Food & Environmental Allergies

Coca, Arthur. *The Pulse Test.* New York: Arco Publishing Company, 1978.

Dadd, Debra Lynn. *The Nontoxic Home*. Los Angeles: Jeremy Tarcher, 1986.

Goldberg, Burton. *Chronic Fatigue Fibromyalgia & Environmental Illness*. Tiberon, Calif.: Future Medicine Publishing, 1998.

Golos, Natalie, and Frances Golos-Golbitz. *If This is Tuesday, It Must Be Chicken*. Los Angeles: Keats Publishing, 1983.

Randolph, Theron, and Ralph Moss. *An Alternative Approach to Allergies*. New York: Harper & Row, 1989.

Rockwell, Sally. *Dr. Sally's Allergy Recipes*. 1997.

———. *The Rotation Game*. 1989.

Rogers, Sherry. *The EI Syndrome Revisited*. SK Publishing, 1996.

Food & Nutrition

Ballantine, Rudolph. *Diet and Nutrition*. Honesdale, Penn.: Himalayan Institute, 1978.

Colbin, Annmarie. *Food & Healing*. New York: Ballantine Books, 1986.

Erasmus, Udo. *Fats that Heal, Fats that Kill*. Burnaby, British Colombia: Alive Books, 1993.

Gottschall, Elaine. *Breaking the Vicious Cycle: Intestinal Health Through Diet*. Formerly published as *Food and the Gut Reaction*. Kirkton Press, 1994.

Price, Weston. *Diet & Physical Degeneration*. Los Angeles: Keats Publishing, 1938.

Robbins, John. *Diet for a New America*. Walpole, N.N.: Stillpoint Publishing, 1987.

———. *May All Be Fed*. William Morrow & Co, 1992.

Shabert, Judith, and Nancy Erlich. *The Ultimate Nutrient, Glutamine*. Garden City Park, N.Y.: Avery Publishing, 1994.

Holistic Self-Care

Borysenko, Joan. *Minding the Body, Mending the Mind*. New York: Bantam Books, 1987.

Gardner, Joy. *The New Healing Yourself*. Freedom, Calif.: The Crossing Press, 1989.

Murray, Michael, and Joseph Pizzorno, eds. *The Encyclopedia of Natural Medicine*. Rocklin, Calif.: Prima Publishing, 1991.

Pizzorno, Joseph. *Total Wellness*. Rocklin, Calif.: Prima Publishing, 1998.

REFERENCES

Chapter 1. Who Can Benefit from This Book?

Burkitt, D. *Eat Right to Stay Healthy and Enjoy Life More.* New York: Arco Publishing, 1979.

Murray, M., and J. Pizzorno. *Encyclopedia of Natural Medicine*, 2nd ed. Rocklin, Calif.: Prima Publishing, 1997.

U.S. Department of Health and Human Services, Public Health Service, National Institutes of Health. *Digestive Diseases in the United States: Epidemiology and Impact.* Publication 94-1447. Washington, D.C.: 1994.

———. "Helicobacter pylori in Peptic Ulcer Disease." National Institutes of Health Consensus Statement 12, no. 4. Washington, D.C.: 1994.

Chapter 2. The American Way of Life Is Hazardous to Your Health

Boris, J., and F.S. Mandel. "Foods And Additives Are Common Causes of The Attention Deficit Hyperactive Disorder in Children." *Annals of Allergy* 72, no. 5 (May 1994): 462–68.

Carter, C.M., et al. "Effects of a New Food Diet in Attention Deficit Disorder." *Archives of Disorders in Children* 69, no. 5 (November 1993): 564–68.

"Exclusive Interview with Gary Gibbs, D.O., Authority on Food Radiation." *Health & Healing* 2, no. 5 (May 1995): 5–6.

Hemilia, H. "Vitamin C and Plasma Cholesterol." *Critical Reviews in Food Science and Nutrition* 32, no. 1 (1992): 35–37.

Jacques, P. "Effect of Vitamin C on High-Density Lipoprotein Cholesterol and Blood Pressure." *Journal of the American College of Nutrition* 11, no. 2 (1992): 139–44.

Jaffe, R., and P. Donovan. *Guided Health, A Constant Professional*

Reference. Reston, Va.: Health Studies Collegium Publishing, 1989.

Kennedy, S.H. "Vitamin Supplements Win Newfound Respect: Skeptics Are Changing Their Minds Over the Value of These Compounds." *Modern Medicine* 60 (July 1992): 15–18.

Neher, J.O., and J.M. Borkan. "A Clinical Approach to Alternative Medicine." *Archives of Family Medicine* 3 (October 1994): 859–61.

Pauling, L. "Prevention and Treatment of Heart Disease: New Research Focus at the Linus Pauling Institute." *Linus Pauling Institute of Science & Medicine Newsletter* (March 1992): 1.

U.S. Department of Agriculture Economic Research Service. *Food Consumption: Prices and Expenditures, 1980–1982.* Washington, D.C.: 1995.

Wolfe, S.M. *Health Letter of The Public Citizen Health Research Group* 5, no. 7 (1989): 1–5.

Chapter 3. A Voyage Through the Digestive System

Bland, J. *20-Day Rejuvenation Diet.* Los Angeles: Keats Publishing, 1997.

Robbins, J. *May All Be Fed.* New York: William Morrow & Co., 1992.

Thompson, T. *Approach to Gastrointestinal Immune Dysfunction and Related Health Problems.* Lecture given at the Fourth International Functional Medicine Meeting, Aspen, Colo. 1997.

Tips, Jack. *The Liver Triad.* Austin, Tex.: Apple A Day Publishing, 1989.

Chapter 4. The Bugs in Your Body! Intestinal Flora

Bland, J., et al. *Clinical Nutrition: A Functional Approach.* Gig Harbor, Wash.: Functional Medicine Institute, 1999.

Carper, Jean. *Food Pharmacy.* New York: Bantam Books, 1988.

Chaitow, L., and N. Trenev. *Probiotics.* London: Thorsons, 1990.

Czerucka, D., I. Roux, and P. Rampal. "Saccharomyces Boulardii Inhibits Secretagogue-Mediated Adenosine 3',5'-Cyclic Monophosphate Induction in Intestinal Cells." *Gastroenterology* 106, no. 1 (January 1994): 65–72.

Galland, Leo. *Dysbiosis & Disease.* Audiotape from Great Smokies Diagnostic Lab and HealthComm International, 1993.

———. "Solving the Digestive Puzzle." Conference manual, Great Smokies Diagnostic Lab and HealthComm International, San Francisco. May 1995.

Gibson, G.R., and M.B. Roberfroid. "Dietary Modulation of the Human Colonic Microbiota: Intoducing the Concept of Probiotics." *Journal of Nutrition* 125, no. 6 (June 1995): 1401–12.

Gibson, G.R., and X. Wang. "Regulatory Effects of Bifidobacteria on the Growth of Other Colonic Bacteria." *Journal of Applied Bacteriology* 77 (1994): 412–20.

Kimmey, M.B., et al. "Prevention of Further Recurrences of Clostridium Difficile Colitis with Saccharomyces Boulardii." *Digestive Diseases & Sciences* 35, no. 7 (July 1990): 897–901.

Macfarlane, G., and J.H. Cummings. "Probiotics and Prebiotics: Can Regulating the Activities of Intestinal Bacteria Benefit Health?" *British Medical Journal* 318 (10 April 1999): 999–1003.

Mitsuuoka, T. "Intestinal Flora & Aging." *Nutrition Reviews* 50, no. 12 (December 1992): 438–46.

Plein, K., and J. Hotz. "Therapeutic Effects of Saccharomyces Boulardii on Mild Residual Symptoms in a Stable Phase of Crohn's Disease with Special Respect to Chronic Diarrhea—A Pilot Study." *Gastroenterology* 31, no. 2 (February 1993): 129–34.

Resnick, Corey, N.D. Telephone conversation. Winter 1994.

Roberfoid, M.B. "Prebiotics and Synbiotics: Concepts and Nutritional Properties." *British Jounral of Nutrition* 80, no. 4 (October 1998): S197–S202.

Sehnert, K. "The Garden Within." *Health World Magazine* (1989): 9.

Sellars, R.L. "Acidophilus Product." *Therapeutic Properties of Fermented Milks*, Elsevier Applied Science, 1991.

Sghir, A., J.M. Chow, and R.I. Mackie. "Continuous Culture Selection of Bifidobacteria and Lactobacilli from Human Fecal Samples Using Fructooligosachharide as a Selective Substrate." *Journal of Applied Microbiology* 84, no. 4 (October 1994): 769–77.

Trenev, Natasha. Telephone conversation. Winter 1994.

Chapter 5. Dysbiosis: A Good Neighborhood Gone Bad

Begley, S. "The end of antibiotics." *Newsweek* (28 March 1994): 46–51.

Bjarnason, I., et al. "Side Effects of Non-Steroidal Anti-Inflammatory Drugs on the Small and Large Intestine in Humans." *Gastroenterology* 104, no. 6 (June 1993): 1832–47.

Bland, J. *Preventive Medicine Update.* May 1994. Audiotape.

Crook, William. *The Yeast Connection and the Woman.* Jackson, Tenn.: Professional Books, 1995.

Garrett, Lori. *The Coming Plague.* New York: Farrar, Straus, Giroux, 1994.

Hoffer, Abraham. Preface to *The Yeast Syndrome*, by John Trowbridge and Morton Walker. New York: Bantam Books, 1986.

Koelz, H. R. "Ulcer Prevention During Anti-Rheumatism Therapy and in Intensive Medicine." *Schweizerische Rundschau fur Medizin Praxis* 3, nos. 25–26 (21 June 1994): 768–71.

Lee, Martin, of the Great Smokies Laboratories. Personal correspondence. Spring 1995.

Loosli, A.R. "Reversing Sports-Related Iron & Zinc Deficiencies." *The Physician & Sportsmedicine* 21, no. 6 (June 1993): 70–78.

McBride, J. "Nutrient Deficiency Unleashes Jekyll-Hyde Virus." *Agricultural Research* 42, no. 8 (August 1994): 14–16.

Mfitsuoka, T. "Intestinal Flora & Aging." *Nutrition Reviews* 50, no. 12 (December 1992): 438–46.

The Nutrition Screening Initiative, American Dietetic Association, the National Council on Aging, and the American Academy of Family Physicians. "Providers Estimate One in Four Seniors Malnourished." *Nutrition Week* (30 April 1993): 3.

Tippett, K., and J.D. Goldman. "Diets More Healthful, But Still Fall Short of Dietary Guidelines." *Food Review, U.S. Department of Agriculture* 17, no. 1 (January–April 1994): 8–14.

Chapter 6. Leaky Gut Syndrome: The Systemic Consequences of Faulty Digestion

D'Adamo, Peter. *Eat Right for Your Type.* New York: Putnam Publishing Group, 1997.

Elisa/Act Handbook. Reston, Va.: Serammune Laboratories, 1994.

Galland, Leo. "Solving the Digestive Puzzle." Conference manual, Great Smokies Diagnostic Lab and HealthComm International, San Francisco, May 1995.

Guide to Health. Fort Lauderdale, Fla.: Immuno Laboratories, Inc., 1994.

"Gut Hyperpermeability." *Serammune Physicians Lab* 2, no. 1 (January 1992).

Jaffe, Russ. Educational brochure. Reston, Va.: Serammune Physicians Lab, 1994.

"The Leaky Gut." Great Smokies Digest (summer 1990): 4.

Lipski, Elizabeth. *Leaky Gut Syndrome.* Los Angeles: Keats Publishing, 1998.

Marks, David, and Laura Marks. "Food Allergy: Manifestations, Evaluation and Management." *Food Allergy, Postgraduate Medicine* 93, no. 2 (1 February 1993): 191–201.

Swanson, Mark. "Comprehensive Digestive Stool Analysis and Intestinal Permeability." Great Smokies Diagnostic Lab, 1993. Audiotape.

Trenev, Natasha. Lecture to California State Meeting IAACN. April 1994.

Chapter 7. Functional Medicine/Functional Testing

Application Guide, Bacterial Overgrowth of the Small Intestine. Asheville, N.C.: Great Smokies Laboratory, 1994.

Application Guide, Functional Liver Testing. Asheville, N.C.: Great Smokies Diagnostic Laboratory, 1994.

Bland, Jeffrey. "New Clinical Breakthroughs in the Management of Chronic Fatigue Syndrome, Intestinal Dysbiosis, Immune Dysregulation and Cellular Toxicity." Gig Harbor, Wash.: Health Comm, 1992.

Gittleman, Ann Louise. *Guess What Came to Dinner?* Garden City Park, N.Y.: Avery Publishing, 1993.

Godiwala, T. et al. New York: American College of Gastroenterology, 1988.

Kirsch, Michael. "Bacterial Overgrowth." *The American Journal of Gastroenterology* 85, no. 3 (1990): 231–37.

Lab manual. Asheville, N.C.: Great Smokies Diagnostic Laboratory, 1995.

Rider, M.S., et al. "Effect of Immune System Imagery on Secretory IgA." *Biofeedback Self Regulation* 15, no. 4 (December 1990): 317–33.

Chapter 8. Moving Toward a Wellness Lifestyle

Eisenberg, D.M., R.B. Davis, S.L. Ettner, S. Appel, S. Wilkey, M. Van Rompay, and R.C. Kessler. "Trends in Alternative Medicine Use in the United States, 1990–1997: Results of a Follow-Up National Survey." *Journal of the American Medical Association* 280, no. 18 (11 November 1998): 1569–75.

Sokol Green, Nancy. *Poisoning Our Children: Surviving in a Toxic World.* Chicago: Noble Press Inc., 1991.

Tubesing, Nancy Loving, and Donald Tubesing. *Structured Exercises in Wellness,* vol. 3. Duluth, Minn.: Whole Person Press, 1986.

Wetzel, M.S., D.M. Eisenberg, and T.J. Kaptchuk. "Courses Involving Complementary and Alternative Medicine at U.S. Medical Schools." *Journal of the American Medical Association* 280, no. 9 (2 September 1998): 784–87.

Chapter 9. First Things First/Detoxification

Jaffe, Russell. Women and Children's Health Update, syllabus. 1994-95.

National Research Council. *Environmental Neurotoxicity.* Washington, D.C.: National Academy Press, 1992.

Sokol Green, Nancy. *Poisoning Our Children: Surviving in a Toxic World.* Chicago: Noble Press Inc., 1991.

Stone, I. *The Healing Factor.* New York: Grosset & Dunlap, 1982.

Ultrabalance Workbook. Gig Harbor, Wash.: Health Comm, Inc., 1988.

Chapter 10. Diet Means "Way of Life"

Carper, J. *The Food Pharmacy.* New York: Bantam Books, 1989.

Erasmus, Udo. *Fats that Heal, Fats that Kill.* Burnaby, British Columbia: Alive Books, 1993.

Jaffe, R., and P. Donovan. *Guided Health, A Constant Professional Reference.* Reston, Va.: Health Studies Collegium Publishing, 1989.

Moore Lappe, Francis. *Diet for a Small Planet.* New York: Ballantine, 1991.

———. *Food First.* Boston: Houghton Mifflin.

Robbins, John. *Diet for a New America*. Walpole, N.H.: Stillpoint.
———. *May All Be Fed*. New York: William Morrow, 1992.
Schauss, Alex. "Dietary Fish Oil Consumption & Fish Oil Supplementation." In *A Textbook for Natural Medicine*, edited by Joseph E. Pizzorno and Michael T. Murray. St. Louis, Mo.: Churchill Livingstone, 1991.
Schnohr, P., et al.. "Egg Consumption and High-Density-Lippoprotein Cholesterol." *Journal of Internal Medicine* 235 (1994): 249–51.
Shinitsky, M. "Egg Consumption, Serum Cholesterol & Membrane Fluidity." *Biomembranes and Nutrition* 195 (1989): 391–400.
Smith, Bob. "Organic Foods vs. Supermarket Foods, Element Levels." *Doctor's Data*, 1993.
Weir, D., and M. Schapiro. *Circle of Poison*. San Francisco: Institute for Food & Development Policy, 1981.

Chapter 12. Natural Therapies for Common Digestive Problems

Aldoori, W.H., et al. "A Prospective Study of Diet and the Risk of Symptomatic Diverticular Disease in Men." *American Journal of Clinical Nutrition* 60 (1994): 757–64.
Aslan, A., and G. Triadafilopoulos. "Fish Oil Fatty Acid Supplementation and Active Ulcerative Colitis: A Double-Blind, Placebo-Controlled Crossover Study." *The American Journal of Gastroenterology* 87, no. 4 (April 1992): 432–33.
Babbs, C.F. "Oxygen Radicals in Ulcerative Colitis." *Free Radical Biological Medicine* 13, no. 2 (1992): 169–81.
Baran, E., and C. Dupont. "Modification of Intestinal Permeability During Food Provocation Procedures in Pediatric Irritable Bowel Syndrome." *Journal of Pediatric Gastroenterology & Nutrition* 11 (1990): 72–77.
Barnard, N. "Fiber, Health, and Research; The Work of Dennis Burkitt, M.D." *PCRM Update* (May/June, 1990): 1-9.
Batmanghelidj, F. *Your Body's Many Cries for Water*. Falls Church, Va.: Global Health Solutions, 1995.
Bell, I.R., et al. "Symptom & Personality Profiles of Young Adults from a College Student Population with Self-Reported Illness from Foods and Chemicals." *Journal of the American College of Nutrition* 12, no. 6 (1993): 693–702.

Biasco, Guido, et al. "Folic Acid Supplementation and Cell Kinetics of Rectal Mucosa in Patients with Ulcerative Colitis." *Cancer Epidemiology, Biomarkers and Prevention* 6 (June 1997): 469–71.

Bjarnason, I. "Intestinal Permeability." *Gut* (1994, Supplement 1): S18–S22.

Bland, J. *Glandular-Based Food Supplements: Helping to Separate Fact from Fiction.* Bellevue, Wash.: Bellevue-Redmond Medical Lab, Inc.

Bleijenberg, G., and H.C. Kuijpers. "Biofeedback Treatment of Constipation: A Comparison of Two Methods." *American Journal of Gastroenterology* 89, no. 7 (July 1994): 1021–26.

Bolin, T.D., A.E. Davis, and V.M. Duncombe. "A Prospective Study of Peristent Diarrhea." *Australia/New Zealand Journal of Medicine* 12, no. 1 (February 1982): 22–26.

Born, P., et al. "Fructose Malabsorption and Irritable Bowel Syndrome." *Gastroenterology* 101, no. 5 (1991): 1454.

Borok, G. "Irritable Bowel Syndrome and Diet." *Gastroenterology Forum* (April 1994): 29.

Boyko, E.J., et al. "Increased Risk of Inflammatory Bowel Disease Associated with Oral Contraceptive Use." *American Journal of Epidemiology* 140, no. 3 (1994): 268–78.

Breneman, J. "Allergy Elimination Diet as the Most Effective Gallbladder Diet." *Annals of Allergy* 26, no. 2 (February 1968): 83–87.

Campan, P. "Pilot Study on n-3 Polyunsaturated Fatty Acids in the Treatment of Human Experimental Gingivitis." *Journal of Clinical Periodontology* 24 (1997): 907–13.

Capper, W., et al. "Gallstones, Gastric Secretion, and Flatulent Dyspepsia." *Lancet* 1 (25 February 1967): 413–15.

Capron, J.P., et al. "Meal Frequency and Duration of Overnight Fast: A Role in Gallstone Formation?" *British Medical Journal* 283 (1981): 1435.

Catassi, C., et al. "Celiac diseases in the year 2000: Exploring the Iceburg." *Lancet* 343 (1994): 200–03.

Challacombe, S.J. "Hematological Abnormalities in Oral Lichen Planus, Candidiasis, Leukoplakia and Non-Specific Stomatitis." *International Journal of Oral Maxillofacial Surgery* 15, no. 1 (February 1986): 72–80.

Charnow, Jody A. "Vitamin A, Fiber May Cut Risk of Duodenal Ulcer." *Medical Tribune* (6 February 1997): 15.

Chen, L. "Bile Acid Pool in the Formation of Pigment Stones: An

Experimental Study." *Chung Hua Wai Ko Tsa Chih* 30, no. 8 (August 1992): 496–98.

Constipation Fact Sheet. Publication no. 92-2754. Washington, D.C.: National Institutes of Health, National Institute of Diabetes and Digestive & Kidney Diseases, 1992.

"Crohn's Disease Linked to Measles." *Medical Tribune* (13 May 1993): 10.

Dieleman, L.A., and W.D. Heizer. "Nutritional Issues in Inflammatory Bowel Disease." *Gastroenteroloy Clinics of North America* 27, no. 2 (June 1998) 435–51.

Di Prisco, M.C. "Possible Relationship Between Allergic Disease and Infection by Giardia Lamblia." *Annals of Allergy* 70 (March 1993): 210–12.

Drinka, Paul, et al. "Nutritional Correlates of Atrophic Glossitis: Possible Role of Vitamin E and Papillary Atrophy." *Journal of the American College of Nutrition* 12, no. 1 (1993): 14–20.

Drinka, P.J., E. Langer, L. Scott, and F. Morrow. "Laboratory Measurements of Nutritional Status as Correlates of Atrophic Glossitis." *Journal of General Internal Medicine* 6, no. 2 (March/April 1991): 137–40.

"Fasting May Cause Stones." *Medical Tribune* (25 July, 1991): 13.

Fernandez-Banares, F., et al. "Enteral Nutrition as a Primary Therapy in Crohn's Disease." *Gut* (1994): S55-S59.

———. "Role of Fructose-Sorbitol Malabsorption and Irritable Bowel Syndrome." *Gastroenterology* 101, no. 5 (November 1991): 1453–54.

Francis, C.W., et al. "Bran and Irritable Bowel Syndrome: Time for Reappraisal." *Lancet* 334 (2 July 1994): 339–40.

Gaby, A., and J. Wright. "Ulcerative Colitis." *Nutrition & Healing* 2, no. 1 (January 1995).

Galland, Leo, M.D. Telephone conversation. June 1995.

———. Telephone conversation. Winter 1995.

Gottschall, E. *Food and the Gut Reaction.* Kirkton, Ontario: Kirkton Press, 1986.

Gross, V., et al. "Free Radicals and Inflammatory Bowel Diseases, Pathophysiology and Therapeutic Implications." *Hepato-Gastroenterology* 41 (1994): 320–27.

Gryboski, J.D. "Ulcerative Colitis in Children 10 Years Old or Younger." *Journal of Pediatric Gastroenterology and Nutrition* 17, no. 1 (July 1993): 24–31.

Hanauer, S.B., M.A. Peppercorn, and D.H. Present. "Current Concepts, New Therapies in IBD." *Patient Care* (August 1992).

Helicobacter pylori in Peptic Ulcer Disease. National Institutes of Health Consensus Statement 12, no. 1 (February 1994).

Hoffman, R. *7 Weeks to a Settled Stomach.* New York: Pocket Books, 1990.

Hotz, J., and K. Plein. "Effectiveness of Plantago Seed Husks in Comparison with Wheat Bran on Stool Frequency and Manifestations of Irritable Colon Syndrome with Constipation." *Medizinische Klinik* 89, no. 12 (15 December 1994): 645–51.

Husebye, E., V. Skar, T. Hoverstad, and K. Melby. "Fasting Hypochlorhydria with Gram Positive Gastric Flora Is Highly Prevalent in Healthy Old People." *Gut* 33 (October 1992): 1331–37.

Jacobs, E.J., and F. White. "Constipation, Laxative Use, and Colon Cancer among Middle-Aged Adults." *Epidemiology* 9, no. 4 (1998): 385–91.

Jancin, Bruce. "Gastroesophageal Disease Linked to Long Antacid Use." *Family Practice News* 26, no. 13 (1 July 1996): 1–2.

Jones, Evan L. "Does DMSO Dissolve Hemorrhoids?" *Cortlandt Forum* 103 (May 1994).

Kimikazu, I., J. Kiyonana, and M. Ishikawa. *Studies on Gamma-Oryzanol II: The Anti-Ulcerogenic Action.* Tokushima: Research Institute, Otsuka Pharmaceutical Co., Ltd., 1976.

Kratzer, W., et al. "Gallstone Prevalence in Relation to Smoking, Alcohol, Coffee Consumption, and Nutrition." *Scandinavian Journal of Gastroenterology* 32 (1997): 953–58.

Lazzari, R., et al. "Sideropenic Anemia and Celiac Disease." *Pediatric Medicine Chir* 16, no. 6 (November/December 1994): 549–50.

Leitzmann, Michael F., et al. "The Relation of Physical Activity to Risk for Symptomatic Gallstone Disease in Men." *Annals of Internal Medicine* 128, no. 6 (15 March 1998): 417–25.

Malstrom, M., O.P. Salo, and F. Fyhrquist. "Immunogenetic Markers and Immune Response in Patients with Recurrent Oral Ulceration." *International Journal of Oral Surgery* 12, no. 1 (February 1983): 23–30.

Markell, E.K., and M.P. Udkow. "Blastocystis Hominis: Pathogen or Fellow Traveler?" *American Journal of Tropical Medicine and Hygeine* 35, no. 5 (September 1986): 1023–26.

Maruyama, K., and K. Kashiwzaki. "Clinical Trial of Gamma-oryzanol on Gastrointestinal Symptoms at 375 Hospitals." Japan: Department of Internal Medicine, Keio University, 1977.

McRorie, J. W., et al. "Psyllium is Superior to Docusate Sodium for Treatment of Chronic Constipation." *Alimentary Pharmacological Therapy* 12 (1998): 491–97.

Mendeloff, A.I., and J.E. Everhart. "Diverticular Disease of the Colon." In *Digestive Diseases in the United States: Epidemiology and Impact.* Washington, D.C.: U.S. Dept. of Health & Human Services, National Institutes of Health, 1994.

Merck Manual, 16th ed. Rahway, N.J.: Merck Research Laboratories, 1992.

Minakuchi, C., et al. "Effectiveness of Gamma-Oryzanol on Various Gastrointestinal Complaints." *Shinyaku to Rinsho* 25, no. 10 (1976): 29.

Moerman, C. "Dietary Risk Factors for Clinical Diagnosed Gallstones in Middle-Aged Men: A 25 Year Follow-up Study." *Annals of Epidemiology* (1994): 248–54.

———. "Dietary Sugar Intake in the Etiology of Biliary Tract Cancer." *International Journal of Epidemiology* 22, no. 2 (1993): 207–13.

Murray, M., and J. Pizzorno. *Encyclopedia of Natural Medicine.* Rocklin, Calif.: Prima Publishing, 1991.

Nellist, C.C. "Elemental Diet Therapy a Good Option for Crohn's." *Family Practice News* (1 March 1994): 7.

Nolan, A., W.B. McIntosh, B.F. Allam, and P.J. Lamey. "Recurrent Apthous Ulceration: Vitamin B_1, B_2, and B_6 Status and Response to Replacement Therapy." *Journal of Oral Pathology and Medicine* 20, no. 8 (September 1991): 389–91.

Ofarrelly, C., et al. "Gliadin Antibodies Identify Gluten-Sensitive Oral Ulceration in the Absence of Villous Atrophy." *Journal of Oral Pathology and Medicine* 20, no. 10 (November 1991): 476–78.

Ozick, L.A., C. Salazar, and S.S. Donelson. "Pathogenesis, Diagnosis and Treatment of Diverticular Disease of the Colon." *Gastroenterologist* 2, no. 4 (December 1994): 299–310.

Palopoli, J., and J. Waxman. "Recurrent Apthous Stomatitis and Vitamin B_{12} Deficiency." *Southern Medical Journal* 83, no. 4 (April 1990): 475–77.

Phillipson, J.D., and C.W. Wright. "Medicinal Plants in Tropical Medicine: Medicinal Plants Against Protozoal Diseases." *Trans-*

actions of the Royal Society of Tropical Medicine and Hygiene 85 (1991): 18–21.

Porter, S.R., C. Scully, and S. Flint. "Hematologic Status in Recurrent Apthous Stomatitis Compared with Other Oral Disease." *Medical Oral Pathology* 66, no. 1 (July 1988): 41–44.

Prudden, John F., and Leslie L. Balassa. "The Biological Activity of Bovine Cartilage Preparations." *Seminars in Arthritis and Rheumatism* 3, no. 4 (Summer 1974): 287–320.

Resnick, C. "The Effects of Gamma-Oryzanol on Ulcers, Gastritis, Hyperlipidemias, and Menopausal Disorders." Research review. Tyler Encapsulations, 1993.

Robinson, R.J., et al. "Effect of a Low-Impact Exercise Program on Bone Mineral Density in Crohn's Disease: A Randomized Controlled Trial." *Gastroenterology* 115 (1998): 36–41.

Roediger, W.E.W. "Decreased Sulfur Amino Acid Intake in Ulcerative Colitis." *Lancet* 351 (23 May 1998): 1555.

Rogers, S. "Chemical Sensitivity: Breaking the Paralyzing Paradigm: How Knowledge of Chemical Sensitivity Enhances the Treatment of Chronic Disease." *Internal Medicine World Report* 7, no. 8 (1992): 13–41.

Rumessen, J.J. "Functional Bowel Disease: The Role of Fructose and Sorbitol." *Gastroenterology* 101 (1991): 1452–60.

Russell, R. *In Clinical Pearls, 1991*, by Kirkham R. Hamilton. IT Services, 1992.

Scheppach, W. "Effects of Short Chain Fatty Acids on Gut Morphology and Function." *Gut* (1994, Supplement 1): S335–S38.

Scheppach, W., et al. "Effect of Butyrate Enemas on the Colonic Mucosa in Distal Ulcerative Colitis." *Gastroenterology* 103 (1992): 51–56.

Seigel, J. "Inflammatory Bowel Disease: Another Possible Effect of the Allergic Diathesis." *Annals of Allergy* 47, no. 2 (August 1981): 92–94.

Seigel, M.A., and B.A. Balciunas. "Medication Can Induce Severe Ulcers." *Journal of the American Dental Association* 122, no. 10 (September 1991): 75–77.

Shabert, J. *The Ultimate Nutrient Glutamine*. Garden City Park, N.Y.: Avery, 1994.

Shibasaki, T. "The Relationship of Nutrition and Dietary Habits to Gingivitis, Dental Calculus Deposit, and Dental Plaque Adhesion in High School Students." *Shoni Shikagaku Zasshi* 27, no. 2 (1989): 415–26.

Siblerud, R.L. "Relationship Between Mercury from Dental Amalgam and Oral Cavity Health." *Annals of Dentistry* (Winter 1990).

Simon, J.A. "Ascorbic Acid and Cholesterol Gallstones." *Medical Hypothesis* 40, no. 2 (February 1993): 81–84.

Simon, J.A., and E.S. Hudes. "Serum Ascorbic Acid and Other Correlates of Gallbladder Disease among U.S. Adults." *American Journal of Public Health* 88, no. 8 (August 1998): 1208–12.

Singh, G. "Recent Considerations in Nonsteriodal Anti-inflammatory Drug Gastropathy." *American Journal of Medicine* 105, no. 1B (27 July 1998): 31S–38S.

Sky, P.R. "Of Parasites and Pollens." *Discover* (September 1993): 56–62.

Thompson, N.P., et al. "Is Measles Vaccination a Risk Factor for Inflammatory Bowel Disease?" *Lancet* 345 (1995): 1071–74.

Tomas-Ridocci, M., et al. "The Efficacy of Plantago Ovata as a Regulator of Intestinal Transit." *Revista Espanola de Enfermedades Digestivas* 82, no. 1 (July 1992): 17–22.

Tuzhilin, S.A., et al. "The Treatment of Patients with Gallstones by Lechitnin." *American Journal of Gastroenterology* 65 (1976): 231.

Vernia, P., et al. "Lactose Intolerance and Irritable Bowel Syndrome: Relative Weight in Inducing Abdominal Symptoms in High Prevalence Area." *Gastroenterology* 102, no. 4 (Part II, April 1992): A530.

Walker, D.M., et al. "Effect of Gluten-Free Diet on Recurrent Apthous Ulceration." *British Journal of Dermatology* 103, no. 1 (July 1980): 111.

Wang, S.W., H.K. Li, J.S. He, and T.A. Yin. "The Trace Element Zinc and Apthosis. The Determination of Plasma Zinc and the Treatment of Apthosis with Zinc." *Revue de Stomatologie et de Chirurgie Maxillo–Faciale* 87, no. 5 (1986): 339–43.

Whitehead, W.E. "Biofeedback Treatment of Gastrointestinal Disorders." *Biofeedback and Self-Regulation* 17, no. 1 (1992): 59–76.

Wilhelmsen, I., and A. Berstad. "Quality of Life and Relapse of Duodenal Ulcer Before and After Eradication of Helicobacter pylori." *Scandinavian Journal of Gastroenterology* 29, no. 10 (October 1994): 874–79.

Wilmore, D. Personal conversation. Spring 1995.

Wilson, J.M. "Hand Washing Reduces Diarrhea Episodes: A Study in Lombok Indonesia." *Transactions of the Royal Society of Tropical Medicine and Hygiene* 85 (1991): 819–21.

Wray, D. "Gluten-Sensitive Recurrent Apthous Stomatitis." *Digestive Disease Sciences* 26, no. 8 (August 1981): 737–40.

Wright, J. *Dr. Wright's Guide to Healing with Nutrition.* Emaus, Penn.: Rodale Books, 1984.

Yoshinari, T. "Usefulness of Hi-Z Fine Granule (Gamma-Oryzanol) for the Treatment of Autonomic Instability in Gastrointestinal System." *Shinyaku to Rinsho* 225, no. 3 (1976): 56.

Chapter 13. Natural Therapies for the Diverse Consequences of Faulty Digestion

Abyad, A., and J.T. Boyer. "Arthritis and Aging." *Current Opinion on Rheumatolology* 4, no. 2 (April 1992): 153–59.

Alteras, I. "The Incidence of Skin Manifestations by Dermatophytes in Patients with Psoriasis." *Mycopathologia* 95, no. 1 (July 1986): 37–39.

Anthony, M. "Platelet Superoxide Dismutase in Migraine and Tension Type Headaches." *Cephalalgia* 14 (1994): 1818–13.

Appleboom, Thierry, and Patrick Durez. "Effect of Milk Product Deprivation on Spondyloarthropathy." *Annals of Rheumatic Diseases* 53, no. 11 (1994): 481–82.

Barrie, S. *Dysbiosis & Immune Disease, a Retrospective Study.* Audiotape from lecture given at the Great Smokies, Asheville, N.C. 1993.

Bates, Betsy. "Low-Fat, High-Carbohydrate Diet Averts Migraines." *Family Practice News* (1 August 1996): 16.

Berbis, P., et al. "Essential Fatty Acids and the Skin." *Allergy Immunology* 22, no. 6 (June 1990): 225–31.

Black, M. "Nicotinic Acid and Headache." *Cortlandt Forum* (August 1990): 26–30.

Bland, J. Advancement in Clinical Nutrition HealthComm 1993–4. Taken from Komaroff, A.L. "Clinical Presentations of Chronic Fatigue Syndrome." In *Chronic Fatigue Syndrome,* edited by Bock and Whelan. New York: Wiley and Sons Ltd.

————. *Applying New Essentials in Nutritional Medicine.* Gig Harbor, Wash.: HealthComm, 1995.

Boris, M., and F.S. Mandel. "Foods and Additives Are Common Causes of the Attention Deficit Hyperactive Disorder in Children." *Annals of Allergy* 72, no. 5 (May 1994): 462–68.

Bornstein, R.A., G.B. Baker, A. Carroll, G. King, J.T. Wong., and A.B. Douglass. "Plasma Amino Acids in Attention Deficit Disorder." *Psychiatry Research* 33, no. 3 (September 1990): 301–6.

Bou-Holaigah, Issam, et al. "The Relationship Between Neurally Mediated Hypotension and the Chronic Fatigue Syndrome." *Journal of the American Medical Association* 74, no. 12 (27 September 1995): 961–67.

Briggs, N.C., and P.H. Levine. "A Comparative Review of Systemic and Neurological Symptomatology of 12 Outbreaks Collectively Described as Chronic Fatigue Syndrome, Epidemic Neuromyasthenia, and Myalgic Encephalomyelitis." *Clinical Infectious Disease* 18 (Supplement, January 1994): S32–S42.

Brzeski, M., et al. "Evening Primrose Oil in Patients with Rheumatoid Arthritis and Side-Effect of Non-Steroidal Anti-Inflammatory Drugs." *British Journal of Rheumatology* 30 (1991): 370–72.

Burks, Wesley A., et al. "Atopic Dermatitis and Food Hypersensitivity Reactions." *Journal of Pediatrics* 132 (1998): 132–36.

Corrocher, R., et al. "Effect of Fish Oil Supplementation on Erythrocyte Lipid Pattern, Malondialdehyde Production and Glutathione-Peroxidase Activity in Psoriasis." *Clin Chim Acta* 179, no. 2 (15 February 1989): 121–31.

Czirjak, L., et al. "Localized Scleroderma after Exposure to Organic Solvents." *Dermatology* 189, no. 4 (1994): 399–401.

Darlington, I.G. "Dietary Therapy for Arthritis." *Nutrition and Rheumatic Diseases* 17, no. 2 (May 1991): 273–85.

Darlington, L.G., and N.W. Ramsey. "Clinical Review of Dietary Therapy for Rheumatoid Arthritis." *British Journal of Rheumatology* 32 (1993): 507–14.

Deal, C.L., et al. "Treatment of Arthritis Pain with Topical Capsaicin: A Double-Blind Trial." *Clinical Therapy* 13, no. 3 (1991): 383–95.

Deluze, C., et al. "Electroacupuncture in Fibromyalgia: Results of a Controlled Trial." *British Medical Journal* 305 (21 November 1992): 1249–51.

Disilvestro, R.A. "Effects of Copper Supplementation on Ceruloplasmin and Copper-Zinc Superoxide Dismutase in Free-Living Rheumatoid Arthritis Patients." *Journal of American College of Nutrition* 11, no. 23 (1992): 177–80.

Dochao, A., et al. "Therapeutic Effects of Vitamin D and Vitamin A in Psoriasis: A 20 year Experiment." *Actas Dermosfiliogr* 66, nos. 3, 4 (1975): 121–30.

Dykman, K.D., C. Tone, C. Ford, and R.A. Dykman. "The Effects of Nutritional Supplements on the Symptoms of Fibromyalgia and Chronic Fatigue Syndrome." *Integrative Physiological and Behavioral Science* 33, no. 1 (January–March 1998): 61–71.

Eleson, S. "The Neurotoxic Etiology of Autistic Spectrum Disorders (56 Patients)." Personal communication found in the proceedings of the Sixth Annual Symposium on Functional Medicine, page 341, at the Institute for Functional Medicine, Gig Harbor, Wash., May 1999.

Edelson, S., and D. Candot. "Autism: Zenobiotic Influences." *Toxicology and Industrial Health* 14 (1998): 553–63.

Eisinger, J., et al. "Glycolysis Abnormalities in Fibromyalgia." *Journal of the American College of Nutrition* 13, no. 2 (1994): 144–48.

Elisa/Act Patient Handbook. Reston, Va.: Serammune Laboratories.

Ellis, C. "Hot Pepper Cure: Capsaicin Relieves Psoriatic Itch." *Modern Medicine* 61 (1993): 31.

———. *Journal of the American Academy of Dermatology* (September 1993).

Etzel, R. "Special Extract of Boswellia Serrata (H-15) in the Treatment of Rheumatoid Arthritis." *Phytomedicine* 3, no. 1 (1996): 91–94.

Fahrer, H., et al. "Diet and Fatty Acids: Can Fish Substitute for Fish Oil?" *Clinical Experiments in Rheumatology* 9, no. 4 (July/August 1991): 403–6.

Fairris, G.M., et al. "The Effect of Supplementation with Selenium and Vitamin E in Psoriasis." *Annals of Clinical Biochemistry* 26 (Part 1, January 1989): 83–88.

Faivelson, S. "Electroacupuncture Tried for Pain of Fibromyalgia." *Medical Tribune* (24 December 1992): 24.

Flynn, M. "The Effect of Folate and Cobalamine on Osteoarthritis and Hands." *Journal of the American College of Nutrition* 13, no. 4 (1994): 351–56.

"A Follow-Up on Malic Acid: CFIDS Buyer's Club." *Health Watch* 3, no. 1 (spring 1993): 1, 3.

Forsyth, Linda M., Harry G. Preuss, Ana L. MacDowell, Leondard Chiazze, Georgre D. Birkmayer, and Joseph A. Bellanti. "Therapeutic Effects of Oral NADH on the Symptoms of Patients with Chronic Fatigue Syndrome." *Annals of Allergy, Asthma, and Immunology* 82, no. 2 (February 1999).

Gabay, C., and M.F. Kahn. "Male-Type Scleroderma: The Role of Occupational Exposure." *Schweiz Med Wocheschr* 122, no. 46 (14 November 1992): 1746–52.

Galland, Leo, M.D. Telephone conversation. June 1995.

Galland, L., M. Lee, H. Bueno, and M.S. Heimowitz. "*Giardia lamblia* Infection as a Cause of Chronic Fatigue." *Journal of Nutritional Medicine* (1990): 27–31.

Gaston, L., et al. "Psychological Stress and Psoriasis: Experimental and Prospective Correlation Studies." *ACTA Dermatolgy and Venereology* (Supplement 156, 1994): 37–43.

Germain, B.F. "Silicone Breast Implants and Rheumatic Disease." *Bulletin on the Rheumatic Diseases* 41, no. 6 (October 1992): 1–4.

Godfrey, P.S., B.K. Toone, M.W. Carney, T.G. Flynn, T. Bottglieri, M. Laundy, I. Chanarin, and E.H. Reynolds. "Enhancement of Recovery from Psychiatric Illness by Methylfolate." *The Lancet* 336, no. 8712 (August 1990): 392–95.

Goldenberg, D.L. "Fibromyalgia, chronic fatigue syndrome, and myofascial pain syndrome" *Current Opinion in Rheumatology* 6, no. 2 (March 1994): 223–33.

Golos, N., and F. Golos-Golbritz. *If It's Tuesday, It Must be Chicken.* Los Angeles: Keats Publishing, 1979.

Grassetto, Maurizio, and Antonella Varotto. "Primary Fibromyalgia Is Responsive to S-Adenosyl-L-Methionine." *Current Therapeutic Research* 55, no. 7 (July 1994): 797–806.

Gray, J.B., and A.M. Martinovic. "Ecoisanoids and Essential Fatty Acid Modulation in Chronic Disease and Chronic Fatigue Syndrome." *Medical Hypothesis* 43 (July 1994): 31–42.

Grimminger, F., et al. "A Double-Blind Randomized, Placebo-Controlled Trial of N-3 Fatty Acid BasedLipid Infusion in Acute, Extended Guttate Psoriasis: Rapid Improvement of Clinical Manifestations and Changes in Neutrophil Leukotriene Profile." *Clinical Investigator* 71 (1993): 634–43.

Gumowski, P., B. Lech, I. Chaves, and J.P. Girard. "Chronic Asthma and Rhinitis Due to *Candida albicans*, Epidermophyton, and Trichophyton." *Annals of Allergy* 59, no. 1 (July 1987): 48–51.

Hagerman, R.J., and A.R. Falkenstein. "An Association Between Recurrent Otitis Media in Infancy and Later Hyperactivity." *Clinical Pediatrics* 26, no. 5 (May 1987): 253–57.

Harvima, R.J., et al. "Screening of Effects of Selenomethionine-Enriched Yeast Supplementation on Various Immunological and Chemical Parameters of Skin and Blood in Psoriatic Patients." *Acta Derm Venereol* 73, no. 2 (April 1993): 88–91.

Hendel, L., et al. "Esophageal Candidosis in Progressive Systemic Sclerosis: Occurrence, Significance, and Treatment with Fluconazole." *Scandinavian Journal of Gastroenterology* 23, no. 10 (December 1988): 1182–86.

Henricksson, A.E.K. "Small Intestinal Bacterial Overgrowth in Patients with Rheumatoid Arthritis." *Annals of Rheumatic Diseases* 52 (1993): 503–10.

Hesse J., et al. "Acupuncture versus Metoprolol in Migraine Prophylaxis: A Randomized Trial of Trigger Point Inactivation." *Journal of Internal Medicine* 235 (1994): 451–56.

Hesse, J., et al. "Acupuncture Compared with Metoprolol for Migraine Gave Mixed Results." *Annals of Internal Medicine* 235 (May 1994): 451–56.

Heuser, G., et al. "Candida albicans and Migraine Headaches: A Possible Link." *Journal of Advancement in Medicine* 5, no. 3 (fall 1992): 177–87.

Hippocrates. "On Airs, Waters, and Places." In *The Genuine Works of Hippocrates*, translated by Francis Adams. London; Leslie P. Adams, Jr., 1849.

Horrobin, D.F. "Fatty Acid Metabolism in Health and Disease: The Role of Delta-6 Desaturase." *American Journal of Clinical Nutrition* 57 (Supplenent 1993): S732–S37.

Horvath, K., G. Stefanatos, K.N. Sokolski, R. Watchel, L. Nabors, and J.T. Tildon. "Improved Social and Language Skills after Secretin Administration in Patients with Autistic Spectrum Disorders." *Journal of the Association Acad Minor Phys* 9, no. 1 (1998): 9–15.

Houston, L. "Dietary Change in Arthritis." *The Practitioner* 238 (June 1994): 443–48.

Ianniello, A., et al. "S-adenosyl-L-methionine in Sjogren's Syndrome and Fibromyalgia." *Current Therapeutic Research* 55, no. 6 (June 1994): 699–706.

Joe, B., and B.R. Lokesh. "Effect of Curcumin and Capsaicin on Arachodonic Acid Metabolism and Lysosomal Enzyme Secretion by Rat Peritoneal Macrophages." *Lipids* 32, no. 11 (1997): 1173–80.

Johnson, E.S., N.P. Kadam, D.M. Hylands, and P.J. Hylands. "Efficacy of Feverfew as Prophylactic Treatment of Migraine." *British Medical Journal* 2291, no. 6495 (31 August 1985): 569–73.

Jones, M. "Migraine Headaches and Food." *NOHA News* 14, no. 2 (spring 1989).

Kalimo, K. "Yeast Allergy in Adult Atopic Dermatitis." *Immunological and Pharmacological Aspects* 4 (1991): 164–67.

Kampf, R. *Schweizerishe Apotheker-Zeitung* 114 (1976): 337–42.

Kanofsky, J. Daniel. "Magnesium Deficiency in Chronic Schizophrenia." *International Journal of Neuroscience* 61 (1991): 87–90.

Keough, C. *Natural Relief for Arthritis*. New York: Pocket Books, 1983.

Kimikazu, I., J. Kiyonana, and M. Ishikawa. *Studies on Gamma-Oryzanol II: The Anti-Ulcerogenic Action, Research Institute*. Tokushima, Japan: Otsuka Pharmaceutical Co., Ltd.

Kjeldsen-Kraugh, Jens. "Dietary Treatment of Rheumatoid Arthritis." *Scandinavian Journal of Rheumatology* (1996). 63.

Kopelson, Jerry. "Clinician of the Month." *Functional Medicine Update* (January 1999).

Kozielec, T., and B. Starobrat-Hermerlin. "Assessment of Magnesium Levels in Children with Attention Deficit Hyperactivity Disorder (ADHD)." *Magnesium Research* 10, no. 2 (1997): 143–48.

Kun, Lee Dae. *Autism Research Review International* 4, no. 2 (1990).

Kuratsune, Hirohiko, et al. "Acylcarnitine and Chronic Fatigue Syndrome." *Carnitine Today* 10 (1997): 195–213.

Kurkcuoglu, N., and F. Alaybeyi. "Topical Capsaicin for Psoriasis." *British Journal of Dermatology* 123, no. 4 (October 1990): 549–50.

Lahesmaa, R., et al. "Molecular Mimicry: Any Role in the Pathogenesis of Spondyloarthropathies?" *Immunology Research* 12, no. 2 (1993): 193–208.

Lamm, S.H. "Silicone Breast Implants and Long-Term Health Effects: When Are Data Adequate?" *Journal of Clinical Epidemiology* 48, no. 4 (April 1995): 507–11.

Lapp, C.W., and P. Cheney. "Chronic Fatigue Syndrome: Self-Care Manual, Febuary 1991." *The CFIDS Chronicle Physicians' Forum* 1, no. 1 (March 1991): 14–17.

Lawrence, R. C., C. G. Helmick, F. C. Arnett, R. A. Deyo, D. T. Felson, E. H. Giannini, S. P. Heyse, R. Hirsch, M. C. Hochberg, G. G. Hunder, M. H. Liang, S. R. Pillemer, V. D. Steen, and F. Wolf. "Estimates of the Prevalence of Arthritis and Selected Musculoskeletal Disorders in the United States." *Arthritis and Rheumatism* 41, no. 5 (May 1998): 778–99.

Leirisalo-Repo, M. "Enteropathic Arthritis, Whipple's Disease, Juvenile Spondyloarthropathy, and Uveitis." *Current Opinion Rheumatology* 6, no. 4 (July 1994): 385–90.

Leung, R.S., et al. "Neutrophil Zinc Levels in Psoriasis and Seborrheoic Dermatitis." *British Journal of Dermatology* 123, no. 3 (September 1990): 319–23.

Leventhal, L.J. , et al. "Treatment of Rheumatoid Arthritis with Gamma-Linolenic Acid." *Annals of Internal Medicine* 119, no. 9 (1 November 1993): 867–73.

Li, M.H., H.L. Zhang, and B.Y. Yang. "Effects of Ginkgo Leave Concentrated Oral Liquor in Treating Asthma." *Chung Kuo Chung Hsi I Chieh Ho Tsa Chih* 17, no. 4 (April 1997): 216–18.

Lyon, M., and J. Cline. "The Effect of an Ioligoantigenic Diet with or without a Prescribed Medical Food Product on the Behavior and Physiological Parameters of Children with Attention Deficit Hyperactivity Disorder." Unpublished data, quoted in the proceedings of the Sixth International Symposium on Functional Medicine, pg. 346, Institute for Functional Medicine, Gig Harbor, Wash., 1999.

"Magnesium Reduces Hyperactivity." *Autism Research Review International* 12, no. 2 (1998): 4.

Machtey, I. "Vitamin E and Arthritis/Vitamin E and Rheumatoid Arthritis." *Arthritis and Rheumatism* 34, no. 9 (September 1991): 1205.

Marks, David, and Laura Marks. "Food Allergy: Manifestations, Evaluation and Management." *Food Allergy, Postgraduate Medicine* 93, no. 2 (1 February 1993): 191–201.

Martelletti, P. "T Cells Expressing IL-2 Receptor in Migraine." *Acta Neurology* 13, no. 5 (October 1991): 448–56.

Matusiewicz, Ryszard. "The Homeopathic Treatment of Corticosteroid-Dependent Asthma: A Double-Blind, Placebo-Controlled Study." *Biomedical Therapy* 15, no. 4 (1997): 117–22.

McCarthy, G,. and D. Kenny. "Dietary Fish Oil and Rheumatic Diseases." *Seminars in Arthritis and Rheumatism* 21, no. 6 (June 1992): 368–75.

McCarty, D.J., et al. "Treatment of Pain Due to Fibromyalgia with Topical Capsaicin: A Pilot Study." *Seminars in Arthritis and Rheumatism* 23, no. 6 (Supplement, June 1994): 41–47.

McCarty, M.F. "Glucosamine for Psoriasis?" *Medical Hypotheses* 48 (1997): 437–41.

———. "The Neglect of Glucosamine as a Treatment for Osteoarthritis—A Personal Perspective." *Medical Hypotheses* 42, no. 5 (May 1994): 323–27.

McMillan, E.M., et al. "Diurnal Stage of Circadian Rhythm of Plasma Zinc in Healthy and Psoriatic Volunteers." *Progressive Clinicial Biological Research* 227B (1987): 295–303.

McSherry, J. "Chronic Fatigue Syndrome: A Fresh Look at an Old Problem." *Canadian Family Physician* 39 (February 1993): 336–40.

Menzel, I., and H. Holzmann. "Reflections on Seborrheic Scalp Eczema and Psoriasis Capillitii in Relation to Intestinal Mycoses." *Z Hautkr* 61, no. 7 (April 1986): 451–54.

Michaelsson, G., and L.K. Ljunghall. "Patients with Dermatitis Herpetiformis, Acne, Psoriasis, and Darier's Disease Have Low Epidermal Zinc Concentrations." *Acta Derm Venereol* 70, no. 4 (1990): 304–8.

Michaelsson, G., et al. "Selenium in Whole Blood and Plasma Is Decreased in Patients with Moderate and Severe Psoriasis." *Acta Derm Venereol* 69, no. 1 (1989): 29–34.

Moldofsky, H. "Fibromyalgia, Sleep Disorder and Chronic Fatigue Syndrome." *Ciba Foundation Symposium* 173 (1993): 262–71, 272–79.

Moreshead, J., and R. Jaffe. "Fibromyalgia: Clinical Success Through Enhanced Host Defenses: A Case-Controlled Outcome Study." IAACN Syllabus, Dallas, Tex. September, 1994.

Mulbert, A.E., et al. "Identification of Nonsteroidal Anti-inflammatory Drug-Induced Gastroduodenal Injury in Children with Juvenile Rheumatoid Arthritis." *Journal of Pediatrics* (April 1993): 645–46.

Murray, M., and J. Pizzorno. *The Encyclopedia of Natural Medicine.* Rocklin, Calif.: Prima, 1991.

Nielsen, G.L., et al. "The Effects of Dietary Supplementation with N-3 Polyunsaturated Fatty Acids in Patients with Rheumatoid Arthritis." *European Journal of Clinical Investigation* 22 (1992): 687–91.

Nietert, Paul J., et al. "Is Occupational Organic Solvent Exposure a Risk Factor for Scleroderma?" *Arthritis and Rheumatism* 41, no. 6 (June 1998): 1111–18.

Nihon Shinkei Seishin Yakurigaku Zasshi 18, no. 3 (June 1998): 71–80.

Noy, S., et al. "Schizophrenia and Autoimmunity—A Possible Etiological Mechanism?" *Neuropsychobiology* 30 (1994): 157–59.

Oliwiecki, S., et al. "Levels of Essential and Other Fatty Acids in Plasma and Red Cell Phospolipids from Normal Controls in Patients with Atopic Eczema." *ACTA Derm Venereol* (Stockholm) 71 (1990): 224–28.

Peet, M., et al. "Essential Fatty Acid Deficiency in Erythrocyte Membranes from Chronic Schizophrenic Patients, and the Clinical Effects of Dietary Supplementation." *Prostaglandins, Leukotrines and Essential Fatty Acids* 55, nos. 1, 2 (1996): 71–75.

Pelmear, P.L., J.O. Roos, and W.M. Maehle. "Occupationally-Induced Scleroderma." *Journal of Occupational Medicine* 34, no. 1 (January 1992): 20–25.

Pignet, M., and A. Lecomte. "The Effects of Harpogophytum Capsules in Degenerative Rheumatology." *Medicine Actuelle* 12, no. 4 (1985): 65–76.

Polli, E., M. Cortellaro, L. Parrini, L. Tessari, and G. Cherie Ligniere. "Pharmacological and Clinical Aspects of S-adenosyl-methionine (SAMe) in Primary Degenerative Arthropathy." *Minerva Medical* 66, no. 83 (5 December 1975): 4443–59.

Procter, A. "Enhancement of Recovery from Psychiatric Illness by Methylfolate." *British Journal of Psychiatry* 159 (August 1991): 271–72.

Randolph, T., and R.W. Moss. *An Alternative Approach to Allergies.* New York: Harper Perennial, 1990.

Resnick, C. "The Effects of Gamma-Oryzanol on Ulcers, Gastritis, Hyperlipidemias, and Menopausal Disorders." In *Research Review*. Greshem, Oreg.: Tyler Encapsulations, 1993.

Rigden, S., and J. Bland. "UltraClear Program and Cost Effectiveness." In *Advancement in Clinical Nutrition*. Gig Harbor, Wash.: HealthComm, 1994.

Robbins, L. "Precipitating Factors in Migraine: A Retrospective Review of 494 Patients." *Headache* 34, no. 4 (April 1994): 214–16.

Rockwell, Sally. *Dr. Sally's Allergy Recipes.* Seattle: Diet Designs, 1997.

Rupprecht, M., et al. "Physical Stress–Induced Secretion of Adrenal and Pituitary Hormones in Patients with Atopic Eczema Compared with Normal Controls." *Experimental and Clinical Endocrinology and Diabetes* 105 (1997): 39–45.

Sampson, H.A. "The Immunopathogenic Role of Food Hypersensitivity in Atopic Dermatitis." *Acta Derm Venereol Suppl* (Stockholm) 176 (1992): 34–37.

Sanchez-Roman, J., et al. "Multiple Clinical and Biological Autoimmune Manifestations in 50 Workers after Occupational Exposure to Silica." *Annals of Rheumatic Disease* 52, no 7 (July 1993): 534–38.

Sazanova, N.E., et al. "Immunological Aspects of Food Intolerance in Children During First Years of Life." *Pediatriia* 3 (1992): 14–18.

Schoenen, J., et al. "Effectiveness of High-Dose Riboflavin in Migraine Prophylaxis: A Randomized Controlled Trial." *Neurology* 50 (1998): 466–70.

Schoenen, J., et al. "High-Dose Riboflavin as a Prophylactic Treatment of Migraine: Results of an Open Pilot Study." *Cephalagia* 14 (1994): 328–29.

Seignalet, J. "Diet, Fasting, and Rheumatoid Arthritis." *Lancet* 339 (4 January 1993): 68–69.

Shafran, S.D., et al. "Chronic Fatigue Syndrome." *American Journal of Medicine* 90 (June 1991): 730–40.

Sharma, Rajiv P., et al. "Acute Dietary Tryptophan Depletion: Effects on Schizophrenic Positive and Negative Symptoms." *Neuropsychobiology* 35 (1997): 5–10.

Silberstein, S.D., and R.B. Lipton. "Epidemiology of Migraine." *Neuroepidemiology* 12, no. 3 (1993): 179–84.

Smith, R. "Chronic Headaches in Family Practice." *Journal of the American Board of Family Practitioners* 5, no. 6 (November/December 1992): 589–99.

Soriani, S., et al. "Serum and Red Blood Cell Magnesium Levels in Juvenile Migraine Patients." *Headache* 35, no. 1 (January 1995): 14-16.

Soyland, E., et al. "Dietary Supplementation with Very Long-Chain Omega-3 Fatty Acids in Patients with Atopic Dermatitis." *British Journal of Dermatology* 130 (1994): 757–64.

Srivastava, K.C., and T. Mustafa. "Ginger (Zingiber officinale) in Rheumatism and Musculoskeletal Disorders." *Medical Hypothesis* 39 (1992): 342–48.

St. Amand, R. Paul, M.D. Communciation with author. [4560 Admiralty Way, Marina Del Ray, Calif. 90292, (310) 577–7510.]

Starobrat-Hemerlin, B. "The Effect of Deficiency of Selected Bioelements on Hyperactivity in Children with Certain Specified Mental Disorders." *Ann Acad Med Stetin* 44 (1998): 297–314.

Starobrat-Hemerlin, B., and R. Kozielec. "The Effects of Magnesium Physiological Supplementation on Hyperactivity in Children with Attention Deficit Hyperactivity Disorder (ADHD). Positive Response to Magnesium Oral Loading Test." *Magnesium Research* 10, no. 2 (1997): 149–56.

Stewart, W.F., A. Schechter, and B.K. Rasmussen. "Migraine Prevalence. A Review of Population-Based Studies." *Neurology* 44, no. 6 (Supplement 4, June 1994): S17–S23.

Strong, A.M.M., et al. "The Effect of Oral Linoleic Acid and Gamma-Linolenic Acid (Efamol)." *British Journal of Clinical Practice* 39, nos. 11–12 (November/December 1985): 444–45.

Sukenik, S., et al. "Treatment of Psoriatic Arthritis at the Dead Sea." *Journal of Rheumatology* 21, no. 7 (July 1994): 1305–9.

Syed, T. A., S. A. Ahmad, A. H. Holt, S. H. Ahmad, and M. Afzal. "Management of Psoriasis with Aloe Vera Extract in a Hydrophilic Cream: A Placebo-Controlled, Double-Blind Study." *Tropical Medicine and Internal Health* 1, no. 4 (August 1996): 505–09.

Tan, Boon B., et al. "Double-Blind Controlled Trial of Effect of Housedust-Mite Allergen Avoidance on Atopic Dermatitis." *Lancet* 347 (26 January 1996): 15–18.

Taubert, K. "Magnesium in Migraine. Results of a Multicenter Pilot Study." *Fortschreit Medizin* 112, no. 24 (30 August 1994): 238–30.

Thomas, J., et al. "Migraine Treatment by Oral Magnesium Intake and Correction of the Irritation of Buccofacial and Cervical Muscles as a Side Effect of Mandibular Imbalance." *Magnesium Research* 7, no. 2 (June 1994): 123–27.

Tiwana, H., C. Wilson, R. S. Walmsley, A. J. Wakefield, M. S.

Smith, N. L. Cox, M. J. Hudson, and A. Ebringer. "Antibody Responses to Gut Bacteria in Ankylosing Spondylitis, Rheumatoid Arthritis, Crohn's Disease, and Ulcerative Colitis." *Rheumatology International* 17, no. 1 (1997): 11–16.

Trock, D.H., et al. "A Double-Blind Trial of the Clinical Effects of Pulsed Electromagnetic Fields in Osteoarthritis." *Journal of Rheumatology* 20, no. 3 (1993): 456–60.

Troughton, P.R., and A.W. Morgan. "Laboratory Findings and Pathology of Psoriatic Arthritis." *Baillieres Clinical Rheumatology* 8, no. 2 (May 1994): 439–63.

Tuthill, R.W. "Hair Lead Levels Related to Children's Classroom Attention-Deficit Disorder." *Archives of Environmental Health* 51, no. 3 (May–June 1996): 214–20.

Uhlig, T., A. Merkenschlager, R. Brandmaier, and J. Egger. "Topographic Mapping of Brain Electrical Activity in Children with Food-Induced Attention Deficit Hyperkinetic Disorder." *European Journal of Pediatrics* 156, no. 7 (July 1997): 557–61.

Wager, W., and U. Nootbaar-Wagner. "Prohpylactic Treatment of Migraine with Gamma-Linolenic and Alpha-Linolenic Acids." *Cephalalagia* 17 (1997): 127–30.

Werbach, M. *Healing with Nutrition*. New York: Harper Collins, 1993.

Yunus, M.B., et al. "Plasma Tryptophan and Other Amino Acids in Primary Fibromyalgia: A Controlled Study." *Journal of Rheumatology* 19, no. 1 (1992): 90–94.

Index